19.95

g. Vastano

Occupational Information

Occupational Information

WHERE TO GET IT AND HOW TO USE IT
IN CAREER EDUCATION, CAREER COUNSELING,
AND CAREER DEVELOPMENT

ROBERT HOPPOCK

Professor Emeritus of Counselor Education
New York University

Fourth Edition

McGraw-Hill Book Company

NEW YORK   ST. LOUIS   SAN FRANCISCO   AUCKLAND   DÜSSELDORF
JOHANNESBURG   KUALA LUMPUR   LONDON   MEXICO   MONTREAL   NEW DELHI
PANAMA   PARIS   SÃO PAULO   SINGAPORE   SIDNEY   TOKYO   TORONTO

Library of Congress Cataloging in Publication Data

Hoppock, Robert, date
    Occupational information.

    Bibliography: p.
    Includes indexes.
    1. Vocational guidance.   2.   Group guidance in
education.   3.   Electronic data processing—Vocational
guidance.   I.   Title.
HF5381.H582   1976   371.4'25   75-11597
ISBN 0-07-030330-4

    4567890DODO798

This book was set in Times Roman by National ShareGraphics, Inc.
The editors were Stephen D. Dragin and Susan Gamer;
the cover was designed by Edward Aho;
the production supervisor was Charles Hess.
R. R. Donnelley & Sons Company was printer and binder.

This book is dedicated
to my grandchildren,
Shawn, Shannon, and Jeanne,
and to all
who will try to help them
and others like them,
as they approach
the sometimes frustrating, sometimes painful,
but when successful
the fantastically rewarding, search
for an occupation in which they can be
reasonably useful and reasonably contented.

No two persons are born exactly alike, but each differs from each in natural endowments, one being suited for one occupation and another for another. . . . All things will be produced in superior quantity and quality and with greater ease, when each man works at a single occupation in accordance with his natural gifts.

PLATO

. . . We must decide what manner of men we wish to be and what calling in life we would follow; and this is the most difficult problem in the world.

CICERO

Contents

Preface

To All Editions

This is a textbook for use in the education of counselors, teachers, psychologists, rehabilitation officers, school and college administrators, social workers, employment interviewers, personnel directors, librarians, parents, clergy, psychiatrists, and others to whom people turn when they want facts about jobs to help them to decide what they will do to earn a living. To my pleasant surprise, the book has also been used by one university as the text for a sophomore course in career planning. Parts of the book may interest economists and sociologists who are concerned with problems of occupational choice, distribution, mobility, and adjustment.

Many of the illustrations in this book are taken from educational institutions. The basic principles, however, remain the same, whether the counselor meets a client in school, in the employment service, in industry, in a social agency, or in a veterans' hospital. The social worker may not organize a course in occupations, but he or she will find most of the teaching techniques useful in a group work program. The counseling psychologist and the employment counselor may approach the client from quite different orientations but both must turn to the same sources for the same facts.

The word "counselor" appears frequently in this book. It is used here to designate anyone who is trying to help another person to choose an occupation or to get occupational information. Counselors may be professional or amateur; they may devote all or part of their time to career guidance; they may help many persons or only one; they may be employed as teachers of occupations or be just friends of the persons who ask for help. They are, in short, the readers of the book, who may never have thought of themselves as counselors but who become counselors the moment they undertake to help another person think through a problem—in this case the problem of planning a career.

The general plan of the book is as follows: Chapters 1 to 6 identify the kinds of occupational information that counselors and clients need and suggest where to get it and how to appraise, classify, and file it. Chapters 7 to 11 discuss basic theories of career choice and development and the use of occupational information in counseling. Chapters 12 to 24 describe a variety of ways in which occupational information may be presented to groups of all kinds. Several of the recommended procedures involve active audience participation in compiling from primary sources the information which members of the group need and want. Chapter 25 summarizes the results of research on the use of occupational information in career guidance. Supplementary material will be found in the Appendixes. For the convenience of the instructor who is teaching occupational information for the first time, suggested lesson plans and assignments are offered, beginning on page 311. Most of the suggestions have been tested in the author's classes. Although the lesson plans and assignments were designed for university courses, some of them could be used in elementary and secondary schools and in other settings with other groups.

To This Edition

To me the most interesting new developments discussed in this edition are:

The rapid and widespread introduction of career education programs in the public schools. See Chapter 12.

The accompanying development of career resource centers, staffed sometimes by competent, professional consultants in occupational information, and sometimes by paraprofessionals about whom I have some reservations. See Chapters 20 and 23.

The increasing use of VIEW decks, job banks, and other computer systems in storing and retrieving occupational information. See Chapter 20.

The creation of the new National Occupational Information Service, in the U. S. Department of Labor, which will try to make more accessible to counselors, teachers, students, and others the rich resources of occupational information compiled by occupational analysts in the public employment services, in other government agencies, and elsewhere. See Chapter 20.

Also included in this edition are:

Brief descriptions of many new ways in which teachers and counselors can make occupational information accessible to students and clients. See Chapters 13 to 21.

The results of new research designed to determine the impact of occupational information upon subsequent occupational adjustment, measured against the ultimate criteria of self-support and job satisfaction. See Chapter 25.

In the bibliography, 291 old references have been deleted; 246 have been retained; and 180 new ones have been added. The result is a compilation of the best publications I have found since I started looking for them in 1924.

The author and publisher of this book are both strongly committed to equal opportunity for employment and promotion at all levels, without regard to sex, race, nationality, or any other irrelevant consideration. We regret that we have not been able to completely eliminate use of the generic *he* in all cases, and beg the indulgence of those who find it offensive, until someone invents a neuter pronoun more acceptable than *it*. Despite the use of the male pronoun, everything in this book is intended to apply equally to both sexes.

ROBERT HOPPOCK

Acknowledgments

To JoAnn Harris Bowlsbey, Alva Cooper, Russell B. Flanders, Harold L. Henderson, Robert F. Herrick, Kenneth B. Hoyt, John Krumboltz, Leon Lewis, Sidney P. Marland, Jr., Nancy D. Stevens, Donald E. Super, and David Winefordner, each of whom has read parts of the manuscript.

To Amelia Ashe, James G. Ashman, Henry Borow, Gene Bottoms, Eileen Brennan, Lowell A. Burkett, Robert Calvert, Jr., Robert E. Campbell, John O. Crites, Calvin J. Daane, Jama Doenges, S. Norman Feingold, Sidney A. Fine, Stephanie Foran, Wanda J. Green, Norman Gysbers, L. Sunny Hansen, James R. Holcomb, John Holland, Warren E. Kauffman, Darryl Laramore, Ethel Lawrence, Bruce McKinlay, Marti Moore, Story Moorefield, Marla Peterson, Stephen Poliacik, Carol Anderson Ramirez, Anne Roe, Daniel Sinick, Eugene Smith, Barry E. Stern, Lucinda E. Thomas, David V. Tiedeman, Barbara B. Varenhorst, Earle E. Vossen, and Bernard Yabroff, each of whom contributed or helped me to find information that I needed.

To the authors not previously acknowledged, who have generously granted permission to use the new quotations from their works, and to the American Personnel and Guidance Association, the University of Minnesota, the National Urban League, and the National Vocational Guidance Association.

To Elaine Seaton, Diane R. Covino, Marie R. Klein, Sylvia Levin, Marilyn B. Paley, Alan S. Rossiter, Mary Lou Westerling, and their colleagues on the staff of the Manhasset Public Library, for their help in finding materials and for making a harried author feel welcome.

To the many other friends, acquaintances, and students whose information and ideas I have appropriated without recognition or recall.

To my daughter, Joan, who typed most of the manuscript, tactfully corrected my mistakes, and helped me to remove the remaining traces of my own male chauvinism.

To my wife and her mother, who patiently endured repeated interruptions in their own work whenever I needed help.

To all these I am greatly indebted and deeply grateful.

ROBERT HOPPOCK

Occupational Information

Chapter 1

Why Study Occupations?

Both the reader and the author of this book have made decisions which we hoped would facilitate our progress in the direction of careers which appeared attractive to us. We shall make more such decisions in the future. Each decision has been or will be based in part upon our own occupational information, however inadequate that information may be.

These decisions, in sequence, help to determine our careers. Together they constitute our choice of an occupation for the near or distant future. As time passes and conditions change, we may or may not change both our jobs and our occupations. We may thus make one or many occupational choices. The more choices we make, the more occupational information we need. There are at least five reasons why the wise choice of an occupation is important and why facts about jobs are essential to this choice.

The Choice of an Occupation May Determine Whether One Will Be Employed or Unemployed In some occupations employment is notoriously irregular; in others it is much more stable and secure. By choosing an occupation in which employment is known to be relatively stable, one may increase the probability of having a job even when millions of other persons are out of work.

In severe economic depressions as many as 75 percent of the workers in some occupations and industries have been unemployed. At the same time less than 10 percent of the workers in other fields were out of work, and in some occupations employment actually increased.

Even in very mild recessions there are striking differences in the rates of unemployment among different groups of workers. In 1972, for example, 10 percent of the workers in construction were unemployed, but only 4 percent of those in transportation and public utilities were out of work.

The Choice of an Occupation May Determine Success or Failure   Many things affect success. They include effort, luck, and knowing the right people. They include also the ability of the worker to perform satisfactorily the tasks assigned to him. People differ in both the nature and the level of their abilities, and occupations differ in the abilities required for their acceptable performance. By choosing an occupation which will utilize one's strengths and make only minimal demands upon one's weaknesses, one may increase the probability of success.

The Choice of an Occupation May Determine Whether One Will Enjoy or Detest His Work   There are probably few, if any, occupations in which workers never have to do anything that they dislike, but there is no need for most of us to work at jobs in which we dislike most of the things we have to do. Despite popular impressions to the contrary, modern mass production does not condemn all factory workers to misery. Robinson [318][1] and others have summarized thirty years of research and 494 attempts to measure the percentage of workers who are dissatisfied with their jobs. The reported percentages range from 0 to 92 with a median of 13 percent dissatisfied. Many of the studies were made on factory populations, several different criteria of job satisfaction were used, and in the vast majority of the studies a minority of the workers was reported to be dissatisfied.

By the wise choice of an occupation one may find a large share of life's pleasures and satisfactions in his work. Although we have had much research on vocational aptitudes and vocational interests, we have had comparatively little on what might be called the emotional fitness of a person for a job or of a job for a person. How important this aspect of vocational choice can be was well expressed years ago by the distinguished psychiatrist, who was then the medical director of the National Committee for Mental Hygiene, Frankwood E. Williams [413].

> One's job must furnish an outlet suitable to one's particular, personal emotional needs. The greatest part of one's emotional life is lived in one's job, not elsewhere, as is commonly supposed. Different professions and vocations . . . offer quite different emotional outlets; even specialties within a profession offer different outlets. One may be more than adequately equipped intellectually, and with special ability for a given profession, but if that profession does not offer the emotional outlet peculiar to one's own needs, unhappiness and discontent follow. Even though material and professional success may come, it is likely to be as dust in the mouth. After considerable

---

[1] Numbers in brackets refer to the bibliography at the back of this book.

trial and error, other partial outlets are found that make the situation bearable, but there is likely to be an element of frustration throughout that makes for unhappiness.

The Choice of an Occupation Influences Almost Every Other Aspect of Life
It determines the persons with whom the worker will associate during much of the day; it thus affects the choice of friends and possibly the choice of a marriage partner. It determines where the family will live, where the children will go to school, and how often they will move. It may affect the frequency with which the worker sees his or her family and the amount of time spent with them. The job helps to determine both the economic and the social status of the entire family. Whether family income will increase or decrease with advancing age, whether it will be stable or erratic, whether it will provide for health and comfort or will actually threaten survival in case of illness may depend on the occupational choices of the breadwinners.

The job may directly affect the worker's physical health. It may strengthen or aggravate feelings of success or failure, of satisfaction or frustration, of acceptance or rejection, and thus may help to determine mental health. In subtle ways the job changes the values, the ideals, the standards, and the daily conduct of the worker.

Occupational Choices Determine How a Democratic Society Will Utilize Its Labor Force   The modest young person who is choosing a field of work may not think much about the impact of this choice upon human welfare, but the aggregate of thousands of such choices may determine where serious shortages and surpluses of workers will occur. Economic rewards, public policy, and military conscription all affect the distribution of the work force, but in a democratic society the final determinant of what any one person will do is that person. When too many persons prepare for a few popular professions and fail to find employment, precious human assets are wasted, and powerful future leaders begin to wonder about the political and economic systems under which they live.

Many investigators have observed the discrepancies between the occupational preferences of students and the occupational distribution of our employed population. One of the most vivid reports was based upon the announced choices of 1,658 boys and girls in the eighth grades of thirty-five public schools in Cincinnati, Ohio, described by Dale [87]:

> What would Cincinnati be like if these eighth grade students became the sole inhabitants of the city, in the jobs of their choice, ten years from now? . . . Health services would be very high, with every eighteen people supporting one doctor. . . . It may be, however, that they would all be needed in a city that had no garbage disposal workers, no laundry workers, and no water supply, since no one chose to do that kind of work. . . . The two bus drivers . . . will find that their customers get tired of waiting, and use the services of the sixty-seven airline pilots. It may be difficult getting . . . to see the forty baseball players.

One need not be a genius to see that some of these students are going to have to revise their choices and that they will need information about many occupations which they are not seriously considering today.

Occupational Information Is Indispensable One cannot choose what one does not know, and many occupations are unknown to most of us. One may stumble into an appropriate occupation by sheer luck, but the wise choice of an occupation requires accurate information about what occupations are available, what they require, and what they offer.

Occupational information alone is not enough. Knowledge and acceptance of one's own aptitudes, abilities, needs, limitations, interests, values, feelings, fears, likes, and dislikes are essential also, as is clear thinking about the relative significance of all the facts. Nothing in this book is intended to imply that any of these other considerations is any less important than occupational information.

It is obvious that knowledge of occupations can be effectively applied only when one knows something about oneself. It is equally obvious that knowledge of oneself can be effectively applied to the choice of an occupation only when one knows something about occupations. Either without the other is incomplete.

WHAT WILL THIS BOOK DO FOR YOU?

The author was once a counselor, starting on his first job and not knowing what to do or how to do it. This book was written to help his students to avoid some of his embarrassing mistakes. The following are some of the things that he hopes you, if you read it, will be better prepared to do than he was.

1 Start a new job in a new school or college, a new agency, or a new community with the comfortable assurance that you know what you will have to learn about occupations, and that you know where and how to learn it from the best sources in the least time with the least wasted effort.

2 With the same assurance, if you are a teacher, take on your share of the career awareness, career orientation, and career education programs in your school or college.

3 Identify the things your student or your client ought to know about an occupation before deciding to prepare for it or to look for a job in it.

4 Help almost any student or client to learn almost anything about almost any occupation.

5 Distinguish between the better and the poorer sources of occupational information, and show your students and clients how to do so.

6 Quickly appraise any library collection of occupational books or any file of occupational pamphlets, remove publications that should be discarded, and replace them with better materials.

7 Tell high school and college students where to look for information about summer jobs.

8 Set up a good filing system for occupational information that will help you to find things when you want them.

9 Recognize the theory of career choice and development which has guided your own actions even if you were unaware of it. Compare your theory with those of others and revise your own if you find revision is needed.

10 Be more aware of the unconscious motivations that may affect your own occupational decisions and those of your clients.

11 Understand why some of your clients do the "stupid" things they do, and how you can or cannot help them. Understand why some psychotherapists do the "stupid" things they do, and how you can or cannot help them.

12 Resolve your own uncertainty about your relationship to recruiting and recruiters for either military or civilian occupations.

13 Distinguish between what you should and should not try to do with occupational information in career counseling.

14 At a moment's notice, go into any group of young people or adults who want to know more about part-time and full-time jobs, and conduct a group conference that will be both productive and interesting.

15 Use your own former students and clients as sources of up-to-date information about the kinds of jobs that are most likely to be open to your present students and clients.

16 Provide encouraging role models for discouraged students or clients who fear there are no jobs for them.

17 Plan and conduct a follow-up study of your former students or clients in which your present students or clients will do most of the work and will enjoy doing it, and in which the cost will be negligible.

18 Plan, arrange, and conduct interesting and instructive plant tours to places where your students and clients may find jobs.

19 Teach a unit or a course in career planning in which neither you nor your students will be bored.

20 Plan and conduct a community survey of jobs that may be open to your students and clients, in which they collect and compile the information and learn something about interviewing.

21 Conduct an interesting and productive case conference for your students or clients, to help them learn more about the decision-making process.

22 Arrange and conduct practice job interviews with local employers.

23 Provide interesting meetings and projects for career clubs.

24 Tell your boss, if you are asked, what a good career information service should provide, and how to provide it.

REVIEW QUESTIONS

1 How may a person increase the probability of having a job even when millions of other persons are unemployed?

2 How may a person increase the probability of success?

3 Is career planning for factory workers a waste of time? Has modern mass production destroyed their opportunity to find job satisfaction?

4 Where is the greatest part of one's emotional life lived?

5 A person may be adequately equipped intellectually, may achieve success, and may yet be unhappy in a job if it does not offer what?

6 What are some of the ways in which one's occupation affects one's family and one's life off the job?

7 What kind of world would we have if occupational choices were based only on the abilities, interests, and needs of the individual?

8 Has anything in this chapter surprised, provoked, or challenged you? Will any of this affect your future thoughts and actions? How?

9 What do you think of vocational counseling services which devote 90 percent of their resources to discovering the needs, abilities, and interests of the client and 10 percent to studying the changing employment market?

Chapter 2

What the Counselor Should Know about Occupations

Definitions In this book the term "occupational information" is used to mean any and all kinds of information regarding any position, job, or occupation, provided only that the information is potentially useful to a person who is choosing an occupation. More briefly stated, occupational information means facts about jobs for use in career planning.

In this and subsequent chapters the word "client" is used to designate any person who seeks the help of any counselor. Obviously, the client may or may not also be a student and often will be if the counselor is employed in a school or college. The word "student" is used to designate any person enrolled in a school or college, who may or may not seek the help of the counselor. Thus a student may or may not also be a client. Any counselor anywhere will, of course, have direct personal contact with clients. The counselor who works in a school or college may also have direct or indirect contact with students who do not seek help but who are served through teachers, group activities, or a course or unit in occupations which the counselor may teach; the counselor therefore has responsibilities to "students" as well as to "clients."

The beginning counselor is likely to be overwhelmed by the infinite variety of the questions clients ask. Obviously one cannot be a walking encyclopedia. One cannot answer every question on the spot. Like every teacher, the counselor must, if honest, frequently admit ignorance.

The impossibility of knowing everything may lead the frightened beginner to take refuge in the idea one need not know anything except where the library is and how to use it. In desperation and ignorance, the beginner may fall back upon the rationalization of the lazy and incompetent by deciding that it is better for clients to search for the answers to their questions without help. Clients should become familiar with the sources of occupational information. What better way is there to become familiar with any tool than by using it? Why not simply send the client to the library for facts about jobs?

There are two important reasons for not taking this easy way out: many of the answers are not to be found in the library or in any publication, and much of the information in print is inaccurate, obsolete, or intentionally misleading. To turn an unsuspecting client loose in even the best library of occupational information is a little like turning one loose in a drugstore to write and fill a prescription. The same may be said of sending a client, unaided, to most of the other sources of occupational information.

Brayfield and Mickelson [27] tabulated the contents of 5,958 occupational publications and found that many occupations were inadequately represented.

The impossibility of knowing everything is no excuse for knowing nothing. No teacher of mathematics can know everything about mathematics, but the teacher does not send students to the library to learn algebra without help. No teacher of French can know everything about the French language, literature, and life, but no teacher sends students to the library to learn French without help. The counselor must do what every teacher does: separate the essential from the nonessential, the important from the less important, and then master the essential information.

What then is essential?

First Jobs The counselor should know where dropouts and graduates got their first jobs. The occupational interests and plans of school and college students often bear little relation to the employment opportunities of the area in which the students will look for work. Consequently, many of them never do find a job in the occupation of their choice. Disappointed and frustrated in their search for employment, too many of them drift into some substitute job in which they are neither effective nor satisfied.

This unhappy situation will be corrected only when students can base their occupational plans upon a realistic view of the kinds of jobs that will be open to them. This realistic view is best obtained by learning what jobs previous dropouts and graduates were able to get. This information is readily available in schools which make annual follow-up studies. The new counselor should inquire of associates and supervisors whether or not such studies have been made. If they have not been, the counselor should proceed promptly to make one, preferably with the aid of students.

Any project of this kind, which involves public relations, should first be discussed with, and approved by, the counselor's immediate superior. If no recent studies have been made, the first one should cover the dropouts and graduates of the past five years unless a sample of several hundred can be obtained from more recent classes. A large sample is necessary in order to reveal clearly which occupations and employers have absorbed the largest numbers of former students.

Once made, the follow-up study should be repeated annually in order to discover changes when they appear. Each study should include, at least, all the dropouts and graduates of the past twelve months. Some schools follow up all former students at intervals of one, three, and five years after separation from school. Others prefer intervals of one, four, and seven years, and still others like one, five, and ten.

High schools need to follow up their alumni after they have completed college and military or alternate service in order to find out where these former students got their first jobs. Without this information the educational guidance as well as the career guidance of prospective college students can be sadly unrealistic.

The follow-up study has two advantages over the community occupational survey as a means of learning what entry jobs are likely to be available. First, it has no geographical limits; it goes wherever the former students have gone and thus reveals the true extent of the employment market with which the counselor must be concerned. Second, it reveals the kinds of jobs which dropouts and graduates are able to get in the open competition of the labor market. Employers may state, quite truthfully, that they frequently do have vacancies which could be filled by inexperienced young workers. The employers may nevertheless not hire beginners when the vacancies occur, if experienced workers are available at that time. Only the follow-up study reveals what kinds of jobs the beginners actually get.

Suggestions for conducting a follow-up study as a class or club project will be found in Chapter 13. If student participation is not feasible, the counselor may conduct the study. If no way can be found to communicate with former students, the counselor can get limited information about them by asking the teachers and students who are still in school to report the nature and place of employment of any former students whom they know.

All that has been said above about students, dropouts, and graduates applies also to the clients of counselors who do not work in schools or colleges. Every counselor should know what has happened to former clients. Every agency which has clients should make periodic follow-up studies of the persons it has served.

Thus rehabilitation counselors, counselors in community vocational guidance and placement services, and counseling psychologists in veterans' hospitals and in private practice all need to know what has become of their former clients. Only in this way can the counselor find out whether the client has been helped or hindered in the attempt to evaluate the probability of finding employment in the chosen occupation.

Principal Employment Opportunities   The counselor should know the other opportunities for dropouts and graduates in the community. No technique is perfect. Desirable and indispensable as the follow-up study is, it will not do the whole job of revealing all employment opportunities to counselor and clients. Dropouts and graduates may have missed some excellent opportunities of which they were unaware. New opportunities may have arisen since the last class entered the employment market. To discover these, a survey of the employment market is desirable.

The extent of the employment market, already revealed by the follow-up studies, will vary greatly from one institution and from one community to another. High school dropouts and graduates usually find their first jobs in or near their home towns, even in suburban areas, but this tendency is not universal. College alumni usually cover a much wider territory, but not always. Amateur counselors in rural areas sometimes assume that employment opportunities near home are too limited to permit much choice, but Raymond Handville found 220 different occupations within a 25-mile radius of a rural school.

Any follow-up is likely to reveal a considerable concentration of alumni employed near the institution. A follow-up of alumni from the high school at Jamestown, New York, revealed that 74 percent of the respondents still gave Jamestown as their address five years after graduation [295]. I have rarely seen a report that more than 50 percent had moved away. Local employment opportunities should never be slighted.

The occupational survey may be as simple or as elaborate as the counselor's resources permit. The beginning counselor, coming into a new college or a new community, should begin the survey by browsing through the classified section of the local telephone directory, observing the kinds of organizations listed therein. Anyone who has not done this before will be surprised at the variety of industries and occupations that might otherwise have been overlooked.

The counselor should next call on the school or college placement officer, if there is one, and on any teachers who have helped their own students to get jobs, then go to the nearest office of the state employment service and to any private employment agencies in the community. The addresses of local employment agencies are usually found in the classified telephone directory; a national directory is published by the National Employment Association [108]. If no office of the state employment service is listed in the local directory, a letter to the state employment service at the state capital will reveal the location of the nearest office.

To each placement officer the counselor should explain that the purpose of this visit is to learn something about the local occupations that are likely to be open to dropouts and graduates, and should ask the placement officer if he can contribute any information or suggest where any might be found. Because the employment agency business is sometimes fiercely competitive, some placement officers are understandably reluctant to reveal trade secrets, including the names of the employers they serve. But most placement officers will be willing to indicate the kinds of jobs they find easy and hard to fill and the kinds of applicants they can and cannot place. Because the interest of any informant may sometimes be served by revealing only part of the truth, the counselor should accept all information gratefully but tentatively and check it against other sources at every opportunity. No information is perfect. No source is infallible. But excellent leads for further investigation may be obtained in a short time with little effort and almost no expense by calling on placement officers and employment agencies.

The counselor should call next on the secretary of the local chamber of commerce, from whom one can usually obtain some information regarding the largest local employers, approximately how many persons they employ, and the nature of their business. If this information is not available locally, it may sometimes be obtained by writing to the state chamber of commerce at the state capital. In a very small community, a call at the local bank or a walk around town may be all that is needed.

After identifying the larger employers, the counselor's next calls should be on the personnel directors or employment managers of these companies and on the officers of the local labor unions with which these companies have contracts. If the counselor also teaches a course or unit in occupations, or another course in which industrial tours are appropriate, time may be saved and service to students may be improved by taking the class on these trips. How to conduct such tours and what questions to ask are described in Chapters 14 and 15. The same questions may be used in a private interview if the counselor goes alone.

The survey activities so far described can be and should be undertaken by the counselor. No appropriation is necessary if the counselor is willing to spend a little money for postage stamps, telephone calls, and local transportation.

When these activities have been completed, the counselor may wish to undertake a more complete survey of the employment market for graduates. This may be done at little or no expense as a student project in a course or unit in occupations, or it may be undertaken by the counselor alone. Suggestions will be found in Chapter 16.

All that has been said above about counselors who work in schools and colleges is equally true of counselors who work in community agencies or elsewhere. Every counselor who attempts to help clients make occupational choices should know the principal employment opportunities of the community.

Student Interest   The counselor should know which occupations are being seriously considered by students. Although the occupational preferences of students are often unrealistic, they are nevertheless important, if only because the students will show little real interest in exploring other occupations until they have explored their first choices. The counselor needs to know which are the currently popular occupations in order to become more familiar with them.

A tabulation of students' occupational preferences can be compiled quickly with the use of a simple mimeographed questionnaire. If mimeographing or other duplicating facilities are not available, plain paper may be used and the questions numbered and read to the students.

If you do not wish to be misled, do not ask only, "What would you *like* to do when you finish school? " This question has been known to draw answers far removed from what the student expects or plans to do. A better approach is probably a series of questions such as, "Considering what you now know of your own abilities, interests, and opportunities, what occupations do you think you are most likely to enter when you finish school? What other occupations are you seriously considering? What others would you like to enter if you could? Would you like to have more information about any of these occupations? If so, which ones? "

The results of this inquiry will interest not only the counselor but other teachers; and the school administrators may like to see a summary of the replies. Local newspapers will usually publish a story on them if given the chance. Again, because publication involves public relations, the counselor should get the approval of the supervisor before approaching the newspapers. Students' names should, of course, not be publicly identified with their choices.

The percentage of truthful responses may be increased by assuring the students that only the counselor and clerical helpers will see the replies. If student clerks are to help in the tabulation, this fact should be stated frankly; the helpers should be chosen for their discretion as well as for their accuracy and then should be strongly indoctrinated in the confidential nature of their work. Truthfulness may be further encouraged by assuring the students that they need not put their names on the papers if they prefer not to. The counselor may, however, wish to risk a little candor in order to preserve identification. If the names are on the papers, these papers can help the counselor to get facts about specific occupations to the students who will be most interested in them.

The Big Three The counselor should know almost everything about three occupations. As noted above, the counselor cannot know everything about every occupation, but should be the community's best expert on at least three. These are, first, the occupation or industry or company which has employed the largest number of dropouts and graduates from the school or of clients from the agency; second, the occupation or industry or company which employs the largest number of persons in the community; and, third, the occupation or industry or company which is currently being seriously considered by the largest number of students or clients. No counselor is too busy to make himself or herself an authority on these three occupations; a counselor who is, is too busy doing the wrong things.

Obviously the counselor should know more than this. Having learned everything possible about these three occupations, by visits, by reading, by talking with alumni and with other employers and employees, the conscientious counselor will need no further urging to extend a knowledge of occupations as far as time and resources permit, for the counselor will have blushed more than once to discover how little he knew about these three occupations, how much of what he did "know" was not true, and how pitiably inadequate are the sources to which he previously referred the clients who came to him for occupational information. The counselor will also have learned how important it is to repeat visits and interviews at least once a year in order to learn what changes have occurred.

The counselor who postpones his or her own study of occupations until he finds the time for it will never find the time. The most effective way for a counselor to do occupational research is to set aside a fixed amount of time at regular intervals and then stick to the schedule as conscientiously as if a class had to be met at this time. The counselors in one large city once set aside one full day a week for research on local occupations. The counselor who finds this schedule impossible may reserve one morning a week or one morning every two weeks. Mornings are suggested rather than afternoons because once the counselor appears in his office, he is likely to find it hard to get away.

A great deal can be accomplished in small units of time if one can just stick to a regular schedule. With as little as one morning every two weeks, the counselor can visit twenty places of employment in a school year. In five years a hundred can be visited. Any counselor who gives less time than this to occupational research should begin to suspect himself of malpractice.

The counselor who also teaches a course in occupations will find time for occupational research automatically provided as he or she takes students to visit local industries, brings alumni back to school for group conferences, and helps students to get the facts they want about the occupations which interest them.

Sources of Information   The counselor should know where to get information about occupations and how to appraise its accuracy. The average counselor is a college graduate who has spent at least sixteen years as a student, looking in books and in libraries for answers to questions. It is not surprising that the library should be first thought of when occupational information is needed. A good library can be a useful source, but it is not the only one, and it is frequently not the best. For some kinds of information on some occupations, it can easily be the worst.

For fifteen years the author of this book planned and edited abstracts of the available literature on more than a hundred occupations. Over and over again, reviewers found the literature to be obsolete, inaccurate, inadequate, intentionally or unintentionally biased. One abstracter examined all the available literature published on one occupation over a period of twenty years and then reported that, twenty years earlier, three original investigations of this occupation had been made in three major cities, and nearly everything written on the occupation since that time had been copied from one of these old studies or from someone else who had copied from the originals.

There is good occupational literature in print, and some of it will be mentioned later in this book. What the beginning counselor needs to learn and to remember is that there is also bad occupational literature and that the average student, teacher, parent, librarian, psychologist, and social worker does not know how to tell the good from the bad.

No one source of occupational information is wholly good or wholly bad. Each source is good for some kinds of information and poor for others. Discriminating counselors must learn, and then must teach their clients, where to look for the facts they want and how to appraise what they find. These topics are discussed in Chapters 4 and 5.

Labor Legislation   One of the first tasks assigned to a school counselor may be the issuance of employment certificates, sometimes called "age certificates," "work permits," or "working papers." These are documents which state and federal laws require job applicants, under age eighteen, to present to employers before the applicants can legally be hired for some kinds of work. Anyone who has any responsibility for career counseling of youth should get and read the free publications on employment certificates and child labor issued by the state departments of education and of labor, and the U.S. Department of Labor. A liberal education awaits the counselor who will visit the state department of labor, confess ignorance, and ask what the counselor should learn and how.

If responsibility for issuing employment certificates is assigned to the counselor, he or she will have repeated opportunities to help young people at a crucial point, when they are making decisions on which they will act immediately. Some students will be frightened by the impending change in their lives, eager to make the right decision, and willing to listen to anyone who is kind, considerate, interested in them and their problems, and possibly well informed. That person could be you.

REVIEW QUESTIONS

1 You have just been employed as a counselor in a community that is new to you. What are the quickest ways for you to learn something about its principal occupations and industries?

2 How can you best obtain a realistic view of the kinds of jobs most likely to be available to your clients?

3 What are the advantages of the follow-up study over the community occupational survey, and vice versa?

4 Since the counselor cannot be a walking encyclopedia of occupational information, what should he do?

5 Why is the occupational informational library an inadequate source of occupational information?

6 Where do the graduates of suburban high schools usually find their first jobs?

7 How many different occupations did Handville find within a 25-mile radius of a rural school?

8 How can a busy counselor find time for occupational research?

9 Where can a counselor get information about "working papers"?

10 Is there anything in this chapter that you can use to improve your work? What? How?

Chapter 3

What the Client Should Know about Occupations

At some time, in some way, with or without the help of a counselor, every person who chooses an occupation looks at the various opportunities which he or she thinks are open to him or her, compares them, and selects the one which has the most appeal. This may be done thoroughly, systematically, and realistically; it may be done casually, impulsively, or fancifully.

Students and clients differ in their need for occupational information, just as they differ in abilities and interests. Some need a great deal of information, some need little or none, and some are already in a position to supply it.

Clients' Needs Differ   The beginning counselor will soon observe a few students whose need for occupational information appears to be negligible. They have career plans with which they are satisfied and which to the counselor seem reasonable. Conceivably, any one of these persons might be more successful and better satisfied in some other occupation, but the average school or college counselor will find little time to explore such a possibility. The competent counselor who knows something about occupations will be much too busy helping clients who obviously need and want help.

Some clients have tentative choices which appear appropriate but which they want the counselor to help them review just to make sure they have not overlooked some consideration of importance. A checklist of questions for use in such cases appears later in this chapter.

Some clients are moving toward appropriate occupational choices on their own initiative. They neither need nor want extensive counseling, but they do need, want, and ask for specific information to use in arriving at their own decisions. One of the counselor's major responsibilities in occupational information is to help these clients to get the information they want, check its accuracy, and see its implications in terms of their own choices. Sources of information are discussed in Chapter 4. The ways in which the facts may affect the job satisfaction of the prospective worker are discussed in Chapter 11.

Other clients are positive about their plans but with less apparent justification. One of the problems which worries counselors most is what to do with the client who is certain of what he or she wants to do but whose choice seems unwise because of the lack of some essential qualification or because employment opportunities are negligible or because some satisfaction is anticipated that the counselor believes the occupation will not yield. There is no easy solution to this problem. If the client seems unable to face reality, psychotherapy may be tried. Even then, the counselor may be wholly ineffective until the client has followed the first choice and failed. If and when this happens, the counselor faces one of the most challenging responsibilities, which is to help such clients find acceptable substitutes for the things they want to do and can't. At this point, occupational information in large doses may be indicated. Before this time, occupational information may or may not be helpful. For further discussion of this problem see Chapter 10.

Somewhat different is the problem of the client who has no idea of what he or she wants to do. Individual counselors differ in their approaches to this problem, but all of them come eventually to the place where they must acquaint the client with the occupations which are open. It is at this point that the counselor begins to use the information compiled from follow-up studies, community occupational surveys, and other sources. For further discussion of this problem see Chapter 10.

Because the adequate presentation of information about a variety of occupations is a long and time-consuming process and because much of the information to be presented is needed by more than one client, a good course in occupations is sometimes a help to both the counselor and the client. Individual interviews will still be necessary, but more interview time can be used to discuss the individual aspects of the problem if the background information has already been presented by the same counselor to the same client in the more economical group situation. For more on this topic see Chapters 12 to 22.

Range of Opportunities Clients should know what jobs are open to them. There has been much research on the range of occupations in which young persons express an interest. In general, the results indicate a disturbingly limited range, which can be quickly and easily extended by presenting information about additional occupations. For ways in which to present additional occupational information, see Chapters 13 to 16.

Sources of Information The client should know where to get information about occupations and how to appraise its accuracy. Contrary to a popular impression among many counselors, the best sources of occupational information are not to be found in libraries, not even in the average couselor's own special library of occupational information. The client cannot be taught what he or she should know about sources by the sink-or-swim method of sending him or her to the library, unaided, to find what often is not there. For more on sources of occupational information and how to make students familiar with them see Chapters 4, 5, and 13 to 16.

How to Choose   The client should know how to choose an occupation. The bases on which some young persons choose their occupations have made more than one counselor shudder. From some vague source they have heard that a specific occupation pays well, is expanding, and offers attractive opportunities for advancement. They have seen one glamorous aspect of the occupation and are attracted by it. They wish to be like someone they admire who is engaged in this field. They have taken an interest test, and it points in this direction. They liked this subject in school or did well on an aptitude test in this area. Any one of these reasons could be a good reason for considering the occupation. No one of them alone nor all of them in combination is sufficient basis for an intelligent choice. There are dozens of other considerations which may have more effect upon the success and satisfaction of the client than any of the items mentioned in this paragraph. How to reach career decisions is readably discussed by Brown [34], Byrn [37], and the College Placement Council [306]. For more on this topic see Chapters 17 to 19.

How to Find a Job   Career counseling which does not stay with the client until he or she has been employed is frequently futile, because the counselor is not present when the client discovers that no one will pay him or her to do just what the counselor and the client have decided the client should do. At this point the counselor may need to help the client to improve his job-hunting techniques or to reconsider the objective. Few clients know the most effective channels for finding vacancies. There is much which they can and should be taught, in the counseling interviews or in a good course or unit in occupations. For more on this subject see the sections "Practice Job Interviews," "Job Clinics," and "Practice on Employment Application Blanks" in Chapter 20.

Significant Specifics   Krumboltz [224] has noted that some clients "not only do . . . not know the answers to some vital questions; they do not even know what questions to ask." The client should know many specific things about an occupation before entering it. Most of these specifics are included in the checklist below. How significant some of these items are in determining the success and satisfaction of the client is discussed more fully in Chapter 11.

Eventually every person who is to be self-supporting comes to the point where he must commit himself to preparing for an occupation or seeking a job in it or accepting or refusing a job that he can have. If he has not previously examined the occupation or the job in terms of what he has to offer it and what it offers him, he may wish to do so at this time. The following checklist of questions which may be applied to any occupation is presented to help the counselor and the client to review a job or an occupation systematically. Not all these questions apply to all jobs, but the counselor will find here most of the important topics to consider. The reader is urged not to skip over this checklist unless he is already familiar with several other lists of this kind. The beginning counselor may find here a number of important considerations which will be new to him and which he should be thinking about from this point on.

A CHECKLIST OF FACTS ABOUT JOBS FOR USE IN CAREER GUIDANCE

Employment prospects

Are workers in demand today? Are they likely to be in demand when the client will be looking for a job? Is employment in this occupation expected to increase or decrease?

Nature of the work

What is the work of a typical day, week, month, year? What are all the things a worker may have to do in this occupation, the pleasant things, the unpleasant things, the big and little tasks, the important responsibilities, and the less glamorous details? Does he or she deal mainly with data, people, or things? With what kinds of tools, machines, and materials does one work? Must one walk, jump, run, balance, climb, crawl, kneel, stand, turn, stoop, crouch, sit, reach, lift, carry, throw, push, pull, handle, finger, feel, talk, hear, or see? Must one travel? Where and when?

Work environment

In what kind of surroundings is the work done? Hot, cold, humid, dry, wet, dusty, dirty, noisy? Indoor or outdoor? Is the worker exposed to sudden changes of temperature, offensive odors, vibration, mechanical hazards, moving objects, burns, electric shock, explosives, radiant energy, toxic conditions, or other hazards? Does the worker work in cramped quarters, in high places, or in any other unusual location? Are lighting, ventilation, and sanitation adequate? Does one work with others, near others, or alone? If with others, what is the worker's relationship to them, and does it place the worker in a position of superiority, inferiority, equality, conflict, or stress?

Qualifications

Age   What are the upper and lower age limits for entrance and retirement?

Sex   Is this predominantly a male or female occupation? Are there reasonable opportunities for both? Is there any more active demand for one than for the other?

Height and weight   Are there any minimum or maximum requirements? What are they?

Other physical requirements Are there any other measurable physical requirements, e.g., 20/20 vision, freedom from color blindness, average or superior hearing, physical strength, etc.?

Aptitudes Has there been any research on aptitudes required, e.g., minimum or maximum intelligence quotient, percentile rank on specific tests of mechanical aptitude, clerical aptitude, finger dexterity, pitch discrimination, reaction time, etc.?

Interests Have any vocational interest inventories been validated against workers in this occupation?

Tools and equipment Must these be supplied by the worker? What is the average cost? Can they be rented or bought on credit?

Legal requirements Is a license or certificate required? What are the requirements for getting it?

Citizenship Is it required?

Residence Must the worker be a resident of the city or state in which he or she is employed?

In what other ways do workers in this occupation differ from other people?

Unions

Is the closed shop common or predominant? If so, what are the requirements for entrance to the union? Initiation fees? Dues? Does the union limit the number admitted?

Discrimination

Despite legal prohibitions, do employers, unions, or training institutions discriminate on the basis of sex, race, religion, marital status, etc.?

Preparation

Distinguish clearly between what is desirable and what is indispensable.

How much and what kind of preparation is required to meet legal requirements and employers' standards?

How long does it take? What does it cost? What does it include?

Where can one get a list of approved schools?

What kind of high school or college program should precede entrance into the professional school? What subjects must or should be chosen?

What provisions, if any, are made for apprenticeship or other training on the job?

Is experience of some kind prerequisite to entrance?

Entrance

How does one get his or her first job? By taking an examination? By applying to employers? By joining a union? By registering with employment agencies? By saving to acquire capital and opening one's own business? How much capital is required?

Advancement

What proportion of workers advance? To what? After how long and after what additional preparation or experience?

What are the related occupations to which this may lead, if any?

Earnings

What are the most dependable average figures on earnings by week, month, or year?

What is the range of the middle 50 percent?

Are earnings higher or lower in certain parts of the United States or in certain branches of the occupation?

Number and distribution of workers

Are the workers evenly distributed in proportion to population or concentrated in certain areas? Where? Why?

Can a person practice this occupation anywhere that he or she may wish to live?

Do conditions in small towns and rural areas differ materially from those in urban centers? How?

Are most of the workers employed by private industry, by government, or by some other kind of organization, or are they self-employed? Are most of the employing organizations large or small?

Advantages and disadvantages

What do workers say they like most and least about their jobs?

Are hours regular or irregular, long or short? Is there frequent overtime or night work? Sunday and holiday work?

What about vacations? Maternity or paternity leave?

Is employment steady, seasonal, or irregular? Does one earn more or less with advancing age?

Is the working lifetime shorter than average, e.g., as for professional athletes?

Are the skills acquired transferable to other occupations?

Is the work hazardous? What about accidents or occupational diseases?

How will the work affect the life style of the worker and the family?

In comparison with other occupations requiring about the same level of ability and training, in what ways is this one more or less attractive?

For college seniors who are comparing potential employers, Sherrill [344] prepared a helpful booklet which includes the following list:

QUESTIONS AND SUBJECTS FREQUENTLY DISCUSSED IN INTERVIEWS

1 The Industry (or Type of Service)

Do the general characteristics of the industry have a definite interest for you?

Is it, or does it promise to be, sound in the national economy?

Has the industry a history of broad usefulness? Are expansions or diversifications contemplated? Are new developments challenging the industry?

2 The Company (or Institution)

Has the company shown substantial growth as reflected by increased production, new products and services, sales over a period of years?

Has there been, or is there promise of, considerable growth of products, technological changes, and facilities which permit upgrading of qualified people? Has the company taken on new acquisitions? Are there prospects of a merger?

How does the company rate with Dun & Bradstreet, Standard & Poor, the local banker, and customers? What reputation does it have with the placement service, the faculty, and alumni?

Have the company's labor and public relations appeared normal over a period of time?

Does the company have today's usual fringe benefits such as group life insurance, hospitalization, sick benefits, retirement, and provisions for continuing education? What are the approximate contributory costs?

3 Stability

Does the whole picture of the industry . . . the company, research and development, diversification of products and services, sales . . . appear progressive in this age of technological progress and obsolescence?

What is the company's financial condition? (Refer to annual statements of assets and liabilities; ratio of research expenditures to sales; the trend of earnings per share of stock. Extremely high or low positions may be important for your inquiry.)

Does the company appear well established and aggressively managed? What is its competitive position?

Does the company have many contracts subject to cancellation? What is the history of professional layoffs? What were the basic causes? (Turnover percentages can be misleading; definitions and interpretations are seldom identical.)

Could this hiring be for temporary work?

4 Assignments

Is the work in line with your interests, and can your education and experience be well applied? What indoctrination, training, and work are offered during the first few years? What challenges are promised for you?

Do you want a job clearly defined with established responsibilities and hours of work?

Are schedules and days of work satisfactory?

Will you receive a permanent assignment or will you be expected to move from one location to another? Will extensive travel or time on business away from home impose restrictions on family or other obligations?

Would it be possible to obtain a transfer to another location should personal reasons demand it?

5　Freedom for Ideas and Methods

Does it appear that you will have reasonable freedom in assignments to use initiative in developing ideas and new methods?

What associations or supervisor's clubs exist on a self-operating basis?

Are there meetings with the new people to discuss problems, ideas, new developments?

6　Professional Status

Does it appear that you will have professional status or managerial responsibilities?

What are some of the privileges accorded a professional employee?

Will you be free to make decisions as you become qualified?

Are professional organizations nearby?

Does the company promote activities aiding professional growth, such as participation in technical societies and seminars?

Are there aspects of publication of technical papers or patents that would add to your professional stature and worth to the company?

7　Advancement

While advancement depends much upon your efforts and abilities, you will want to consider all aspects of the business and your probable place in the organizational structure. What are the factors which seem unfavorable for your future advancement?

Is there evidence of real flexibility in management?

Will additional work become available to permit promotion as you develop new abilities?

Are there many cases of promotions through reassignments and transfers?

Do promotions come primarily from within the company or are outsiders brought in for key jobs to a large extent?

8　Salary

What is the present average salary for those in your classification and state of preparation?

Consider reasons for unusually low or high salary offers.

Is the beginning salary apt to be static?

What is your salary potential? Are there many cases of salaries increasing as responsibilities increase?

Are there periodic reviews? On a merit basis? When and by whom?

Are salaries adjusted on an overall basis . . . as for a change in the cost of living?

9 Continuing Education

Are there colleges within commuting distance offering courses useful to you?

Does the company encourage continuing education and does it subsidize tuition?

Does the company provide technical programs designed to strengthen the employee and the company?

10 Location (or Possible Future Locations)

Is the area you are considering suitable for your progress and happiness? A number of factors deserve special attention if you have a family. Do you desire residence in a metropolitan or suburban area? Would living a considerable distance from home town and family obligations impose problems? Consider the effects of nearby institutions, community safety, health, welfare, available utilities, organized protection, the school system, and city management.

Are you seriously concerned about climate, excessive humidity, noise, odors?

11 Off-the-Job Conditions

Does the community appear progressive for your interests in recreational, social, professional, or other areas of activity?

What community activities now engage the interests of employees and their families?

How will family members adjust to the new environment? Do the townspeople seem friendly and willing to aid newcomers?

Are churches and service organizations adequate?

12 Housing

Is housing available within a reasonable distance?

Are suitable rentals within your means?

Does the company assist in relocations? To what extent?

Does property appear a sound investment if you later want to sell?

13 Transportation

Are transportation and communication services satisfactory? Consider main highways, rail, and air facilities.

Consider time and cost of daily travel to and from work.

14 Cost of Living

Cost of living varies with location and depends primarily on what people are accustomed to and how they want to live.

Consider any special costs required by the job . . . expense of living in a specified area, social expectations, frequent assignments away from home.

Are there nearby business institutions (service, commerce, manufacturing) to help keep local taxation levies at a reasonable level?

15 Temporary Employment (Undergraduate and Postgraduate)

Is work available during periods before military service or intermittent periods while you are continuing your education?

What are the requirements for leaves-of-absence?

16 Military Commitments

Will the company consider your employment in the event of probable military call after graduation?

Does the company cooperate with requirements for summer camp (ROTC), National Guard, or reserve meetings? Is a salary adjustment made?

What is the policy regarding work and salary upon return from service?

17 Corporate Attitudes and Characteristics

A company or other organization, like an individual, has certain predominant characteristics—the traits, interests, abilities which underlie its strengths and weaknesses. Some indicators of such character are participations in civic, government, and educational affairs; its attentions to individual improvements, high ethical standards, and dealer and stockholder relationships. If you believe certain outstanding characteristics of a company will affect your progress and success, now is the time to investigate thoroughly.

In what ways does the company or its representatives serve in community affairs, service organizations, government? How extensively is safety promoted on the job and off, and how does the company's annual frequency rate compare with the industry's average? How many serve in youth organizations or lead in other public services? What meetings at colleges and technical groups are usually attended by company representatives? Will you be in line for any of these meetings?

From the preceding questions one counselor compiled a shorter list for college seniors to ask campus recruiters.

REVIEW QUESTIONS

1 How do clients differ in their need for occupational information?
2 How can the range of occupations in which young persons express an interest be quickly and easily extended?
3 Where can you get for your clients a readable pamphlet on how to reach career decisions?
4 Career counseling which stops short of placement is frequently futile. Why?
5 What are some of the characteristics of the work environment that should be considered by a person choosing an occupation?
6 What are some of the physical requirements that a candidate for employment may have to meet?
7 What should a person who is choosing an occupation know about unions in any field one thinks of entering?

8 In considering preparation for an occupation, what should the client and counselor "distinguish clearly between"?

9 What are some of the different ways in which one may get one's first job?

10 List some of the important considerations in the choice of an occupation that you think might be overlooked by a person who did not use a checklist similar to the one in this chapter.

11 How can you use what you have learned from this chapter?

Chapter 4

Sources of Occupational Information

One part of a counselor's work is to answer questions about occupations from clients, teachers, parents, and others. Often the counselor will not know the answers, but he or she will know more than the questioner about where and how to find them. The purpose of this chapter and the next one is to help the counselor to find the information desired on any occupation and to appraise its accuracy.

Not every question can be answered. No one can predict with certainty the average earnings of plumbers four years ahead. No one can say precisely what combination of aptitudes and interests contributes most to successful teaching. But a great many questions can be answered, and reasonably good guesses can be made about many others if the counselor knows where and how to look for the necessary information.

ORIGINAL SOURCES

The original sources of all occupational information are very simple, very easy to remember. They are the worker who does the job, the person who pays him to do it, and the government bureau which issues licenses and regulates employment.

All other sources of occupational information are intermediate sources which, in some way at some time, obtained their information from these original sources or from someone else who went to the original sources.

The ultimate recourse for the counselor or client who wants occupational information and has trouble finding it is to turn to these original sources. The difficulties in doing so are obvious. Except in the government bureaus, the persons may be hard to find or reluctant to answer. Those who can be reached may provide an atypical or a biased sample. They may have reasons for revealing only part of the truth or for stretching it a little. Despite the difficulties, the original source is often the best source and sometimes the only source from which to seek the desired information.

Workers and employers can be found in several ways: by examining the classified telephone directory; by consulting local offices of the state employment service and other placement services; by consulting the local chamber of commerce, labor unions, professional and trade associations, and banks; by asking one's students or clients to list the occupations of their relatives and friends; by making follow-up studies of former students and clients; and by making occupational surveys of the employment market.

When the original sources have already been consulted by a competent inquirer who has compiled and published the results, the counselor may, of course, turn first to such reports. Part of this chapter is devoted to explaining where and how such reports may be found. The succeeding chapter suggests how they may be appraised so that the client may be protected from information that is obsolete, incomplete, or intentionally or unintentionally biased.

Overs [296] has called attention to the importance of covert occupational information which "is generally unwritten, . . . is not expressed publicly, [and] may be denied . . . by responsible authorities although its validity may be high as measured by administrative actions." Covert information may reveal that a job is more or less desirable, that employers are more or less selective than overt information implies. "For instance, in intermediate level and higher level civil service positions . . . most applicants are hired by their prospective supervisors through personal contact and then ways are found to cover them into the civil service system."

Covert occupational information may be obtained from present and former clients, from follow-up studies, from informal talks with employers, employees, and union officers, from plant tours, from fellow counselors, and from observation—"i.e., clients in certain categories get jobs while clients in other categories don't." Some sociological studies [297] of occupations provide a rich source of covert information.

"The counselor who achieves practical results . . . collects and uses this covert information. . . . The counselor who accepts the official [statements] at face value . . . is often confronting his client with a false occupational reality."

The total volume of information available in publications is impressive—dangerously so. Its sheer quantity may lead the counselor to the erroneous conclusion that a good library is a sufficient source of occupational information. It is not. The counselor who depends upon a library for all occupational information will be unable to answer many of the questions that come to him, and the clients will be unable to find the answers without help.

The author and his students once undertook to find the answers to questions which counselors had been asked but which they could not answer, such as, "How do you get to be a tombstone cutter? What do Good Humor drivers do in the winter?" We found the answers, and we kept a record of where we found them. Most of the answers came from workers and their employers.

This chapter is intended to serve as a convenient reference to which the counselor may turn as questions arise. While there is no need to memorize every detail, the counselor is urged to read the chapter carefully in order to see what surprises it may contain; the beginner will be likely to find several, and even the experienced counselor may find one or two, as the author did when he prepared this material.

PUBLICATIONS

Publications Usually Available in Schools and Colleges   Perhaps the most widely used of all sources of occupational information is the *Occupational Outlook Handbook* [292] published biennially by the U.S. Bureau of Labor Statistics. It describes several hundred occupations. The descriptions include the nature of the work, where workers are employed, training, other qualifications, advancement, employment outlook, earnings, working conditions, and where to go for more information. The *Occupational Outlook for College Graduates* [291] is an abridged edition of the handbook. The *Occupational Outlook Quarterly*, from the same publisher, provides supplementary information between the biennial editions of the handbook. While no publication of this kind can ever be perfect, the handbook is generally conceded to be the best document of its kind currently available. Most counselors who are looking for occupational information turn to it first. Some schools place a copy in every homeroom. Old editions should be discarded and replaced as new editions are published. In some ways similar to the handbook is Hopke's *Encyclopedia of Careers and Vocational Guidance* [171].

Most schools and colleges maintain a collection of occupational pamphlets. Some publishers now offer collections of this kind, complete with filing cabinet, filing system, file folders, occupational pamphlets, and a service for supplying new materials as they are published. Some of these kits are described in Chapters 5 and 6.

Most college placement offices maintain a file of recruiting brochures, supplied by the companies which hope to hire some of the students about to graduate. Some of these brochures provide excellent descriptions of the jobs available. Regrettably, most of the brochures deal in glittering generalities and exemplify all the dangers of recruiting literature discussed in Chapter 5.

Also available in most college placement offices is the *College Placement Annual* [68], a directory of employers who recruit on college campuses. It indicates the jobs for which these employers expect to hire college graduates during the year ahead. The companies are arranged alphabetically and indexed geographically and by major job categories. Also indexed are companies that recruit for foreign employment, those that offer summer jobs, and those that recruit holders of doctoral degrees and experienced college alumni. For Canadians there are the *Directory: Employers of New University Graduates* [102], the *Directory:*

Employers of New Community College Graduates [101], and other publications of the Department of Manpower and Immigration, Ottawa.

Other Major Reference Works for the Counselor's Library   Less widely used but valuable for reference are the following, which belong in every counselor's library:

The *Dictionary of Occupational Titles* [98], which is usually referred to as the *D.O.T.*, contains very brief descriptions of thousands of occupations. The titles are classified by categories and subordinate groups, and identified by code numbers, by worker trait requirements, and in other ways. How the *D.O.T.* may be used in counseling is discussed in Chapter 10; filing systems based on the *D.O.T.* are discussed in Chapter 6. There is also a *Canadian Classification and Dictionary of Occupations* [42].

The local classified telephone directory. This provides a quick and easy way of revealing to the student or client the wide range of occupations locally available and the names of possible employers. It can also reveal how limited are the opportunities for employment in some of the glamour fields. See also the *National Minority Business Directory* [279] and the *Guide to Minority Business Directories* [151].

Building a library of occupational information is described in Chapter 5.

Where and How to Find Other Publications   To locate books, pamphlets, and magazine articles describing different occupations, consult current and back issues of the *Career Index* [47], the *Career Guidance Index* [46], the *Counselors' Information Service* [77], the *Guidance Exchange* [145], the *Guide to Local Occupational Information* [150], the *Guide to Indexes as a Resource for Occupations and Careers* [149], the "Career Media" section in some issues of the *Journal of College Placement* [211], and the lists of "Current Career Literature" recommended by the Career Information Review Service of the National Vocational Guidance Association and published in the *Vocational Guidance Quarterly* [401]. Earlier publications recommended by the Career Information Review Service may be found in the *NVGA Bibliography of Current Career Information* [281].

The beginning counselor should write to the publishers of these indexes, ask for descriptive literature and sample copies, compare them, select and subscribe to the one which seems best for his purposes, and be sure to save all issues for future reference.

One of these indexes should be among the first purchases made for any library of occupational information, for several reasons. As a file of back issues accumulates, the index will become the counselor's best guide to the most recently published information on any and all occupations. By calling the counselor's attention to several publications on the same subject, the index will facilitate more discriminating purchase; sometimes an inexpensive pamphlet will be better than an expensive book. Much free material is listed, and some of it is good. The index will more than pay for itself in what it will save on the purchase of new materials.

Another excellent bibliography is Forrester's *Occupational Literature* [126].

Being a single volume which covers the publications of several years, this is more convenient to use than the periodical indexes. Its one disadvantage is that it is published less frequently and thus includes none of the new publications which have come out since the last edition went to press.

After consulting these bibliographies, ask your students if any of them have relatives in the occupation from whom they can borrow occupational books or magazines for you to consult. Consult the card index and the pamphlet files of local libraries. Ask your librarian for back issues of professional journals and trade papers related to the occupation you are investigating.

To locate technical journals in any field consult *Ulrich's International Periodicals Directory* [393] and *The Standard Periodical Directory* [372]. For articles in general magazines consult the *Readers' Guide to Periodical Literature* [314]; for recent news about any occupation watch the local newspapers and *The New York Times Index* [283]. All these are available in most large libraries and in many smaller ones.

Career World [49] is a readable periodical for students; it describes opportunities in a wide variety of occupations and frequently refers to sources of further information.

For guides to audiovisual materials containing occupational information see Chapter 20.

When you do not find the information you want among the publications or when you suspect that the publications are out of date, biased, or otherwise inaccurate, consult the other sources listed below for information on specific topics.

KINDS OF INFORMATION AND WHERE TO FIND THEM

Employment Opportunities   To determine the kinds of jobs most likely to be open to dropouts, graduates, or members of any other group, examine the results of follow-up studies to see what jobs were obtained by former members of the same group. Consult employment offices, and make a survey of employers. Review the discussion of these sources in Chapter 2.

Ask your school, college, or local librarian for other directories of employers.

For information about government jobs, write to federal, state, county, and city civil service commissions, and talk with the persons who represent your district in all elective offices. Ask the U.S. Civil Service Commission for the address of the Federal Job Information Center nearest to you.

The author hopes the reader will tolerate and possibly share his desire to help those who would devote their lives to working for world peace, and who seek information on how to do it. Among the best references on this subject are *Action and Careers in a New Age* [3], Calvert's *Your Future in International Service* [39] and the *Guide to Alternative Service* [146]. Information on opportunities in vocations for social change is available from several organizations listed in *Working Loose* [418].

Summer Jobs   Information on summer jobs for high school and college students, teachers, and others may be obtained from:

College Placement Annual [68]. Look in the table of contents for the index to companies which hire college students for summer jobs. Then see the descriptions of the companies, arranged alphabetically in the front of the book.

B'nai B'rith Career and Counseling Services, 1640 Rhode Island Ave., N.W., Washington, D.C. 20036

Commission on Voluntary Service and Action, 475 Riverside Dr., New York, N.Y. 10027

Committee on Employment Opportunities Abroad, Council on Student Travel, 777 United Nations Plaza, New York, N.Y. 10017

Coordination Committee for International Voluntary Service (UNESCO), 1 Rue Miollis, Paris 15e, France

Council on International Educational Exchange, 777 United Nations Plaza, New York, N.Y. 10017

Federal, state, county, and city civil service commissions

National Directory Service, 266 Ludlow Ave., Cincinnati, Ohio 45220

UNESCO Publications Center, 650 First Ave., New York, N.Y.

U.S. Department of Labor, Manpower Administration, Washington, D.C.

U.S. National Student Association, 2115 S St., N.W., Washington, D.C.

Your own state employment service at the state capital

Employment in Foreign Countries   For information regarding employment opportunities outside the United States, write to:

Associate Commissioner for International Education, U.S. Office of Education, Washington, D.C.

B'nai B'rith Career and Counseling Services, 1640 Rhode Island Ave., N.W., Washington, D.C. 20036

Chamber of Commerce of the U.S.A., Washington, D.C. 20006

Commission on Voluntary Service and Action, 475 Riverside Dr., New York, N.Y. 10027

Commission on Youth Projects, 475 Riverside Dr., New York, N.Y. 10027

Committee on Employment Opportunities Abroad, Council on Student Travel, 777 United Nations Plaza, New York, N.Y. 10017

Coordination Committee for International Voluntary Service (UNESCO), 1 Rue Miollis, Paris 15e, France

Council on International Educational Exchange, 777 United Nations Plaza, New York, N.Y. 10017

Foreign Policy Association, 345 E. 46 St., New York, N.Y. 10017

Department of Manpower and Immigration, Ottawa, Ontario, Canada

Hill International Publications, East Islip, N.Y.

Institute of International Education, 809 United Nations Plaza, New York, N.Y. 10017

National Council of the Churches of Christ, 475 Riverside Dr., New York, N.Y. 10027

National Directory Service, 266 Ludlow Ave., Cincinnati, Ohio 45220

National Employment Services, Inc., 1612 K St., N.W., Washington, D.C.

UNESCO Publications Center, 650 First Ave., New York, N.Y.

U.S. Civil Service Commission, Washington, D.C.

U.S. Department of Defense: Overseas Dependents Schools, Washington, D.C. 20301

U.S. Department of Labor, Manpower Administration, Washington, D.C.
U.S. National Student Association, 2115 S St., N.W., Washington, D.C.

Supply and Demand for Workers   Ask school and college placement offices
and public employment services; they are in the best position to observe the
supply and demand for workers in the occupations which they handle. Information from these sources is seldom more than twenty-four hours old. It is comparatively free from bias. In periods of depression, when many occupations are overcrowded, the employment office is favorably situated to observe where the
crowding is least severe.

The information obtained from local agencies usually reflects local conditions, which may or may not follow national trends. For a broader picture, consult the *Occupational Outlook Handbook* [292] and write to the U.S. Bureau of
Labor Statistics, Washington, for any reports released since the last handbook
went to press. In Canada see *Supply, Demand and Salaries, New Graduates of
Universities and Community Colleges* [385].

Read slowly and carefully all statements about the occupational outlook.
The hasty reader can easily draw the wrong inference from such statements as the
following, if he fails to notice and to emphasize the words which I have put in
capital letters.

> Opportunities for TALENTED . . . are expected to be good.
>
> WELL-QUALIFIED beginners with . . . TALENT will have good employ-
> ment opportunities.
>
> Employers were actively seeking young . . . with EXCEPTIONAL TALENT.
>
> Employment opportunities are favorable for TALENTED and WELL-
> TRAINED. . . . People with less ability and training are likely to encounter KEEN
> COMPETITION.

The correct inference from each of these statements may well be, "You had
better have a second-choice occupation in reserve if you want to eat." In contrast, observe the following quotations from the same publication.

> . . . are expected to have very good employment opportunities. . . . NOT
> ENOUGH GRADUATES to satisfy the demand.
>
> A nationwide SHORTAGE of trained . . .

Consider also the shades of meaning indicated by the words used to describe
growth or decline in expected numbers employed: "very rapid," "rapid," "moderate," "slow," and "little or no change"; and the terms which describe the demand for workers as compared to the supply: "excellent," "very good," "good or
favorable," "may face competition," and "keen competition." For more on this
see the introductory section of the handbook.

Be cautious about accepting statements of employers, employees, professional and trade associations, labor unions, and training institutions; frequently
they have a selfish interest in increasing or restricting the supply of workers.

Employers seldom find the ideal applicant for work. Even in periods of
unemployment, employers can and often will say quite truthfully, "There is still

plenty of room for good people." Because the counselor deals most of the time with average persons, one must remember to emphasize the word "good" in the employer's statement. What the counselor considers good will sometimes be far removed from what the employer had in mind. Trade associations and other associations of employers are subject to similar bias.

Employees are subject to the same bias in reverse. Not all of them are as successful as they would like to be. It is easy for them to believe that they would have been more successful if they had had less competition. It is not surprising that they notice, remember, and repeat anything which supports the opinion that their field is overcrowded. Labor unions and associations of professional workers are subject to similar bias. During economic depressions, it is common to find a professional association reporting that its field is overcrowded and rare to find one that encourages the recruitment of new workers. Labor unions quite frankly restrict the number of apprentices and the admission of new members to the union; some professional associations do the same thing less openly.

Not to be confused with the professional association is the association of professional schools, which reverses the bias again. When enrollments decline, educational administrators become apprehensive. College professors and vocational schoolteachers share their concern. Budgets are threatened. Salary increments and promotions are delayed. When enrollments go up, faculty meetings are concerned with excluding the incompetent applicant for admission in order to maintain standards, but when enrollments go down, more attention is focused on recruitment. Even the reputable, accredited, and endowed colleges have not been above stretching the truth a bit in some of their recruiting literature. Associations of schools and colleges reflect the biases of their members.

Bearing in mind the cautions mentioned above, it is sometimes possible to get useful information from professional and trade associations, e.g., figures on the number of professionally trained persons graduated and the number of new persons hired in one year.

Future Prospects   Consult the *Occupational Outlook Handbook* [292]. Write to the U.S. Bureau of Labor Statistics, Washington. Write to the state department of labor and the state employment service; some states have produced and published projections of the employment outlook in their own areas. For local conditions, interview local employers and the officers of local unions and compare what they say. Beware of biases noted above.

The forecast of prospects should extend into the future at least as far as the prospective worker's full-time education. Failure to consider this fact can result in some sad disappointments. When there is a widely advertised shortage of workers in any occupation, there is a tendency to assume that the shortage will still exist when the present high school seniors are ready to look for jobs. Actually, by that time, so many other persons may have responded to the shortage and the demand may have so changed that there will be a surplus instead of a shortage of applicants for work. Conversely, a widely advertised surplus of workers can so discourage new entrants as to create a shortage in a few years. One cannot assume that surpluses and shortages will reverse themselves, but neither can one assume that they will not. Always one must look for the best available predictions and never forget that prediction is a hazardous business at best.

Dickinson [97] has noted that when one is comparing the number of new entrants who can be absorbed in an occupation with the number of persons in training for the occupation, it is important to remember that "very sizable percentages of those gaining degrees in such fields of study do not choose to enter these professions."

Nature of the Work   Consult the *Dictionary of Occupational Titles* [98]. Visit and observe workers at their work. Ask several persons engaged in the occupation to tell you all the things they do and to indicate which things occupy most of their time. One of the best ways to do this is to ask the worker to describe in sequence everything that he has done since coming to work this morning and how much time was spent on each task, then ask what he did the day before that was different, then what else he has done as a part of his job during the past week, month, year. Without a detailed review of this kind, workers often forget to mention some of their activities.

Ask employers if they have any written job descriptions that you may see. See Pearson [302] for a sample of the kinds of occupational information that some companies provide for their own employees.

Work Environment   Go to see it if you can. Ask several workers and employers. Because working conditions in the same occupation may vary from one place of employment to another, be careful not to generalize from too few observations. Examine Overs and Deutsch [297], *Sociological Studies of Occupations* [364], and back issues of the *Sociological Abstracts* [363].

Qualifications for Employment   Ask employers not only what qualifications they seek but also what they have accepted. Distinguish between the qualifications which are indispensable and those which are desirable. Remember that few workers have all the desirable qualities.

For civil service jobs, consult the announcements of the most recent examinations. To get civil service announcements, write to the federal, state, county, and city civil service commissions.

Physical Demands   Do not overlook the physical demands of the occupation, which are often at least as important as the mental qualifications and which are sometimes much easier to discover. The first aptitude test applied to prospective soda dispensers by one vocational school is a tape measure around the hips; too much bulk at this point makes the worker a traffic hazard behind the counter. Some large cities have minimum and maximum height and weight requirements for police officers and firefighters. One city will hire no teacher who weighs more than 300 pounds. Color blindness may handicap a chemist, a commercial artist, or a house painter. High blood pressure will exclude a truck driver from employment with some companies. A person who cannot stand on his feet all day will have to find an unusually favorable environment to earn a living as a dentist or retail salesperson. For facts on physical demands, ask local employers and employees, consult the *Dictionary of Occupational Titles* [98], the U.S. Employment Service, and the federal, state, county, and city civil service commissions.

Aptitudes   Read Super and Crites [382]. See also the sections on worker trait groups in the *Dictionary of Occupational Titles* [98]. For more recent research, consult the back issues of the *Psychological Abstracts* [311]. In conversations with employers, beware of vague statements about such general characteristics as initiative, dependability, honesty, punctuality, and industry, which are needed in nearly all occupations. The statements may be true enough, but they are of little help to the person who is trying to choose between occupations.

Interests   Consult the manual of instructions which accompanies available interest blanks to see if any research has been done on the relationship between scores on these blanks and success or satisfaction in the occupation. Beware of scores on blanks that have not been adequately validated. See also Super and Crites [382]. For more recent research, consult the back issues of the *Psychological Abstracts* [311].

Tools and Equipment   Ask local employers, employees, and unions. Write to business, professional, and trade associations listed in the *Encyclopedia of Associations* [116] and in *National Trade and Professional Associations of the United States and Labor Unions* [280].

Legal Requirements   Write to the appropriate city, county, state, and federal licensing boards. If you do not know the name and address of the correct board, send your question to the mayor, governor, or President, and ask him to route it to the proper department. Double check by asking local employers and employees.

Do not assume that a license is not required until you have made inquiries of all of the above. The number of licensed occupations increases continually. Some occupations are licensed by some states or cities and not by others. Among the workers who must have licenses, in some or all places in the United States, are airplane mechanics, apprentice seamen, architects, auctioneers, awning contractors, barbers, beekeepers, boxers, cement-block manufacturers, chauffeurs, commission merchants, cosmetologists, dealers in firearms, dental hygienists, food handlers, fur dealers, gasoline-service-station attendants, ice-cream manufacturers, insurance agents, journeyman electricians, junk dealers, kennel owners, landscape gardeners, manicurists, minnow dealers, morticians, motor-vehicle dealers, nursery dealers, optometrists, parking-lot attendants, plumbers, public librarians, real estate salespersons, registered and practical nurses, residential builders, stationary engineers, structural welders, syrup manufacturers, teachers, veterinarians, and many others.

Among the government agencies which issue these licenses are the municipal departments of health, fire, police, buildings, and safety engineering; the state departments of aeronautics, agriculture, banking, conservation, health, education, insurance, labor, police, state, social welfare; the athletic board of control; the state board of libraries; the liquor-control commission; the U.S. Department of Agriculture; Coast Guard; Federal Aviation Agency; Federal Communications Commission; Interstate Commerce Commission; and U.S. Treasury Department. See also the section "Labor Legislation" in Chapter 2.

Unions   Consult officers of local unions regarding requirements and costs of admission to the union. Ask both the union and the employers about closed-shop contracts and about what percentage of employees are union members.

Consult the *Directory of National Unions and Employee Associations* [105] and *National Trade and Professional Associations of the United States and Labor Unions* [280]. Select the appropriate unions, and write to them. The constitution and bylaws of a national union may say nothing about racial discrimination in the admission of new members, and national policy may even forbid such discrimination, but a union local may nevertheless find ways to discriminate, just as employers may evade the laws which prohibit them from discriminating. Because it may be impolitic for a union to tell the whole story, the counselor should always ask former students and clients about their experiences in applying for union membership.

Discrimination   Ask employers, employees, and former students. Do not ask employers and unions, "Do you discriminate? " Ask employers, "How many blacks do you employ now? In what jobs? " Ask unions, "How many of your members are blacks? " Ask similar questions about all other groups with which you are concerned. Other groups subject to discrimination include Jews; Catholics; Protestants; Communists; alleged Communists; Chinese, Japanese, Mexicans, Puerto Ricans, and other persons with distinctly foreign names, speech, or appearance; women; married women; pacifists; nonveterans; former prisoners; and persons over forty years of age.

Discriminatory practices include refusal to admit to union membership, refusal to refer qualified workers for employment, refusal to hire, unequal working conditions, refusal to upgrade, and dismissal without cause. Discrimination is practiced by government agencies as well as by private employers and labor unions and by individuals within these organizations even in opposition to organization policy.

For further information on discrimination against blacks and Jews, write to the National Urban League, 55 E. 52 St., New York, N.Y., and to the B'nai B'rith Career and Counseling Services, 1640 Rhode Island Ave., N.W., Washington, D.C. 20036.[1]

Preparation   See the sections on "Qualifications for Employment," "Legal Requirements," and "Unions" above; see "Approved Schools and Apprenticeship" below; see the discussion of "Preparation" in Chapter 11.

---

[1] The addresses here and on subsequent pages were correct at date of publication but should be checked by any reader using this list.

Approved Schools   Consult directories such as:

Accredited Institutions of Higher Education [1]
Accredited Post Secondary Institutions and Programs [2]
American Junior Colleges [7]
American Universities and Colleges [8]
College Blue Book: Occupational Education [332]
College Guide for Jewish Youth [67]
Colleges Classified [69]
Directory, National Association of Trade and Technical Schools [103]
Directory of Post Secondary Schools with Occupational Programs [106]
Directory of Secondary Schools with Occupational Curriculums [107]
Education Directory: Higher Education [114]
Guide to College Majors [147]
A Guide to Graduate Study. Programs Leading to the Ph.D. Degree [148]
Lovejoy's College Guide [249]
S.O.S. Guidance Research Information Booklets [191]
Technician Education Yearbook [388]
Universities and Colleges of Canada [394]

Write to business, trade, and professional associations listed in the *Encyclopedia of Associations* [116] and in *National Trade and Professional Associations of the United States and Labor Unions* [280]. Schools approved by some of the professional associations are so identified in some of the other directories.

Write to the U.S. Office of Education, Washington, D.C., and to your own state department of education for their most recent directories of approved and accredited vocational and professional schools and colleges and for a list of other directories of schools and colleges.

Write to the Accrediting Commission of the National Home Study Council, 1601–18 St., N.W., Washington, D.C., for its most recent list of approved correspondence schools [104]. Although correspondence study is even less likely than residence study to assure the student of subsequent employment, it can be of considerable value to the person who has a job and wants to become more proficient at it.

Shoemaker [345] asked university department heads to recommend "some schools that are considered 'good' in your area of specialization." He got 133 responses from 91 areas of specialization.

The applicant who is not admitted to the college of his choice can sometimes find a school that will accept him if he seeks help from the following:

College Admissions Assistance Center, 887 Seventh Ave., New York, N.Y. 10019

College Search Selection Service, 1 du Pont Circle, Washington, D.C. 20036

National Association of College Admissions Counselors, 9933 Lawler Ave., Skokie, Ill. 60076

Private College Admissions Center, 1738 Wisconsin Ave., Washington, D.C. 20007

Apprenticeship Ask the person in charge of apprenticeship or of vocational education in your school. Ask employers. Ask union locals. Ask the nearest office of your state employment service. Write to the Bureau of Apprenticeship and Training, U.S. Department of Labor, Washington 20210, for the addresses of the nearest regional and state apprenticeship agencies; then write to them. Ask the state agency if there are any apprenticeship councils near you, and consult them.

Apprentices are now trained in more than 300 occupations. Among these are aircraft-engine mechanic, automobile mechanic, boat-builder, bookbinder, brick-layer, business-machine mechanic, cabinetmaker, carpenter, commercial photographer, cook, dental mechanic, electrician, engraver, jeweler, machinist, meat-cutter, painter, patternmaker, photoengraver, plasterer, plumber, printer, refrigeration and air-conditioning mechanic, sewing-machine mechanic, sheet-metal worker, stonemason, tailor, tool and die maker, upholsterer, and watchmaker.

Methods of Entrance Ask employers, employees, and former students how a beginner gets the first job.

Capital Ask proprietors and bankers how much capital a beginner needs to start in business. Write to the United States Small Business Administration, Washington.

Advancement Ask both employers and employees. Inquire what percentage of beginning workers subsequently advances to each level.

Related Occupations Consult the *Dictionary of Occupational Titles* [98]. Ask employers, employees, and the local office of the state employment service.

Earnings Write to the U.S. Bureau of Labor Statistics, Washington. It publishes reports on earnings in the whole range of occupations from the unskilled to professional and administrative. Write to the professional, trade, and business associations in the *Encyclopedia of Associations* [116], the directory of *National Trade and Professional Associations of the United States and Labor Unions* [280], and the *Directory of National Unions and Employee Associations* [105]. For prevailing wages in local industry, try the local office of the state employment service. Try also the state department of labor. In large cities consult the local office of the U.S. Department of Labor. Ask local employers and unions, and compare their answers. Be sure to specify whether you are inquiring about wages for beginners or for experienced workers.

Starting salaries currently offered to college seniors in different curricula, by companies in different industries, are reported periodically in the College Placement Council's *Salary Survey* [334].

Beware of figures which may be accurate but misleading. Perhaps the most misleading of all are the top earnings of the most successful persons in an occupation. These are frequently reported in newspapers and in popular magazines. The optimistic young person may readily assume that if someone else can earn that much, perhaps he can, too. Perhaps so, but the probabilities may be a thousand to one against it.

We know so little about how to predict the earning power of any individual that the best guess we can make usually is that a man or woman will earn about what the average worker earns in the occupation that he or she enters. Consequently the best figures to use in comparing occupations are the median, or the range of the middle 50 percent. Means may have to be used when medians are not available; means are less desirable because they may be unduly affected by the extremely high earnings of extremely few persons.

Even median earnings can be misleading if one does not consider the working lifetime. Showgirls are old at twenty-three. Professional boxers are finished in their thirties. Heavy laborers may be unable to stand the physical strain in their forties and fifties. The choice of an occupation should be made only after a realistic look at probable life earnings. These are admittedly difficult to predict, but we can at least warn the young hopeful that in certain occupations earnings will be likely to decline with advancing age. Some data on life earnings have been published by the U.S. Bureau of the Census.

Hourly, daily, and weekly rates of pay can also be misleading. Coal miners, furriers, and gardeners are employed in seasonal industries; they must expect several weeks or months of unemployment each year. Hourly, daily, and weekly earnings must be converted into annual earnings before they can be used properly in career guidance. In the conversion, allowance should be made for unemployment compensation.

The person who wants a steady job in a seasonal occupation may find it by looking long enough. Some large companies, for example, hire carpenters for maintenance work and keep them busy all the time; such carpenters are usually paid less per hour than carpenters whose work is intermittent.

Other persons, who budget their expenditures carefully, enjoy the vacations provided by seasonal unemployment, during which they may collect unemployment compensation. It is, of course, not the counselor's responsibility to decide whether continuous or intermittent employment is preferable; it is the counselor's responsibility to see that the client knows which kind of employment he or she is choosing.

Number and Distribution of Workers   Write to the Bureau of the Census, U.S. Department of Commerce, Washington. Ask which census publication will give you the information you want.

If the facts you want have not been published, ask the Bureau of the Census if and how the data may be obtained. Some data are tabulated but not published, and transcripts of these data may be obtained at cost. Additional tabulations also may be contracted for under a cost arrangement.

It is possible to obtain data on the number employed in different occupations by age, race, and sex in any locality in the United States.

Hours   Ask local employers and employees. For national figures write to the U.S. Bureau of Labor Statistics, Washington; to the professional, trade, and business associations in the *Encyclopedia of Associations* [116], the directory of

National Trade and Professional Associations of the United States and Labor Unions [280], and the *Directory of National Unions and Employee Associations* [105].

Vacations Ask employers and employees.

Stability of Employment Ask employers and employees how the number of persons employed was affected by the last economic recession, the last big war, and the end of the war. Ask also about seasonal changes, effects of weather, strikes, and anything else which may interfere with steady employment for a normal working lifetime. Consult the *Occupational Outlook Handbook* [292].

Some occupations are particularly responsive to increases or decreases in public appropriations. Employers and employees can usually report with some accuracy, and often with some feeling, the effects of public spending in the past and the extent to which employment in their field is or is not affected by it.

If one wishes to work in a seasonal occupation, he will, of course, find employment prospects best at the time of the year when employment is rising. Employers can usually predict when this time will be. In retail selling, for example, employment rises sharply before Christmas and declines sharply after, and this happens year after year through periods of prosperity and depression.

Hazards Ask employers and employees, professional associations, and labor unions about accidents and occupational diseases. Write to the U.S. Bureau of Labor Statistics, Washington, D.C. 20212, and to the National Safety Council, Chicago, Illinois 60611.

Advantages, Disadvantages, and Satisfactions Ask several workers in the occupation, "What are the three things you like best about your job? What are the three things you like least about it? " See Rosen and others [323].

FINALLY

As the need for facts about jobs arises, the counselor who hopes to be effective will not rely solely upon the facts in the files or upon the occupational information that can be compiled by a client who has had no training in occupational research. The counselor who wants to do the job well will go out and talk with the employers and the employees of the community. He will turn to the telephone more often than to the files. How one community agency used a volunteer worker to get facts about jobs by means of field visits and telephone inquiries has been described by Miller [264].

REVIEW QUESTIONS

1 What are the original sources of all occupational information?
2 What sources provided most of the answers to questions that counselors could not answer?

3 What indexes periodically list new books, pamphlets, and magazine articles containing occupational information?

4 Which are the best sources of information on the relative supply and demand for workers in different occupations? Which are the biased sources, and why are they biased?

5 Which is the best source of information on future prospects for employment in many occupations?

6 Which is the best source of information on legal requirements for entrance to an occupation?

7 What are some of the groups that are subject to discrimination in employment other than Jews, blacks, and women?

8 Where can you write for general information about apprenticeship?

9 What organization publishes reports on earnings in the whole range of occupations?

10 What questions should be asked about stability of employment?

11 One of your clients wants to know all about an occupation that you have never even heard of. To what sources will you turn for information and in what sequence?

12 Your colleagues on your job know that you are taking this course. They ask you to talk to them for ten minutes about sources of occupational information. What will you tell them?

13 Is there anything in this chapter that you can use to improve your work? What? How?

Chapter 5

Appraising Occupational Literature

The dubious quality of many books, pamphlets, and magazine articles which purport to describe occupations has been mentioned in preceding chapters. One very important responsibility of the counselor or teacher is to examine and appraise the accuracy of every piece of occupational literature to which clients or students will be referred.

If the beginning counselor gets his or her first job in an organization which already has a substantial library of occupational information and if responsibility for the quality of this library has been assigned to some other member of the organization, the beginner should, of course, not be obnoxious by openly questioning or criticizing the quality of a colleague's work. But neither should one assume that he can refer his clients to this library without first examining and appraising the materials that clients will use.

Under these circumstances, the beginner may ask the librarian to indicate the materials available and to explain the preferred procedures for using them; then the counselor should examine them as thoroughly as time permits. Usually, there will not be time to do a very thorough job at this point.

Thereafter, every time the counselor refers a client to published occupational information, he should do one of two things: first, refer the client only to specific publications which the counselor has already examined and appraised, or, second, go with the client to the library and appraise each publication in the client's presence, at the same time teaching the client a little about how to appraise such materials. The counselor can avoid implied criticism of the librarian by explaining to the client that this library must serve the needs of many persons and that publications useful to other persons for their purposes may not be useful to this client.

If the counselor also teaches a course or unit in occupations to the students he counsels, he can and should include in this course both instruction and practice in the appraisal of occupational literature, but he can never escape ethical and professional responsibility for knowing the quality of the publications to which he refers his students any more than he can escape responsibility for knowing the validity of the aptitude tests he uses.

If the counselor is to be responsible for the purchase of new materials, he should then order publications only on approval and reserve sufficient time to appraise each accession before it goes onto the shelves or into the files. He should also make a thorough examination of the occupational literature on hand when he arrives and ask the librarian if some way can be devised to separate the best materials from the others. In this connection, he must, of course, remember that he and his clients are not the only users of the library and that the librarian may not be able to do everything that would be desirable from the counselor's point of view.

FIVE CRITICAL QUESTIONS

In appraising occupational literature, the counselor will do well to memorize and always to ask himself at least these five questions: When? Where? Who? Why? How?

When? If the reader will go to any school or college library, ask to see the occupational shelves, and examine the copyright dates of the books thereon, he will find, almost invariably, at least one book that is twenty-five years old resting on the same shelf with books published in the current year, and there will be nothing to warn the unsuspecting reader that the statements in the older volume may be a quarter century behind the times.

Most counselors maintain a file of occupational pamphlets, to which new materials are added periodically, and from which no one ever throws anything away. Examination of one such file revealed 900 pamphlets that were more than five years old. Of these 300 were over ten years old, 20 were over twenty years old, and a few had been published thirty years before [184]. Occupational books and pamphlets that are obsolete should be burned or sold as scrap paper or at least transferred to the historical section of the library.

The date by which to judge a book is not the date which appears on the title page. This date is usually the year in which the volume was printed. The book may have been written years earlier and reprinted without revision. The important date is the first copyright date, which usually appears in small print on the back of the title page. Later copyright dates for revised editions may or may not be significant. A book can be technically considered "revised" if the author changes one comma to a semicolon, and some revised versions seem to have enjoyed just about this much change.

Certain kinds of occupational information become obsolete more quickly than others. The ratio of supply to demand for beginners in engineering has changed radically within one year. Appropriate aptitudes and interests change only as the nature of the work changes. Hours and conditions of employment may change with each union contract negotiation. Hazards may change as rapidly as industrial processes. Industrial occupations may be wiped out completely by technological improvement, but it may take a thousand years to get an obsolete subject out of a school or college curriculum.

In appraising any publication, counselors should consider how rapid is the rate of change in the kind of information they seek. They may then decide how old a publication may be and still serve their purposes. Beginners may not be very confident in judging the rate of obsolescence, but if they will only pause long enough to consider it, they will avoid the inexcusable malpractice of referring clients to sources that are obviously out of date.

Where? All original occupational research has some kind of geographical limitation. It may cover conditions in one company, one city, one state, or one nation. In time it may cover one world. At present, much occupational literature purports to be national in its application but is based upon only scattered research covering a much smaller area or on the author's experience and reading. Careful appraisal therefore requires careful scrutiny of the research evidence upon which the author has based his statements. Is there any? If so, was the evidence compiled in the area in which the reader expects to seek employment? If not, are conditions likely to be similar or different in the two areas? Teachers' salaries and training requirements, for example, tend to be much higher in wealthy urban or suburban areas than in poorer rural areas. Inability to gain entrance to an exclusive union may exclude an urban boy from a preferred occupation but be a matter of no concern to the resident of a small town where the workers are not organized.

Who? Experienced workers in occupational research soon learn that certain of their colleagues invariably do careful, scholarly research and make only conservative statements which can be adequately documented. Other writers and some publishers become known for the superficial, inadequate, or biased nature of their material.

The beginning counselor will be somewhat at a loss to appraise the quality of authorship but can begin by noting anything that may be said about the author's qualifications and by asking for such information when the publishers do not supply it. In general, the best material is that written by persons whose full-time job is occupational research, such as the occupational research workers in the U.S. Bureau of Labor Statistics, the U.S. Employment Service, the state employment services, and the Women's Bureau of the U.S. Department of Labor. But these are not the only sources of good material.

Two of the best occupational descriptions that I have seen were "A Day with a Social Worker" [92] by Margaret O'Rourke Montgomery and "It's All in a Day's Work" [379] by Donald E. Super. The former reported in complete detail everything that one social worker did from 9:00 A.M. to 6:15 P.M. on a typical day; the latter reported in similar detail the activities of a college professor for an entire week. Similar but briefer descriptions of the work done in sixty-five occupations, with comments on how the jobs affected the home lives of some of the workers, are in Norton [287].

Why?   Some occupational literature is written solely for purposes of professional vocational guidance by persons who have no desire to do other than present the pertinent facts as accurately as possible.

Some is written for purposes of entertainment; most articles in popular magazines are in this category. Material for these articles is selected because it makes interesting reading. Important facts may be omitted if they are dull. Peak salaries may be stated, and average salaries omitted. Glamorous activities may be described at length; the more time-consuming routine aspects of the job may be barely mentioned. As entertainment, for the general reader who is not choosing an occupation, such literature has its place. As occupational information, it often leaves the reader with a false impression.

Some occupational literature is written for the purpose of recruiting students or workers. This is particularly dangerous because so much of it is free; consequently, it finds its way into school and college libraries and into college placement offices in disproportionately large quantities. It is often biased, emphasizing the attractions of the occupation, omitting or slighting its disadvantages, and sometimes intentionally conveying a false impression regarding opportunities, requirements, or rewards. The actual statements made are often true, as are the statements in patent-medicine advertising, but the total impression is often just as misleading and just as intentionally so. It is a sad commentary on our professions and our professional schools, but it is indisputably true that some of the most respected of them have not been above creating false impressions in order to recruit high school and college students. The deliberate misrepresentation employed by some recruiting officers for military services has been notorious for centuries. Gullible school counselors have been unwitting partners to the deception.

Be cautious when appraising information about occupations found in periodicals which carry a substantial amount of recruitment advertising. Look elsewhere for information about the disadvantages of occupations and about possible false statements by recruiting officers; further information on this may be obtained from the American Friends Service Committee, 160 N. 15 St., Philadelphia, Pa. 19102.

Southern and Colver [368] recommended that recruiting literature be used in counseling because of the useful information it contains but cautioned the counselor about his or her responsibilities when it is used:

> Many counselors tend to feel that the use of free material, especially recruitment material, is not an acceptable practice. We question the wisdom of such an attitude. . . .
> Every company realizes that only a small percentage of those people who read

the literature will apply for jobs, but that most readers are prospective customers, now or at some time in the future. In using this material for occupational information, the counselor has a responsibility for making the client fully aware of the fact that this is advertising and public relations material, as well as occupational information.

A few occupational articles are written for the express purpose of discouraging competition. In periods of general unemployment, nearly all occupations are temporarily "overcrowded." It is not unusual, at such times, for professional associations and labor unions to encourage the publication of news stories and magazine articles which describe the low earnings and the extensive unemployment among their own members. All that they say may be true, but if the same situation exists in most other occupations, the impression created may be misleading.

Biography and fiction are sometimes recommended for student reading because of their occupational content. A few such publications are good, but many biographies describe occupational conditions faced by the subject twenty or thirty years ago and do not warn the reader that conditions have changed. Many books of fiction convey mistakenly glamorous impressions of occupations. Both biography and fiction are usually written for purposes of entertainment rather than education. Necessarily they give most of their space to the entertaining aspects of whatever they present.

How? This question applies both to how the facts were collected and to how they are presented.

Questionnaire research has been described as a method of summarizing ignorance. Much occupational information has been collected by questionnaire. If the data sought concern matters on which the respondent is well informed, such as his or her own hours and earnings, if the sample is adequate, and if there is no incentive for giving false replies, the questionnaire may be the best possible method of compilation. If the data concern matters of opinion, on which the respondent is ignorant or biased, the results may do more harm than good. Most workers really know very little about the aptitudes which determine success or failure in their work, although many of them think they know a great deal. The same may be said of supply and demand for workers.

Some occupational literature is based solely on library research. It is as good or as bad as the original studies which the author consulted. Usually these studies are not identified, and the reader can only guess how good or how recent they were. This kind of "research" is often found in textbooks on occupations.

By inquiring about, and by carefully noting, how the information for any publication was collected, the counselor can sometimes get a much clearer idea of its probable accuracy. Guidelines for preparing and evaluating career films, filmstrips, and printed materials [152] have been published by the National Vocational Guidance Association and revised from time to time. These standards are used by the association to appraise new occupational pamphlets as they appear. Recommended publications are listed periodically in the *Vocational Guidance Quarterly* [401].

Using similar criteria, Hill [165] developed *The Ohio University Check List*

and Rating Device for Evaluating Occupational Literature used "in helping counselor trainees to develop skill in evaluating . . . occupational literature."

How the facts are presented may determine whether or not the publication
will be read and understood by the persons whom the counselor seeks to help.
The difficult reading level of many occupational publications has been explored
by Brayfield and Reed [28], by Diener and Kaczkowski [99], by Ruth [333], by
Sharp [342], and by Watson, Rundquist, and Cottle [406]. The *New Rochester
Occupational Reading Series* [142] includes fifty stories about young workers,
written at reading levels from grades two to six, for "students of junior and senior
high school age who are retarded, slow, or reluctant learners." Splaver [369, 370]
and Oxhandler [298] have studied what makes occupational books and pamphlets popular. Unfortunately, the counselor often will have little opportunity to
select publications on the basis of readability, popularity, or suitability. By the
time one has eliminated those which are obsolete, biased, or otherwise unacceptable, there will frequently be little left from which to choose. The most readable
material is of little value if the content is false. Accurate material is of little value
to readers who will not read it; it can, however, be read by counselors, who
probably ought to read much more occupational literature than they usually do.

There are usually several students in any grade whose reading level is *above*
the grade average. Italia Claps has reported that some of her fifth- and sixth-
grade children were enthusiastic readers of the *Occupational Outlook Handbook.*

TO SAVE TIME

The order of the five questions "When? Where? Who? Why? and How?" is
intended to save the counselor's time. If one begins by asking "When?" it will be
found sometimes that one can reject a reference on this basis alone, without
bothering to ask the other questions. "Where?" may reveal that the source of the
data was too remote or too different from the area in which the client hopes to
work. If the publication passes these two tests, "Who?" may indicate that the
publication is so good or so bad that the remaining questions are needed only to
confirm the counselor's judgment of the author. "Why?" will often spot a piece of
recruiting literature to be avoided. Each of these first four questions can be asked
and answered quickly for many publications, and a large number can be rejected
or identified as questionable without further examination. Some of the questionable publications may be kept in the counselor's personal library for such use as he
or she cares to make of them (perhaps as horrible examples in a course or unit in
occupations), but they should not be placed on open shelves or in open files for
indiscriminate use by all students.

REVIEWS BY EXPERTS

If examination by the counselor indicates that a publication is probably acceptable, the counselor may then try to find someone engaged in the occupation who
will read it as a check on the counselor's judgment. Often the parent of some

student can be found to do this. Many parents and alumni are pleased at being asked to help, and good public relations may thus be incidentally established. Excerpts from the reader's report may, with permission, be copied and pasted in the front of the publication for permanent record and as an aid to others who consult the publication. If this is done, the reviewer's name and position should be appended to the excerpts, along with the date of the review.

ANNUAL BOOK BURNING

Every library of occupational information should be thoroughly weeded once a year, at which time all obsolete publications should be removed. This need not be an onerous task. A student clerk can remove from the shelves and the files all publications which are more than five years old. The counselor who knows the literature can quickly decide which of these items to discard and which to keep for another year.

If you decide to keep anything that is more than five years old, put on the front cover some warning that the material may be out of date, for example a red label reading:

OUT OF DATE
This document is more than five years old. Some of the information in it may now be out of date. Ask your counselor where to get more recent information.

For more on this subject see "Renovating an Occupational Information File" [184].

HOW TO BUILD A LIBRARY OF OCCUPATIONAL INFORMATION

Occupational Information Kits, Collections, and Pamphlet Series   The quickest and easiest way to acquire a library of occupational information is to buy it ready-made. Several publishers have produced sets of occupational pamphlets which cover many of the popular occupations. Some schools and libraries have bought complete sets of these pamphlets and then discovered that much of what they bought was already obsolete and should be discarded.
Caution. Before ordering any complete set of occupational pamphlets, ask the publisher for the copyright date of each pamphlet in the series, or order the set on approval and do not pay the bill until you have examined the copyright dates yourself.

The principal publishers of occupational pamphlets are listed in Appendix A of this book.

Science Research Associates, Inc., sells a Career Information Kit [48] which contains a collection of pamphlets from several publishers. Chronicle Guidance Publications offers an Occupational Library [290] containing its own pamphlets plus reprints of articles from various magazines. Careers (Largo, Fla.) publishes its own Desk-Top Career Kit [95].

The ready-made pamphlet collection certainly saves the counselor considerable time that would otherwise be spent in reviewing, appraising, selecting, and purchasing individual pamphlets. This saving is an obvious advantage. There are less obvious disadvantages.

The pamphlets included may not all be appropriate for the persons who are to read them. If they are not, some money will be wasted.

The pamphlets included may not be the best on the subject if the best title was produced by another publisher.

Nearly every publisher who produces a set of pamphlets continues to produce new ones and to revise his old ones. But the revisions are not always made as frequently as they should be, nor are they always adequate. In the meantime, every publisher is tempted to sell surplus publications even after they are obsolete; not all publishers resist the temptation.

Occasions are almost sure to arise when the counselor will want more information than the best pamphlet file can provide. He will need and want to supplement the pamphlet file with books which describe one or more occupations. And he will want to buy new pamphlets from many publishers as they appear.

For these reasons, the counselor will need to supplement and extend any collection of occupational pamphlets which he may buy ready-made. He may even prefer to build his own collection from the start. How to do this is described below.

To Supplement the Pamphlet Collection If you are in a school or college, ask all your students to answer the following questions on a mimeographed form:

When you think about what you will do after you finish school or college, which occupations are of most interest to you?

Would you like to read books and pamphlets which describe the opportunities and requirements in any of these occupations?

Which ones?

Tabulate the replies to the last question. Note the occupations in which the largest numbers of your students are interested.

If you are in a counseling organization where you meet your clients only one at a time, keep a record of the occupations in which they indicate an interest, until you feel that you have a good sample.

Examine your present library to see if you have enough recent material on each of these occupations. If you have not, make a note to order more.

Subscribe to one or more of the indexes listed in Chapter 4 under "Publications," after comparing them as suggested there. Order all back issues of the current year and bound volumes for the five years preceding the current year.

From the back issues of the index select the publications needed to fill the gaps in your present library. Read carefully the annotations of all publications before you order them. Take one occupation at a time, and compare the available publications on it as to content, recency of publication, cost, and probable value to your students.

Order all publications on approval, and appraise them as suggested in this chapter.

Before placing any publication in the files or on the shelves, write the copyright date on the front cover. If the document is not dated, write the date received. This date will help to remind you and your students to consider the possible obsolescence of the materials when you consult them. It will save hours of time when you weed your files.

If you keep and file any recruiting literature from employers, schools, or military services, put on the front cover some warning about recruiting literature, for example, a red label reading:

WARNING
This document comes from an author or publisher who could conceivably wish to recruit students or workers. Recruiting literature often says more about the attractions of an occupation than about the disadvantages. Ask your counselor about the disadvantages.

If possible, do not spend your entire first year's book budget at one time. Save from one-third to two-thirds of it to purchase future publications as they appear. Ask your supervisor if present regulations regarding book requisitions will permit you to order publications as you need them. If the answer is no, ask if the regulations can be changed. If the answer is still no, keep a record of the things you want and order them at the prescribed times.

Examine each new issue of the index when it arrives. Order immediately all the free and inexpensive pamphlets that you think will be of value to your students. The free publications that you can collect in this way will more than justify the cost of your subscription to the index.

Order books that cost more than a dollar only when you are sure you will have use for them. If you are not sure, order when a need for the books arises. Occasionally, you will regret having done this. You will need the books sooner than you can get them, or you will find them out of print when you want them. These annoyances are preferable to dissipating your book budget on publications you will never use.

Keep in close touch with your librarian to find out which publications on which occupations appear to be in greatest demand. Occasionally examine the library books yourself, and note which have been taken out most frequently.

If your budget is limited, you may find the Kiwanis or Rotary Club willing to contribute to it. Or you may get the school and the public librarian to divide between them the purchase of the materials you want so that unnecessary duplication is reduced or eliminated.

If your budget is very small, limit most of your purchases to inexpensive pamphlets and to books which describe more than one occupation. The smaller your budget, the more you need a good current bibliography to bring you information about all the new publications that you can get free of charge.

When Funds Are Inadequate   The author's students have asked, "When we can't buy all that we ought to buy, what should we buy first?" The author suggests that the first money available be used to provide the following, in this order.

The *Dictionary of Occupational Titles* [98] and the latest supplements to it.

One copy of the latest edition of the *Occupational Outlook Handbook* [292].

One copy of the local classified telephone directory, which can usually be obtained free from the business office of the local telephone company.

A simple, inexpensive filing system. See Chapter 6 for suggestions.

An annual subscription to one of the indexes listed in Chapter 4 under "Publications."

A list or a card file of employers which have hired former students or clients, cross-indexed by occupation. See Chapter 13 for suggestions on inexpensive follow-up studies.

A list or card file of other employers who have said they will hire students, alumni, or clients, similarly cross-indexed by occupation. See Chapter 16 for suggestions on inexpensive surveys of entry jobs.

One copy of the *College Placement Annual* [68].

Your own notes on jobs in local plants to which you have taken students or clients for plant tours. See Chapter 14.

Your own notes which you have taken during group conferences which you have arranged for your students and clients. See Chapter 15.

Clippings from newspapers and magazines which your students will bring to you at your request. Be sure to caution them not to deface publications which do not belong to them.

Free and inexpensive publications selected from the index you have chosen, appraised as suggested in this chapter.

REVIEW QUESTIONS

1 What should the counselor do whenever he or she refers a client to published occupational information?
2 What five questions should the counselor memorize and always ask about any piece of occupational literature?
3 What should be done with occupational books and pamphlets that are obsolete?
4 By what date should one judge a book for obsolescence?
5 What are some of the kinds of occupational information that change rapidly?
6 Why is it important to know where occupational information was collected?
7 Why do articles in popular magazines sometimes give false impressions of occupations?
8 Why is recruiting literature particularly dangerous?
9 What are the weaknesses of biography and fiction as sources of occupational information?
10 Who should check the counselor's judgment of occupational literature?
11 How often should a library of occupational information be thoroughly weeded?
12 When funds are inadequate, what are the first things to buy?
13 You are a counselor in a school, college, or agency which has a collection of occupational information in its library. The librarian asks you to review the collection and recommend which publications should be kept and which removed. How will you proceed?
14 Will anything in this chapter affect your future thoughts and actions? What? How?

Chapter 6

Classifying and Filing Occupational Information

The industrious counselor soon collects occupational pamphlets, books, and clippings by the hundreds. To these he or she adds notes on the information obtained from tours of local industries, from conversations with workers in different occupations, from follow-up studies of dropouts and alumni, and from other sources. Soon the volume of such material becomes so large that it must be classified and filed, so that one can find what one has on any occupation when and as it is needed.

Depending on where one works, the counselor may or may not have the help of a librarian. If such help is available, the librarian may already have established a file of occupational information. The counselor may find that the existing file serves all essential purposes, that the librarian will be pleased to receive and to file any new material that the counselor may acquire, and that the counselor can attend to other matters.

On the other hand there may be no librarian and no filing system, or the librarian may want the help of the counselor in setting up an occupational file, or the librarian and the counselor and their common administrator may agree that the counselor should maintain a separate file of occupational information; Le May and Warnath [240] found that college students preferred that files for their use be housed in the student union. In this case the sooner the counselor starts, the better. John G. Odgers suggested that "once he has accumulated a hundred or more pieces of occupational information . . . he may find the job of getting everything classified and filed is overwhelming. His best bet is to . . . classify and file materials as they arrive. Otherwise he may find himself with a week's work and no week in which to do it."

NOW WHERE DID I PUT THAT?

Many problems in filing arise from the fact that an occupation is a hard thing to define. Actually an occupation is just a classification of jobs which have something in common. Since jobs may have many things in common, they may be classified in many ways.

Jobs may be classified according to the activities involved, such as selling, teaching, typing.

Jobs may be classified according to their function, such as research, finance, manufacturing, distribution, education.

Jobs may be classified according to the product which they produce, such as automobiles, chemicals, steel.

Jobs may be classified according to the employer, for example American Cyanamid, General Electric, F. W. Woolworth.

Jobs may be classified according to the expressed interests of students or clients.

Jobs may be classified according to measured interest patterns, such as artistic, computational, persuasive.

Jobs may be classified according to the school subjects which help to prepare workers for them, such as mathematical, musical, scientific.

Jobs may be classified in other ways that may occur to the reader and in still other ways that have not yet been conceived.

Depending upon which classification is adopted as the basis for a filing system, information about the job of a salesperson for the Ford Motor Company might be filed under any one of the following headings: selling, distribution, automobiles, Ford, persuasive occupations, business education. If the person who files occupational materials is not to be hopelessly confused, if the person who wants to find information in the files is not to be continually frustrated, someone must do some pretty clear thinking about how to classify jobs and occupations and the publications which describe them.

In their search for the ideal, counselors have tried several different ways of classifying and filing occupational information. Some of these ways are described and compared below.

CLASSIFICATION AND FILING SYSTEMS

Alphabetic Files   Many counselors and librarians begin by classifying and filing their occupational information alphabetically by the name of the occupation. This appears at first to be simple, easy, and logical. Anyone who knows the alphabet can go to such a file and use it with a minimum of instruction. Materials on any one occupation are filed and found together. Or are they?

When the assembled collection of occupational information is small, the alphabetic file may be reasonably satisfactory, but it does have disadvantages. Materials on related occupations are not grouped together unless they can all be filed under the same occupational title. Some occupations have more than one title. The counselor or librarian must decide whether materials on accounting and on bookkeeping will be filed together or separately. Similar decisions must be made for electrical engineering and mechanical engineering, for electrical engineering and electrical contracting, for electrical contracting and general contracting. Each time such a decision is made, it must be recorded, so that similar material may be similarly filed in the future. Numerous cross-reference cards must be placed in the file or in a separate cross index.

If the counselor finds that some original decisions on classification were unwise or inconsistent, materials must be refiled. As the number of occupational titles in the file rises into the hundreds, the number of decisions that must be made and remembered or recorded can become a bit of a burden. There is always a risk that valuable materials will be lost in the file because the counselor failed to think of one important title for cross indexing.

The counselor who prefers the alphabetic file can escape some of the difficulties by purchasing and following an alphabetic filing plan such as the Bennett plan, which is described below. In this plan hundreds of decisions have already been made and recorded.

United States Census Classification   In the hope of avoiding some of the disadvantages of the alphabetic file, counselors have sought and tried other classification systems. In the early days of vocational guidance many filing systems were based upon the occupational and industrial classifications of the United States census, because these were then the most complete classifications that were readily available. The census provided an alphabetic and a classified index covering several thousand titles, which were classified in occupational and industrial categories. It thus relieved the counselor of many decisions regarding classification and of the necessity for devising and labeling many cross references, since the census index could be used as a substitute for cross references.

The census has been largely abandoned as a basis for occupational filing systems since the publication of the *Dictionary of Occupational Titles.*

The *Dictionary of Occupational Titles* Classification   As a basis for occupational filing systems the *D.O.T.* has all the advantages of the census, plus some new ones.

Thousands of job titles are listed and are defined in short paragraphs. Thousands of alternate titles are listed and cross-indexed. Each title is assigned a code number.

The code number for any occupational title can be found in one part of the *D.O.T.* The occupational title for any code number can be found in another part.

In filing systems which are based on the *D.O.T.*, the appropriate *D.O.T.* code number is written on each publication. The publication is placed in a folder which bears the same code number. Folders are placed in the file in numerical order, rather than alphabetic. Occupational titles are written on the folders beside the code numbers. The code numbers have been so devised that consecutive numbers are assigned to closely related occupations; hence consecutive folders contain materials on related occupations.

The counselor can now avoid many of the difficulties of classification and cross-indexing by following the *D.O.T.* classification. Thousands of decisions have already been made for him and recorded in the *D.O.T.* The counselor will find that he or she still has some decisions to make, but not so many as with any other system.

The disadvantage of systems based on the *D.O.T.* is that a reader, a student, or a client must have the system explained to him before he can use the files, and he must refer frequently to the *D.O.T.* in order to find the code numbers of the occupations on which he is seeking information.

The *D.O.T.* has been revised at intervals of ten to fifteen years. The counselor, of course, can decide whether or not he or she wishes to incorporate future revisions in the filing system. The necessary changes will take some time, but they can be made readily with the help of the *Conversion Table of Code and Title Changes* [73] which usually is published after each revision.

Filing plans which are based on the *D.O.T.* are described in more detail later in this chapter.

Classification by Industry   Clients and students sometimes want to know what kinds of occupations may be found in specific industries, particularly if such industries are important sources of employment in the areas in which the clients expect to look for work, for example, the automobile industry in Detroit, the insurance business in Hartford, and the steel industry in Pittsburgh. Clients whose occupational preferences may lead them into any of several industries— for example, machinists and office machine operators—may wish to compare different industries. An industry itself, for purposes of recruitment or goodwill, may publish a pamphlet describing employment opportunities in the industry. A good deal of useful occupational information is published on an industry basis and is much more readily classified and filed by the industry than by the occupations within the industry.

Some means of filing such information by industry should be provided in any occupational filing system. The most complete and convenient basis for a filing system by industries in the United States is to be found in the *Standard Industrial Classification Manual* [371]. If you work outside the United States, you may prefer the *International Standard Classification of Occupations,* published by the International Labour Office, Geneva, Switzerland.

Industries are arranged alphabetically in one part of the manual and numerically in another, thus resembling the arrangements in the *D.O.T.* For filing by industry this manual may be used in the same way that the *D.O.T.* is used for filing by occupation.

How to use the *Standard Industrial Classification Manual* in filing is described further in the section below on homemade filing plans.

Classification by Employer   Colleges which are visited by recruiting officers from large companies often receive recruiting booklets and other publications about the companies. Public schools in industrial cities collect information about local employers as a result of tours, conferences, and follow-up studies. Such material may be filed by industry according to the *Standard Industrial Classification Manual* and arranged alphabetically by company within the industry.

If the collection of industrial materials consists almost exclusively of company publications, some institutions may find that a simple alphabetic file by company name is preferable to the industrial classification.

Publications of some diversified companies may cover several different industries. General Motors and Chrysler, for example, manufacture refrigeration equipment as well as automobiles. Omnibus publications which cover several industries as well as several occupations require special indexing, which is described in detail later in this chapter under "Homemade Plans."

Geographical Files   Some placement officers file some of their occupational information geographically by state and city. This is a convenient means of handling material which applicants may wish to consult when they are looking for work in certain localities. For example, the college student who wants to return home may wish to compile a list of potential employers from business directories, classified telephone directories, company brochures, and annual reports. The student who has been offered a teaching position in a public school system may want to see everything the placement office has on the local schools.

Geographical filing is not a convenient way of handling information on companies with numerous locations, such as Bethlehem Steel. Nor is it a serviceable plan for filing information on occupations which can be practiced almost universally, such as painting.

Academic-subject Classifications   Students sometimes become interested and proficient in a school or college subject and want to know what occupations it may lead to. Teachers sometimes wish to tell their students about occupations related to their subjects. Consequently some attempts have been made to group occupations by related academic subjects, particularly in occupational pamphlets published by colleges for their own students or for recruiting purposes.

Occupational filing systems are seldom based upon academic-subject classifications, because so many occupations cannot be clearly identified with any one subject and because so many other occupations could be equally well assigned to any of several different subjects.

Career Clusters   To facilitate the exploration of a wide range of occupations in career education programs, the U.S. Office of Education suggested that all the jobs in the *Dictionary of Occupational Titles* might be grouped into fifteen clusters: construction, manufacturing, transportation, agri-business and natural resources, marine science, environmental, business and office, marketing and distribution, communications and media, hospitality and recreation, personal service, public services, health, consumer and homemaking, and fine arts and humanities.

Measured-interest Classifications   Some counselors have filed occupational information in the categories which are found on vocational interest inventories. This kind of classification has obvious advantages when discussing interest scores. Information on closely related occupations will be found in adjacent folders. The major disadvantage is that the filing system may have to be completely revised if the institution ever decides to drop one interest inventory in favor of another with a different set of categories.

Expressed Interest Classifications Cooley [74] analyzed "student perceptions to determine clusters of occupations which are viewed similarly by the people who have to make distinctions among them as they move into the world of work." In a five-year, overlapping longitudinal study, he found the occupational plans of 150 fifth-grade boys with above-average general intelligence "to be based primarily on interest. At first, the only stable distinction among plans was the dichotomy" of science technology versus all other occupations.

> Of course, most of the boys gave more specific plans, but the boy who talked civil engineering one time in an interview perhaps was talking physics or even biochemistry in a subsequent interview. Also, those who said lawyer one time may have been talking business the next time. There was a great tendency of stability within this very broad dichotomy, science technology or not. . . .
>   During and following junior high school it was possible to detect ability discriminations. For example, some of the science-technology group began to talk about professional careers in this broad area and others began to talk about being electricians or mechanics. Here again the ability discriminations were very gross, so that up through high school only four occupational categories were needed; namely, (*a*) college in science technology, (*b*) college in something other than science technology, (*c*) technology without college, and (*d*) neither college nor technology. The students did not seem to make consistent finer discriminations. . . . It was not possible to find attributes which could significantly distinguish between those planning to be lawyers and businessmen or between future chemists and engineers. During college it was possible to make finer distinctions with respect to college science majors. These distinctions were based primarily on what might be called values. . . .

Cooley did not propose a filing plan, but his classifications may be helpful to teachers and counselors who wish to discuss broad areas of occupations with students, or who wish to arrange exhibits, meetings, tours, printed materials, etc., in similarly broad categories.

Bennett Occupations Filing Plan and Bibliography Published by Interstate Printers and Publishers, Inc., Danville, Ill. 61832,[1] this is an alphabetic filing plan in which the subject headings are adapted from the *D.O.T.*, but the *D.O.T.* code numbers are not used.

All the subject headings and cross-references are combined in a single alphabetic list and numbered consecutively. These are followed by headings that are supplements for related materials.

The printed labels may be pasted on folders as the need for them arises, but

---

[1] The addresses given in this chapter were correct at date of publication but should be checked by any reader who wishes to write to these sources.

it is more efficient to paste them all on empty folders and cross-reference cards when the file is started.

To file materials by this plan, the counselor first examines the material to determine the content, then searches in the printed list of headings for the one which seems most appropriate. This heading and its corresponding number are written on the material to facilitate later refiling, and the material is then placed in the appropriate folder.

The subject headings in this plan include industries as well as occupations and other supplementary headings, as noted above.

Nothing is said about what to do if no appropriate subject heading can be found in the printed list. Presumably the counselor can invent new headings and insert new folders for them, either in alphabetic order or as additional supplements at the back of the file.

Omnibus materials which cover several unrelated occupations are provided with a folder labeled "COLLECTIONS (Several jobs described in one publication)." No suggestions are offered for indexing the contents of such publications by occupation. Cross-reference notations could, of course, be placed in all other appropriate folders. This plan is designed for filing unbound occupational information, but the subject headings can also be used for books, films, and tape recordings.

Career Information Kit   This is produced by Science Research Associates, Inc., Chicago, Illinois 60611, and is available in a corrugated case or a portable metal file containing over 500 publications on occupations.

The filing plan uses a numerical system based upon job-family relationships but not upon the *D.O.T.* Major occupational fields are divided into occupational areas and job titles; a separate folder is provided for each. Within categories the folders are arranged alphabetically and numbered accordingly. The code number and title appear on each folder.

The manual of directions contains a complete list of the code numbers and titles, arranged as they appear on the folders, and an alphabetic index which shows the code number for each occupation. Included in the index are Dewey decimal classification numbers to facilitate the location of related materials in general libraries.

To file occupational materials by this plan, the counselor first examines the material in order to identify the occupation which it covers. He then refers to the alphabetic cross-reference list to find the code number for this occupation. He writes this code number on the material to facilitate later refiling, and then he places the material in the appropriate folder which bears this code number.

Nothing is said in the manual about how to file omnibus materials which cover several unrelated occupations. The plan does not include directions for shelving books, films, and tape recordings. It does not include directions for filing materials which describe industries rather than specific occupations, except to a limited extent in the subdivisions of major fields.

Career Information System   As this book goes to press, the Appalachia

Educational Laboratory in Charleston, West Virginia, is developing a Career Information System (CIS) based upon the worker trait groups of the *Dictionary of Occupational Titles*. This system includes a filing plan with a table to convert *D.O.T.* code numbers to worker trait group (W.T.G) numbers.

To file an occupational brief in this system, first find the job title and the code number in the *D.O.T.* Then find the W.T.G. number in the conversion table. Write the W.T.G. number on the occupational brief and file it in a folder which has been previously numbered for that W.T.G. To retrieve the publication, follow the same procedure to find the W.T.G. number. Then look in the file for the folder with this W.T.G. number. Look in this folder for the publication.

Occupational Library   This is published by Chronicle Guidance Publications, Inc., Moravia, New York 13118, and is available with over 600 occupational briefs, reprints, and posters and with or without a portable metal filing cabinet.

The filing plan uses a numerical system based upon the three-digit code of the *D.O.T.* Major occupational categories are divided into main occupational divisions and then into specific occupational subgroups. Folders are arranged by *D.O.T.* number; the code number and title appear on each folder.

The manual of directions contains a complete list of the code numbers and titles arranged as they appear on the folders, and an alphabetic index which shows the code number for each occupation. Included in the index are Dewey decimal classification numbers to facilitate the location of related materials in general libraries.

To file occupational materials by this plan, the counselor first examines the material in order to identify the occupation which it covers. He then refers to the alphabetic cross-reference list to find the code number for this occupation. He writes this code number on the material to facilitate later refiling, and then he places the material in the appropriate folder which bears this code number. If the occupational title is not found in the alpabetic cross-reference list, the counselor refers to the *D.O.T.* to get the code number.

Nothing is said in the manual about how to file omnibus materials which cover several unrelated occupations. The plan does not include directions for shelving books, films, and tapes. It does not include directions for filing materials which describe industries rather than specific occupations, except in seven broad occupational fields for which folders are provided.

Homemade Plans   After examining the filing plans which others have devised, the counselor may decide that no one of them exactly meets his needs. For counselors who wish to devise their own filing systems, the following suggestions are offered:

Base your plan on the *D.O.T.* This will not solve all your problems, but it will save you the decisions that have already been made about how to classify and file material on thousands of job titles.

Use the *Standard Industrial Classification Manual* as a guide to filing industrial materials which cannot be filed under *D.O.T.* code numbers.

Use a steel filing cabinet of letter size or larger to hold light, fragile materials such as your own notes, clippings, pictures, reprints, posters which can be folded, and small pamphlets. Place these materials in manila file folders. When the contents of a single folder become too bulky or heavy, remove them from the manila folder and put them in a heavier folder, such as the Vertical File Pocket No. 1514C made by the Oxford Pendaflex Corp., Garden City, New York.

Use bookshelves to hold books, tape recordings, films, and other materials that are too bulky or too heavy for the file folders. These may all be kept on the same shelves, or books may be kept in one place, tape recordings in another, and films in another. Either way, the arrangement should be by *D.O.T.* or *S.I.C.M.* code number.

How to use the D.O.T. Begin with nothing in the file and nothing on the shelves. For your first attempt at filing, select some small pamphlet which deals with a single, well-known occupation. Proceed as follows:

1 Review the section above on "The *Dictionary of Occupational Titles* Classification."
2 Consult the *D.O.T.*
3 In this find the title of the occupation which your pamphlet describes; beside it will be the code number.
4 Copy this code number on the pamphlet.
5 Copy the code number and the occupational title on a file folder.
6 Put the pamphlet in the folder.
7 Put the folder in the filing cabinet.

Repeat this process with additional materials on other occupations. As each new folder is added to the file, place it in numerical order in relation to the other folders. For protection against damage, place fragile clippings in transparent covers or in envelopes before putting them in folders with other materials; copy the *D.O.T.* number on the envelope, as well as on the clipping and the folder.

When you have trouble deciding where to file something, put it aside until you have filed everything that you can file easily. By then you will be more familiar with the *D.O.T.*, and you may have less trouble with the difficult pieces.

Difficulties in finding D.O.T. code numbers Although the *D.O.T.* defines and cross-indexes thousands of occupational titles, you will sometimes find that you have information on an occupation which you cannot readily locate in the Dictionary. When this happens, review carefully the sections of the *D.O.T.* which explain alternate titles and how to find them. If this fails to solve your problem, the authors of the *D.O.T.* suggest that when users of this publication need additional job definitions, new code numbers, or clarification of the classifications, they should write to the Manpower Administration, U.S. Employment Service, Department of Labor, Washington, D.C. 20213.

How to use the Standard Industrial Classification Manual When you wish to file something which describes an industry rather than an occupation, if you cannot logically file it in any *D.O.T.* category, the time has come to set up an industrial file, separate from your occupational file. Be sure to keep the two files separate and clearly labeled, because they will have separate systems of code numbers.

For your first attempt at filing industrial materials, select some simple pamphlet or document which describes a single, well-known industry. Proceed as follows:

1 Review the section above on "Classification by Industry."
2 Consult the *Standard Industrial Classification Manual.*
3 Look in the alphabetic index for the title of the industry which your document describes; beside it will be the code number.
4 Copy this code number on the document you wish to file.
5 Copy the code number and the industrial title on a file folder.
6 Put the document in the folder.
7 Put the folder in the industrial section of your files.

Repeat this process with additional materials on other industries. As each new folder is added to the file, place it in numerical order, in relation to the other folders, in the industrial section of your files.

To illustrate this procedure, if you wish to file a document that describes the past and probable future growth of commercial airlines and you try to file it under a *D.O.T.* code number, you will find yourself in trouble. The future growth of airlines affects the future prospects for employment and advancement of all kinds of workers in airline companies. So you decide that this document should go in your industrial file.

Difficulties in finding Standard Industrial Classification Manual code numbers If you are doubtful about which of two classification code numbers to use, or if you cannot find the industry in the alphabetic indexes, refer to the complete classification structure with descriptions of the industries to be included in each classification. If you still cannot find the industry listed, choose the code which comes closest to it. Whenever you have difficulty in choosing a code number, add a card to your cross-index file, and place on this card the title of the industry and the code number that you have chosen, so that you can readily find the material when you want it. If the industry may be known by two or more names, such as oil and petroleum, put in a separate card for each name.

If a publication deals primarily with industrial rather than occupational information but contains useful information on some occupations, it may be placed in the proper industrial classification and cross-indexed in the occupational card file.

You will not need 20,000 folders Although the *D.O.T.* and the *Standard Industrial Classification Manual* provide code numbers for several thousand occupations and industries, you will not need an equal number of folders. You will probably never have materials to file on more than a few hundred occupations. Even if you should have, both code systems are so devised that you can easily file the materials on related occupations in a single folder by simply shortening the code number that you write on the folder.

Shelving books, films, and recordings Occupational books are handled in the same way as notes, clippings, and pamphlets, except that the classification number is recorded on the spine of the book and on the title page and the books are arranged numerically on the shelves. Films and tape recordings may be placed on the shelves with the books after the proper code numbers have been written on the containers.

Omnibus books, pamphlets, films, and recordings Books and other publications which describe several unrelated occupations cannot be properly classified under any one code number. They can readily be overlooked when you are seeking information on a specific occupation if you do not recall which omnibus book contains information on which occupation.

If such books are worth buying, they are worth using, and they can be fully utilized only if they are adequately cross-indexed. The clerical labor of cross-indexing a book that describes fifty or a hundred occupations is forbidding to busy counselors who have no clerical help, but the job must be done if the books are to be used. There are too many such books for the counselor or the client to examine all of them each time information on one occupation is needed. If you have one or more bright students as volunteer or paid clerical assistants, they can be taught to classify and cross-index the information in such books, with some help from you when they encounter difficulty.

Whoever does the indexing must first determine, for each occupation covered, whether or not the information in the book is of sufficient potential value to merit indexing. Casual mention of an occupation, in one or two sentences, is scarcely worth indexing if you have better material on the same subject. Each occupation to be indexed is then found in the *D.O.T.*, the code number and title of the occupation are written on an index card, the book containing the information is identified on the same card, and the card is placed in the file. These index cards may be the same size as the file folders and may be placed in their proper numerical position in the filing cabinet, or they may be smaller cards kept in a separate file and arranged numerically therein. The books may then be arranged on the shelves by author or title, in a separate section for omnibus books. Films, tape recordings, and large pamphlets may be handled in the same way as books. Fragile materials may be filed in folders in a separate omnibus section of the filing cabinet, in which these materials are arranged by author or title.

All that has been said about occupations in this section on omnibus books applies equally to industries and industrial classification, except that the *Standard Industrial Classification Manual* should be used in place of the *D.O.T.*

Alternative procedures The counselor who prefers may use pamphlet boxes instead of file folders, and shelves instead of a filing cabinet. *D.O.T.* code numbers and occupational titles will then appear on the pamphlet boxes instead of on file folders. Large, sturdy pamphlet boxes can be purchased from stationery stores and from library supply houses such as Gaylord Bros. of Syracuse, New York 13201 and Stockton, California 95201.

Some schools prefer filing cabinets consisting of many drawers in which the pamphlets lie flat. *D.O.T.* code numbers are combined so that the number of categories is reduced to the number of drawers in the file. Purcell [312] described such a file, which was introduced because in the former vertical file ". . . pamphlets were frequently misfiled, folders were continually flopping over, and not infrequently, entire folders were found out of sequence." To make the change to the new system four temporary employees worked one week. They discarded obsolete materials and marked the publication date and code number of all materials retained. "Students seem to enjoy using the file and can locate material quickly. Being able to remove an entire drawer of materials and carry it over to the work table for use is a real boon; and we find that under this system very few materials are misfiled." An alphabetic index to the file may be mounted on the wall above the cabinets.

Other Plans   Burianek and Tennyson [36] described a display rack for filing which ". . . has proved effective in motivating students to peruse occupational pamphlets. In a reception room where the study chairs face the display rack, a waiting youngster . . . tends to reach up and pull out a folder. . . ."

Diamond [96] described a similar rack which was used by fifteen times as many students as had ever used the materials before.

Chervenik [54] described a similar plan for use in a university counseling office.

Corre [75] described a system based on the U.S. census in which the occupations are arranged alphabetically within the major groups.

Frank and Patten [130] described a homemade filing plan similar to the one suggested above. It uses both the *D.O.T.* and the *S.I.C.M.*

Gachet [132] described a plan designed for women college students, based on the *D.O.T.* and cross-indexed under fifty-three occupational classifications that were arranged alphabetically.

Huey [193] described a plan based on the U.S. census, which provided for cross-indexing of omnibus materials.

Kirk and Michels [219] described the filing plan used in the Counseling Center of the University of California at Berkeley. The plan includes subdivisions on occupations, trends and outlook, legislation, special groups, training, employment, scholarships, planning, and adjustment.

LeMay [239] described a loose-leaf notebook in which each page contains one job title, the corresponding *D.O.T.* number, and a list of all the sources from which the school has obtained useful information on the occupation, in pamphlet or other form. Counselors find the book helpful when they wish to reorder lost publications or seek additional information.

Munschauer [273] published the Cornell Career Center Classification Chart, in an article which also mentions several useful publications.

Neal [282] described an alphabetic filing plan with cross-indexing and a plan for shelving books.

Schubert [341] described a plan based on the interest categories of the Kuder Preference Record.

Wyatt [420] described a display rack for company literature used in a college placement office.

TIME REQUIRED

The task of filing occupational information is not so formidable as it may appear to one who has just read this lengthy explanation. If no unusual difficulties are encountered, an experienced counselor should be able to find the correct code number, write the number on a pamphlet and a folder, and place both of them in the files in less than five minutes. A counselor who devotes ten minutes a day to filing, who works five days a week, forty weeks a year, could file 400 new pieces of occupational information each year. Few counselors will add even half that number of new publications to their libraries in an average year.

COST

A good occupational library with a homemade filing plan can be started and maintained at modest cost. The essential items are:

Initial expenses
   1   Steel filing cabinet
500   Manila file folders
 50   Heavy file folders
   1   Bookcase
   1   *Dictionary of Occupational Titles*
   1   *Standard Industrial Classification Manual*

Recurring annual expenditures
   1   Annual subscription to one of the indexes to new occupational books and pamphlets described in Chapter 4
       New file folders as needed
200   New books and pamphlets

CHARACTERISTICS OF A GOOD FILING SYSTEM

Before deciding upon a classification system, before choosing or devising a filing plan, the reader may wish to compare each possib;lity with the following suggested characteristics of a good filing system.

1 It should provide a safe place for housing written and printed documents, clippings from newspapers and magazines, posters, pictures, films, tape recordings, pamphlets, books, and anything else that may contain useful occupational information.

2 It should provide one and only one designated location for each item to be filed, so that there may be no confusion about where to file an item or where to find it.

3 It should be easy to use, so that all who use it can find what they want with a minimum of time and effort.

4 It should bring together as many as possible of the materials on any one occupation or industry or employer.

5 It should bring together related occupations or industries or employers.

6 It should provide some means of quickly finding material in omnibus books and other publications which describe several different occupations.

7 It should be expandable, so that it can grow as the collection grows.

8 It should provide for filing and finding related materials, such as the results of follow-up studies and community occupational surveys.

COMPARATIVE APPRAISAL OF FILING PLANS

The reader of this book will probably do better to choose his own filing plan than to follow anyone else's judgment. However, the author's students have asked for the author's judgment, so here it is.

For High Schools, Colleges, Libraries, and Other Community Agencies For most counselors in these institutions, I would choose one of the following in this order of preference:

1 *A homemade plan,* because it is the only one that provides for adequate indexing of industrial as well as occupational materials, using both the *D.O.T.* and the *Standard Industrial Classification Manual,* and because it is the only one that provides directions for shelving books, films, and recordings.

2 *The Chronicle plan,* because it is based on the *D.O.T.* and it can be purchased with or without a collection of pamphlets.

3 *The Bennett plan* for those who want an alphabetic file rather than one which uses *D.O.T.* code numbers.

4 *The Science Research Associates kit* if the purchaser is just starting to collect occupational information and has no substantial investment in publications which might be duplicated.

All these plans have the disadvantage of requiring a little time to learn how to file material and to find it. This may even be an advantage if it prevents the counselor from sending a client to the files alone when the counselor ought to go along.

Although the last three plans do not provide directions for shelving books, films, and recordings or for indexing omnibus books, the directions under homemade plans may be adapted for use in combination with any of these plans.

For Employment Offices Which Use the D.O.T. Code For these I would choose for the reasons stated above:

1 *A homemade plan*
2 *The Chronicle plan*

For Teachers Colleges For placement officers in teachers colleges, whose only interest is jobs in education, I would choose:

A geographical file by state and city for information on potential employers, particularly public schools and colleges.

For Teachers For teachers of academic subjects whose only interest in occupational information is in connection with their own subjects, I would choose:

An academic subject file. While the total amount of material is small, some simple alphabetic arrangement within the subject field may serve all essential purposes. When and if the collection becomes large, I would switch to one of the four plans listed above for counselors.

For elementary school teachers whose major interest is in career education programs of occupational awareness, I would choose

A career cluster file.

For Students For the student or client who is collecting information on a small number of occupations to help in the choice of an occupation, I would choose:

An alphabetic file, because it is the simplest to use when the number of occupations and the amount of material are small. If he loses anything in the files he can search the entire collection in a short time. If he is in doubt about where to file something, he can put it in a "Miscellaneous" category and examine this category every time he seeks material on any subject.

SUGGESTIONS FOR BEGINNERS

Because occupational information may be classified in so many different ways, no filing system will ever be perfect. Because information may be sought for so many different purposes, no filing system will yield all its useful contents with uniform speed and precision. Don't expect too much. Don't try to do too much. And don't blame yourself or your files when they do not work perfectly for all purposes.

Spend an evening with all the volumes of the *Dictionary of Occupational Titles* and the *Standard Industrial Classification Manual.* Read the introductory and explanatory parts of each volume. Examine the remaining contents. Take time to understand what the classification structure is and to see how you can use it for your own purposes. Take several of your own occupational materials and decide how you would classify and file them if you were to develop your own filing system.

If you have the time and the inclination, write for and examine the filing plans listed above. Get them on approval, and try filing and finding the same materials in these systems.

Select the system which seems best to meet your needs, which you find easy to understand and comfortable to work with. Install it, use it, change and adapt it to suit your own purposes, and use plenty of cross-references.

Once a year go through your file, weeding out and throwing away every document that is more than five years old unless you have some good reason for keeping it. Your student clerk can remove these obsolete materials for you. Then it will not take much of your time to look at them and tell him which to put back.

To facilitate weeding, put the copyright date or the accession date on the front of each pamphlet before you file it.

Jerome J. Leksa has suggested putting in the file one or more pink cards for each counselor on the staff, with the counselor's name on each of his or her cards. The cards would be the same size as the file folders, and would replace the folders when they were removed for use. Thus any other counselor seeking the same file would know where to look for it.

FILING RELATED MATERIALS

The counselor needs some place to file information on child labor laws, work certificates, unemployment insurance, and other materials that are related to occupational information but that do not describe occupations or industries.

Baer and Roeber [13] prepared a filing plan for "supplementary occupational and educational information" on sixty-six topics including apprenticeships, automation, child labor, community agencies, dropouts, employment agencies, handicapped individuals, job finding, job satisfaction, labor laws, labor organizations, and scholarships.

A counselor's professional file [78]   This provides printed folders for articulation, associations, counseling, educational information, evaluation, group guidance, mental hygiene, placement, publishers, testing, and other topics.

ON COOPERATION WITH THE LIBRARIAN

The counselor who starts on a new job may find that the librarian in the institution already has an occupational file but that the filing system does not serve the counselor's purposes. The librarian will usually be a staff colleague of equal rank to whom the counselor cannot issue orders and with whom he will wish to establish and maintain cordial working relationships.

Librarians have their problems, too. They must try to meet the needs and the demands of the entire staff and clientele. These demands sometimes conflict; they sometimes cannot be met with the staff at the librarian's disposal. Administrative policy or library practice may discourage the development of separate departmental libraries, and this may bring the librarian into conflict with counselors and others who would like to have their own separate bookshelves and pamphlet files in their own offices. Librarians have learned from sad experience that complex filing systems discourage readers from using the files. The librarian who has a file that seems to serve and satisfy the readers may be understandably reluctant to change it.

Before the counselor concludes that an existing system is inadequate, he or she should recall that no filing system is perfect. Each system has some advantages and some disadvantages. Each will serve one purpose best, at the expense of other purposes. The counselor who wants to maintain good human relations will respect the needs of colleagues who use the same files. If careful examination reveals that the existing files will not meet the counselor's reasonable needs, there are several things one may do.

If the librarian is cooperative, the whole problem may be discussed freely and some solution reached. In rare cases the librarian may welcome the help of the counselor in revising the files, may offer to change the filing system, or may invite the counselor to assume responsibility for this part of the library. More frequently, perhaps, the librarian will suggest that the counselor set up a separate file of occupational information in his or her own office. The counselor, in turn, will recognize that the librarian must serve other staff members whose needs may conflict with those of the counselor; will recognize that the librarian may know some things the counselor does not know about the ways in which students and others use the files; and will respect the librarian's professional training and experience in selecting, acquiring, housing, and distributing all kinds of library materials. The cooperative counselor will be willing to give a little in the interest of his or her colleagues and of cordial human relations.

If the librarian is unapproachable, the counselor may get along as well as possible with the files as they exist, or set up a file in the counseling office. If a separate file is contemplated, the counselor may be wise to discuss this possibility with the immediate superior before mentioning it to anyone else. If the librarian disapproves and resents the separate file, personnel problems may be created that will be worse than the filing problems.

If the librarian is approachable but insecure or reluctant to make immediate changes, the counselor may become the most frequent user of the files and ask the librarian for help whenever having difficulty. After the librarian has had time to acquire some confidence in the counselor's integrity and competence, the counselor may offer help in acquiring new materials. Later he or she may offer to help weed out the obsolete. Eventually the librarian may be willing to consider the counselor's offer to revise the filing system.

Important as a good filing system can be, it may in the long run be less important than good working relationships. A librarian can be of great help to young people who seek occupational information and to the counselor who is trying to help them. Everyone in the school, from the principal to the janitor, is going to be asked by some student at some time for information about some occupation. If the counselor has alienated colleagues, the students will get poorer service than if the staff is working together in friendly cooperation with mutual consideration for one another's needs and problems and limitations.

REVIEW QUESTIONS

1 What are some of the different ways in which jobs can be classified?
2 You are a member of a committee appointed to recommend a filing system for the occupational information that is to be collected in the library of a new high school. Your colleagues favor an alphabetic system because of its simplicity. They ask you what are its disadvantages. What will you tell them?
3 After you have answered the preceding question, one person asks if the *D.O.T.* provides an adequate guide for filing all the materials that your collection will be likely to include. How will you answer?
4 You are a college placement officer. You have a collection of recruiting pamphlets filed by companies. You have just hired a new assistant who wants to change to an alphabetic filing system by occupation. Will you approve the change? Why? Why not?
5 You are a dormitory counselor in a small college. Your dean has asked you to start a collection of occupational information for the use of students and faculty advisers.

Some faculty members want the materials filed by academic subjects. Will you follow their wishes or suggest another method? If so, what? Why?

6 You are a counselor in a psychological testing center, or in a rehabilitation center, and you are assigned to reorganize the collection of occupational information. Some of your colleagues want the material filed by interest classifications on one of the vocational interest inventories which they use. What will you do? Why?

7 You are employed as a counselor in the high school or the undergraduate college that you attended. You are free to file occupational information in any way you choose. How will you file it? Why? How will you file omnibus books? Tape recordings?

8 How much of your time as a counselor will you need to spend in filing occupational information in order to keep your collection up to date?

Chapter 7

Theories of Occupational Choice and Career Development

Any attempt to help any person make career plans or occupational choices implies some theory of choice or development. Such a theory expresses our expectation, or belief, or hypothesis about the way in which plans or choices are made.

Thus counseling implies a belief that decisions are influenced by what the counselor says or does, or by what happens to the client in the counseling relationship. The use of vocational aptitude tests and interest inventories implies a belief that decisions are influenced by the information which these instruments may contribute to the client's knowledge of himself. The provision of occupational information implies a belief that decisions are influenced by what the client knows about occupations.

There are many theories of occupational choice and career development—too many for all of them to be reviewed in a book devoted to another subject. But explanation and discussion of a selected sample of theories may help the counselor to see more clearly the beliefs implied in his own behavior, and perhaps to reconsider some of the things that he does.

Several excerpts from other writers are presented and discussed in this chapter. The quotations are necessarily brief. From much longer documents, I have chosen the parts which seem to me most pertinent to a book on occupational information; these are not always the quotations most likely to interest other research workers. Nor do these brief passages really do justice to the writers. The reader who is interested in theory is urged to read each writer's full statement in the original, plus Osipow [294]; Roth, Henshenson, and Hilliard [327]; Whiteley and Resnikoff [411]; and Zytowski [426].

The quotations include theories which have been carefully drafted and documented, research evidence which supports or challenges the theories, hypotheses proposed for further investigation, conclusions from research completed, and some casual but provocative expressions of opinion. Some of the writers explain occupational choice in terms of external economic, sociologic, and educational influences; others find their explanations in the conscious and unconscious internal motivations of the individual. There is sharp conflict on some points, considerable agreement on others.

In this chapter each writer's statement is first presented with a minimum of comment. The arrangement is alphabetic. Comparison and discussion follow in the latter part of the chapter. The student who is approaching this subject for the first time may find the conflicting statements somewhat confusing, especially if he tries to remember them all. This chapter may be more useful to the beginner if he will read it as he might examine a display of merchandise in a store, looking at each excerpt critically, rejecting those ideas which contribute nothing to his own thinking, and marking for review those which provoke his interest.

THE THEORIES

Brill [31] In his *Basic Principles of Psychoanalysis* Brill suggested that

> . . . the normal individual needs no advice or suggestion in the selection of a vocation, he usually senses best what activity to follow. . . .
> The surgeon and the butcher have both conquered their sadistic impulses and sublimate the same for useful purposes. . . .
> The professions of prize fighters, wrestlers, bullfighters, warriors, and mighty hunters are direct descendants of pure sadism, and the need for the sadistic outlet is well shown by the popularity of these vocations. . . .
> Unconscious and sometimes conscious feelings of guilt and remorse as a reaction to real or imaginary sins are often the basis of theological callings. . . . The actor and the professional soldier are sublimated exhibitionists par excellence; the latter is also unconsciously dominated by a strong aggressive component. . . .
> There is always some psychic determinant which laid the foundation for the later vocation, and if not interfered with the individual is unconsciously guided to express his sublimation in that particular form. . . .
> As in the selection of a mate, a sensitive person needs no advice and wants none in choosing his vocation; and fools will fail in spite of the best guidance. . . .

Caplow [44] Caplow reviewed the evidence from sociologic research on occupational choice and concluded that

> . . . Error and accident often play a larger part than the subject himself is willing to concede.
> . . . Almost all farmers are recruited from farmers' sons.
> . . . Occupational choices are made at a time when the student is still remote from the world of work. They are made in terms of school requirements, which may call for quite different abilities and tastes from those which will be related to the eventual job.

. . . Occupational choices are made in the schoolroom, under the impersonal pressure of the curriculum, and remote from many of the realities of the working situation. . . .

Realistic choices typically involve the abandonment of old aspirations in favor of more limited objectives. . . . Not until late in his career will the average man be able to sum up his total expectations with some degree of finality and measure them against his remaining aspirations so as to arrive at a permanent sense of frustration, a permanent glow of complacency, or an irregular oscillation from one to the other.

Clark The effect of earnings on job choice has been discussed by economists ever since the division of labor was invented. Difference of opinion exists as to the relative importance of income and other influences, and individual differences in responsiveness to income are conceded, but few would deny that a substantial change in rates of pay is a potent force in moving workers from one occupation to another. This aspect of occupational choice was discussed at length by Clark [61] in his *Economic Theory and Correct Occupation Distribution*, in which he expressed the conviction that "Proper information regarding wages, if sufficiently impressed upon people, will lead to correct choice of occupation and correct number, provided barriers to occupations have been removed."

Dawis, Lofquist, and Weiss [91] In their studies of vocational rehabilitation, Dawis, Lofquist, and Weiss formulated the following Theory of Work Adjustment:

Each individual seeks to achieve and maintain correspondence with his environment. . . . Work represents a major environment to which most individuals must relate. . . . Correspondence can be described in terms of the individual fulfilling the requirements of the work environment, and the work environment fulfilling the requirements of the individual. . . . The continuous and dynamic process by which the individual seeks to achieve and maintain correspondence with his work environment is called work adjustment. . . . Stability of the correspondence between the individual and the work environment is manifested as tenure in the job. . . . Tenure is a function of correspondence between the individual and his work environment. . . . Satisfactoriness and satisfaction indicate the correspondence between the individual and his work environment. . . . The levels of satisfactoriness and satisfaction observed for a group of individuals with substantial tenure in a specific work environment establish the limits of satisfactoriness and satisfaction from which tenure can be predicted for other individuals. . . . The work personalities of individuals who fall within the limits of satisfactoriness and satisfaction for which substantial tenure can be predicted, may be inferred to be correspondent with the specific work environment. . . . Work personality-work environment correspondence . . . can be used to predict satisfactoriness and satisfaction, indicators of correspondence in the work adjustment process. . . . Work personality-work environment correspondence can be used to predict tenure.

Forer [125] Forer found the explanation of occupational choices largely in the personality and the emotional needs of the individual, often operating unconsciously:

1 Choice of a vocation is not primarily rational or logical, but is a somewhat blind, impulsive, emotional, and automatic process and is not always subject to practical and reasonable considerations.

2 Primary reasons for selecting a particular vocation are unconscious in the

sense that when the individual is pressed to elaborate beyond the superficial rationalization of economic advantage and opportunity, he is forced to admit that he does not know why; he simply has to build bridges or can't stand paper work. These activities have immediate appeal or distaste for him. We are saying that interests and references have unconscious roots. . . .

3 Both of these factors point ultimately to the purposive nature of occupational choice. Obviously it is necessary for most persons to find gainful employment. But the economic motive is secondary. Occupational choice, the specific occupation chosen or the fact of lack of preference, is an expression of basic personality organization and can and should satisfy basic needs.

4 Selection of a vocation, like the expression of other interests, is a personal process, a culmination of the individual's unique psychological development. . . .

Ginzberg, Ginsburg, Axelrad, and Herma [141]   These authors shocked professional career counselors in 1951 when they accused the profession of having no theoretical foundation. Their accusation was promptly, angrily, and not very convincingly rebutted by some leaders in the profession, but it stimulated much of the subsequent development of and research on theory.

For about twenty years what came to be called the Ginzberg theory was frequently quoted and widely accepted. It was based on a study of eighty-one persons, in which the authors

. . . found that the process of occupational decision-making could be analyzed in terms of three periods—fantasy, tentative, and realistic choices. These can be differentiated by the way in which the individual "translates" his impulses and needs into an occupational choice. In the fantasy period the youngster thinks about an occupation in terms of his wish to be an adult. He cannot assess his capacities or the opportunities and limitations of reality. He believes that he can be whatever he wants to be. His translations are arbitrary.

The tentative period is characterized by the individual's recognition of the problem of deciding on a future occupation. The solution must be sought in terms of probable future satisfactions rather than in terms of current satisfactions. During this period, however, the translation is still almost exclusively in terms of subjective factors: interests, capacities, and values. In fact, as most individuals reach the end of this period, they recognize that their approach has been too subjective. They, therefore, consider their choices tentative, for they realize that an effective resolution requires the incorporation of reality considerations and this will be possible only on the basis of additional experience.

During the realistic period, the translation is so heavily weighted by reality considerations that a synthesis is difficult. The individual recognizes that he must work out a compromise between what he wants and the opportunities which are available to him. . . .

This, then, is our general theory. First, occupational choice is a process which takes place over a minimum of six or seven years, and more typically, over ten years or more. Secondly, since each decision during adolescence is related to one's experience up to that point, and in turn has an influence on the future, the process of decision-making is basically irreversible. Finally, since occupational choice involves the balancing of a series of subjective elements with the opportunities and limitations of reality, the crystallization of occupational choice inevitably has the quality of a compromise.

In 1972 Ginzberg [140] published a restatement of the theory, based upon all of the research which had been done in the interim. In this restatement he wrote:

We no longer consider the process of occupational decision-making as limited to a decade; we now believe that the process is open-ended, that it can coexist with the individual's working life.

Little is left of our original emphasis on irreversibility. The principal challenge that young people face during their teens is to develop a strategy that will keep their options open, at least to the extent of assuring their admission to college or getting a job with a preferred employer.

The reformulation of our theory of occupational choice, then, follows in brief:

Occupational choice is a process that remains open as long as one makes and expects to make decisions about his work and career. In many instances, it is coterminous with his working life.

While the successive decisions that a young person makes during the preparatory period will have a shaping influence on his later career, so will the continuing changes that he undergoes in work and life.

People make decisions about jobs and careers with an aim of optimizing their satisfactions by finding the best possible fit between their priority needs and desires and the opportunities and constraints that they confront in the world of work.

Our reformulated theory is that *occupational choice is a lifelong process of decision-making in which the individual seeks to find the optimal fit between his career preparation and goals and the realities of the world of work.*

While young people who grow up in adverse circumstances have fewer effective options through which to shape their lives and careers, all people have some options and the majority has a great many.

The critical issue is whether or not they take advantage of the options.

Holland [168, 169]   Holland summarized his theory in these words:

These working assumptions constitute the heart of the theory. . . .

In our culture, most persons can be categorized as one of six types—Realistic, Intellectual,[1] *Social, Conventional, Enterprising, and Artistic. . . .*

There are six kinds of environments: Realistic, Intellectual,[1] *Social, Conventional, Enterprising, and Artistic. . . .*

People search for environments and vocations that will permit them to exercise their skills and abilities, to express their attitudes and values, to take on agreeable problems and roles, and to avoid disagreeable ones. Consequently, Realistic types seek Realistic environments, Intellectual[1] types seek Intellectual[1] environments, and so forth. To a lesser degree, environments also search for people through recruiting practices. The person's search for environments is carried on in many ways, at several levels of consciousness, and over a long period of time. . . .

As a child grows up, he learns through his parents, social class, schools, and community what he does well, what he does poorly, and what he likes to do. He also acquires some useful though not always accurate vocational images . . . . When he graduates from school and takes his first job, his choice is a resolution of a complex set of forces that include his hierarchy of choices . . . the range of job opportunities available to him, the influence of parents and friends, and various chance factors. In the present theory, a person's first and subsequent decisions are explained in terms of personality pattern and environmental model only. A more complete theory would incorporate economic and sociological influence.

A persons's behavior can be explained by the interaction of his personality pattern and his environment.

Hollingshead [170]   From his research on *Elmtown's Youth,* Hollingshead reported that

The pattern of vocational choices corresponds roughly with the job patterns associat-

---

[1] Holland subsequently substituted the word "Investigative" for "Intellectual."

ed with each class in the adult work world. Therefore, we believe that the adolescents' ideas of desirable jobs are a reflection of their experiences in the class and family culture complexes. . . .

The surprising thing to us is not the high percentage of youngsters in class II who want to go into business and the professions, but the low percentage in classes IV and V. Apparently these lower class youngsters, on the average, have adjusted their job desires to what they may hope to achieve. By so doing, they have limited their horizons to the class horizon, and in the process they have unconsciously placed themselves in such a position that they will occupy in the class system the same levels as their parents.

Kline and Schneck [220] In reporting "An Hypnotic Experimental Approach to the Genesis of Occupational Interests and Choice," Kline and Schneck expressed their belief that

What has not been stressed in vocational guidance is the origin of vocational interests, their relationship to personality organisation and their relationship to individual aptitudes. There is evidence that changes in personality organisation greatly influence not only occupational interests but the level of job adjustment, and that in fact the prescribed approach to vocational maladjustment in a great number of cases appears to be psychotherapy rather than vocational guidance. A manipulation of the expressed occupational interests of an individual does not in fact prove to effect adjustment in cases of vocational maladjustment. Psychotherapy involving distinct changes in personality organisation has on the other hand been capable of altering occupational factors to the extent of effecting adjustment out of maladjustment.

In their experiment Kline and Schneck placed three persons under hypnosis and then said to them, "I'm going to count from one to five and when I reach five you will be able to visualize a scene involving an occupation for which you have a real interest, even though this interest may be unknown to you now."

One subject was a married woman, age twenty-four, about to be fired from her job as a clerical office worker because of frequent clashes with her supervisor. Under hypnosis she said, "I am a singer and I am singing before a large audience. They like me very much and ask me to sing again. They give me a lot of attention and applause." The examiner asked, "Why do you really enjoy it?" The woman replied, "Because I am showing my mother that I can be successful and that people really do like me."

Another subject was a twenty-three-year-old actress who repeatedly failed just as she seemed to be on the verge of success. Under hypnosis she first saw herself drawing fashion copy, next as an executive in an office. Then she said, "I'm resisting myself. I won't let myself think of other jobs. I can't. Please—no more scenes. I'm afraid I will find out that I really don't want to be an actress and will want to go into some other type of work, and I'm afraid that people will laugh at me if I should."

Miller and Form [263] In their book on *Industrial Sociology* Miller and Form expressed the following view:

The network of interrelated social factors that have been demonstrated to be associated with occupational levels might become the basis of a *social* causation theory of career patterns. Such a theory would impute the origin and development of a career to those social factors that have been identified. Relationships can be demonstrated between occupational level of a worker and (1) the father's occupation, (2) the historical circumstances, (3) the father's income and education, (4) financial aid and influential contacts, (5) social and economic conditions. An accurate weighing of the facts will demonstrate that the social background of the worker is a base of opportunities and limitations. As opportunities are enlarged the *possibilities* of occupational mobility are increased. Personal motivation and native ability are necessary to an enlarging career pattern. However, there is good evidence that the social backgrounds of workers are the crucial determiners in the *number* who are able to come into various occupational levels. . . .

Social background, native ability, historical circumstance, and acquired personality *traits* are the influences determining a given career pattern. These forces may be considered as intertwined and pulling upon each worker with different intensities at various times in his career. By the time a man or woman reaches 35 or 40 years of age the forces often become equilibrated, and what the occupational history is from 35 years to 60 years is a fair index of whatever stability the worker will experience.

Roe [319]   Roe saw

. . . the job as a source of satisfaction of many needs. . . . When I speak of the job . . . I mean not only what he does but the total setting within which he does it. A major part of most jobs, in terms of the satisfactions to be derived from them, is the social interaction, and the social status which is linked to the job. . . . The intrinsic interest of the task varies pretty constantly with the level of the job . . . and as the relative importance of intrinsic interest declines, the importance of the job setting increases. . . . To understand how a man functions in a job one must know what his needs are and where and how they are satisfied. . . .

All persons have physiological needs which

. . . can vary only within a very limited range, but . . . need for understanding, need for beauty, etc., will have extremely wide variation among individuals. . . . For example, aesthetic needs are very strong in some individuals, and may then be extremely important in vocational choice, but of no importance at all for other persons.
. . . The modes and degrees of need satisfaction determine which needs will become the strongest motivators. The nature of the motivation may be quite unconscious.

Roe accepted Maslow's [253] concept of a hierarchy of needs, which Roe listed in the following order:

1 The physiological needs.
2 The safety needs.
3 The need for belongingness and love.
4 The need for importance, respect, self-esteem, independence.
5 The need for information.
6 The need for understanding.
7 The need for beauty.
8 The need for self-actualization.

In this list the lower-numbered needs are frequently referred to as the basic or "lower order" needs. The higher-numbered are called the "higher order" needs.
Roe suggested that:

Needs, for which even minimum satisfaction is rarely achieved, will, if higher order, become in effect expunged, or will, if lower order, prevent the appearance of higher order needs, and will become dominant and restricting motivators. . . .

A child whose expressions of natural curiosity are thoroughly blocked may cease to be curious. . . .

Needs, the satisfaction of which is delayed but eventually accomplished, will become (unconscious) motivators, depending largely upon the degree of satisfaction felt. . . .

This is the key to the development of interests.

Interests . . . are . . . the focus of effortless, active attention, which becomes progressively differentiated. . . .

The first and greatest differentiation is between person-directed attention and non-person-directed attention. Person-directed attention may refer to other persons or to the self, and it may be a resultant of excessive thwarting from persons, or of major satisfactions connected with persons. And I think that this differentiation is probably fixed for all practical purposes . . . by kindergarten age. . . .

What the counselor needs to know is the major orientation of the child, his patterns of interpersonal relations, and especially the situations which the child finds satisfying and those which he dislikes. The counselor should be able to extract from these experiences some estimate of the need hierarchy of the child, and of need strengths. . . . The counselor must also know what the socio-economic background of the family is, and what their attitudes and value systems are, and their expectations for the child. . . .

If high school is to be the last of formal educational training . . . specific vocational counseling is necessary, and I would strongly urge that it not be primarily task oriented, but be oriented first to the general situation and then to the specific task. And that it include some discussion of what satisfactions the job can and cannot be expected to supply. . . .

At the college level ". . . the importance of the task is very much greater. This is largely because of the shift from extrinsic to intrinsic interests occurring with difference in job level."

See also chapters by Roe in Whiteley and Resnikoff [411].

Schaffer [338] Schaffer studied job satisfaction as related to need satisfaction among seventy-two employed men, most of whom were in professional and semiprofessional occupations. His theory formally stated is this:

Over-all satisfaction will vary directly with the extent to which those needs of an individual which can be satisfied in a job are actually satisfied; the stronger the need, the more closely will job satisfaction depend on its fulfillment. . . .

The most accurate prediction of over-all job satisfaction can be made from the measure of the extent to which each person's strongest two or three needs are satisfied. . . .

Twelve needs . . . were chosen. . . .

A *Recognition and Approbation.* The need to have one's self, one's works, and other things associated with one's self known and approved by others.

B *Affection and Interpersonal Relationships.* The need to have a feeling of acceptance by and belongingness with other people. The need to have people with whom to form these affective relationships.

C *Mastery and Achievement.* The need to perform satisfactorily according to one's own standards. The need to perform well in accordance with the self-perception of one's abilities.

D *Dominance.* The need to have power and control of others.

E *Social Welfare.* The need to help others, and to have one's efforts result in benefits to others.

F *Self-expression.* The need to have one's behavior consistent with one's self-concept.

G *Socioeconomic Status.* The need to maintain one's self and one's family in accordance with certain group standards with respect to material matters.

H *Moral Value Scheme.* The need to have one's behavior consistent with some moral code or structure.

I *Dependence.* The need to be controlled by others. Dislike of responsibility for one's own behavior.

J *Creativity and Challenge.* The need for meeting new problems requiring initiative and inventiveness, and for producing new and original works.

K *Economic Security.* The need to feel assured of a continuing income. Unwillingness to "take a chance" in any financial matters.

L *Independence.* The need to direct one's own behavior rather than to be subject to the direction of others.

Super In 1953 Super proposed "A Theory of Vocational Development" [381], which he has since revised and expanded.

From *The Psychology of Careers* [380]:

The term *vocational choice,* widely used in discussions and studies of vocational development and adjustment, conveys a misleading notion of neatness and precision in time. . . .

Choice is, in fact, a process rather than an event. . . . The term should denote a whole series of choices, generally resulting in the elimination of some alternatives and the retention of others, until in due course the narrowing down process results in what might perhaps be called an occupational choice. . . .

Vocational development is conceived of as one aspect of individual development. . . .

Vocational maturity is used to denote the degree of development, the place reached on the continuum of vocational development from exploration to decline. . . .

The choice of an occupation is one of the points in life at which a young person is called upon to state rather explicitly his concept of himself, to say definitely "I am this or that kind of person."

Similarly, holding and adjusting to a job is for the typical beginning worker a process of finding out, first, whether that job permits him to play the kind of role he wants to play; secondly, whether the role the job makes him play is compatible with his self-concept—whether the unforeseen elements in it can be assimilated into the self or modified to suit the self; and, finally, it is a process of testing his self-concept against reality, of finding out whether he can actually live up to his picture of himself.

From *Career Development: Self-Concept Theory* [384]:

Elements of a self-concept theory of vocational development . . . may be identified as the processes of formation, translation, and implementation of the self concept.

Self-concept formation. In infancy the individual begins the process of forming a concept of himself, developing a sense of identity as a person distinct from but at the same time resembling other persons. This is essentially an exploratory process which goes on throughout the entire course of life until selfhood ceases and identity is lost to the sight of man as we know him. How does this concept of self evolve?

Exploration appears to be the first phase. . . . The self is an object of exploration as it develops and changes; so, too, is the environment.

Self differentiation is a second phase . . . the baby notes "This is I, that is someone else." He goes on to ask, "What am I like?" . . .

Identification is another process which goes on more or less simultaneously with differentiation. . . . The boy, whose father was at first his only male object of identification, finds that he can resemble a number of other males and assume a variety of masculine roles, can choose his identification on the basis of what appeals to him most. . . .

Role playing is a type of behavior which accompanies or follows identification. . . . Whether the role playing is largely imaginative or overtly participatory it gives some opportunity to try the role on for size, to see how valid the concept of oneself as a left-handed baseball player, or as a student of biology preparing to be a physician, actually is.

Reality testing stems as readily from role playing as role playing does from identification. Life offers many opportunities for reality testing, in the form of children's play, . . . in school courses, . . . in extracurricular activities, . . . and in part-time or temporary employment. . . . These reality testing experiences strengthen or modify self concepts, and confirm or contradict the way in which they have been tentatively translated into an occupational role.

Translation of self concepts into occupational terms. The translation proceeds in several ways. . . . Identification with an adult. . . . Experience. . . . Awareness of the fact that one has attributes which are said to be important in a certain field of work. . . .

Implementation of the self concepts. The implementation or actualizing of self concepts is the result of these processes as professional training is entered or as education is completed and the young man or woman moves from school or college into the world of work. . . .

These appear to be the elements of a self-concept theory of vocational development.

Since the publication of his theory, Super and his associates have done considerable research on his concept of vocational maturity, attempting to measure it and to determine how it develops from ninth grade until some years after the individual has left full-time education for full-time employment. The research has been summarized by Osipow [294], by Crites [81], and by Super in Whiteley and Resnikoff [411], in which Super wrote:

Despite the hope that I hold for a phenomenological approach, I am reluctant to be identified . . . as a self-concept theorist. This is because, as normally understood, this term seems to leave out of consideration the objective situational and personal variables which . . . I have taken very much into account.

If, then, my approach must be labelled, let it be as differential-developmental-social-phenomenological psychology. For it is only as we make use of all of these fields and also of aspects of sociological and economic theory that we will eventually construct a theory of vocational development that deals adequately with the complex processes by which people progress through the sequence of positions constituting a career.

Tiedeman [390]   Tiedeman said:

The conception of choos*ing* is now the primary conception in my evolving theory of the personally-determined career. . . .

Career development is not all thought; career development is the exercise of thought in work activities in ways such that action is somewhat guided by thought. However, action influences thought as well as the reverse. . . .

The adequate exercise of choice requires full use of thought, a conscious mechanism. . . .

Behavioral science does not honor the possibility of thought in any form except that of the investigator. . . .

Personal determination in career development originates from purposeful action provided that such action becomes related to the career realm of the person's experience. The cultivation of a union of purposeful action with career requires careful consideration of the mechanisms of time and sequence by subject and counselor. When the subject and counselor focus upon the previously explicated mechanisms of time and sequence in relation to the processes involved in vocational choosing, unconscious, pre-conscious, and conscious mechanisms provide means of analyzing the objects and bases of choice in the development of the personally-determined career. The expansion of career development through the incorporation into personal and career continuities of the discontinuities of new career opportunities gives rise to the processes of differentiation and integration associated with such incorporation. The attainment of integration during the incorporation of discontinuity into continuity requires commitment to such incorporation as well as the assumption of tentativeness towards that incorporation so that the person is master, not slave, of the possibility.

Obviously the development of maturity which incorporates the personally-determined career is a matter of considerable duration in the life of man. In fact, I am of the view that maturity is an always evolving condition, never an attained condition. Nevertheless, I do believe that patterns are discernible at different ages in relation to different problems in the evolution of career. . . .

A curriculum will have to be constructed which will teach students how to use . . . educational and vocational information . . . in the framing of vocational decisions. The assumption of responsibility during choice in vocational decisions will be the primary goal of this instruction. . . .

The *procedure* of making decisions will then become the explicit context within which the counselor's discourse in this task will find focus. Finally, the *process* of making informed decisions will become the professional context within which the counselor must operate. In other words, case by case, year after year, the counselor must focus upon the developed awareness of the student concerning *his* process of decision making in educational and vocational realms.

See also Miller and Tiedeman [262].

Warner and Abegglen [403]   Warner and Abegglen analyzed the social origins and careers of 8,000 major business executives in the United States. On the basis of incidence in the population, they computed how many persons from various kinds of families might be expected to become business leaders if family background had no effect upon occupational success. They then observed how many persons from each group did become business leaders. They found that

For every 10 men who might have been expected to be business leaders on the basis of their occupational backgrounds and the proportion of such men in the general occupational population, there were approximately 80 sons of business leaders; 40 sons of small business men, about 40 sons of professional men, and slightly over 10 sons of foremen. . . . Fewer than 2 out of the expected 10 turn up for the semiskilled or unskilled and almost none for farm laborers. . . .

A comparison of the findings of 1928 . . . indicate . . . an increase in the proportion of the men who come from the lower ranks. . . .

Geographical regions . . . contributed disproportionately. . . . Corrected for the size of the population . . . the . . . Middle Atlantic states rank first. . . .

Most of the men of the business elite were born in the big cities. . . .

Seventy-six per cent of the men studied had gone to college, 57 per cent had graduated. . . .

The laborer who "marries the boss's daughter" takes almost exactly the same amount of time for achievement as the one who marries someone from his own level of origin (25.9 years for the first, 26.1 for the latter).

COMMENTS ON THEORIES

The theories described above are pioneer attempts to find some rational explanation and some basis for understanding of what happens when a person chooses an occupation. They are theories in the broadest sense. Some have been called assumptions or postulates or hypotheses. All of them are based upon some evidence; all of them will require much more evidence before any one of them can be regarded as established. In the meantime, the counselor must rely upon his own experience and his own judgment in comparing conflicting theories, in accepting ideas which make sense to him, in rejecting those which do not, and in formulating his own theory to guide his own actions.

It is imperative that the counselor never forget that *any* theory, no matter how plausible, is *only* a theory until adequate research establishes it as a fact. A theory may be an *aid* to our thinking; it is never a *substitute* for thinking.

The comments which follow may be of some help to the reader in identifying the areas of agreement and the points of conflict among the theories described above, and in considering the implications of these theories for the use of occupational information in counseling and in teaching. The opinions expressed are the author's own, subject to all the errors of judgment based on inadequate data and subject to revision as these errors become apparent.

Vocational Choice or Vocational Development?   Super [380] has noted that "the term *vocational choice* . . . conveys a misleading notion of neatness and precision in time," whereas "choice is, in fact, a process rather than an event."

The concept of vocational development does not, of course, deny the fact that every individual must someday decide that he will or will not accept a job that has been offered. One may, indeed, have to make several such decisions. Each decision will be affected by one's development up to that point. Whether each decision is good or bad will always depend in part upon the accuracy and adequacy of the information which one has about the occupation under consideration.

The use of the term *vocational choice* or *occupational choice* in this book on occupational information is not intended to imply that a person makes only one such choice in a lifetime, nor that any such choice is unaffected by one's vocational development and vocational maturity. In this book the term *vocational choice* is used to refer to those occasions on which a person decides, tentatively or finally, that he will prepare for, look for, or accept a job in one occupation rather than another. Obviously a person may make any number of such choices in a lifetime.

I have no quarrel with Super or with Super's theory. Though I prefer the term *needs* to *self-concepts,* this preference is only for a term that seems to me to include a little more of a person's potential motivations. And Super has repeatedly emphasized his belief that accurate occupational information is essential to good career planning. If we differ at all, I think it is only on our assessment of the possibility of producing a larger number of good occupational decisions by providing more and better occupational information in the early stages of vocational development.

Super and Overstreet [383] concluded that ". . . the typical ninth-grade boy has not yet reached a stage at which wisdom of vocational preference can be expected." They also noted that "the . . . information which these boys had about . . . duties, conditions of work, and other important characteristics" of their preferred occupations was found to be limited.

We do not yet know how wise ninth-grade boys might be about their vocational preferences if they did have accurate and adequate information about occupations. We do know that many college seniors are as naïve and as bewildered as ninth-grade boys. And we do know that a few individuals do make stable choices even before the ninth grade.

We do not know why the vocational choices of some persons improve with age while others seem never to get any better and still others seem to need no improvement. On theoretical grounds it seems possible that occupational information may have something to do with this phenomenon. Perhaps the person who makes the good early choice has had the good fortune to *discover* an appropriate occupation early in life. Perhaps the person whose choices never improve never does find a job that is right for him. Perhaps for other persons vocational choice improves as the individual discovers more ways of making a living and learns more about them. To the extent that this hypothesis proves to be true, we might hope to help young people to reach wiser decisions earlier in life if we could increase the accuracy and the adequacy of the occupational information at their disposal.

Something of this sort was doubtless hoped for when courses in occupations were first introduced into the public schools. Something of this sort may explain why the choices of some students who have had courses in occupations have proved to be better than the choices of comparable students who did not have such courses. For a review of the research evidence on the effectiveness of courses in occupations, see Chapter 25.

Super wants to be sure we do not overlook the fact that while

> . . . information is essential—so is knowing whether or not, and how, it applies to oneself. Information is screened by the individual—how good is his screening? It is important to take self-concepts into account, to provide opportunities for and to evaluate exploratory behavior, and to counsel concerning both of these.

I want to be sure the information the client screens is adequate and accurate when he gets it.

We agree that both of these concerns are pertinent and important.

Osipow [294], in his evaluation of Super's theory, concluded:

> The research and data relevant to the concept of vocational development seem to indicate a steady and reasonably predictable increase in both the amount of attention and the sophistication of that attention given to vocational choice tasks through the adolescent years. . . . As vocational decisions require a person to explicitly state his

conception of himself, people with accurate information about themselves and the world are most likely to make sound vocational decisions.

Zaccaria [423], in his review, observed, "Super's theory is perhaps the broadest and most widely accepted of the contemporary theories of vocational development."

Unconscious Motivations Much of the career counseling of the past appears to have been based upon the assumption that occupational choices are made intellectually in terms of what the client knows about occupations and about himself or herself. Currently there appears to be increasing recognition of the extent to which the client's emotional needs may affect his choices, with or without his awareness of these needs, as may be noted in the excerpts above from Brill, Forer, Kline and Schneck, and Roe. As with every new idea there are, and will continue to be, extremists who explain everything in terms of their one pet idea. Thus Brill sees no need for counseling or for testing or for occupational information; the client's emotions will lead to a wise choice if the rest of us will only let the person alone. In response to this blithe assumption, one may observe that the client's emotions can affect choices among only those occupations of which the client is aware and that the emotional response to any contemplated choice is a response to what the client believes the occupation to be. Emotional responses sometimes change with alacrity when clients learn how mistaken were their concepts of what specific occupations involve.

Competent counselors will not discard all their previous knowledge and experience when they discover unconscious motivations; they will, perhaps, find it a little easier to understand why their clients sometimes appear to act irrationally. As we learn more about emotions and their effect upon choices, we may learn how to help clients to become more aware of their emotional needs and to act effectively to meet them. As we learn to do this, career counseling will make increasingly important contributions to the emotional health and welfare of the client as well as to the client's economic and social adjustment. So long as people choose occupations, there will be need for someone to help them to learn what occupations are accessible to them, what these occupations offer that may meet their needs, and what each occupation requires in exchange.

Is Vocational Adjustment Basically Emotional? There probably are some persons who are so maladjusted emotionally, who find it so difficult to live comfortably with themselves and with others, that they would be ineffective and dissatisfied in almost any occupation. Others may be so concerned with their own emotional anxieties that they find it impossible to face reality or to think rationally about the choice of an occupation. Such persons may well need psychotherapy more than they need vocational guidance, as Kline and Schneck suggest. Recognition of this fact has led some observers to assume that all vocational indecision and dissatisfaction is merely a symptom of emotional maladjustment, that the "real" problem is always within the individual, and that if the counselor can deal effectively with this "real" problem, the client will then be able to solve his own vocational problems without the help of occupational information or aptitude tests or "vocational" counseling.

In conflict with this assumption is the evidence of conspicuous change in vocational adjustment which has followed change in external conditions. Many an unhappy worker has become a contented worker overnight by a fortunate change of employment; basic emotional maladjustments are not cured so quickly.

Gaudet and Kulick [135] studied the emotional adjustment of ". . . individuals who seek vocational and educational guidance." They could find no noticeable difference between the ". . . emotional, social, and familial adjustment" of these clients and the emotional, social, and familial adjustment of "a normative sample" of the total population.

Instead of assuming that all vocational maladjustment is caused by emotional maladjustment, we might get nearer the truth if we explored the hypothesis that *in some cases* emotional maladjustment causes vocational maladjustment while *in some cases* vocational maladjustment causes emotional maladjustment. The frustration of daily competition in work at which one is obviously inept, with support for one's family dependent upon satisfactory performance, is hardly conducive to mental health.

It is probably true that a normally versatile person can succeed well enough to make a living in any one of several occupations. It is also true that most of us can think of several occupations in which our own limitations would put us at a serious disadvantage. Success and satisfaction and mental health may well depend upon finding one of the former and avoiding all of the latter.

The experience of psychiatrists with this problem of choosing an occupation is reflected in Menninger's [259] comment:

> Perhaps three-fourths of the patients who come to psychiatrists are suffering from an incapacitating impairment of their satisfaction in work or their ability to work. In many it is their chief complaint. . . .
>
> Another index of our lack of scientific thinking in regard to the function of labor is our colossal ignorance and neglect of the problem of vocational choice. Here is one of the momentous decisions that cast the lives of human beings in fixed though diverse channels. Perhaps next to the choice of a marital partner, it is the most important and far-reaching decision made by the individual. . . .
>
> If one has occasion to observe in a young adolescent about to be graduated from high school his struggles over a choice of college and, particularly, over his course of study in that college, one cannot but be grateful to those who have made some effort to put at his disposal a survey of the complicated activities of life in which he will soon be forced to participate in some capacity or other.

There is no essential conflict between psychotherapy and vocational counseling. Some persons need one; some need the other; some need both. In the case of those who need both, each may reinforce the other.

Recent literature on counseling has frequently mentioned that a client who needs and wants psychotherapy may present a vocational problem as an excuse for an initial interview, during which he may observe the counselor and decide whether or not to discuss his other problems. It is certainly desirable that counselors be aware of this possibility and alert to detect what the client does need and want. It is equally desirable that the counselor remember Gaudet and Kulick's evidence that most of the persons who seek vocational and educational guidance are normal people, that not every client is psychopathic or emotionally maladjusted or even unduly anxious about his problems. For more on this see Hoppock [180].

Psychotherapists are exposed daily to an atypical sample of the population. It is not surprising that they, like the rest of us, sometimes generalize from their own experience, without adequate allowance for the limitations which their specialization has imposed upon their experience. No reasonable person would deny the great unmet need for therapy among multitudes of unhappy people. But the research on happiness in marriage, in work, in life as a whole has seldom shown a majority of the population to be unhappy. As a species of the animal kingdom, man has made a fairly tolerable adjustment.

There are a great many people in the world who are doing a pretty good job of handling their own emotional problems without professional assistance, who neither need nor want psychotherapy, but who do sometimes want and need information on which to base important decisions. Providing such information, tailored to their needs, and helping them to explore its significance in relation to their problems are essential parts of a counselor's professional responsibility. When the client's problem is the choice of an occupation, the counselor has an inescapable responsibility to use all his professional knowledge and skill to help the client to get the essential information about the occupations under consideration and to see to it that the information is accurate. Facts about jobs are quite as important as feelings about them.

To answer the question posed at the beginning of this section, vocational adjustment is basically emotional in some cases, but the evidence to date suggests that these cases constitute a minority of those who seek vocational and educational guidance. For the majority of clients, emotional needs are a part of the problem of choice, but they are not the whole problem. Clients do have economic needs and physical needs as well as emotional needs, and the client whose emotional needs are not met in his job can often correct this situation more readily by changing his job than by changing himself.

In a twenty-seven-year follow-up on job satisfaction of employed adults, Hoppock [177] found that ". . . changes in jobs did change job satisfaction promptly and in both directions" and that ". . . the greatest increases in job satisfaction were achieved by those who changed jobs."

Sociologic and Economic Influences   However potent may be the emotional and intellectual factors in determining occupational choice, there can be no escaping the fact that all effective choices *must* be made from the employment opportunities to which the client has access and *will* be made from those of which he is aware. Caplow, Clark, Hollingshead, Miller and Form, and Warner and Abegglen have given us convincing evidence that economic and sociologic factors do limit the range of occupations to which a person has access, do direct attention to some occupations and away from others, and do affect the occupational distribution of the population.

Most counselors come from middle-class homes with middle-class values and middle-class awareness of middle-class opportunities. Only through disillusioning experience do some counselors learn that not all their clients share their values or respond as the counselors do to what they regard as attractive opportunities. Counselors who would work effectively with clients whose backgrounds differ from their own will study the economics of the labor market and the sociology of work as industriously as they study psychology. They will listen to their clients and the clients' parents as much as they talk to them. Slowly they will learn some of the economic and family and cultural influences which lead their clients to do things that sometimes appear incomprehensible to members of other cultures. The reader who wishes to explore this area of human knowledge will do well to start with Caplow's [44] fascinating and scholarly review of *The Sociology of Work* and follow this with Nosow and Form's *Man, Work, and Society* [288], Slocum's *Occupational Careers—A Sociological Perspective* [358], Hall's *Occupations and the Social Structure* [153], and Krause's *Sociology of Occupations* [221].

The teacher who feels underpaid, who toys with the idea that he might quit his job, go into business for himself, and make a lot of money, may be no more attuned to reality than the six-year-old child who plans to be an airline pilot or the retarded student who plans to be a physician. The desire for wealth, status, glamour, or anything else may lead a person to choose an occupation that he thinks will bring him these things. If he shows no interest in considering the demand for workers and his own qualifications for the work, he may reasonably be suspected of fantasy at any age.

One of the less pleasant tasks of the counselor is that of helping such persons to discover and to face reality before they burn their bridges behind them. One of the really professional tasks of the counselor is the highly technical job of determining what the demand for workers really is and what qualifications really are essential to success.

Economists, Sociologists, Psychologists, and Educators There is no major conflict among the carefully formulated theories and the observations of economists, sociologists, psychologists, and educators unless one wishes to assert that the influence which one sees is the dominant influence.

Most reasonable people will agree that most of us need to earn a living, that we would like it to be a good living, and that few of us will accept a job without knowing what it pays. The need to earn a living is one of the basic needs which most of us seek to meet when we choose an occupation.

Most reasonable people will agree that the family and the social class in which we were reared helped to determine the occupations with which we were familiar, the occupations in which employment opportunities were presented to us, the occupations which we considered respectable and questionable, and some of the social needs that we sought to meet in our occupational choices. Even the persons who rebel against their families are influenced by them, and one can hardly deny the evidence that social origins have affected the occupational distribution of our population.

Most reasonable people will agree that there are observable differences in vocational interest and aptitude, that the same occupation may appear attractive to one person and repulsive to another, and that emotional needs do influence occupational choices consciously or unconsciously.

Most reasonable people will agree that there are some occupations which are extremely difficult to enter without the prescribed preparation and that education or the lack of it may permit or prevent a person from entering such an occupation.

Economists, sociologists, psychologists, and educators all are presumably correct when they assert that the forces with which they deal do affect occupational choice. Each of them may also correctly assert that in some cases the dominant influence is to be found in his field. Each of them is probably wrong if he or she thinks that all occupational choices, or even a majority of them, are dominated by the considerations which dominate his or her own interest. Occupational choice is not the exclusive province of the economist or the sociologist or the psychologist or the educator. It is the province of the person who is doing the choosing and who should be able to command the help of all the related disciplines in learning how best to make a choice.

IMPLICATIONS FOR COUNSELORS

Despite the differences which have been noted above, all the theories appear to have much more in common than in contrast.

Areas of Agreement   There appears to be either explicit or tacit agreement that both occupations and people differ; that the choice of an occupation may help or hinder success and satisfaction; that choices are affected by needs and should be affected also by abilities and by employment opportunities; that some choices are realistic, some fantastic, and some in between; that many persons make several different choices before committing themselves to any one choice; that choices may continue to change throughout the working lifetime of the individual; and that a counselor may sometimes help a person to make better choices than the person would make without help.

Reality Testing   There is explicit agreement on the necessity for reality testing as a part of occupational choice.

Well-intentioned but uninformed commencement orators, inspirational teachers, and amateur counselors contribute to fantasy as they eloquently assure the younger generation that perseverance and determination can overcome all obstacles to a cherished goal. Perhaps school counselors should suggest to their colleagues on the faculty that inspiration of this kind be tempered by reality.

Today there is much concern with disadvantaged youth and with efforts to raise their level of aspiration. It is difficult to express any reservations about these efforts without appearing to oppose equal opportunity for all. But good intentions do not guarantee good results.

Rich or poor, privileged or persecuted, we each have our own abilities and limitations, to which our own aspirations must be reasonably related. An indiscriminate effort to raise the aspirations of *all* disadvantaged youth may succeed only in aggravating the frustrations of those *individuals* who lack the qualifications to achieve their newly acquired aspirations.

Let us by all means remove racial barriers, but let us also remember that in any group of students anywhere there are very likely to exist some who could wisely raise their level of aspiration and some who could wisely lower it.

Counselors Should See Their Clients through Placement   Ultimately every client tests his or her occupational choice against the realities of occupational life when trying to make a living. Too often the client cannot get a job in the occupation of choice. He or she needs a job, and takes what can be gotten. It is at this point of placement that much career counseling breaks down because neither the client nor the counselor did enough reality testing in anticipation, during the process of career counseling. Because the client who fails to get a job seldom returns to the original counselor, the counselor seldom learns of these failures.

We could make tremendous improvements in the quality of career guidance if we could require all counselors to do what rehabilitation counselors were once required to do—follow the client through the process of placement and stay with him until his record indicates that the placement and the counseling have been successful. There would be some red faces among counselors when they experienced this kind of reality testing for the first time, and the embarrassment of the counselors might in turn provide the motivation needed to make future counseling more realistic.

Far too many counselors now are able to dispose of their clients before the success or failure of the counseling can be tested against reality. School and college counselors can dispose of their problems by graduating them. Client-centered counselors are relieved of their failures when the client no longer returns for counseling. Testing centers can get rid of their clients when the testing results have been interpreted. Counseling psychologists in veterans' hospitals can dispose of their patients by turning them over to the state employment service when the patients are ready to look for a job. Thus the counselors themselves can escape reality testing of their own work.

Fantasy in Counseling   Too much of our career counseling today operates almost exclusively in terms of interests, capacities, and values. The situation is bad enough in some of our public schools which give little attention to the realities of the employment market. The situation is even worse in some of our college counseling centers which are separate from the college placement centers, in some of the counseling psychology programs in the Veterans Administration, and in some of the counseling agencies operated by psychologists in private practice.

Most of the professional employees of these agencies are psychometrists, clinical psychologists, and counseling psychologists, who are well trained to deal with the subjective factors. In the same agencies there are comparatively few counselors who are equally well trained to deal with the reality considerations, who have the technical knowledge of occupations and the professional skill to help the client to work out a compromise between what he wants and what he can get. The imbalance of professional competence which prevails in such agencies today may permit a service which is better than none, as some evaluations already indicate, but it hardly seems calculated to produce the best results in terms of realistic choices.

There is fantasy in the belief that good career counseling can be provided by psychologists who know all about values and emotions and interests and capacities and who are not equally competent in the area of occupational information. What we now have in career counseling is far too many psychologists who regard placement as a dirty word and any direct contact with the employment market as degrading. If we are not someday to be charged with quackery, we should have in all career counseling services as many persons who are skilled in occupational information as we have persons who are skilled in psychology, or we should have a new breed of counselor whose training, experience, and competence in economics, in occupational information, and in placement equals his or her training, experience, and competence in psychology, in psychometrics, and in psychotherapy.

Perhaps because so many college counseling centers have shown so little interest in the realities of the employment market, many college placement offices have changed their names to "career counseling and placement office," "office of career planning," or something similar, and have hired persons with some professional preparation for career counseling. If these offices do not neglect their placement function or let the two functions be separated, we may get some improvement in the career counseling of college students. The quality will deteriorate wherever college administrators permit career counseling to be separated from placement, and wherever directors of career counseling permit their counselors to escape the chastening experience of seeing their own clients through placement.

One of the most important uses of occupational information in counseling is in helping the client to test the reality of any choice against all the pertinent, known facts about the demand for workers, the qualifications for employment, and the ways in which the occupation may or may not meet the needs of the client if he or she is able to get and hold a job. How occupational information may be used to do this is discussed later in this book.

Self-appraisal   There is one aspect of occupational choice that has been mentioned infrequently in the theories and in the other literature of vocational guidance. We have impressive evidence of the inability of many persons to estimate their own aptitude for activities in which they have had little opportunity to experiment. From this evidence we may easily but mistakenly infer that the average person has little ability to estimate his aptitude for anything.

On the contrary, most persons, by the time they are ready for full-time employment, have had thousands of opportunities to try to do thousands of different things and to observe whether they do them better or less well than other people. The duties of most occupations include many activities in which the average person has had many opportunities to participate. A person who knows enough about an occupation to be thoroughly familiar with all the duties and activities that the occupation involves will often avoid choosing that occupation if it is one of those for which he is least fitted, and will often lean toward it if it is one of those occupations for which he has more appropriate aptitudes. When people appear not to do this, their choices may be based upon inadequate knowledge of the occupation as well as upon ignorance of themselves. To the extent that we can help individuals to become thoroughly familiar with the activities of the principal occupations that are open to them, we may hope to contribute significantly to their adjustment even in some of the occupations for which no aptitude tests are yet available.

REVIEW QUESTIONS

1   Which of all these theories most nearly approximates your own?
2   With which do you disagree most vigorously? Why?
3   To what extent do you think your past vocational choices have been affected by anything mentioned in any of these theories?
4   How will your future counseling or teaching be affected by anything you have read in this chapter?

Chapter 8

A Composite Theory
for Counselors

Theories serve two purposes: for the research worker they provide hypotheses to be investigated; for the counselor they provide a way to make some sense out of the otherwise bewildering behavior of other people. In this chapter we are concerned with the counselor, and with how theories of occupational choice and career development can help him or her.

When a person acts the way we expect him to act, he confirms and supports the theories on which we operate. We feel reassured, successful, and confident. And we keep on doing what we are doing.

When a person does not act the way we expect him to act, when he acts in a way directly contrary to our expectations, he contradicts the theories on which we operate. We feel insecure, uncertain of our success, and doubtful of our methods. We may even feel impatient with the person who obstinately refuses to act in the way our theories have led us to expect that he will act. But when we recover from our impatience, we begin to reexamine our theories, to look for others which offer better explanations of the way people behave and better bases for anticipating how our students and clients will respond to our efforts as counselors.

Not for many years, if ever, will we have enough research evidence to confirm or contradict each of the many theories of occupational choice and career development already proposed, not to mention the new theories not yet devised. In the meantime, counselors must do the best they can.

What can a counselor extract from the conflicting theories now available? Must these theories only add to his confusion? Or can they help him to understand the behavior of the persons he tries to serve? Admittedly, what the counselor can infer from theories yet unconfirmed will be speculative. But examination and comparison of several theories may provide the counselor with a broader base for his own speculations and thus bring him a little nearer to truth, whatever that truth may be.

The existence of several conflicting theories suggests the possibility that there may be some truth in all of them. The basic principle of individual differences, so familiar to counselors, suggests the same possibility. One theory may explain the behavior of some persons, but we may need another theory to explain the behavior of others.

The remainder of this chapter is the result of one counselor's attempts to understand the behavior of the persons who have sought his help in making their plans and choices at various stages in their career development. This is presented not as a neat hypothesis for research, but as a series of speculations as to why people behave as they do when they are trying to reach career decisions. It will be apparent that these speculations draw freely on several of the theories reviewed in the preceding chapter.

A COMPOSITE THEORY

1 Occupations are chosen to meet needs.

2 The occupation that we choose is the one that we believe will best meet the needs that most concern us.

3 Needs may be intellectually perceived, or they may be only vaguely felt as attractions which draw us in certain directions. In either case, they may influence choices.

4 Career development begins when we first become aware that an occupation can help to meet our needs.

5 Career development progresses and occupational choice improves as we become better able to anticipate how well a prospective occupation will meet our needs. Our capacity thus to anticipate depends upon our knowledge of ourselves, our knowledge of occupations, and our ability to think clearly.

6 Information about ourselves affects occupational choice by helping us to recognize what we want and what we have to offer in exchange.

7 Information about occupations affects occupational choice by helping us to discover the occupations that may meet our needs, what these occupations offer to us, and what they will demand of us.

8 Job satisfaction depends upon the extent to which the job that we hold meets the needs that we feel it should meet. The degree of satisfaction is determined by the ratio between what we have and what we want.

9 Satisfaction can result from a job that meets our needs today, or from a job that promises to meet them in the future, or from a job that we think will help us to get the job we want.

10   Occupational choice is always subject to change when we believe that a change will better meet our needs.

EXPLANATIONS

Most human action is caused by feelings, by our desire to be more comfortable or less uncomfortable, more satisfied or less frustrated, in short, by our desire to feel better than we do. Human action is affected by intellect only after feelings have indicated that some kind of action is desirable and only to the extent that our intellect can convince us that a particular course of action will improve or relieve our feeling tone. Intellect gives direction to our actions when factual information or logical reasoning indicates that one course of action is more likely than another to bring us the satisfactions that we seek.

It may appear that human action sometimes is caused, not by a desire to feel better than we do, but by a desire to maintain the comfortable state that we have already attained. Certainly the latter desire can provide motivation for action, but only when we feel some concern that our comfortable state may deteriorate if we do not act. We then act to relieve our concern. In relieving our concern, we feel better. Thus we act in order to feel better.

It may appear that some persons enjoy unhappiness, persecute themselves, or sacrifice themselves for others. Such actions may not make the individual either happy or satisfied. They are, nevertheless, undertaken in the hope that they will make the individual less unhappy than he or she would be if any other course of action were followed. To the martyr, death is preferable to capitulation. He or she may be an atheist who expects no reward in heaven and yet prefers death to life on terms that would be intolerable. The person who persecutes himself or herself does so in order to relieve a feeling of guilt or because for some other reason relief or satisfaction is found in unhappiness. Paradoxical as it appears, perverted as it may be, the person seeks unhappiness in order to enjoy it.

The client who is unable to face reality may distort information about occupations just as he may distort information about himself. He may accept those facts which support a course of action that appeals to him while rejecting those facts which he finds disturbing. Wishful thinking is a fairly common characteristic of the human race. When people appear not to act rationally in choosing an occupation, their failure to do so may be traced to one of three causes: inadequate information about themselves, inadequate information about occupations, or inability to think clearly. Inability to face reality is one kind of inability to think clearly.

As noted previously, an occupation is only a name for a group of jobs which have something in common. The specific jobs within one occupation may differ in many ways. They may involve different supervisors, different employers, different locations, different physical surroundings, different associates. Because of these differences a person may be satisfied in one job and dissatisfied in another job in the same occupation if one of the jobs meets more of the person's needs than the other.

Needs and values sometimes change. A young person's eagerness for adventure may be replaced in later years by a preference for stability. An occupation which meets the needs of a client at age twenty may no longer meet his or her needs at age fifty. Participation in an occupation, daily association with the kinds of people who are attracted to it, acceptance of, and conformity to, the mores of the occupational group can in time have a subtle but substantial effect on a person's values. The result may be to make the occupation appear either more or less desirable than it seemed at first. If changes in needs and values are antici- pated, they may affect the original choice of an occupation; if they are not anticipated, they may lead a person to change his occupation in later life.

Economic factors affect occupational choice by helping to determine the age at which a person terminates his or her formal education and enters the labor market on a full-time basis. The economic cycle, moving from periods of prosper- ity to depression and back again, helps to determine the number and nature of the employment opportunities available at the time a person is looking for a job. Immediate and potential future earnings affect the extent to which a contemplat- ed occupation may be expected to meet one's economic needs.

Education influences occupational choice by opening the doors to some occupations that would otherwise be closed, by making a person aware of occu- pations of which he had no previous knowledge, by arousing or discouraging his interest in them, by providing tryout experiences which lead the student to antici- pate success or failure in specific activities. For some students, school or college provides a new social group with which they identify and which profoundly influences the social and economic needs which they feel their occupations must meet.

Psychological factors influence occupational choice by helping to determine the extent to which one perceives one's own needs, accepts or suppresses them, faces the realities of employment opportunities and of his own abilities and limi- tations, and thinks clearly about all these facts. The extent to which aptitudes and interests are general or specific will probably be argued as long as there are psychologists to speculate and statisticians to calculate probabilities, but there is little doubt that interests help to determine the occupations a person will consider and that aptitudes help to determine whether or not he or she will achieve enough success to get and to hold the job that has been chosen.

Sociologic factors affect occupational choice by helping to determine the occupations with which a person is familiar, by virtue of his or her contacts with family and friends. The cultural pattern of the social group in which a person has been reared and of the social group with which one currently identifies oneself helps to determine the occupations which will be considered socially acceptable and socially preferred. Social patterns of exclusion or acceptance help to de- termine the occupations which are available to the individual; thus a union may admit relatives of members in preference to others, an employer may discrimi- nate on racial or religious grounds, the qualifications for a job may include social contacts and social skills which are seldom acquired except through family asso- ciations. All these factors affect occupational choice by helping to determine the employment opportunities that will be available to an individual and those which he or she will consider, by influencing the social needs which one will feel that one's occupation must meet and the extent to which he or she will expect any contemplated occupation to meet these needs.

THE THEORY IN OPERATION

How this theory may help us to understand the phenomena of occupational choice may be suggested by the following examples.

Perhaps the simplest illustration is one that has appeared in times of economic depression. A person is unemployed and destitute and hungry. He takes the first job he can get, despite the fact that the work is offensive to him and does not meet many of his obvious needs. At the moment the need of which he is most aware is the need for food. He will be miserable until that need is met. Other needs can wait. This job offers the most acceptable, available way to meet the need that he feels most acutely. He takes the job. Later, on a full stomach, with this job for temporary security, he will look for another job that will provide food and also meet more of his other needs.

At the other end of the scale is the complex case of the individual who is only vaguely aware, if at all, of the emotional needs which drive him toward a particular occupation. Thus, a brilliant student who has little skill in teaching, even less patience with slower learners, and no genuine desire to help others to learn may nevertheless choose teaching as his occupation because the only real success he has ever achieved has been in the classroom and he fears to leave the environment in which he has enjoyed success or because something in his past experience has left him with a desire to dominate other people and teaching is the only occupation in which he sees an opportunity to do so. He may not be conscious of either of these motives and yet may be driven by them more compulsively than if he were aware of them. He may even become a teacher and remain a teacher all his life, despite the fact that neither he nor his students really enjoy his teaching, because he never finds any other occupation that offers him the security of the familiar classroom or the opportunity to play the dominant role.

Abnormal as well as normal needs may find expression in the choice of an occupation, sometimes with unfortunate results. Comfort [70], in his book *Authority and Delinquency in the Modern State: A Criminological Approach to the Problem of Power,* has observed:

> There are many occupations in modern society, almost all of them concerned with the executive side of power, which confer a limited license for the infliction of pain or of arbitrary authority, and these occupations are of a type indispensable to the present pattern of life. . . . Tolerated delinquents appear in centralized cultures at two distinct levels. They may enter and control the machinery of legislative and political power, as policy-makers and rulers. They may also be found, and tend in general to be more numerous, in the machinery of enforcement which intervenes between the policy-maker and the citizen. We owe our present recognition of the presence and the role of these tolerated delinquents, and of their capacity for mischief, to the rise of totalitarian states, but the reappearance of delinquency and military tyranny as socially accepted policies in civilized states has led, and must lead, to a scrutiny of similar mechanisms within the social democracies. . . . By comparison with other employments, the enforcement services offer poor remuneration and a severer discipline. . . . There is, therefore, in centralized societies, a tendency for the personnel of these occupations to be drawn increasingly from those whose main preoccupation is a desire for authority, for power of control and of direction over others.

How the Theory May Help Us to Understand Others   The needs and the demands of individuals are probably as varied and as complex as the individuals themselves, but if the individual sees or even subconsciously feels any way in which the choice of an occupation may help to meet his needs, then his needs will affect his choice. It is desirable that we as counselors understand this, not because the understanding will enable us to solve all the complex problems that will be brought to us, but because we may then better understand the less complex cases and be of more help to them. Without this understanding we may be baffled by the choices of individuals whose emotional needs or value patterns differ from ours. A choice that seems illogical to us, and would indeed be illogical if we made it for ourselves, becomes logical when we understand the needs and the values of the person who makes it.

Thus we smile and dismiss as fantasy the occupational choice of the little child who announces his serious intention to be a firefighter when he grows up. It may not occur to us that the child, dominated by adults from morning until night and protected from every danger that can be anticipated, may feel a real need to be important and to embark upon some adventure more thrilling than the exploration of his own backyard. In terms of the needs that he feels and of the occupations with which he is familiar, his choice may be as logical as ours. In his place we might well make the same choice, and some of us did.

We consider immature the choice of the adolescent who is determined to enter the occupation of a current adult hero, for which work our student obviously lacks essential aptitudes. We overlook, perhaps, the fact that the adolescent is here showing the first sign of maturity. He or she is breaking away from home ties and has a real need to identify with, and try to be like, some adult outside the family, as in the past he tried to be like his parents. Knowing as little as he does about vocational aptitudes and about the requirements of occupations and being not yet ready to stand alone, we too might find security in such an occupational choice, and some of us did.

If we can even suspect the emotional needs behind what look to us like irrational choices, we may be more tolerant of them. If we can occasionally understand the connection between these needs and choices, we may then be of more help to our clients, sometimes by simply waiting for them to mature a little more, sometimes by helping them to understand and accept themselves, sometimes by helping them to discover more effective and attractive ways to satisfy their needs.

We are still a long way from having research data on how well specific occupations may satisfy specific emotional needs. A beginning has been made by Borgen and others [23], who compiled data showing the extent to which needs may be satisfied in each of eighty-one occupations, as judged by 2,976 "immediate supervisors of jobs in several hundred firms."

A fascinating discussion, in lay language, of how different occupations may meet different emotional needs appears in Brown [33].

Aptitudes and Interests Are Not Enough   Perhaps this theory may explain in part the skepticism of some observers regarding the kind of career guidance that is given by counselors whose major interest is in aptitude and interest tests.

Aptitude and interest are important, but they are only parts of the total picture of the client. A person may have a perfect pattern of measured aptitudes and interests for a specific occupation and firmly reject it if it fails to meet the needs which are most important to the individual. The person may be happier and, conceivably, more effective in an occupation for which he has only average qualifications if the occupation meets more of the needs which are high in the person's scale of values.

Thus a parent who values his role as a parent higher than his occupational success may reject a job for which he has perfect aptitudes, because it would require him to leave his family or to move them to a location that would aggravate one child's allergies.

Another person may value leisure more than money, prestige, or achievement and be happier in a job that is "beneath him" than in one which would utilize more of his talents but consume more of his time.

Another may prefer steady work and an assured weekly income in a job that he does moderately well rather than higher but irregular earnings in a field for which he may have superior aptitude and interest.

A child may feel a need to conform to or to resist his parents' wishes, to remain near them or to get away from them. His choice may be influenced more by such considerations than by others which may appear more rational to the counselor.

The person who likes to think of himself as a superior being whom others respect and admire may be strongly attracted to any occupation which permits him to be the center of attention. Given the requisite abilities, he may become a supervisor or employer, an expert tax consultant, a lawyer, physician, nurse, police officer, receptionist, or information clerk.

The person who feels secure only when he has someone else to tell him what to do may like to think of himself as the loyal, obedient, trusted assistant to someone whose strength and courage and competence he admires and in whose care he feels safe. Depending on his abilities, he may meet his needs as a confidential assistant to the president of a corporation, as a private secretary, as a member of the clergy in a church with a strong hierarchy, or as a statistical clerk, a soldier, or a domestic servant.

The compassionate idealist may be able to think of himself comfortably only as a person whose life is devoted to the service of others. He may be so selfish in some respects that his friends are skeptical of his ideals; yet he may be unable to respect himself unless he can do something that he feels will leave the world a better place because he was here. Depending on his abilities, he may find satisfaction as a social worker, a political reformer, an inventor, an entrepreneur, a union organizer, or a Salvation Army musician.

All of the examples above and below may of course apply as readily to female as to male workers.

How the Theory Explains Illogical Choices A person chooses and prepares for an occupation, accepts or rejects a job that is offered, remains in or leaves a job because he expects or hopes that this course of action will make him feel better. Most of us have seen ourselves, in some situation, act contrary to our intellectual convictions about what was the proper course of action. We could not explain to others or even to ourselves why we behaved so illogically. We only knew that we "just had to do it" or that we "just couldn't bring ourselves to do it." In these words we were saying that all our neat, logical processes had not really convinced us that the "logical" course of action would make us feel better.

When a young person chooses an occupation for which he or she is obviously not fitted, tenaciously resists all logical arguments against it, and stubbornly ignores the evidence of inability to meet even the minimum qualifications, this amounts to telling us that something in this job promises to fulfill some important emotional need. He will not give up this path to its fulfillment until he can find some more promising way in which to achieve the same satisfaction or relief that he thinks this occupation would bring. If counselor and client can learn about other occupations, in which the client can earn a living and can also achieve some of the desired emotional satisfactions—then the counselor may be able to help the client to a more realistic choice.

One may, of course, try to change a client's emotional cravings or to find ways of meeting them outside the occupation. This is sometimes desirable and sometimes successful. In most cases there is nothing wrong with the emotional needs that the client feels, there is nothing wrong about the desire to satisfy these needs through work, but the client does require help in finding an occupation which will fulfill certain needs and in which a job can be found and held.

Needs May Lead Us to Satisfactions   Fortunately, emotional needs do not always lead us to irrational occupational choices. They are, perhaps, more likely to lead us to occupations in which we may find reasonable satisfaction and success if we can be patient and industrious enough to examine the occupations that are open to us, to compare them in terms of what they can offer us and what we can offer them, and if we can be realistic enough to face facts, including the fact that we are unlikely ever to achieve complete satisfaction and that life would be pretty dull if we did.

If our knowledge of ourselves or of occupations is insufficient, we are less likely to make a wise choice and more likely to cling stubbornly to an unrealistic choice because it offers the only route we can see to what we want. We may then find ourselves unemployed because we chose an occupation in which jobs are scarce or unsuccessful because we chose a job for which we lack the requisite abilities or unhappy because we were misinformed about what the work was really like.

Conscious Choice May Not Be Necessary   Career development begins when a person first becomes aware that an occupation might be a means of meeting the needs that he feels. Occupational choice may take place at any time thereafter. Choices may change as frequently as a person's awareness of his needs changes or as frequently as he discovers that another occupation might better meet his needs. Some persons choose early and never change—like Mozart, who was playing the piano at the age of four and composing at seven. Some persons never do find an occupation which meets enough of their needs to give them any real feeling of satisfaction. Some persons achieve satisfaction without ever having made an occupational choice in the sense in which counselors usually think of choice.

Much of our career guidance to date appears to have been based upon the assumption that our objective is to help someone reach an occupational choice which both he and we will consider appropriate. Until this choice has been consciously identified and announced, we feel that the client still needs counseling and that our job as career counselors or teachers of occupations is incomplete. Once the choice is announced, if we consider it a good choice, we enjoy a sense of successful achievement and are disposed to direct our attention elsewhere.

All this may be quite appropriate in some cases; it is not necessarily appropriate or logical in all cases. The wise and conscious choice of an occupation is not an end in itself; it is a means to an end. It is an intermediate objective. The ultimate objective is an individual who is reasonably useful and reasonably contented in his work. It is conceivable that this objective may sometimes be attained without the individual ever having consciously chosen a career.

We do not yet have sufficient evidence to prove that conscious occupational choice is either essential or not essential to good occupational adjustment. Perhaps one of the readers of this book will someday do the research to provide us with such evidence. Meanwhile, it seems at least conceivable that some persons may learn a good deal about themselves and a good deal about occupations and yet never make an occupational choice until they are offered a specific job which they must either accept or reject. It seems conceivable, also, that at this point their knowledge of occupations and of themselves may enable them to make wiser decisions than they would have made without such knowledge. The teacher of occupations may thus contribute to improved occupational adjustment, even if the students do not reach final occupational choices before they finish the course. Career development may proceed even though the results are not immediately apparent. Or it may not.

Needs Are Not Always Complex   Many persons do not ask or expect from their jobs much more than a fairly steady income that will enable them to maintain the modest standard of living to which they are accustomed. Not everyone is ambitious. Not everyone wants to be promoted and to assume added responsibilities. One student wrote, "I suppose that I am one of those people that . . . never use all their abilities. But I'm satisfied if I get by. All I want out of life is a steady job and money enough to buy a home, raise a family, and enjoy life without killing myself doing it."

Such persons do not talk much about "choosing an occupation"; they just "get a job," and when it terminates, they get another. Simple as this process may appear, it does involve an occupational choice every time the individual decides to look for a job in one place rather than another and every time that one decides to accept or reject a job that has been offered. Thus an unemployed person who has always worked in a retail store and liked it may refuse even to apply for a factory job until he has exhausted every possibility of finding another job in retailing. Though he may say he is only looking for a job, he is at the same time making an occupational choice just as truly as is the high school or college senior who makes the same decision about where to look for work and whose decision has been preceded by aptitude and interest testing, counseling, and the examination of a wide range of occupational possibilities.

Much of our most successful career guidance is done on this simple level, with persons whose demands are modest enough to be met without great difficulty and who can be helped to find the kinds of jobs they want by counselors, placement officers, and teachers of occupations who know the local employment market. It is, perhaps, regrettable that so little of our discussion of occupational choice has dealt with these simple cases, for our preoccupation with the complex problems has led too many beginning counselors to measure their own success by their ability to satisfy the client whose demands preclude any reasonable possibility of satisfaction.

How Occupational Information Helps   All the facts about jobs with which this book is concerned are important because they help us to discover what jobs are available, what these jobs offer that may satisfy our needs, and what these jobs demand of us in return.

Courses and units in occupations may be useful in helping students to discover and to compare occupations which promise to meet their needs. While no one wants to dispense with individual counseling, it is conceivable that in some cases the course may be more effective than counseling, because students do not understand themselves and their needs well enough to reveal them to the counselor. But they do feel needs, and when they see an occupation that promises to meet these needs, they may feel strongly attracted to it. Without the opportunity to see it, as part of a general survey of occupations, neither they nor the counselor might ever have thought of it—students because they were unaware of its existence or its nature, the counselor because he or she was unaware of the need.

Needs are met in many ways, not all of them occupational. But when occupations are being chosen to meet needs, as they will be, the more occupations we counselors know and the more we know about them, the better is the chance that we will be able to help our clients to find occupations that will meet their needs and in which they can also get and hold jobs.

The ability to get and hold a job cannot be overlooked, even in a discussion of needs. The best occupation in the world will not meet our client's needs if he cannot get a job in it or hold it after he gets it or if he will not move to where the work must be done. Ultimately the compelling need for most of us is to eat; the occupational choice which overlooks this need is hardly realistic, however well it might serve as an emotional outlet. This is one more reason why we as counselors need a realistic knowledge of the occupations available to those we try to help.

One of the most cogent illustrations of this need for realistic occupational information occurs many times each year. A person recovers from an illness. He is warned that if he returns to his former occupation, he may have a relapse. He looks for other work but finds none. His family suffers because of his inability to support them. He feels that he has failed them, that his life is futile. He wants to live, but he also wants to feel useful. He wants his own self-respect and the respect of others. He loves his family and wants to provide for them. Eventually, his desire to support his family becomes greater than his desire to protect his health. He is offered a job in his old occupation. He takes it. He has a relapse. The job failed to meet the need which may be most apparent to others—the need to protect his health. It did meet the need which at the moment he felt most strongly—the need to support himself and his family and to regain his self-respect. Adequate occupational information, provided perhaps by a rehabilitation counselor, might have helped him to find a way to be self-supporting without jeopardizing his health.

Implications for Counselors   The use of occupational information is discussed later in this book. At this point, however, the author's students have asked, "What are the implications of this theory for counselors?" The following are suggested in response to this question:

The counselor should always remember that the needs of the client may differ from the needs of the counselor.

The counselor should operate within the framework of the client's needs.

The counselor should provide every possible opportunity for the client to identify and to express his or her own needs.

The counselor should be alert to notice and to remember the needs which the client reveals.

The counselor should help the client to get whatever information the client wants about himself or herself and about occupations.

The counselor should help the client to discover the occupations which may meet his or her needs.

The counselor should help the client to anticipate how well any contemplated occupation will meet the client's needs.

The counselor should get the occupational information which the counselor needs in order to help the client to meet his or her needs.

The counselor should stay with the client through the process of placement in order to provide the further counseling that will be needed if the desired job is not available.

The counselor should follow up the client some months after placement in order to see how well the job is meeting the needs which the client thought it would meet.

REVIEW QUESTIONS

1   Of all the statements in this chapter, which one could you endorse most heartily? About which one are you most skeptical? Why?

2   Will anything in this chapter affect your future thoughts and actions? What? How?

3   How do economic factors affect occupational choice?

4   How does education influence occupational choice?

5   How do psychological factors affect occupational choice?

6   How do sociologic factors affect occupational choice?

7   Some psychologists believe that only psychologists should be permitted to do career counseling. What do you think? Why?

8 Why do some persons reject occupations for which they are well equipped in aptitude and interest?

9 Why do some clients stubbornly cling to occupational choices in the face of overwhelming evidence that the choices are not realistic?

10 What are some of the implications of this chapter for counselors?

Chapter 9

Contributions of Client-centered and Behavioral Counseling to Career Counseling

The development and success of "nondirective," or "client-centered," counseling as a contribution to psychotherapy have led counselors in other fields properly to consider the possible uses of the client-centered approach in their own work.

It is one purpose of this chapter to discuss the contributions and limitations of client-centered procedures in career counseling before discussing the use of occupational information in counseling. The reader who is not already familiar with client-centered counseling will find it described in Rogers [320, 321]. In the first of these two books, what is now called "client-centered" counseling was described as "nondirective" counseling. The terms "nondirective" and "client-centered" are now used interchangeably. An excellent summary of client-centered philosophy may be found in Rogers [322].

Another purpose of this chapter is to describe and discuss the contributions and limitations of behavioral counseling in career counseling. The reader who is not familiar with behavioral counseling will find it described in Krumboltz and Thoresen [227]. An excellent briefer description may be found in Krumboltz [222]. The application of behavioral counseling to career decision making is described in detail in Krumboltz and Baker [225].

The Nondirective Approach The completely nondirective approach to counseling may be summarized as follows: the nondirective counselor seeks to understand, accept, reflect, and clarify the feelings of the client; the counselor scrupulously refrains from directing the conversation, conveys little or no information, makes no suggestions, expresses no approval or disapproval, and generally seeks to focus his or her own and the client's attention upon the feelings being expressed by the client rather than upon the intellectual content of what the client says.

In contrast to this, the directive counselor assumes responsibility for directing the interview, asks questions, answers questions, supplies information and suggestions, and may or may not tell the client what he or she thinks the client should do.

Originally the proponents of nondirective counseling insisted that any digression from nondirective procedures tended to disturb the essential relationship between counselor and client and thus to impair the effectiveness of counseling. Recently there has been less insistence on this point. Many counselors who regard themselves as client-centered are no longer wholly nondirective in their counseling procedures. Many counselors who do not regard themselves as nondirective do sometimes use nondirective techniques.

Patterson [300] has well expressed the current view of many counselors:

> The client-centered approach is essentially an *attitude* rather than a series of techniques. The attitude may be implemented in different ways in different situations. In counseling on problems of personal adjustment the techniques of simple acceptance and reflection of feeling are sufficient. In counseling dealing with problems of vocational choice, tests may be used and occupational information provided. It is, or should be, done in ways which are consistent with the basic attitudes or assumptions of client-centered counseling. . . .

Although at the present time most counselors profess to be client-centered in attitude, Murphy's [277] revealing study "Counselor Dominance" suggests that counselors are often more dominant than they think they are, and also more dominant than they think they should be.

Terminology is now a bit confusing, since the reader often is not sure whether the writer is using the terms "nondirective" and "client-centered" to designate an attitude or a technique. In the remainder of this chapter these terms are used to designate the techniques of acceptance and reflection of feeling as described in Roger's *Counseling and Psychotherapy* [321].

The Potential Value   The potential value of client-centered counseling in career counseling is considerable. Through client-centered counseling, both counselor and client may achieve a clearer understanding of the nature of the client's problems; of the client's feelings about them, his values, his conflicts, his perception and acceptance of reality; and of the bearing of accepted facts upon the client's own problems and plans. Client-centered counseling may relieve some of the client's emotional conflicts, so that he may function at a higher level of efficiency in trying to solve his own problems. The client may then be better able to perceive and accept and deal with facts which are readily obtainable but which he has previously overlooked or refused to face.

If, on the other hand, the counselor spends too little time listening to the client, accepting and reflecting the client's feelings, trying to understand the client's internal conflicts and values, the counselor may easily mistake the nature of the problem on which the client wants help. Or the counselor may identify the problem but overlook values, anxieties, or other feelings of the client that will be among the major determinants of the client's success and satisfaction. Disturbing and disconcerting facts presented to the client may be silently rejected or discounted, so that they will not function in the client's perception of reality. Dependence upon the counselor may be welcomed by the client as an escape from the discomfort of facing and dealing with his problem.

The Inescapable Limitation   The inescapable limitation of the *exclusively* nondirective approach to career counseling is that it functions solely within the clients' perception of reality. If the clients' perceptions are false, if they are dealing intellectually and emotionally with misconceptions of their own abilities and limitations or with mistaken concepts of occupational opportunities and requirements, they may make decisions and plans that are wholly unrealistic. If pertinent facts to correct the clients' misconceptions are not readily accessible, if nothing in their experience or in the counseling suggests to them that their perception is false, they may take actions that would be wholly logical in terms of their own perception but that are almost certain to lead to failure, frustration, and further maladjustment.

For example, if a person whose qualifications are minimal chooses an occupation that is chronically overcrowded, the client may very well find it impossible to get a job. This would hardly be the best way for him or her to become self-supporting—economically or psychologically. If a person whose qualifications are adequate chooses an occupation without learning the exact nature of the work, the job may well be found distressingly different from expectations; this would hardly be the best way for the person to achieve emotional equanimity or job satisfaction.

Client-centered counseling was developed by social workers and clinical psychologists whose major interest was in the internal emotional conflicts of anxious, unhappy persons. Client-centered counseling was designed to help such persons to resolve their internal conflicts, recognize and accept their own emotions, clarify their own value patterns, enhance their own feelings of worth and competence, and lead their own lives according to their own standards with less concern for the approval or disapproval of others. Client-centered counseling was not designed to help a person to find out where to get a job or what kind of activity any specific occupation involves. Client-centered counseling was intended to help remove emotional obstacles to the perception and acceptance of reality, which obstacles may prevent a person from thinking clearly even when all pertinent facts are available to him. Client-centered procedures can be very helpful in career counseling; they were never intended to do the whole job of career counseling.

Behavioral Counseling   To the behavioral counselor, the purpose of counseling is to help the client learn skills and behaviors which will enable the client to achieve the particular satisfactions he or she wants. The behavioral counselor is less concerned with helping the client to plan one career or to find a particular job than with modifying and if possible improving the behavior by which the client seeks to solve these and other problems.

The behavioral counselor and the client begin by defining the problem in behavioral terms. For example, if the client has been trying unsuccessfully to choose an occupation for which to prepare or in which to seek a job, the problem is to help the client to learn the decision-making behaviors so that he or she will reach the wisest possible decision.

Specific goals need to be identified; for example, the client has found certain desired information, or has narrowed a career choice to three areas and been satisfied with this decision for three weeks, or has found a job which satisfies his or her three most urgent needs.

The next step is to select and schedule specific actions which the client will take; and, if necessary, to provide certain reinforcements in the form of small intermediate rewards as each step in the program is completed.

The behavioral counselor will use directive, nondirective, measurement, therapy, learning, or any other techniques that he or she thinks will help the client to reach the client's objective.

The Potential Values   The potential values of behavioral counseling in career counseling are in its systematic approach, its insistence upon clearly defined goals, its provision of specific behaviors for reaching them, and its objective measures of determining when the goals have been reached.

The behavioral counselor is accountable to the client, who must confirm the counselor's understanding of the problem before counseling can begin. One could almost say that every one of us is a walking bundle of problems, most of which we handle well enough to survive. At a given moment the client may seek help on any one of his or her problems. The behavioral counselor will not condescendingly label this as the "presenting" problem, while secretly identifying another as the "real" problem. Instead, he or she recognizes that all counselors are exposed to the temptation to work on the problems that interest them, and that this temptation may confuse their own judgment as to what the "real" problem is. By insisting that counselor and client agree upon the problem they are to attack, and by insisting upon objective measures of determining when the goal has been reached, the behavioral counselor seeks to protect both himself and his clients from diverting their efforts from the client's problem to what might conceivably be the counselor's problem.

Since many problems can be handled by the client alone, once he or she knows how to attack them, the behavioral counselor, when successful, enhances the client's self-reliance.

The Possible Limitations   The limitations of the behavioral approach to career counseling are not necessarily inescapable, but they do appear in some of the work reported to date.

When desired changes in a client's behavior become clearly visible, the counselor may be pleased—so pleased that he is satisfied to stop at this point and to assume that the new behavior will enable the client to solve his own problem without further help from the counselor. Maybe it will; maybe it will not.

For example, if a liberal arts college senior needs a job for next year, but has no idea what kind of work she wants to do, and if the counselor helps this client to plan and to follow a program of information-seeking behavior, and the client reaches a decision, the client and the counselor may both feel successful and satisfied. But if the client got her occupational information from the typical file of obsolete pamphlets, and her information about her aptitudes and interests from inadequately validated tests and inventories with inappropriate norms, the client may later find herself employed in a job that she hates, or still trying to find a job in an area in which she cannot compete.

There is nothing in behavioral counseling that need prevent a counselor from making sure that the client will use good sources of information; but neither is there any assurance that the counselor will take this precaution.

Conclusion The purpose of career counseling, as perceived in this book, is to help the client in some way to progress toward, and ultimately to establish himself or herself in, a career in which the client can be reasonably useful and reasonably contented.

Client-centered counseling may help the client to progress toward this objective by helping him better to understand how he feels about the whole process and what he wants to do about it.

Behavioral counseling may help the client to progress toward this objective by helping him to discover, to learn, and to use the kind of behavior that he and his counselor agree is needed if the client is to get what or where he wants to get.

The career counselor gladly welcomes the help and will use the techniques of both client-centered and behavioral counseling, as he or she will use any other ethical technique in the effort to help the client to become reasonably useful and reasonably contented in his work.

All three counselors recognize that human beings in a changing world may have to change their specific objectives and behaviors and jobs from time to time and may or may not need help in doing so.

REVIEW QUESTIONS

1 In career counseling, what are the potential values of client-centered counseling and of behavioral counseling?

2 What is the inescapable limitation of the exclusively nondirective approach to career counseling?

3 What are the possible limitations of behavioral counseling in career counseling?

4 How do the purposes of client-centered counseling and of behavioral counseling differ from the purposes of career counseling?

5 In what kinds of situations would *you* begin a career counseling interview nondirectively? In what kind would you not? Why?

6 In what kinds of situations would *you* employ behavioral counseling in career counseling? In what kinds would you not? Why?

7 Will anything in this chapter affect your future thoughts and actions? What? How?

Chapter 10

The Use of Occupational Information in Counseling — General Aspects

Occupational information is used in counseling for the same basic purpose for which the counselor uses any other kind of information. The purpose is to help clients to clarify the goal that each wants to reach and to move in the direction in which each wants to go, so long as the goal and the means of attaining it are not injurious to others.

WHAT COUNSELING IS NOT

It is not the purpose of counseling to recruit clients for occupations in which they are needed or which the counselor considers desirable.

It is not the purpose of counseling to divert clients from occupations for which the counselor believes them to be unqualified or of which the counselor disapproves.

It is not the purpose of counseling to encourage the bright student to go to college and the slow student to go to work.

It is not the purpose of counseling to substitute the values, the ideals, the ambitions, or the judgment of the counselor for those of the client, no matter how strongly the counselor may feel that he or she knows best.

It is not the purpose of counseling to make decisions for the client or even to bring the client to the point of decision.

THE PURPOSE OF COUNSELING

The purpose of counseling is to help the client to recognize his or her own needs and values, to see how these affect the goals that the client seeks to reach, to identify these goals and to arrange them as well as possible in order of priority, to discover the possible courses of action which may bring the client closer to the goals sought, and to anticipate as accurately as possible the results of each course of action in terms of the individual's goals.

What clients decide and when they decide it are their business. The only exception to this limitation on the counselor's functions occurs when a client clearly intends to do something that will seriously injure another person. In such a case, the counselor may step out of the role of counselor and try to prevent the injury. He should recognize that when he does this, he ceases to be a counselor, and he may find it difficult to resume the counselor's role.

Not everyone who seeks the counselor's help wants or needs to go through the full process of counseling as described above. Many want only a small amount of help on one small part of the total process. They may prefer to handle the remainder of the process alone or with the help of other persons. In such cases the counselor does what he can, within the limits of what he is asked to do. If he thinks he might be helpful in additional ways, he may offer his services, but he does not intrude where he is not wanted.

John Odgers has observed that

> . . . a sizeable chunk of our population really have no preference—and should not be frightened or made perplexed or anxious by having a counselor stress the importance of choice. If Shartle's analysis is true—and there are many jobs which require no particular aptitude patterns, competencies, or training—then we may be doing a disservice by pushing *some* folks through a choice process which implies that they must really know themselves inside out—and know many details about many jobs.
> . . . Many people are relatively easily satisfied—and can do an acceptable job and get satisfaction from any of various jobs. . . . I have in mind a young man (about 30) who in the last ten years has been reasonably well adjusted as an ad clipper in a newspaper clipping service, a bread route man, a drill press operator, and a traveling salesman of housetrailer equipment. He left the first job because of salary, the second because lack of seniority got him bumped to a rural route with long hours, the third because of a prolonged strike. He never worried about self-concept, aptitudes, fantasies or the fact that he quit school just before graduating. He was concerned about a living wage, decent working conditions and hours, employment secruity, etc. . . . His best counselor was the want-ad section of the paper. I'm not saying we shouldn't help fellows like this—but we shouldn't get them to thinking they are (or have) problems. Maybe it's fortunate that most of this type never get to a counselor.

To avoid misunderstanding, the reader is urged to keep in mind that this chapter deals only with *the use of occupational information* in counseling. The omission of other aspects of the counseling process from this discussion is not intended to imply that they are any less important.

THE USE OF OCCUPATIONAL INFORMATION

Individual goals differ, counseling techniques differ with them, and so does the use of occupational information in counseling. The goal may be as simple as finding a temporary job for the Christmas holidays or as complex as trying to discover whether or not a change of employment will help to relieve a serious case of emotional disturbance.

Occupational information is useful in counseling when and to the extent that it can help a client to solve a problem. If the client is fully capable of solving the problem as soon as he or she has the necessary information, counseling may consist only of providing the information or of telling the client where to find it; some counselors would not even call this counseling. But when the client needs help to get the essential information, to appraise its accuracy, or to see how it relates to the problem, or when the client needs help in considering his or her own reaction to the information, then there may be need for all the competence and skill and patience that the counselor may possess.

The first step in counseling is to discover, and if necessary to help clients to discover, what it is that they want. Is the client seeking release from a feeling of anxiety or fear or insecurity? Is he a reasonably happy and contented individual who wants help in finding a job? Is he lacking any conscious occupational preference but facing a decision which will tend to restrict his future range of occupational choice? Has he a tentative choice that he wishes to review to see if it makes sense? Is he using questions about occupations as a means of getting acquainted with the counselor before bringing up some other problem?

The counselor will probably begin nondirectively, encourage his client to talk as long and as freely as the client will or as the counselor's time permits, until both client and counselor believe that the nature of the problem has been pretty well identified and agreed upon. Thereafter, counseling procedure may vary with the nature of the problem. If the problem does not involve career planning, the remainder of this chapter will not apply.

The inexperienced counselor may find helpful suggestions in Appendix D.

The Client with No Preferences   One of the most common and most difficult problems is that of the client who has no occupational choice and who comes to the counselor with the attitude, "You are the expert; you tell me what to do." The counselor—who, of course, cannot accept this responsibility for leading another person's life—may even believe that this attitude of dependence requires some exploration in the counseling situation.

If the counselor decides, immediately or later, to try to help the client reach an occupational choice, the counselor may begin by helping the client to review all that his past experiences may reveal about his needs, values, ambitions, and anxieties; his abilities, limitations, likes, and dislikes. Some counselors ask their clients to try to recall all their past successes: the activities that gave them a sense of achievement, pride, and satisfaction. Some explore the previous jobs and other activities that the client liked or disliked, and the extent of involvement in these activities with data, people, and things. The counselor or the client may wish to use physical examinations or psychological tests or sociologic inquiries or other means to add to their information about the individual.

The client with no discernible preferences faces a problem that can be both perplexing and frightening. It is perhaps because of the prevalence of this problem that vocational aptitude tests and interest inventories have been so frequently used by counselors and so eagerly sought by a credulous public. Such tests are sometimes helpful in directing the attention of the client to occupations that might otherwise be overlooked, among which may be found an appropriate occupation. They are among many tools that the skillful counselor uses in helping the client to discover possible occupations and to anticipate his probable success and satisfaction in them. Other personal characteristics, leisure-time activities, previous education, and work experience all may be used as possible clues to occupations that may be considered.

Whether the counselor and client decide that much or little time needs to be spent in studying the individual, sooner or later they reach the point at which possible occupations must be examined to see which appear to be the most reasonable choices.

It is at this point that counseling breaks down if the counselor is not well informed about occupations. Here the weak counselor pools his own ignorance of occupations with the ignorance of the client and from this shallow pool tries to help the client to select an appropriate occupation. Here the well-informed counselor may achieve some brilliant and effortless successes by the simple process of suggesting acceptable occupations or jobs unknown to the client. How readily the counselor can do this will depend in part upon how modest or excessive are the demands of the client. If all that the client wants is a job that he can do, for which he needs no further preparation, and that offers average or better earnings, the counselor who has the results of follow-up studies and community surveys may be well equipped to make suggestions. If the client's goals are more complex, he and the counselor together may need to go beyond their present knowledge and explore the possibilities in a wider variety of occupations. At this point, they may turn to more extensive lists of occupations such as those in the *Occupational Outlook Handbook* [292] and the *Dictionary of Occupational Titles* [98].

Although the *D.O.T.* was prepared for the use of employment service interviewers in classifying applicants for work and in classifying employers' job orders, it can be effectively used in counseling if the counselor will take several hours to examine it in leisurely fashion, to read the introductory and explanatory sections, and to practice using it on the kinds of problems that he and his clients are trying to solve.

One way to start is to select from the *D.O.T.* all of those occupations which either the client or the counselor thinks might be appropriate, and arrange these in the order in which the client may wish to examine them. The sections of the *D.O.T.* that are most likely to be helpful in compiling a list of occupations to explore are the worker trait requirements, the occupational group arrangement of job titles, and the industry arrangement of titles. Before using any of these, be sure to examine the entire *D.O.T.*

Computers will produce lists of occupations which appear to be consistent with the client's abilities, interests, values, etc., and will provide brief descriptions of the occupations suggested. See Chapter 20 for more on computers.

The Appalachia Educational Laboratory at Charleston, W. Va., has designed a manual system by which the client may find, in the *Dictionary of Occupa-*

tional Titles, the worker trait groups most likely to include occupations of interest to him. The system also refers the client to specific pages in the *Occupational Outlook Handbook,* the *Encyclopedia of Careers and Vocational Guidance,* and the *D.O.T.* for further information about each occupation. If the client wants still more information, the system will refer him to other printed materials filed and indexed by worker trait groups.

Chronicle Guidance Publications has a somewhat similar manual system [293] using the worker trait groups to help the client find occupations he may wish to explore.

All this may lead to no immediate occupational choice that will be definite and satisfying. The client may find something unsatisfactory about every occupation that the counselor can suggest; he may even reject the entire *Dictionary of Occupational Titles* and in effect say to the counselor, "See! You can't find anything that I like, either." This can, does, and will happen.

The counselor can, of course, escape this experience of rejection by refusing to make any suggestions, and there may be counselors who believe that this procedure would be best for the client. Certainly it bears some resemblance to the client-centered counseling which has proved so effective in helping people with their emotional problems. Until we have more evidence to indicate what kind of occupational counseling is most effective, the author of this book inclines to the belief that there may still be some value in making available to the student the occupational information that he wants, even if he does not always use it to our satisfaction. Certainly every successful placement officer and career counselor can recall instances in which satisfying occupational choices and improved occupational adjustment have followed the presentation of appropriate occupational information.

If the counselor is convinced that the client is unable to face reality or to make a decision, the counselor may work on this obstacle as a counseling problem; if the counselor lacks the time or the competence to deal with it, he may attempt referral or simply accept the fact and direct his attention to persons he can help.

Meanwhile the counselor's efforts may not have been wasted. To the extent that he has helped the client to know more about himself and more about occupations, to that extent he may have prepared the client to make a wiser decision when he finally goes looking for a job and must accept or reject a job that is offered to him. As noted in Chapter 8, some persons never will make an occupational choice until this time. Others may just not be ready to make a decision now but will be later.

Because counselors seldom have time to explore all the potential occupations with each client, the course in occupations may serve to supplement counseling by making the client more aware of occupations that might meet his needs. When the client has discovered something attractive, he may return for further counseling.

Some high school counselors try to dispose of the problem by recommending that the student attend a liberal arts college. But many colleges offer little or no career counseling, and some believe they should offer none. Before suggesting college as a solution, the counselor might well write to some college presidents and ask:

> Do you welcome students who have no clearly defined career objective?
> In what ways do you try to help them? When?
> Can you send me a list of the present occupations of your recent graduates?
> Do you have a career counseling and placement office?
> Does your curriculum include an elective course in career planning, which

provides a realistic review of the employment opportunities for your graduates?

The Tentative Choice　Less baffling is the problem of the client who has one or more tentative occupational choices and who seeks help in reviewing or comparing them. In this case again, the counselor may begin by encouraging the client to talk until both counselor and client are agreed on what the problem is and on what the client wants to find in and through his or her occupation. Then, together, they may review the checklist in Chapter 3 and consider each item in turn to see what it may reveal about the wisdom of a contemplated choice.

Time may be saved by considering first those items most likely to lead to a quick rejection if the client is misinformed. Time may be saved, also, by going all the way through the checklist on the basis of the client's and counselor's present knowledge of the occupation and simply marking those items on which more information is needed before compiling the additional information. Somewhere along the way, the checklist may call attention to a consideration which will convince the client that this occupation is not for him. If so, the time that might have been spent in compiling additional information on this occupation can be saved for the study of some more promising possibility. Should this happen, it may be wise to verify the facts which led to the rejection before the decision is made final.

Should this first review of the checklist leave the occupation still open to consideration, the counselor and client may then proceed to look for the additional facts they need, following the suggestions in Chapter 4. When the facts have been assembled, the checklist may be reexamined in the light of the new information. This time the client may find it helpful to list, on one side of a sheet of paper, all the reasons why this occupation appears attractive and on the other side all the reasons against choosing it, then to select the five strongest reasons on each side of the sheet, weigh them, and see if they point to any clear conclusion. If they do not, decision may be delayed pending similar study of other occupations which may be similarly summarized and with which the first occupation may be compared. In this kind of intensive study of an occupation the counselor or client may find it convenient to use the "Outline for the Study of an Occupation" in Appendix C. Tryout experiences in summer vacations, in part-time jobs, or in a program of cooperative work-experience education may be especially helpful at this point.

Should this further study and comparison still not lead to a decision with which the student is content, additional occupations may be similarly reviewed and compared until a satisfactory occupation is discovered or the client becomes exhausted and gives up or the counselor has exhausted the available time and resources or the time arrives at which the client must find immediate employment. In some cases no decision will be reached until the client is ready to go to work, at which time he or she must accept or reject any jobs which may be offered. When the client finally finds and accepts one, a decision for the present has been made. It may not be a permanent decision. Like many successful persons, the worker may change jobs several times in the first few years and may even become a "job hopper" who never settles down. The counselor cannot assume responsibility for preventing this; he or she can only offer all the help that knowledge and skill enable him or her to give. Decisions are made or not made by the client. But to the extent that the counselor has helped the client to become better acquainted with himself and with occupations, there is hope that the client may make better choices than would have been possible otherwise.

Occasionally the client's choice will be between two occupations, or two facets of an occupation, neither of which requires further preparation. For example, should a prospective teacher of science, who has met all certification requirements, look for a job in a high school or a junior college, in a small town or a large city? Should a high school senior, with stenographic skills, take a civil service examination or look for a job in private industry? In such cases, it may be desirable to look for jobs in both areas, see what jobs are available, and make the final choice between specific job offers. Such a choice is sometimes much easier to make and more satisfying when made.

Occasionally, tentative choices can be confirmed or canceled by a preliminary exploration of the job market. One widow had no marketable skills other than those of homemaker and hostess. She was attracted by an advertisement of a school which offered training for hotel hostesses. Her counselor suggested that she call on several hotel managers, ask them about the job market for persons like herself, and inquire about the manager's opinion of the school. One manager hired her on the spot.

Similar exploration of the employment market is often advisable *before* the client begins professional preparation. The tendency of too many students, parents, teachers, and counselors is to assume that jobs will be available for students who complete their professional or vocational programs with satisfactory records. Too often young graduates find too late that they have prepared for an occupation in which they have little chance of finding a job.

The Impossible Choice   In some ways the most difficult of counseling problems is that of the client who comes for help on how to achieve the impossible—how to enter and succeed in an occupation in which the client is almost certain not to find a job. Some clients are realistic enough to accept the facts when they have them and to revise their plans. The more pertinent and convincing the facts that the counselor has to present, the better is the probability of a realistic decision. But some persons, like those described in Chapter 8, will cling desperately to an unrealistic choice because they can see no other course of action that holds out any more hope of achieving certain satisfactions which they feel they must have.

In some cases of this kind there is nothing to do but to let the persons try, and fail, and then to help them to make a better second choice when they are ready to do so. In other cases, a well-informed, ingenious, and persistent counselor can find out what are the basic satisfactions the individual is seeking in an occupation and can find substitute occupations which will offer the client even more attractive prospects of getting what he wants.

It is in such cases that the counselor's knowledge of occupations within occupations may be invaluable. The average client knows so little about occupations that the announced choice may be much less specific than it appears to be. As the counselor helps the client to learn more about the broad area of preference, the client may discover an occupation which he can enter and which will please him as much as the choice first announced. The *Dictionary of Occupational Titles* may be helpful in the search for such a related occupation.

Another troublesome problem for counselors is the parent who insists that a child prepare for an occupation which the child and the counselor agree to be inappropriate. The parent may refuse to discuss the wisdom of the choice but be eager to help the child to learn more about the occupation; in this process, the parent may discover what the counselor wanted to tell him, or he may find an acceptable and more appropriate related occupation. This approach will not always work, but it is sometimes worth trying when every other approach has failed.

The modest counselor, of course, will not be hasty about deciding that his client cannot get and hold a job in the chosen occupation. There is at least one high school counselor who was told by *his* high school counselor that he would never graduate from college. There is at least one student who graduated at the head of the class in one of our best engineering colleges who would never have been admitted to most schools of engineering. More than one slow student has acquired a professional degree by spreading college work over a longer period of time and has subsequently done a creditable job.

Changing Occupations   The problem of changing jobs in the hope of finding more satisfaction, higher earnings, or better opportunities for advancement is essentially similar to the problem of the client who has two tentative choices, and the checklist in Chapter 3 may be used to compare the present and prospective jobs.

Sometimes a person who has been less successful than expected contemplates a change of occupation in the hope of doing better. When the person is better qualified for a different occupation or seems likely to find more satisfaction in the work itself, such a change may be desirable. There are cases, however, in which a person really likes the work, is well qualified for it, is even reluctant to leave it, but feels that perhaps he or she should change because someone has said there is more money in another field or because friends or relatives are making more money in other occupations. In such cases it is sometimes helpful to raise the question, "If this new job offered you exactly the same salary and the same opportunities for advancement as your present job, would you change jobs?" If the answer is no, then the most careful scrutiny of the proposed occupation is indicated, in order to see if it really does offer anything better than the client's present field of work. Also helpful in discussing proposed changes may be the question, "Where do you hope to be ten years from now?" The answer to this question sometimes reveals goals not indicated in previous conversation.

When a person is forced to change occupations because his or her own has become obsolete or for some other compelling reason, a closely related occupation may offer a better prospect of prompt employment with less sacrifice in earnings than would a change to a wholly new occupation. Related occupations may be discovered by following the directions in the *Dictionary of Occupational Titles.*

Recruiting Workers for Shortage Fields   From time to time, there is pressure on counselors to encourage students to enter occupations in which a shortage of workers is regarded as a threat to the welfare of the nation.

The history of occupational choice and distribution clearly reveals that when an acute shortage of workers occurs, certain events follow. Wages and salaries increase. The shortage and the increased incomes are widely publicized. Large numbers of new workers move into the shortage fields or into preparation for them. The shortage is overcompensated, and a surplus develops. Sometimes these events occur in rapid succession, as when huge numbers of workers moved into munitions factories in the early days of World War II. Sometimes it takes years for the supply to catch up with the demand, but it always does unless some artificial obstacle is imposed. By frequently raising the standards for medical education, the medical profession has restricted the number and size of medical schools and the number of new competitors who could enter the field. Labor unions achieve the same result by restricting admissions to the union. Where there is no such restriction and the supply does not increase, the demand is less acute than it appears to be. Sometimes the demand is not yet great enough to raise the earnings of the workers above the earnings of workers in more popular occupations for which the same workers can qualify.

The counselor and the client should carefully distinguish between a social "need" for more workers and an economic "demand" for them. The need may be there; the jobs may not. Sometimes society will not pay for the services that some of us think it needs.

How should the counselor respond to requests for aid in recruiting workers for shortage fields? If the counselor does everything that he is asked to do, he will soon find that he is successfully recruiting workers who will, in his judgment, be neither successful nor satisfied in the jobs to which he has enticed them. Is this the counselor's function? If not, should he do selective recruiting and lure only those who seem to have appropriate qualifications? This procedure would certainly be better than indiscriminate recruiting. But suppose the client would be even more successful and happy in some other field? Or suppose he is equally qualified for two fields which are both short of workers? Should the counselor encourage the client to go where he thinks he will be most successful and best satisfied or where the recruiting officers are busiest at the moment?

To the author of this book there can be only one acceptable answer to these questions. The counselor is not a recruiting officer and he should never permit himself to become one. Employers, training institutions, and professional associations can be depended upon to publicize any genuine shortage and to urge all qualified candidates to apply. The nation will survive without the counselor adding his or her influence. Under the seductive blandishments of the recruiters, the client needs one competent person who can be trusted to put the client's interest first and to help him to think clearly about what *he* wants to do. The counselor who permits any other interest to creep into his or her activities has ceased to be a counselor.

Counselors need not become belligerent on this point. They can respect the convictions, the motives, and the integrity of sincere recruiters. They can help recruiters to make accessible to clients the factual information about supply and demand which clients need in order to appraise prospects of employment. They can accept the literature which is offered and even distribute some of it. They can invite recruiting officers to answer questions in group conferences *which the counselors will attend.* But every time a counselor does one of these things, he or she assumes an obligation to find and to verify and to present to students or clients an equal amount of pertinent data regarding the disadvantages of doing what the recruiter has proposed. Such data may include distasteful aspects of the work, earnings in the lower half of the distribution, hazards, unfavorable working conditions, and the possibility that by the time the client has completed training, the demand for workers may have been met.

So long as the United States remains a democracy, so long as we value the welfare and the freedom of the individual above the planning functions of the state, the counselor must counsel in terms of the needs and values of the client. The needs of society function in counseling only to the extent that the client values them and wishes to consider them in reaching a decision. The counselor who intentionally permits his or her own values or the values of a professional group or of a government agency to take precedence over the values of the client has not only done the client a disservice, he or she has also undermined the foundation of freedom—the right of the individual to the pursuit of happiness as *he* chooses to pursue it.

It has been both alleged and denied that some recruiting officers promise more than their employers later deliver. Any client who is promised a specific job or training program should be urged to ask the recruiting officer to put the promise in writing and sign it, before the client signs anything. Civilian employees can, of course, resign if promises are not fulfilled. Military recruits may find resignation a little difficult.

Military Occupations   Military service is an occupation. In career counseling it should be treated as such. There are certain obvious differences between military and civilian careers. In times of war, or of peacetime conscription, the person who is eligible to be drafted has lost much of his freedom of choice, unless he is prepared to suffer certain unpleasant consequences. The soldier may be called upon to risk his life. He is given a certain limited license to inflict pain and death in ways that would be considered illegal or immoral without the license. Nevertheless, the differences between military and civilian occupations are not greater than the differences between various civilian occupations, and they do not require different treatment by the counselor. Police officers also have a limited license to inflict pain and death. Firefighters also risk their lives. Family pressure can restrict freedom of occupational choice as effectively as legal pressure.

It is the responsibility of the counselor to make available to his clients the same kind of information about military occupations that he provides about civilian occupations, and in much the same ways. The head of enlisted classification in the United States Navy [65] has said in print that " . . . it is not the place of civilian counselors to augment the recruiting forces of the Armed Services." Nor is it the function of the counselor to dissuade the client who proposes to enlist. Neither patriotism nor pacifism justifies the counselor in substituting his values for the client's values. Nor can the counselor escape responsibility for helping the client to get *all* the pertinent facts before the client decides what to do. Ask any group of veterans how their own military experience compared with the glamorous recruiting literature of the military services, and the question is usually answered by laughter.

Current practice in counseling on military occupations leaves much to be desired, because so much of it is based upon information received from, or presented by, recruiting officers, who can hardly be considered unbiased sources of information. Recruiting officers and recruiting literature are available to any counselor on request. They can be useful in providing factual information about the requirements of the various services; they cannot be expected to say very much about the disadvantages of the service they represent. Among the better methods of acquainting students with military occupations are follow-up studies of former students now in military or alternate service, group conferences with servicemen and veterans, including those who have chosen alternate service, and tours of military installations and of veterans' hospitals. In collecting or presenting information about civilian occupations, most counselors agree that both employers and employees should be used; this principle applies with equal force to military occupations.

In the presentation of information about military occupations, the existence of conscientious objectors to war is generally ignored. But there are still more than 100,000 Quakers in the United States, plus a substantial number of Catholics, Jews, and other Protestants who believe that war is morally wrong and who will not participate in it under any circumstances. If an idealistic client has some doubts about war as a means of resolving conflicts, he is likely to be reminded of his patriotic duty. But the military services do not want conscientious objectors, and draft laws usually provide alternate service opportunities for them. The Selective Service System has published, in English, French, and Spanish editions, a free pamphlet, *Conscientious Objectors* [72] which describes these legal provisions.

At any future time the United States may or may not have an all-volunteer military service. Whenever conscription is in effect, the counselor who really believes that he should present to clients *all* the opportunities that are available to them should at least inform himself and his clients about the provisions which the government has made for conscientious objectors. These provisions may not be restricted to members of the historic peace churches. Draft laws usually provide that any person who is conscientiously opposed to war, by reason of religious training and belief, and who can convince the authorities of his sincerity, may be assigned to certain designated forms of civilian service in lieu of military service. The counselor may obtain more detailed information about these provisions from, or may refer the client for information to, the Central Committee for Conscientious Objectors, 2006 Walnut Street, Philadelphia, Pa., and to the National Interreligious Service Board for Conscientious Objectors, 15 St. and New York Ave., N.W., Washington D.C. 20005.

Many religious denominations offer help to their own members who are conscientious objectors. Information about the beliefs of conscientious objectors can be obtained from the Fellowship of Reconciliation, Box 271, Nyack, N.Y., and from the national headquarters of several religious denominations.

The counselor who is himself a conscientious objector, who believes that all war is morally wrong, may feel that he must disqualify himself from helping any client to choose or plan a military career; the counselor who believes that military service should be accepted as a patriotic duty may feel that he must disqualify himself from helping any client to avoid military service. Both counselors may, of course, feel free to help the client who already shares the counselor's values and wants help only in implementing them.

Occupational Information in Psychotherapy Reference was made in Chapter 7 to the relationship between emotional and vocational maladjustment and to the possibility that either might cause the other. When the psychotherapist suspects that an inappropriate occupation is either causing or aggravating an emotional disturbance, he may wish to review his patient's occupational choice and perhaps help him to find a more congenial field of work. Even though the change may not solve the whole problem, it may bring temporary relief that will facilitate therapy.

The author is indebted to one of his former students for the report of a client who had an excessive fear of disease and an aversion to filth and who found intolerable his work as a clinical laboratory technician, in which he was called upon to examine specimens from persons who were seriously ill. Before undertaking therapy for the fears, the counselor helped his client to choose a new occupation and to find a new job as a polisher of newly made dentures, in which activity his aversion to all blemishes became a vocational asset and his work brought recurring satisfaction.

The psychotherapist who wishes to become a career counselor to a patient or the counselor who is called in as a consultant to a therapist may find some help in the following suggestions:

Explore as thoroughly as possible the patient's feelings about the job, and try to determine whether the aversion is to some essential and inescapable part of the occupation itself or to some characteristic of the present job which might not be present in another job in the same occupation. Sometimes a person who is upset will be so anxious to get away from the frustrating situation that he will be inclined to change his occupation, when all that he really need do is to change his job. An unnecessary change of occupation may be undesirable, because it may involve discarding valuable and marketable experience and starting over again at a beginner's salary. The resultant financial strain may add new aggravations to the emotional problem. An occupation is only a name for a group of jobs which have many things in common. Even in so well-defined an occupation as that of the registered nurse, there is great variety of activity, environment, supervision, and responsibility, which depend in part upon whether the nurse works in a home, a hospital, a social agency, a school, or an industry. In each of these locales there is great variety in jobs from one employer to another. Sometimes the aversion to a job is caused by tyrannical supervision or intolerable working conditions or hours of work or distance from home or some other characteristic of the particular position, which could be remedied simply by finding a more acceptable job in the same occupation.

If it appears that no change of this kind will achieve the desired result and that a change of occupation might, then the counselor and client may examine lists of occupations, select those which seem to have possibilities, and review them as suggested above in the section, "The Tentative Choice." Obviously, in their review, they will pay special attention to the things which have most disturbed the client in the last job. In so doing, there is some danger that equally irritating but different characteristics of the new job may be overlooked. It is, consequently, imperative that the review of occupations be preceded or accompanied by a thorough examination of the client's needs and values, likes and dislikes, abilities, limitations, and anxieties. The review should include the most meticulous scrutiny of all the duties that may be involved in any contemplated occupation, of the kinds of surroundings in which they are performed, and of the client's feeling about every aspect of the occupation. Failure to examine the occupation in sufficient detail may result in a new choice that will be no better than the old occupation, and this unhappy result may lead, in turn, to the erroneous conclusion that no change of occupation would be helpful.

THE BASIC PROBLEM

Stated in the simplest possible terms, the basic problem in all career counseling is to help clients find out what they hope to get from their jobs, what they have to offer in exchange for what they hope to get, and in what occupations they will have the best chance of getting what they want.

Finding out what the client most wants from a job is sometimes the most difficult task of all, because consciously even he may not know. One may have a strong urge to be conspicuous or to dominate, or may seek other satisfactions which are socially unacceptable and which he cannot admit either to himself or to the counselor. But the desire may nevertheless be there, and it may be strong enough to cause the rejection of a choice that would otherwise be logical. Faced with apparently illogical rejections of logical choices, the counselor will do well to look for goals not yet revealed.

Because of the difficulty, sometimes perhaps the impossibility, of bringing all emotional needs and desires to the conscious intellectual level, the client will sometimes make what is for him a wise choice, although it may appear unwise to everyone, including himself. Strong feelings are sometimes a better guide to action than strong intellects.

To the beginning counselor a final word of reassurance may be welcome. A great deal has been written about counseling, but not much is really known about it, despite the impressive technical language in the literature. Basically, a counselor in any organization is just a person who has been given a little extra time so that he or she may try to do better what the other members of the staff have always tried to do as well as they could. A counselor does not have to be omniscient in order to be useful. Anything that one can do better than the average professional worker in the organization may represent an improvement in service to the client. At the very least, the counselor can listen longer than any colleagues. The counselor can take more time and more care in trying to find out what the client needs and wants. The counselor can spend more time in trying to meet the client's needs. And the counselor can devote more time to making himself or herself more competent to do this job.

The counselor will not always be sure what will best serve the client's needs. As long as the counselor lives, no matter how competent one becomes, this kind of uncertainty must be faced. At times the counselor will feel as bewildered as the client. At such times, it may help to remember that the function of the counselor is not to solve the client's problem for him. It is to make available to the client all the help that the counselor can provide. If with this help the client still cannot solve his problem, the failure is not necessarily the fault of the counselor or of the client either. Man's knowledge of how to solve human problems is still incomplete. It is possible that there may be problems which cannot be solved. The justification of the counselor's existence is found, not in the ability to solve all problems or to help all people, but in the ability to give enough help to enough people to be worth what the counselor costs.

REVIEW QUESTIONS

1   Do you agree or disagree with the author's statement of what the purpose of counseling is and is not? Why?

2   How would you use occupational information in counseling the client who has no occupational preferences, the client who has a tentative choice, the client whose choice is unrealistic, the client who is thinking of changing a job?

3   When everyone agrees that too many or too few persons are preparing for an important occupation, what do you think should be done about it? Why? How?

4   What would you do if your boss asked you to put on a campaign to recruit more students for science and mathematics courses?

5 A psychiatrist asks your help in working with a patient who wants to change jobs. What suggestions will you offer to the psychiatrist?

6 Do you agree that strong feelings may sometimes be a better guide to action than strong intellects? Why? Why not?

7 Where does the discouraged counselor find the justification for his existence?

8 How can you use what you have learned from this chapter?

The Use of Occupational Information in Counseling — Answering Questions

One of the most common uses of occupational information in counseling is to answer questions raised by clients. Many persons who come to counselors want nothing more than accurate factual information, on the basis of which they intend to make their own decisions without further help. Others want some interpretation of the facts in relation to their own objectives. Where to get the facts has already been discussed in Chapter 4. The significance of these facts in occupational choice and some of the ways in which they may affect the job satisfaction of the client are discussed in the following pages.

By this time the reader may be a bit surprised at the repetition of section heads in Chapters 3, 4, and 11. The three chapters could have been combined; for some purposes combination would be desirable. But when the reader wishes to use these chapters for later reference, he may find it more convenient to have them separated. The author suggests that the beginner in counseling underscore those parts of Chapter 11 which are new to him and which he wishes to remember and that he review this chapter from time to time until these parts are permanently incorporated in his professional resources. The author suggests that Chapter 3 be used as a checklist with clients in those interviews in which the client seeks help in examining prospective occupations and that Chapter 4 be used mainly for reference when additional information is needed. Chapters 4 and 11 should not be used as interview guides, because they do not include all the specifics listed in Chapter 3.

Employment Prospects   At certain times and in certain occupations, the demand for workers is so much greater than the supply that even substandard applicants have excellent prospects of employment. This was true of the demand for social workers in the early days of the Roosevelt-Hopkins relief program of the 1930s, for machinists and machine operators in the early 1940s, for stenographers and elementary school teachers in the early 1950s, for engineers in the early 1960s.

If a person is looking for temporary employment, he or she may find a job more readily and may make more money in one of these shortage areas than in an occupation for which the person is better qualified, but if a permanent job is sought it may be wiser to choose a field in which he or she will be able to compete when the demand returns to normal or when the supply approaches and perhaps exceeds the demand. If a person is well qualified for a shortage area, the excessive demand for workers may enable the job seeker to advance more rapidly than would be possible in another field.

Conversely, an excessive supply of applicants may well discourage the average or substandard candidate but need not force the superior applicant to look elsewhere. Even in a crowded occupation there may be room for the person with qualifications in the top 1 or 2 percent. The person who chooses the overcrowded field should, however, have more than youthful optimism to support a judgment of his or her own superiority.

Shortages of workers may occur because the occupation is poorly paid. Comparison of earnings in occupations which require the same level of training sometimes reveals surprising differences.

For the person whose entrance to the occupation will be delayed by some years of preparation, current supply and demand may be less important than the forecast of employment prospects for the time when one expects to enter the labor market. For more on this see Chapter 4.

Long-range growth prospects in an occupation or industry, of course, mean greater opportunities for continuous employment, advancement, and increasing income. How much industries may differ in their rate of growth is indicated by the following figures on the increases and decreases in the number of employees in different fields from 1947 to 1972.

	Percent
Bituminous coal mining	− 66
Railroads	− 63
Meat products	+ 25
Finance, insurance, and real estate	+ 124
State and local government	+ 197

Technological change often causes employment to decline in some occupations and concurrently to increase in others. The automobile industry, for example, helped to reduce the employment of blacksmiths by about 200,000, while it created jobs for 750,000 automobile mechanics [Wolfbein, 417].

The more the counselor can learn about the probable future growth or decline of the major industries and occupations in the employment market, the more helpful he or she can be to the client.

Nature of the Work   Popular impressions of the work done in many occupations are so erroneous that this item warrants the most diligent and exhaustive investigation. Often the client's consideration of an occupation will terminate as soon as he or she gets the full picture of the work that it involves and of the amount of time devoted to different tasks.

The reader is invited to pause at this point and ask, "How many things do I have to do in my job that I did not anticipate when I took it?" There are few if any jobs in which the workers never have to do anything that they dislike, but the amount of time that one will spend in distasteful activities can be affected considerably by the choice of an occupation. One of the best investments the counselor can make of his or her time is in learning exactly what people do in the occupations that interest his or her clients, and how much of their time they spend doing it.

Work Environment   Excessive heat, cold, humidity, dust, dirt, noise, or offensive odors are in themselves sufficient reasons for some persons to leave a job or to discard an occupation from further consideration, while an air-conditioned office, attractively furnished, in a good neighborhood for lunch-hour shopping may tip the scales in favor of one job over another. The fact that some of these considerations are unimportant in the counselor's scale of values, if they are, does not mean that they are unimportant to clients. And the counselor who takes a class in occupations to visit a bakery, a laundry, a foundry, a forge, a meat-packing plant, a fertilizer factory, a cement plant, and a boiler shop may change some of his or her own ideas about the importance of environment.

If there is anything unusually attractive or repulsive or hazardous about the work environment, this fact should be noted and discussed in counseling and in terms of the client's values. At least one person has said he wanted "a greasy job." One group of garbage collectors was once reported to have a deficient sense of smell. Before any occupational choice is considered final, the client should visit several places in which the work is done, in order to see, hear, feel, and smell the surroundings. Visiting several places is desirable, because the environment may vary from one company to another.

Some persons prefer to work alone. One taxi driver quit his job three times, but returned to it each time in order to escape the close supervision that he encountered in other jobs. When the client will not work alone, an important part of the environment is the kind of people with whom he or she will work. Are they people that one will understand and like, with whom one can and will establish cordial working relationships? Or are there substantial differences in background or in values that will be a barrier to comfortable human relations on the job? Will the client find in this occupation the kinds of people with whom he or she wants to spend the largest part of life? Because in many jobs human relationships are so important, this factor may have a significant bearing upon success as well as satisfaction. Equally important may be the frequency with which the job permits the worker to direct the behavior of others or requires the worker to follow their directions. Consider the nurse aid and the traffic police officer. In a perceptive article, "Occupations with the Upper Hand," Pohlman [307] notes, "To have power in an occupation, one does not need either a managerial position or a high status occupation. . . . There may be a good bit of prestige in low status occupations." For an excellent discussion of the psychosocial aspects of work, see Samler [336].

Some of the best information on the social climate in different occupations is found not in the books and pamphlets prepared for counselors and their clients, but in the reports of occupational sociologists. The following excerpts are from the *Abstracts of Sociological Literature on Occupations* by Overs and Deutsch [297]:

> A set of unofficial . . . work rules exists among the letter carriers, many of which are in direct violation of the official regulations. . . .
>
> The official job description is devised so that it will take the carrier exactly eight hours to sort and deliver the mail. . . . Usually, however, he alters the order in which he is supposed to deliver the mail; he may walk criss-cross, skip certain loops in his walk, make frequent stops at the relay box, cut across lawns, or devise other short cuts. He may also violate the official rules by holding over some of the mail for the next day's delivery in order to "even out" the differences in the amount of mail on the various days. The carrier then may spend the left-over time in a number of ways: he may go home and return to the station at the officially prescribed time; he may go shopping; he may join fellow carriers at a nearby tavern; he may sit in his car and read; or he may extend his lunch period beyond the official 30 minutes. . . .
>
> The carrier is not to return early too frequently. If he does, the supervisor will interpret the situation as one which indicates that the route is too short.
>
> The norms also prescribe that the regular summer substitute for a given route should always return somewhat later than the prescribed time. Admonitions such as "Don't kill the route" are given to the substitute to emphasize the unofficial role expectations. If the substitute should violate this important norm, the group will penalize him by withholding needed information or deliberately interfering with the rule breaker's activity. For instance, when a substitute who is known to deviate from the unofficial norms is assigned a new route and asks about details of the route, he will be told that he can find all he needs to know in the Order Book. His questions about particular hazards on the route—such as vicious dogs—will remain unanswered. At times, the deviant may find that labels on the mail bundles for his route have been deliberately mixed up. . . .
>
> The mass-mortuary . . . is characterized by impersonality. . . . "Time, not rapport, becomes the essence." . . .
>
> The mass-mortuary often draws its clientele by mass advertising from the large trade area extending beyond a single community. . . .
>
> The establishment's relationship to the survivors is analogous to the buyer-seller type of contractual relationship. . . .
>
> In contrast to the mass-mortuary, "the local funeral home operates on the premise that the clientele . . . should receive personal, . . . sympathetic understanding, in a social, or status-connected relationship to the funeral." . . .
>
> "The local funeral home is organized so that the clientele can always feel certain

they will have their funeral services handled by THE funeral director, whom they know personally." . . .

"If you don't have the kind of personality that will permit you to give comfort and sincere sympathy to the people, you just don't stay in the game," remarked one funeral director. . . .

The business goal of the local funeral home is defined according to community attitudes. These attitudes usually permit profitable operations so that the funeral director can live a comfortable, middle-class, quasi-professional existence. "Should it appear . . . that the funeral director is 'profiteering in sorrow,' community sanctions in the form of withdrawal of trade and 'talk' will either force his operations into an approved form, or eventually he will be out of business."

In many instances, the local funeral home performs services at a loss; in other instances, it may make up the differences. There may be charity cases for which the funeral director never sends the bill. In contrast, mass-mortuary practices approve the use of collection agencies to collect from survivors—a practice which not only collects the debt but includes, as well, interest on the unpaid balance.

Fifty-one per cent of the ministers and forty-one per cent of the priests believed the funeral director exploited or took advantage of a family's grief.

For the most part, clergymen did not meet with funeral directors socially, even though there was continuous contact throughout the years, and even though there was associational contact. This absence of social contact suggested that the clergy do not perceive of funeral directors as status equals.

Qualifications   See Chapter 4 on qualifications, physical demands, aptitudes, interests, legal requirements, discrimination, apprenticeship, capital.

In appraising aptitude for any occupations, beginning counselors are sometimes disturbingly naïve. So, too, are some experienced counselors and some psychologists. The beginner may assume that a test which is called a test of mechanical aptitude must be a test of mechanical aptitude. Actually it may be only a test which its author and publisher hope will measure mechanical aptitude. The trained counselor and psychologist have learned to look for coefficients of validity as evidence of the degree to which a test does measure what it purports to measure, but too frequently they accept a low coefficient as evidence of acceptable validity, or they assume that a high coefficient, obtained against criteria of success in one occupation in one company, justifies the use of the test to measure aptitude for related jobs in the same company or for similar jobs in other companies.

Actually, very few tests have been adequately validated for use in individual vocational guidance, and those which have been seldom purport to measure even half of whatever determines success in the occupation. This is not a book on aptitude testing, and there is not room here for adequate explanation and illustrations, but all counselors who expect to use the results of aptitude tests should scrupulously examine the evidence of the validity of their tests for the purpose for which they propose to use them and be guided accordingly. For more on this see Super and Crites [382].

The counselor should also look for information about critical scores for employment and for success in the occupation and if possible in the company the client is considering. Regrettably, such scores are seldom available, and without them test interpretation for career guidance is dubious at best.

This does not mean that aptitude tests should not be used in career guidance. They should be used, and the counselor who uses them should know enough about the tests and enough about occupations to help the client to interpret the results for what they are worth, and no more.

Unions Although the closed shop is legally prohibited in some places, it can still be found in other places. If the closed shop predominates in the community in which the client wants to work and if the client would rather change his occupation than change his home, the ability of the client to gain admission to the union may be the most important consideration of all. Many unions restrict the admission of new members, and at times some admit only the relatives of union members. It is imperative that the counselor be adequately informed about union entrance requirements in the community, that the information be up to date, and that this aspect of occupational choice be fully discussed with the client in order to determine how it may affect the client's ability to get a job.

The client who is willing to change locations can find several states in which the closed shop is illegal. In rural areas and in small towns there are often no unions.

Discrimination Despite legal prohibitions, discrimination still exists. Although one may find little of it in one occupation and much in another, there are few, if any, occupations which are completely closed. There are women auto mechanics, carpenters, machinists, and plumbers. There are successful black architects who serve wealthy white clients, and black school administrators who supervise white teachers. Many large corporations actively recruit college graduates from minority groups. Within a single organization discrimination may exist in one department and not in another.

Counselors, therefore, should not be too ready to discourage the competent young person who wishes to compete in a field where he or she will be subject even to widespread discrimination. It is the counselor's responsibility to help the client to get as much accurate information as possible about the nature and the extent of the discrimination that the client will probably encounter; it is not the responsibility of the counselor to decide how the client should act in the light of this information. Courageous persons who take long chances and succeed help to lower the barriers of discrimination for those who will come later, but the individual should know the chance he or she is taking when taking it and be prepared to face the risks. The client should not be shoved into a situation that he would rather avoid just because the counselor wants vicariously to fight discrimination, nor should the client be discouraged from taking risks that the client recognizes just because the counselor is cautious. As a private citizen, the counselor is, of course, free to follow his or her own conscience. The counselor may even have a civic obligation to work toward anything that he or she believes will improve the community, but must not substitute his or her own values for those of the client in the counseling situation.

The harsh facts of discrimination are threatening enough to scare anyone who has to face them. The unemployment rate for black teenagers is usually about double the rate for white teenagers.

Weaver [407] suggested that:

In addition to finding out whether there are any employment opportunities for him at all in the field of his choice, a minority youth will need to look for answers to these questions: If there is discrimination, is it national, or is it confined to a particular locale? If minority workers are hired in this field, what is the degree of acceptance by co-workers on the job? What is the degree of acceptance by unions or professional organizations in the field? Once he is hired, can he expect reasonable equality of working conditions and opportunities for advancement? Is there a pay differential? What has been the past history in the field with reference to dismissal policy: Are the minority workers the first to go, regardless of merit and length of service?

In seeking the answers to these questions, do not forget to consult your own alumni and employed students and their parents.

Preparation   School counselors, who should be experts on preparation, make some of their worst mistakes in this area. Because we people in school business are so convinced of the value of education, we tend to confuse that which is desirable and that which is essential. Perhaps without meaning to do so, we place undue emphasis on preparation that may be desirable but is not indispensable. Thus we discourage clients from considering certain occupations unless they can get all the preparation that we recommend. One college student gave up consideration of the ministry when told he would have to study Greek and Hebrew, but one of his friends became a lay preacher without ever going to college at all. Latin is no longer required or even recommended by most medical schools. It is imperative that counselors know and explain to their clients the difference between essential and desirable preparation and the many ways in which both kinds of preparation can be obtained through work-study programs, apprenticeship, night school, on-the-job training, scholarships, and tuition remission.

Where legal requirements must be met, the counselor has an obligation to see that the schools which the client considers entering have been approved and accepted by the legal board which issues the licenses. The author recalls two students who had completed a full year of graduate study in a school that was not accredited and were forced to repeat the same courses in an accredited university before they could be certified for public school counseling. Another student had two years of post-high school study at an institute which was not accredited; both years of work had to be repeated before he could get his degree from an accredited university.

Employers' standards may be either higher or lower than licensing requirements, depending on the state of the labor market. In depression periods, much more than the minimum legal training may be needed to get a job. When workers are scarce, emergency certificates may be issued to applicants who do not meet the legal standards.

Advancement   Clients differ greatly in the value they place on advancement. Some will risk everything for it. Others dislike responsibility and will refuse a promotion that is offered to them. Some prefer an assured though moderate advancement in earnings and status to the more spectacular advancement which they might achieve by taking more risks.

The cautious ones can often find what they seek in very large organizations, where promotion from within is company policy, where union contracts provide for increased earnings, security, and privileges as one acquires seniority, and where there frequently may be found a bureaucracy not unlike that in the civil service and in public education. For an enlightening discussion of this topic see Caplow [44]. The risk takers are more likely to find their opportunities in small companies which are growing rapidly, in new industries, and in the volatile industries which are discussed later in this chapter. Caplow notes that individual earnings in medium-sized businesses are often larger than in huge corporations and that persons who have reached the top managerial level in a small business sometimes move successfully from one type of business to another type at the top level.

The most rapid upward movement is more likely to be found where success depends upon the personal characteristics of the worker rather than upon training and experience. Actors, athletes, authors, and salespersons, if they are good enough to reach the top, can often do so in much less time than actuaries, metallurgists, pharmacists, and teachers. Workers who go into business for themselves, whether as barbers, beauticians, printers, funeral directors, or real estate brokers, can increase their earnings as rapidly as their own abilities and taxes will permit. They can also lose their shirts.

Pitt and Smith [305] have called attention to one aspect of advancement that is seldom mentioned in the literature on occupations:

> For example, great merchandising organizations such as Procter and Gamble require a number of chemists. But the major emphasis in such an organization is on sales and promotion. The young man who chooses chemistry as a career should realize that in such organizations the top executive jobs are almost invariably filled from the sales, merchandising, and advertising departments. . . . However, should a young man's interests include both chemistry and a desire for administrative responsibility, he had best look for employment in some of the basic chemical companies, such as du Pont or Olin-Mathieson, where the working chemist can aspire, with greater possibility of success, to a top administrative post.

Pitt and Smith noted how the same principle applies in other industries to engineers, purchasing agents, psychologists, etc.

In general, opportunities for advancement tend to be overemphasized in choosing an occupation. Our American culture places such a high value on financial success and we talk so much in school about our land of opportunity that we tend to leave students with the expectation that all, or nearly all, of them will advance to positions of prestige, influence, and affluence. Actually, most of them will remain at, or near, the level at which they get their first jobs. Salary schedules may provide modest increases in earnings as the years go by, but regardless of the economic system, one can have only a limited number of corporation presidents or cabinet ministers or commissars.

We might do our clients a better service if we concerned ourselves less with advancement and concentrated our efforts on increasing the probability that our clients would choose occupations in which they would be reasonably effective and reasonably happy in the entry job. Superior performance in the first job offers about as good a prospect of advancement as one may reasonably expect. Of course, if two occupations are equally attractive otherwise and one is growing while the other declines, there is no need to choose the poorer prospect.

Earnings   Glenn E. Grube asked high school students to estimate the weekly earnings of beginning workers in several occupations. The estimates for some of the occupations were: laboratory assistant, $30 to $200; plumber, $25 to $220; teacher $40 to $200; typist $10 to $100.

Not infrequently the clients' expectations of their own earning power are based upon what they have read or heard about the exceptionally high earnings of a few individuals. Unless they can get and accept a more realistic view of their prospects, they may persist in choosing occupations for which they are poorly equipped, or in which average earnings are actually very low. By presenting the best reports on the entire range of earnings in the occupation and especially on the median earnings and on the earnings of the middle 50 percent, the counselor can help correct such false impressions.

One of the best ways in which to help students to get a realistic appraisal of their probable earning power is to have them conduct a follow-up study through their course or unit in occupations and thus to see for themselves how much the former students of their own school are now making. Some of the author's interviews with prospective graduate students who thought of leaving well-paid business jobs in order to become school counselors have terminated as soon as earnings figures from follow-up studies were produced. Accurate figures on median earnings may also help the client who is offered a job and must decide to take it or wait for something better.

In some occupations, earnings are higher in some parts of the country than in others. Teachers, for example, are paid much more in certain large cities and wealthy suburbs than in less affluent communities. It is sometimes important to inquire into local salaries and the cost of living in the territory in which the client wishes to work. One of the author's students, who is a New York City teacher, has wanted for several years to live and work in the South but has not yet found a job that pays anywhere near his present salary.

Sometimes earning prospects can be enhanced by a simple shift from one branch of an occupation to another. At times, for example, certain types of office-machine operators have earned much more than typists or even stenographers, despite the fact that their work required less training and simpler skills. The counselor needs to know rates of pay in different branches of an occupation and in different local companies, as well as in the occupation as a whole. See Chapter 4 for sources.

Number of Workers   The more persons there are employed in an occupation and the older they are, the better are the prospects that some vacancies will exist whenever an applicant is looking for a job. Despite the rapid growth of some occupations, most vacancies in most fields result from the resignation, retirement, or death of employees. In a very small occupation, one may wait months for a suitable vacancy to occur. In a large occupation, hundreds of vacancies occur every day. The person who wants to avoid unemployment may find the larger occupations more attractive.

Distribution of Workers   Some occupations are concentrated in certain areas. A person with a strong aversion to living in these areas may be severely handicapped if he chooses one of these occupations. Even if he likes the area, should health or other considerations ever force him to move, he may be forced to change his occupation. Other occupations are practiced almost everywhere and permit their workers to live wherever they choose. This fact can be of special importance to marriage partners who both work, if either may be transferred.

Television and theatrical entertainment are centered in New York and Hollywood. A mining engineer may be sent to foreign countries but may also be far from the conveniences of the large city. Advancement in some large companies may require moving to distant places. Accountants, automobile mechanics, bill collectors, bus drivers, carpenters, county farm agents, dentists, electricians, beauticians, nurses, plumbers, stenographers, and teachers can find employment in every state in the country.

Even when employment is nationwide, there may be geographical differences in the occupation. Specialization in medicine is easier to arrange in a large city than in a country village. Veterinarians in wealthy suburbs treat more pets than pigs.

Likes and Dislikes   Few things can so quickly change one's impressions of an occupation as asking several persons who are in it to say what they like and dislike about it. A mass of useful occupational information can be picked up by asking this question of friends and acquaintances as a part of casual conversation. Certainly no review of a potential occupation, in a counseling interview, should be considered complete until the counselor or the client has asked this question of several persons engaged in the occupation. Then comes the question the client must face: "How do you think you would feel about these things?"

Hours   The girl who has to work evenings, while her girl friend entertains her boy friend, is not likely to be wholly satisfied with her job, but students who hope to work their way through college may find evening jobs that suit their needs exactly. There are individual differences in the hours that people prefer to work, and there may be excellent reasons for the preferences. There is almost endless variety in the hours at which work must be done, and the counselor who knows occupations can be of real service to some clients simply by making them aware of the occupations which will permit them to work at the hours which facilitate the kinds of lives they wish to live.

More of the world's work than most of us realize is done at unusual or irregular hours. Perishable food comes into the big city during the night, is auctioned to wholesalers, and resold to retailers while the rest of us sleep. Bread is baked, milk is bottled, and pastry cooks arrive at restaurants before the sun rises. Truck drivers pound the highways at high speed throughout the night, while police officers, ambulance drivers, and interns pick up the pieces of the celebrators who drink and drive. Telegraph operators convey the urgent messages; postal employees sort and forward the millions of letters picked up in the evening collections. Bus and taxi drivers take us home from the theater and return with others who are on their way to work. Electric line workers repair broken wires in midnight blizzards, while short-order cooks in all-night restaurants stand ready to serve them when they can take time to eat. Radio, television, and theatrical stars work when the rest of us wish to be entertained, as do the ticket sellers, ushers, stage hands, electricians and projector operators. Music and drama critics and newspaper reporters cover the news when it occurs; editors, printers, and others bring it to us at breakfast. Many of these jobs require Sunday and holiday work, with off days during the week, sometimes on a rotating schedule and sometimes not.

Some editorial workers on weekly magazines work thirty-five hours in two days and have the remainder of the week off. Some railway and airline employees work long hours and then lay off for a day or two. Some bus drivers and telephone operators work split shifts during the morning and evening rush hours with time off in between. Some jobs which must be covered twenty-four hours a day have rotating shifts, so that an employee works from 8 A.M. to 4 P.M. one week, from 4 P.M. to midnight the next, and from midnight to 8 A.M. the next. Some similar jobs put all beginners on the less popular shifts and let the employees with seniority choose their shifts. Some jobs, like night clerk in a small hotel, require the employee's presence but involve little actual work, which makes them ideal for students, who can use the quiet hours for study. Some department stores employ a special staff to work only on Sunday afternoons, taking telephone orders for merchandise advertised in Sunday newspapers.

Florence Broadley has suggested that such odd-hour jobs may relieve some handicapped workers of the difficulties which they experience in traveling during rush hours.

Vacations   Some teachers, perhaps some counselors, would frown upon a student who proposed to choose a career in terms of vacations offered, but the same teachers would think twice before giving up their own free summers. When the vacation arrangements in an occupation are unusually attractive or unattractive, this fact should be noted in counseling and considered in terms of how important vacations are in the client's scale of values.

Stability of Employment   Anyone who has been out of work in a period of economic depression knows how very important stability of employment can be. Yet this consideration may be overlooked by the optimistic young person who has never been close to the misery of unemployment. Even here the counselor should not substitute his or her own scale of values for that of the client, but the counselor does have a responsibility for making certain that the client who is about to choose an occupation in which jobs are not steady knows what may lie ahead.

Some persons are cautious and prefer a steady job even at the expense of higher earnings and more rapid advancement. Others are more inclined to take risks and to look for their security in their own ability to survive whatever calamities may befall. It is not the function of the counselor to convince the client that he should be either more or less cautious than he appears to be; it is the function of the counselor to help the client to find out just what kind of security he wants, how much he wants it, and where he can get it.

One of the author's acquaintances resigns from his job each spring and finds a new job each fall, so that he may devote his summers to coaching the young amateur ballplayers of his community and managing their teams, meanwhile earning a bare subsistence by umpiring the weekend games of semiprofessional teams in the vicinity. He is unmarried. Baseball is his major interest in life. He has not found a way to make baseball support him, but he has found a way in which he can support baseball; he is happy and useful leading the kind of life that he wants to lead.

Occupations differ even more than most of us realize in the continuity of employment which they provide. Some are obviously seasonal, such as those in summer or winter resort hotels. In general, the least stable occupations are those which provide goods or services the purchase of which can be postponed for months or years. Among these are luxuries, such as furs, jewelry, entertainment, and vacation travel, and the capital goods or "hard" goods, such as buildings, machinery, automobiles, refrigerators, and washing machines. In general, the more stable occupations are those which provide goods or services the purchase of which cannot or will not be postponed for very long. These are found in the consumer goods or "soft" goods industries: the grocery stores which stock our daily supplies of food; the utilities which provide us with water, gas, electricity, communication, and transportation; the public schools, police and fire departments, and other government services. Banks and insurance companies usually have lower rates of unemployment than many other businesses.

Because many occupations may be practiced in any of several different industries and companies, the place where one finds employment may have as much bearing on stability as the occupation. Stable companies can usually be identified from their past record of earnings and employment. Such a company may be entered at almost any time a job is available, without much concern about the stage of the economic cycle. Volatile industries and companies can also be identified from their past record, but it is much more difficult to determine whether the current trend is up or down or about to change. Prediction of changing conditions is always precarious. Some help may be obtained by talking with persons in the industry and by reading business and financial publications and the reports of investment-information services. These publications may be found in the libraries of schools of commerce, in the business and economics sections of public libraries, and in the offices of banks and brokers. Librarians are usually glad to help the reader to find what he wants.

Sometimes one needs only a little common sense to anticipate what will happen. No crystal ball is needed to predict that employment in the manufacture of military equipment will rise and fall with military appropriations. In January, 1941, before World War II, the Grumman Aircraft Engineering Corporation at Bethpage, New York, had 2,116 employees. In the midst of wartime production, in September, 1943, the same company had 25,527 employees. After the war, employment dropped to 4,670 in January, 1946. Volatile industries of this kind provide phenomenal opportunities for rapid advancement of the person who has what it takes and who is employed at or near the start of the upswing. They may also provide comparably rapid demotion or separation when the boom ends, except for those who have made themselves so valuable that they become an essential part of the permanent staff.

Within the same industry or company there are sometimes substantial differences in stability of employment. In one period of only three months, in the metalworking industries, unemployment increased by 95 percent among the unskilled and by only 8 percent among the skilled workers [Wolfbein, 417]. Even professional workers are not exempt from the threat of unemployment. The cancellation of a single government contract for military equipment has caused the immediate layoff of 11,000 workers including 1,000 engineers.

In Conclusion   It is now, perhaps, apparent why the author of this book insists that the counselor cannot discharge his responsibilities by referring his client to the library for occupational information. There are too many things the client needs to know that cannot be found in any library. There are too many things that may affect his or her success and satisfaction which he or she may be unaware should even be considered.

Because so many occupational books and pamphlets are obsolete or biased, the counselor who refers a client to any occupational file should go with the client, teach him how to appraise occupational literature (see Chapter 5), and help him to select what he will read.

There is more to career counseling than aptitude and interest testing. There is more to career counseling than psychotherapy. There is more to career counseling than the choice of next year's courses. The clients who come to a professional counselor for help in planning careers have a right to expect that the counselor will be competent to help them, and will help them, to clarify the needs that they hope their occupations will meet, to find out what occupations are available that may meet their needs, and to compare these occupations in terms of probable success and satisfaction in each.

Service to the client may include psychotherapy if needed. It may include aptitude and interest testing if there are appropriate tests available. It may include educational guidance if the client is ready for it. It must also include, if the client desires, a careful review of all the considerations that may affect his or her choice and of all the pertinent facts about himself and about the occupation. To purport to offer career counseling, to accept a fee or a salary for doing so, and then to deliver only educational advice, psychometrics, or psychotherapy raises some questions about either the competence or the integrity of the counselor.

REVIEW QUESTIONS

1 What kind of client may be wise to choose an occupation which is not the one for which he or she is best qualified?
2 For what kind of client is current supply and demand less important than future supply and demand?

3   Why is it so important to explore in detail the nature of the work in a contemplated occupation?

4   What are some of the characteristics of the work environment that may affect job satisfaction?

5   Why should a client see his or her contemplated occupation in several places of employment before making a choice final?

6   Why is it imperative that the counselor be as well informed about union entrance requirements in the community as he is about college entrance requirements?

7   Do you agree or disagree with the author's statement about overemphasis on advancement?

8   What is one of the best ways to help students get a realistic appraisal of their probable earning power?

9   Why should the size of an occupation be considered before choosing it?

10   How may the geographical distribution of workers affect occupational choice?

11   What are some of the occupations which have odd hours that you have not previously thought of in this connection?

12   Which occupations tend to provide stable employment?

13   Why do some workers in an occupation have stable jobs while other workers in the same occupation are frequently unemployed?

14   Will anything in this chapter affect your future thoughts and actions? What? How?

Chapter 12

Career Education and the Teaching of Occupations

The term and the concept of "career education" began to attract wide attention in 1971, when Sidney P. Marland, Jr., then U.S. Commissioner of Education, in an address to the National Association of Secondary School Principals proposed that all education be thought of as preparation for a career. While Marland "conscientiously avoided trying to lay down a precise definition for career education," subsequent publications from his office suggested that the focus from kindergarten to grade six be on "career awareness," from grade seven to grade ten on "career exploration," and from grade eleven to grade twelve or beyond on "career preparation." Thus the elementary school would help children to become better acquainted with the great variety of occupations potentially available to them. The junior high or middle school would help its pupils to compare different clusters of occupations, to select a few of them for more intensive investigation, and to select one cluster for which they would begin to prepare. Senior high school students would begin their career preparation, some in vocational courses and some in college preparatory programs.

Commissioner Marland implemented his proposal with substantial grants from the discretionary funds at his disposal. Exemplary projects were developed in all of the fifty states.

Career education obviously includes occupational information. As noted above, two of the major purposes of career education are career awareness and career exploration, and the more specific purposes of these include the following:

1 To make students, from kindergarten to college, more aware of the many ways in which they may earn the money to support themselves and their families, make their contributions to the common good, and enjoy the satisfactions that many people do find in their work.

2 To reassure those who arrive at the kindergarten already convinced that no one will ever hire them for anything but the least desirable jobs; this kind of despair is sometimes found among children from the minority groups, which have suffered so much from racial and other forms of prejudice. To show these children that some former pupils, much like themselves, do have desirable jobs; and that, although prejudice still exists, it is not always insurmountable.

3 To help students to choose, among the many occupations, a cluster of related occupations for which they will begin to prepare themselves.

4 To show students some of the ways in which the things they learn in school may help them later in their work.

The career education programs designed for these purposes include the presentation of occupational information to students, by classroom teachers, as part of whatever subjects the teachers are teaching.

Occupational information is presented also in units or courses in occupations, taught by school counselors or by teachers specially trained and hired for this specific purpose.

The methods used to present occupational information include many of those described in the remaining chapters of this book.

Marland suggested also an experience-based career education at the secondary school level. As a first step in this direction four programs were funded, in Charleston, West Virginia; Oakland, California; Philadelphia, Pennsylvania; and Portland/Tigard, Oregon. Twelfth-grade students ranging from the educationally retarded to National Merit Scholars spent weeks or months visiting local places of employment, observing a wide range of career opportunities, and working at tasks related to one or more occupations in one or more work sites, all in the hope of helping them to make better career plans and decisions. Academic work necessary to qualify for a high school diploma was provided, and so far as possible it was related to the work interests and activities of the students. Instruction in career development and decision making was included. Each student's program was designed to meet his or her individual needs.

At the end of the first experimental year some students had changed their career plans, saying, "It wasn't what I had imagined" and "I saw right on the job that I couldn't take it." Others had their choices confirmed: "It was just the thing I was looking for." Some focused on career objectives previously unfamiliar to them.

The experimental programs were expensive, in some cases with a ratio as low as 1:2 between staff members and students. Presumably future programs would not require so much developmental work and evaluation, and could be much less expensive.

Marland did not propose to substitute the teaching of occupations for the teaching of reading, writing, and arithmetic. He did propose that every teacher make the pupils aware of the occupational uses of every subject that he or she teaches. Marland described [252] career education as

> . . . the companion to academic preparation at every grade level, from kindergarten through graduate school . . . to enable every . . . person to enter and do well in a career carefully chosen from among many, no matter at what point he or she leaves formal education. . . . Career education . . . is not an anti-intellectual conspiracy. It is not a way to discourage poor and minority young people from going to college.

Marland's proposal was enthusiastically received by many persons, but not by everyone; and, as usual, some of the exemplary programs ended when the federal grants expired.

There has been some opposition from those who perceive career education as a threat to liberal education.

There has been uneasiness among vocational educators who fear that career education may compete for funds previously allocated to the more intensive career preparation provided in vocational schools and courses. Others have wondered how many subject teachers can be persuaded to participate.

Psychologists have criticized the shortness of the exploratory process, as well as the classification base of the clusters. Twelve other clusters of occupations, based upon client needs, have been suggested by Rosen and others [323].

The National Urban League [80] has expressed its concern in these words:

> The same teachers and counselors who have been misdirecting Blacks in the past will be responsible for implementing Career Education. . . .
> Education should not only prepare people for jobs, but also for survival and community involvement in a prejudiced society. The ability to analyze, criticize and change the repressive aspects of our society are vital educational tools as well. . . .
> There must be guarantees that minority students will not be channeled into low-paying service jobs and that their decision not to pursue a B.A. is truly their own. . . .
> If career education is to be more than job training for poor people in a cheap labor market, the ultimate consumers—students—must be directly involved in the planning process, making certain that they are not funnelled into deadend occupations, and forgotten.

It is unquestionably true that many of us white counselors and teachers have, with good intentions, done things which black counselors would not have done. We have not always been right, and we may well heed the admonition of our black friends to reexamine both our motives and the effects of our actions. Inviting minority-group children and their parents to participate in planning, and in appraising our results, may help us to clarify our motives and improve our methods. Marland has endorsed this suggestion.

Predictions are hazardous, but we may venture the guess that career education, vocational education, and liberal education will all survive. The words and the methods may change, but there will always be teachers and administrators who will want to help students with their problems and who will find ways to do so, from kindergarten to graduate school. Surviving also will be some of the methods described in this and in subsequent chapters of this book.

Some local career education staffs include a coordinator of relations with local business and industry and a placement coordinator who helps students to find part-time jobs, and graduates to secure full-time employment. Some have career counselors.

Some school counselors have taken the leadership in developing local programs. Others have participated in career education activities, sometimes enthusiastically, sometimes reluctantly. Some counselors have perceived career education as a supporting service; others have feared it as a potential competitor for local funds.

Local and state directors of career education include both former counselors and former teachers of vocational education.

Since 1971, publishers have been producing so many books and other materials on career education that any recommended list would soon be obsolete. Most of these materials have been reviewed or advertised in such professional journals as the *Vocational Guidance Quarterly* [401] and the *American Vocational Journal* [9]. Two of the early, basic books are by Herr [161] and by Hoyt, Evans, Mackin, and Mangum [192].

Further information on all aspects of career education may be obtained from state directors of career education, from the ERIC Clearinghouse on Career Education at Northern Illinois University, DeKalb, Illinois and from the Division of Career Education, U.S. Office of Education, Washington, D.C.

The first known course in occupations was taught in 1908 at Westport, Connecticut, by George H. Boyden, high school principal, at the suggestion of Superintendent William A. Wheatley [Brewer, 30]. The first known college course in occupations was offered in 1917 at the College of the Pacific [Maverick, 254].

Hutson [196] has noted that in 1916

> . . . the course in vocations was given national standing by its acceptance as an element in the program of studies recommended for secondary schools by the Committee on Social Studies of the Commission on the Reorganization of Secondary Education of the National Education Association. The Committee called the course "vocational civics" and recommended it for the ninth grade. They expressed the belief that pupils of that age are ready to consider their choice of vocation and that such a course would minister to that need. They felt that it might induce pupils and parents to see the economic value of high-school education and thus influence length of stay in school. More important than its meaning for vocational guidance, however, in the minds of this committee, was its possible contribution to civic attitudes and understandings. . . .
>
> The recommendation of the Committee on Social Studies must have had some influence. The output of textbooks for the course on occupations was considerable during the '20s and the '30s, suggesting that a market must have developed. On the other hand, vocational civics must be reckoned the youngest member of the social studies family and the one with least prestige. It is not supported by any college department, such as history, political science, economics, or sociology. . . . Any subject with a pedigree so obscure must have some difficulty in becoming established.

There are fewer textbooks for high school courses in occupations today than there were in the 1920s and 1930s. In many schools a course in vocational civics or in occupations has been introduced and later dropped. Why?

The most likely explanation appears to be that many teachers were assigned to teach the course with no preparation in how to teach it and with no desire to teach it. For example, the author of this book once received a letter which read in part: "I am a Latin teacher. Next year I have to teach occupations. Please tell me what to do." Such teachers understandably did a poor job. They and their students and their supervisors were disappointed in the results.

Despite a discouraging start, the course in occupations has persisted. Each year some schools drop it, others introduce it. Although no figures are available, there appears to be increasing interest in the course at the college level. Where a counselor really believes that a course in occupations is needed, the course is likely to appear. If the counselor moves to another school or college and his or her successor has other interests, the course is likely to be dropped.

While the full-semester or full-year course struggles for acceptance, short units on occupations are included in many social studies courses. The units vary in length from one week to ten or more. Apparently it is easier to introduce a new unit than a new course. Once introduced, the unit is less conspicuous and hence perhaps less likely to be dropped. Since most social studies teachers have had no preparation for teaching such units, there seems little reason to expect that they are superior to the earlier courses in vocational civics. In a few schools the counselor teaches the unit on occupations, with presumably better results.

A unit well taught may have real value, particularly if the teacher does not try to do more than can be done well in the time available. For a summary of research on the teaching of occupations in units and in courses see Chapter 25. For further discussion of units and how to teach them see the section "Presenting Occupational Information through Other Subjects" in Chapter 20.

The Vocational Education Act of 1963 revived interest in the course in occupations. With the aid of federal funds and a new group of pioneers, some states are now experimenting with pilot programs. With state supervisors assigned full time to develop and improve these programs, and with in-service training under way, we may hope to see gradual improvement in the quality of the teaching.

As this book goes to press, North Carolina has 250 certified teachers of a ninth-grade course called "Introduction to Vocations." Six educational consultants have as a part of their responsibility helping teachers of this course. Clary and Beam [63] have described the program. Further information may be obtained from T. N. Stephens, Chief Consultant, Middle Grades Occupational Exploration, Division of Occupational Education, State Department of Public Instruction, Raleigh, North Carolina. See also Hopke [172].

In New Jersey, two state supervisors are assigned to help 2,400 teachers of Introduction to Vocations in the seventh to twelfth grades and in adult classes of 261 schools. Further information on this program may be obtained from John W. Williams, Supervisor, Introduction to Vocations, Vocational Division, State Department of Education, Trenton, N.J.

Georgia has 127 full-time coordinators of a junior high school Program of Education and Career Exploration (PECE), all of whom were selected by their principals and superintendents and trained for this task in a special program at the University of Georgia, described by Swain [387]. PECE includes short periods of work experience in several different settings, with related group discussion and other classroom exploratory activities. Further information may be obtained from Milton Adams, State Department of Education, Atlanta, Georgia.

We shall get good courses in occupations only when they are taught by teachers who are as well informed in the subject matter and as well trained in methods of teaching this course as the teachers of other subjects are for courses in their fields. Perhaps it is time for more of us to think about setting some certification standards for teachers of occupations.

REASONS FOR TEACHING OCCUPATIONS

It Saves Time   Part of the counselor's time is devoted to answering questions of clients. Many of these questions are matters of common interest; they come up again and again. When the counselor finds that it takes thirty interviews to give thirty clients substantially the same information, time can be saved by getting the thirty together and giving the facts to all of them at once.

It Provides a Background of Related Information That Improves Counseling   A course meeting five periods a week for a full semester provides time for both student and counselor to study and discuss problems of common interest to the group. By the simple arithmetical process of dividing the number of students into the number of hours which the average counselor has free for interviews, it becomes at once apparent that the average student in the average school or college is lucky to get as much as an hour or two a year of the counselor's time. In the occupations class the student may be in direct contact with the counselor as much as sixty or more hours.

The economies of time inherent in teaching occupations make it possible to provide the student with a background of factual information against which to discuss the individual aspects of the student's problem. In the interview itself the time usually spent on presenting general information may be devoted to the applications of this information to the problems of the client.

It Gives the Counselor an Opportunity to Know the Clients Better   One of the axioms of guidance is that the counselor must know and understand the clients whom he or she counsels. A course in occupations will not provide the counselor with all that one needs to know. But when the counselor spends half his time in counseling and the other half teaching occupations, he has many opportunities in the classroom to observe the students and to get acquainted with them before and after they come to see him individually.

It Focuses Collective Judgment on Common Problems   Some problems are matters of common interest. Large numbers of students have to make inquiries and decisions on these problems at about the same time. They like to talk about the issues involved. They ought to talk about them. A course in occupations provides an opportunity for students to compare opinions and judgments, not only with one counselor and a few friends, but also with a group of perhaps thirty other students facing the same problem. Members of the group may contribute to one another and to the counselor new ideas and new information that the individual interview would not produce.

It Provides Some Assurance That the Problem Cases Will Not Monopolize the Counselor's Time   It is the normal student, who needs only a little accurate information and a little related counseling in order to solve his or her own problem, with whom the guidance worker has the highest probability of successful results. It is this normal student who gets the least attention in the school that tries to do all its guidance by individual counseling. Despite the best of intentions on the part of both the counselor and the administrator, the problem case always seems to be more urgent. Without a course in occupations the counselor may find that he is investing most of his time where there is the least chance of success.

It Can Be Provided without Increasing the School Budget   If occupations is introduced into the curriculum as a substitute for some less important subject, no addition to the instructional budget is required. This has been done in some states by direction from the state department of education. Some large high schools and colleges have simply made occupations an elective subject and let the students, by their choice of subjects, determine which other courses would have fewer sections.

It May Permit a Part-time Counselor to Spend Full Time on Guidance and Thus to Become More Competent   By including occupations in the instructional program and assigning the counselor to teach the course, it is sometimes possible to relieve the counselor of a teaching assignment in another subject. Thus are provided both the opportunity and the incentive for the counselor to become as competent in his field as the teachers of other subjects are in theirs.

It Keeps the Counselor Up to Date   One of the great weaknesses in the guidance programs of many schools is the fact that the teachers and counselors know so many things about occupations that are not true. If the course in occupations includes plant tours and group conferences, as described later in this book, the participating counselor has his own knowledge of occupations automatically checked and revised every term.

Counselors Recognize the Need for It   Hyde [197] got more than 400 counselors in New York State to list the duties which they regarded as most important. When forty-two separate duties were arranged in order of importance, according to the judgment of these counselors, "group guidance on occupational information" and "group guidance on high school education" were ranked number nine and number ten, respectively. Preceding them in the list were individual counseling with students on six different kinds of problems and conferences with parents and with other members of the school staff. All other duties of counselors—testing, scheduling, compiling cumulative records, program making, supervising student activities, committee work, discipline, forwarding transcripts, correspondence, faculty meetings, reports, etc.—were considered less important than group guidance on occupational information and on high school education.

When the counselors and other guidance workers in Hyde's study were classified by grade level, type of school, etc., into eighteen smaller groups, sixteen of the eighteen groups said they thought they should be devoting more time to "group guidance on occupational information." No group thought they should give less time to it.

SHOULD IT BE REQUIRED?

Opinions differ as to whether occupations courses in high school and college should be required or elective. Bedell and Nelson [16] reported that 87 percent of 311 high school educators ". . . feel that occupational information should be a required part of the high school curriculum." Reports of current practice may be found in a series of articles by Calvert, Carter, Gorman, Hardenbergh, Hoppock, Lowenstein, Murphy, Sinick, Stevens, and Tuxill [40, 51, 52, 173, 183, 185, 187, 188, 251, 348–357, 373–375]. In general, courses in occupations which are offered at the junior high school level appear to be required more often than they are elective. Courses offered in senior high school and college appear more frequently to be elective.

However good the theoretical argument for the required course, the author is convinced that every course should begin as an elective. Too few teachers know how to teach occupations effectively. Too many of the present courses are of little or no value. Keeping the course elective keeps the teacher alert. If the course dies, the students will bury it. When the students who have had the course vote overwhelmingly in favor of making it a required subject, there may be reason for doing so, but when they do that, compulsion probably will not be needed.

SHOULD CREDIT BE GIVEN?

Credit toward graduation is given for occupations courses in many schools and colleges today. Current practice is reported in the articles by Calvert and others mentioned above. In general, the more common practice appears to be to give credit for courses in occupations on the same basis as for other academic subjects. The author is aware of no valid reason why credit should be withheld.

HOW TO FIND SPACE IN THE CURRICULUM

No one who really hopes to see education improved is much impressed by the argument that no new subject can be added because the curriculum is already filled. To accept this argument is to accept the premise that the best subjects are those which got into the curriculum first. If we accepted this premise, we should still require four years of Greek for high school graduation. A new elective subject can be added to any curriculum no matter how crowded when the responsible authorities want to add it. When they do not want to add it, the full curriculum provides a convenient excuse.

Even college-preparatory students usually have room for a few free electives, and Lowenstein [250] has now shown us that college freshmen who had a course in occupations as high school seniors made better grades in college than students from the same school who did not have the course. Some college admissions officers will accept occupations as an academic subject for full academic credit if it is offered by the school as a part of its social studies program and is listed under social studies on the high school transcript. If, however, the transcript classifies occupations with the courses in woodworking and industrial arts, the admissions officer may treat it as a shop course for which he will allow less credit or none.

When Thomas E. Christensen, director of guidance at Worcester, Massachusetts, wanted to add a new elective course in self-appraisal and careers to the high school curriculum, he wrote to the admissions officers of several New England colleges and asked if they would accept this new course as an appropriate academic elective subject for admission to college. Brown, Dartmouth, Harvard, and MIT said they would.

Some schools, of course, may find it easier to introduce a new subject in the general curriculum than in the college preparatory. General-course students certainly need vocational guidance as much as anyone. If pioneer counselors can learn to do a really effective job of teaching occupations in the general curriculum, time will ultimately be found for similar work in other programs.

Some schools have offered summer courses in career exploration. See Stiles [376]. Marland's experience-based career education, described above, devoted a large part of the senior year to it.

WHEN TO TEACH OCCUPATIONS

One accepted principle of educational psychology is that the best time to learn anything is just before we are going to use it. It is then that our interest is highest; it is then that there is the least danger that our knowledge will become obsolete before we use it. The most appropriate time to teach occupations is, therefore, just before or at the time that large enough numbers of persons will need and want substantially the same kinds of occupational information, specifically, during the last term preceding the point at which substantial numbers of students terminate their full-time schooling. Local statistics provide the best basis for locating this point. Likely points are:

Last term preceding end of compulsory attendance
Last term of elementary school
Last term of junior high school or middle school
Last term of senior high school, whether academic, vocational, or comprehensive
Last term of technical institute, business school, or two-year or four-year college
Last term of graduate school

There may be two or more points in any school at which the dropout rate is high enough to warrant a course in occupations.

It is sometimes suggested that a high school course in occupations for students who expect to graduate should be offered in the eleventh grade or the tenth or the ninth, so that the course may help the students to choose their other courses. Certainly students should have all the help they need in planning their high school programs. Some consideration of broad occupational objectives is probably appropriate at this time, but we cannot expect most ninth-grade students, at the age of fourteen, to make occupational choices that they will not want to change before they graduate.

Anyone who has counseled students knows that they make plenty of occupational choices in the elementary school. The same students continue to make more and different occupational choices in high school and in college. The student who graduates and goes immediately to work is more likely to act on the most recent occupational choice than on the choice that was made one or two or three years before.

The first job determines the kind of experience a young person will have to offer when looking for a second job. The first job determines the field in which he will make many of the personal contacts that may lead to the second job. The first job, therefore, may influence the choice of the second job more than we realize. In the same way, the second job may influence the third, and so on, until at the age of forty some persons find themselves trapped in occupations in which they never intended to remain more than a few months. Because of the crucial importance of the first job, it is desirable that the course in occupations be offered at the time when this first job is most likely to be chosen, and that time is when or just before the student goes out to look for a job.

This does not mean that career education programs should be abandoned. The course in occupations is a concentrated form of career education, designed to deliver additional occupational information at the points where it is most needed.

In Vocational and Professional Schools   Most occupations include a variety of jobs among which a choice must be made at the point of placement. A civil engineer may choose between companies which build highways, bridges, dams, and buildings and companies which do not specialize. The civil engineer may work for the government, for industry, or as a teacher in school or college. Some of the potential jobs are stable; some are not. Some are hazardous; some are not. Some provide opportunities for rapid advancement; some do not. A carpenter, plumber, or electrician may work in building construction where the worker will be paid at the top union scale and be frequently unemployed, or may choose a maintenance job in a large retail store or univeristy and be steadily employed at a lower union rate.

In any vocational or professional school may be found seniors who are only vaguely aware of the variety of opportunities available to them and of the effect which their choice among these opportunities may have upon their future lives. Here also may be students who have decided not to enter the field for which they are trained and who need much the same kind of career guidance as the seniors in liberal arts colleges and in the general courses of the high schools. Hence courses in occupations belong in the senior years of vocational and professional schools as well as in other schools and colleges. Such courses have been taught in colleges and departments of agriculture, biology, business, engineering, psychology, and others.

Failures Due to Wrong Timing   Failure to recognize the principle that the best time to learn anything is just before we are going to use it has been responsible for the failure of some attempts at teaching occupations. Historically, vocational guidance was introduced into the public schools of the United States at a time when large numbers of students dropped out of school at the end of the seventh or eighth grade. At that time some courses in occupational information were wisely placed in those grades. Today large numbers of students finish high school before they go to work. They need occupational information in the twelfth grade. They get it in the twelfth grade in some cities. But other schools still teach occupations in the eighth or ninth grade to students who plan to finish high school, and then wonder why the students show so little interest in it.

Elementary and junior high school courses do better when they focus their attention on the problem of educational planning, on the choice of high school subjects; occupational information is then introduced as it is related to this immediate problem. Occupational objectives are not ignored; they are kept as flexible as possible. The emphasis is on a comparison of the broad groups of occupations to which the different high school curricula may lead. Students are helped to compare these groups rather than the specific occupations within the groups. Attention is focused less on the distant objective and more on the immediate decision regarding next year's program. Students, parents, and teachers all can see some sense in this.

Even this plan cannot be blindly copied. The principle is the thing. If large numbers of students still leave one school at the end of the eighth grade, then there is need in that school for occupational information in the last half of the eighth grade.

At the college level the same principles apply. The student who will spend four years in college may need some occupational information in the freshman year as a partial basis for planning his college program. He or she will need more in the senior year when he or she is about to look for a job. Courses are currently offered at both points.

In a "two part look at Career Planning Courses," Powell and McGuire [309] described a one-hour-credit, career planning course, called "Personal Adjustment to Business," offered for thirty years by the College of Business Administration at Indiana University and required of all seniors; and an elective, two-quarter-hour-credit, career planning course offered to liberal arts students at Augustana College, elected mainly by freshmen and sophomores but open to all. Both courses were taught by placement officers.

Faul [119] described one of the most comprehensive college courses in vocational planning, ". . . designed particularly for the student . . . unsure of his vocational goal." The course included self-appraisal, laboratory study, visits to various occupational programs offered by the college, guest speakers from local business and industry, practice with job application forms and letters, practice job interviews which were tape-recorded and played back, and interviews and meetings with the college placement counselor.

An excellent review of college courses in careers appears in Morse and Dressel's stimulating book, *General Education for Personal Maturity* [269]. Four chapters describe the courses at four colleges in some detail. A perceptive appraisal is provided in a concluding chapter by Borow. Other college courses have been described in articles by Calvert, Carter, Fowler, Hardenbergh, Hoppock, Lowenstein, Murphy, Salinger, Stevens, and Tuxill [40, 51, 52, 128, 173, 183, 185, 188, 251, 335, 373, 375]. For an excellent historical and evaluative treatment of college courses in careers, see Holcomb [167].

While the author of this book favors semester or year courses at strategic points, not everyone agrees. Some high schools have offered a four-year program of group guidance taught by the school counselors and meeting one, two, or three periods a week.

Weaver [407] has proposed that

> . . . occupational instruction be provided in each of the four high school grades and that general orientation to the world of work be provided in the last year or so of elementary school. . . . Time can be allocated in segments of increasing length . . . two weeks in the ninth grade, three weeks in the tenth, four weeks in the eleventh, and eight weeks in the twelfth. With allowances made for holidays, the total would be 17 weeks, or the equivalent of one semester.

For college students, Crosby [83] has proposed that

> Vocational guidance should begin in the freshman year and continue through college. It is desirable if it can be designed as a regular course with students meeting once a week, with attendance required, at least until the individual has demonstrated that he is capable of making wise vocational plans and carrying them out. Work during the first two years should include a general introduction to the field, a survey of the various occupations of interest to college graduates, problems involved in self-analysis, and finally a comparison of both subjective and objective factors considered important in choosing a vocation. During the last two years students should concentrate on preparation for placement, first in a general way by exploring employment possibilities, studying company policies, job requirements and duties, salary scales, and promotional opportunities. By the senior year students should register for placement, assemble references, write letters of application, prepare for interviews, and ultimately choose the job which seems to offer the greatest number of satisfactions as well as the best opportunity for personal growth.

The research on vocational development by Super and others, discussed in Chapter 7, has certainly lent support to the view that occupational information should be presented to students continually rather than periodically. With such a program I have no quarrel, *provided it does include* adequate exposure to facts about jobs at those strategic points at which the student is most likely to act on his preferences rather than just to dream about them.

If we could give students accurate information about jobs whenever the students show an interest in their own vocational development, whether this be in kindergarten or in graduate school or in every grade between, we could surely increase the probability of wiser decisions when the student finally goes to look for a job.

Super and Overstreet's [383] research on the vocational maturity of 105 ninth-grade boys in Middletown, New York, confirmed many of the conclusions which experienced teachers and counselors had drawn from their work with ninth-grade students. For example:

> Preferences expressed at the ninth-grade level should not be viewed as definite vocational objectives. . . .
> Vocational objectives should be kept as general as possible early in the student's experience. . . .
> The task of the vocational counselor in the ninth-grade is essentially a matter of furthering vocational development rather than of fostering specific vocational choices.

In their recommendations Super and Overstreet did not mention the prospective dropout who will quit school and go to work at the end of the ninth grade. Despite vocational immaturity, the dropout must make immediate decisions as to where he or she will look for a job and whether or not to take a specific job that is open. These are occupational choices of a highly specific nature and of great potential impact on the future career development of the individual. In work with prospective dropouts, helping them to make specific occupational choices is very much a part of the counselor's job.

In discussing the implications of their research Super and Overstreet suggested that helping the ninth-grade boy

> . . . to get a better understanding of the currently preferred field is not sufficient; he needs to know about other types of occupations which may in due course appeal to him more, and particularly to develop a perspective on the world of work which will enable him to orient himself more quickly to unfamiliar occupations. He needs to know what to look for, where to find out about it. . . . He needs a general framework of occupational information, plus knowledge of how to fill in the details of any part of that framework.

COMBINING EDUCATIONAL AND VOCATIONAL GUIDANCE

At some points in the school program, one group of students may need educational information more than vocational, while another group in the same grade needs vocational information more than educational. For example, in a twelfth-grade class of 100 students, 35 may be going to college and 65 may be looking for jobs. In a large school there should be separate classes for these two groups. Undecided students should have the privilege of attending both classes. In small schools it may be necessary to treat both problems in one class. Where this is done, the teacher must clearly recognize that he or she is teaching two separate subjects, focused on two different problems, and must be extremely careful not to confuse them in his or her own thinking and planning. The teacher may have to use some of the techniques of the rural teacher who has eight grades in a single class in a one-room schoolhouse.

COURSES FOR DROPOUTS

As long ago as 1940 Bergstresser [19] described a course in occupations for prospective dropouts:

In the attempt to meet the special needs of the *pupils* who indicate their intention of *leaving school* at the age of sixteen, the *Providence* schools have inaugurated a new type of course which is called a *pre-employment class.* The teachers of these classes are called pre-employment counselors; they have all had special training in guidance and are especially qualified by experience and interest to deal successfully with the type of young people enrolled in these classes. The pre-employment counselors have these pupils for all of their school work excepting shop courses. In the pre-employment class the counselor devotes a great deal of time and effort to giving the pupils specific, practical preparation for meeting their individual problems of occupational and social post-school adjustment. The counselor also attempts, however, to give the pupils a certain amount of modified instruction in English and social studies. The counselors are given a very free hand to experiment with teaching materials which will function successfully with the pupils, all of whom are, of course, poorly endowed with academic and reading ability.

More recently Flynn and others [124] described a similar course taught to ninth-grade students in Huntington, New York, following which nearly all the prospective dropouts decided to stay in school.

Gardner [134] proposed that the school extend its services to dropouts and graduates after they have terminated their formal education.

Once the young person has left school . . . his educational or vocational future . . . is not usually regarded as a responsibility of the school. But it should be. We should not simply turn these boys and girls out on the streets. They need advice. They need jobs. They need to be helped to think constructively about their own abilities and limitations, about job opportunities, and about their further learning and growth. Bright youngsters are not directed to a library and told to get their own education; they are given guidance. Similarly the young people who go out into the world after high school—and even more urgently those who drop out before graduation from high school—should be helped in order to assure that the years immediately ahead will be years of continued self-development.

To be specific, every high school in the land should provide *continuing* vocational and educational counseling for all who leave school short of college. These services should be available until the boy or girl reaches the age of 21. As things stand today the high school does not provide such follow-up.

The personnel responsible for this service should be professionally equipped to appraise the young person's potentialities. They should be fully acquainted with the kinds of training available outside the formal system, and thoroughly informed on opportunities for work in the area.

Conant [71] strongly endorsed the Gardner recommendation: "To my mind, *guidance officers, especially in the large cities, ought to be given the responsibility for following the post-high school careers of youth from the time they leave school until they are twenty-one years of age."*

Schreader [340] described a start in the direction recommended by Gardner. The Detroit Job Upgrading Program

. . . is to help unemployed young people, 16 to 21 years of age, who have left school before graduation. . . .

Approximately thirty young people are enrolled in each of the seven Job Upgrading units at any one time. These groups meet with their teacher coordinator for three hours each morning Monday through Friday. . . .

Individual conferences, group discussions, filling out application blanks, practice interviews, field trips, educational movies, and parties make up the training. In all activities getting along with others, good manners, good grooming practices, promptness, and care in the completion of each assigned task are stressed as a necessity to becoming a successful worker. . . .

For the young people who need more intensive training . . . there is a six-week subsidized work experience in the afternoons. . . .

Every effort is made to help these young people obtain full time jobs. An important phase of the program is the follow-up service for the first six months they are in private employment.

Slotkin [361] described a similar experimental project which

. . . provides a concentrated pre-certification, pre-employment course of at least 20 days duration to boys and girls who are ready to leave school but are not employed. The objective here is to help students achieve clear, realistic vocational goals; prepare them for entrance employment; and screen them for further guidance and referral.

Upon successful completion of the course, students are placed in employment by the New York State Employment Service. The school counselor visits each boy or girl on the job about once a month until the young person reaches age 17. Those who lose their jobs are required to return to school for further job placement, or for return to full-time or part-time school.

In a later article on the same project Slotkin [359] reported:

The course emphasized job finding . . . techniques and some minimum skills in such things as stock taking, wrapping, typewriting, and traveling about New York City. . . . Stress was placed on the importance of attaining a clear, realistic goal, and the ways in which this can be accomplished. . . .

Since this project dealt with the most alienated and least capable boys and girls, it was to be expected that the first work experience for many would be unsuccessful and disappointing. Patience and persistence were the two principal elements of the post-course follow-up. . . . The record for patience and persistence was established in making seventeen job placements for one boy in a three-month period, the seventeenth being successful.

In the two years since its inception several hundred boys and girls have been served. . . . The unemployment rate of the "graduates" has been checked on four different occasions. . . . At its highest the unemployment rate was less than half that of all sixteen-year-old dropouts, and at its best it was half that of the general population.

GROUP GUIDANCE FOR ALUMNI

Although most modern schools probably would accept the idea that their responsibility to the student and to the community does not end when a student drops out or graduates, relatively few schools have done anything to help their former students during the difficult period of transition and adjustment to work. Some vocational schools provide coordinators who call on young workers and their employers during the first few months of employment. Evening schools and continuation schools serve those who come to them. But the graduate or dropout from the average high school is usually ignored.

Someday, perhaps, a three-year senior high school which now has three counselors, each of whom follows one class through its three years in the school, will add a fourth counselor and then have each counselor follow each class for four years, including the year after graduation. Then, perhaps, we shall have an evening course in occupations, meeting once or twice a week, to which the young alumni and dropouts will be invited and in which they will have opportunity to discuss their common problems of adjustment to work. Topics for discussion may include how to find a job; how to get along with the boss and with fellow workers; whether or not to join a union; when, how, and if one should ask for a raise; how to make suggestions; whether or not to continue education on a part-time basis and where and how to do so; how to build a new social life around community activities to replace the life formerly centered around the school; how to budget, spend, and save money; how to invest savings. Included in the program for this group may well be some social activities to help them maintain old friendships and old contacts during the disconcerting period in which they are learning how to make new ones in a strange environment.

GROUP GUIDANCE FOR ADULTS

Cronin [82, 378] conducted the Seven College Vocational Workshops over a period of four years at Barnard College. Nine successive workshops drew a combined attendance of 422 married women graduates of 123 colleges. Ages ranged from 29 to 70, most of them between 35 and 50.

Each workshop met from 10 A.M. to 2 P.M., once a week for ten weeks. The programs varied, but each included speakers who described the opportunities for mature college women in a wide range of occupations, such as education, social service, science, health, library work, personnel, research, publishing, finance, and public relations; plus opportunities for volunteer work in social and political organizations, how to prepare a résumé of one's qualifications, how to write a letter of application for a job, techniques of job hunting, and what to do during a job interview. Most of the speakers donated their services. After the first workshop three or four "alumnae" from previous workshops were included in the program. Their "true-life stories were encouraging . . . to the students who had begun to acquire know-how and confidence but who were still daunted by the thought of actually braving 'the real world.' "

Follow-up returns from 319 participants revealed approximately 30 percent in paid employment, 30 percent in volunteer work, and 25 percent enrolled in some kind of formal education.

The Seven College workshops have been widely copied and adapted by other colleges, by adult schools, and by community agencies. Programs have varied from one-day sessions to full-semester courses. Commenting on these, Cronin wrote:

> It is our conviction that the ten (or perhaps twelve) week vestibule type of course such as ours is infinitely more effective than the quick-shot career days type of program. . . . For the first four to six weeks SCVW women responded slowly and timidly, though enthusiastically. During the second half of each Workshop they showed that they were getting their bearings, evaluating facts and eliminating fantasies, developing self-knowledge and confidence. Most significant, perhaps, was the inestimable value of the interaction of group members on one another. They derived great comfort from recognizing the similarities in their viewpoints and needs, and a

warm *esprit de corps* developed within the ten weeks. There seemed to be no competition among them but instead there was great reciprocal admiration of individuals' courage and potentialities. It was fascinating to observe this recurring phenomenon.

Somewhat similar courses have been offered at other colleges and by public schools. Some courses have been open to anyone, male or female, who wished to learn more about the opportunities for full-time, part-time, or volunteer work.

Lapidos [231] reported bringing together a group of refugees ". . . for occupational orientation . . . as to what to expect from the American job scene, pay scales, role of unions, training facilities for English, obtaining of social security cards and other basic facts."

Group instruction and other activities, designed to help adults and others to learn effective job hunting techniques, are described in Chapter 20; see the sections "Practice Job Interviews," "Job Clinics," and "Practice on Employment Application Blanks."

WHAT TO INCLUDE

The content of the course in occupations will vary with the purpose, the grade level, the school, the counselor, and the students. No course of study, however perfectly it may function in one school, should ever be adopted in another without critical review by teacher and students to see if it really does meet their own needs better than any other course. Every course of study should be custom-made to fit the needs of the group that it is to serve. Every course should be reviewed annually by teacher and students to see how it may be improved for the next group that is to get it.

We educators are always setting out to reform the world in one semester. One of our worst mistakes is our attempt to do too much. Some of our programs are a hodgepodge, thrown together in the pious hope that if we try enough things, something will probably work, and after all "it won't do the students any harm, will it?"

If our teaching of occupations is to be effective, we must face the fact that some things cannot be done in groups. For some students guidance is a highly individual matter, requiring individual attention in individual interviews. No teaching job is perfect. Some students always miss some points. Some will need facts that are not of sufficiently common interest to warrant inclusion in a group program. Additional information will still have to be given out in the interview. The limitations of the group technique must be clearly recognized. Then we must slough off the things we cannot do and concentrate our efforts on doing well the things that we can reasonably hope to accomplish.

The first rule in planning a course, therefore, is *don't try to do too much.*

The second rule is to *let the students help to plan the course.* Explain to them the general purpose. Describe and list for them some of the things that may be done. Let them suggest others. Let them indicate in some way which items they want most to have included. Then plan the course. We do not have to let the students make the final decision, but if we are going to help students with their problems, certainly we should let them tell us what the problems are.

Following are listed some topics that may be included and some questions that may be answered in courses in occupations. From this list the teacher may select and suggest those which appear to be of probable interest and value to the students. The important thing is to find out what problems the students have now, which of these are of common interest, what factual information will help to solve them, and how best to get and present that information. This is a job for real teachers and for counselors who know their business. It is a job that cannot be done by buying a textbook and following it mechanically.

Because educational planning and occupational planning are so closely related, they are often combined in the same course. Suggested topics in the area of educational guidance are therefore included.

Educational Guidance   We teachers are so familiar with our schools and their programs that we sometimes forget how little our beginning students know about them. John Brewer used to tell of the boy who wanted to know what "al-jib′er-a" was. Biology, geometry, and physics are strange and meaningless words to students who have not encountered them before and, perhaps, to parents of limited education.

College students have their troubles, too. One elects astronomy because he thinks it will be fun on a clear night to point out Mars, Venus, and Saturn to his admiring friends. He expects to learn interesting conversational facts about the heavens; he anticipates a pleasant, not-too-difficult experience, something like an extended visit to a planetarium. Too late, perhaps, he discovers that the course may be just a very advanced study of mathematics.

Because students do not know the nature of subjects nor the goals to which subjects lead, they need and seek information and help in choosing their courses. Some of the information students need concerns their own individual problems and may best be given in individual counseling. Some of it is purely factual and of interest to all and may more economically be given in group guidance.

The strategic times for educational guidance are just before important choices must be made. In large cities with numerous, specialized, four-year vocational high schools, the last half of the eighth grade is the key spot.

The application of this principle is less clear in the choice of a college because of some uncertainty as to when the final choice will be made. No one would question the convenience, to all concerned, of a choice made in the eighth or ninth grade and not subsequently altered. No one would deny that even in schools with good guidance programs, many students reconsider and change their choices in the senior year. Arguing about the undesirability of this procrastination will not change the fact that many students never make final decisions until they must.

It seems desirable, then, that some general consideration be given to types of colleges, and to differences in college entrance requirements, in the eighth- or ninth-grade course on educational opportunities, and that this problem be reviewed in more detail in the eleventh or twelfth grade for the students who are reconsidering their decisions at this point. The latter course should be open to any students in the tenth grade who feel a need for it.

Questions   The group presentation of educational information may save the time of the counselor in answering such questions as the following:

About possible choices: What is the choice that must be made now? Is it between subjects, between curricula, between schools, or between colleges? What are the alternatives?

About the nature of each possible choice: What is a curriculum? How many curricula are there? What subjects do they include? Suppose I don't like the one I choose: may I change?

What does each subject involve? What do you do in the classroom? What kind of homework do you have? What do you learn? Do you have to be bright to learn it?

What is a liberal arts college, a business college, a junior college, a community college, a technical institute? How do they differ? What colleges should I know about and consider? Which ones can I get into? What courses do they offer? What do they cost? Can I get a scholarship?

About where the choices lead: If I take this course, what will it get me? If I study typewriting, can I get a job in an office? If I take home economics, can I be a hospital dietitian? What courses do I need to become a nurse? What is the difference between the general course and the commercial? Will I get a job in an orchestra if I go to the High School of Music and Art? If I take the commercial course now and find out later that I can go to college, will I be able to get in? If I take the college course and find I can't go, will I be prepared for a job?

If I go to college, will I get a better job? What else will a college education give me? What kinds of jobs do liberal arts graduates get, engineering graduates, technical institute graduates?

Some schools have provided courses in which students surveyed possible sources of information about colleges, made trips to colleges, visited college classrooms and laboratories, and discussed fraternities and sororities with college students.

Perhaps one of the most urgent responsibilities we have in educational guidance is to warn students about gyp schools, which employ high-pressure salespersons but which are not accredited. Further discussion of this problem appears in Chapter 20.

No matter how many questions are anticipated, there will always be others. Ample time must be provided in the course to consider any pertinent problems that the students wish to raise.

Occupational Guidance   The primary purpose of courses and units in occupations usually has been to provide a background of information about occupational opportunities. It has been assumed that the probability of wise occupational decisions would increase with the student's knowledge of the jobs he or she might get, and much of the experimental evidence lends support to this assumption. The evidence is reviewed in Chapter 25.

If we may assume that the job of educational guidance has been properly done and that related occupational information has been introduced as needed, then the proper time for orientation to occupational opportunities is just before the student goes out to look for a job. For prospective graduates this means the last half of the senior year. For prospective dropouts it means just before they drop out. In small schools prospective dropouts may be invited to join the course planned for seniors. In larger schools separate courses may be organized for those who expect to leave before graduation. The same basic principle applies to elementary schools, secondary schools, colleges, graduate schools, and institutions in the field of adult education. If large numbers terminate their education and go to work at the end of the twelfth and fourteenth grades, then these are the grades in which to teach occupations.

The course in occupations undertakes to save the time of the counselor in answering such questions as the following:

What jobs are open to us? What jobs did previous dropouts and graduates get? Where? What places hire the largest numbers of young people? In what kinds of business can I be my own employer?

What do you have to do in them? What is a typical day's work? How does it differ from what most people think it involves?

What does it take to get them? Are there rigid requirements of age, height, weight, vision, and union membership? What aptitudes are essential and desirable? Must you have a license? How do you get it?

What preparation is required? How much? What kind? Do I have it?

What of the future? Which occupations and which businesses are growing? Which are declining? What are the opportunities for advancement?

What do they pay? At the beginning, after five years, after ten? Is the work steady, or are there layoffs in slack seasons and in depressions?

What do the workers like and dislike about them?

These few questions expand rapidly into dozens of others related to them. A detailed outline for the study of any one occupation appears in Chapter 3.

The occupations selected for study should include the following, in order of importance:

1 The occupations in which substantial proportions of former students have found employment
2 Other major occupations in the geographical area in which dropouts and graduates look for jobs
3 Other occupations of interest to the students

It is not uncommon practice to begin with the occupations in which the students are most interested. There are obvious psychological advantages in this procedure, provided it does not prevent a reasonable allocation of time to the occupations which most of them are likely to enter.

Numerous studies have revealed the sharp contrast between the occupations in which high school seniors express an interest and the occupations in which follow-up studies show them to be employed a year later. It becomes, therefore, the responsibility of the teacher to see that they learn something about the occupations in which they are most likely to find employment. Half of the students in any class will be below the median ability level of the group. Approximately half of the occupations studied should accordingly be occupations open to students below this median level of ability.

Another important caution for the teacher of occupations is to keep attention focused on beginning jobs. High school students do not choose jobs as bankers, buyers, and fashion designers. They may think they do, but what they really choose are beginning jobs as bank clerks, salesclerks, and alteration workers. College graduates may start a little higher, but not much. They may hope some day to reach the top, but cold statistics indicate that very few of them do. No amount of education, no amount of inspiration, and no amount of career guidance will change the fact that the great bulk of human workers must always be employed on the lower levels. The reader has no doubt heard remarks about organizations which had too many chiefs and not enough Indians.

Because most of our students will remain in, or near, the jobs at which they begin, it is imperative that most of our attention be given to such jobs. Opportunities for promotion need not be concealed, but they should not be overemphasized. If we are going to be realistic and truthful and if we are not going to contribute to future frustration, we must abandon the inspirational ballyhoo that anyone can be president, and we must encourage our students to choose occupations in which they may hope to be reasonably contented if cherished promotions do not materialize.

An excellent example of the kind of realistic occupational information that students need and that schools can supply may be found in Christensen's resource units [58], from which the following excerpts are taken:

> Since many of our present students will find employment in Worcester either after high school graduation or post high school education they should become acquainted with Worcester's occupational opportunitites. . . .
>
> In recent years about one-half of Worcester's high school graduates have gone into full-time jobs.
>
> The majority of boys who go to work after high school graduation are employed in manufacturing or related trade industries.
>
> Most girls who go to work immediately after high school graduation do clerical work.
>
> For the past few years, most of the girls who go into clerical work have begun work in finance, insurance, or real estate industries.
>
> Some girls also go into offices of manufacturing plants, and into stores to do clerical work.
>
> Entry jobs in the factory itself for both boys and girls include bench assemblers, scraper hands, and foundry helpers, also stock boys. . . .
>
> More people in Worcester find work in the metal-working industries than in any other area of industry.
>
> Metal-working industries include many skilled and semi-skilled jobs.
>
> In the metal-working industries, there are opportunities as electricians, machine tool operators, machinists, moulders, pattern makers, sheet metal workers and structural workers.
>
> Training for some of the jobs in the metal-working industries must be acquired either through long apprenticeship or in the Worcester Boys' Trade High School and for others, through on-the-job training. . . .

There are a number of printing companies in Worcester which offer opportunities for those who have had some training in printing at Boys' or Girls' Trade High Schools. . . .

High school graduates without clerical training have been employed as general clerks, file clerks, messengers, office machine operators and telephone operators.

The follow-up study of the Guidance Departments each year shows the number of graduates entering the various Worcester industries. . . .

Four out of five persons remain in Worcester to earn a living. . . .

Most craftsmen learn their skills through apprenticeship under the supervision of a journeyman.

Carpenters, construction laborers, painters, and plumbers in manufacturing and construction industries lead the number of skilled workers. . . .

Most semi-skilled work is routine, but it appeals to many workers for they like to work with machines and find satisfaction in being able to see what they have done for the day.

Operative work requires little physical strength, because most machines are controlled by levers. Those who enter operative occupations must be able to stand the routine work and must have patience and coordination to learn to operate a machine fast enough to earn good wages.

Selling is not a typical entry occupation for young people. Only about 1% of the female graduates enter selling occupations and 4% of the males. . . .

The semi-professions include many workers such as technicians who assist engineers, scientists, physicians, and other personnel.

Some of these technicians include draftsmen, engineering aides, electronic, laboratory, or x-ray technicians. . . .

Approximately two years of formal training is required for semi-professional occupations. Training can be obtained in technical institutes and junior colleges. . . .

Because of the great number of college students graduating today, we shall have many more business administration graduates seeking executive positions in industry in the future.

There will continue to be opportunities for persons without college degrees, however, especially in small self-managed businesses. . . .

A survey of the Worcester job conferences revealed that a majority of the students were interested in and attended conferences on professional occupations, yet only 9% actually enter schools for professional training. . . .

There is one large category of employment frequently omitted from courses and units in occupations. It is the area of self-employment. Every town has its independent grocers, clothing merchants, barbers, beauty-parlor operators, small building contractors, plumbers, electricians, etc., who are their own employers. Most of them have a certain aptitude and skill in the management of their own affairs. It is just as much the job of the counselor to reveal opportunities for the utilization of this aptitude as it is to reveal opportunities for musical, artistic, or any other talent.

In self-employment the danger of failure and the rewards of success both tend to be higher than in other kinds of work. The risks should not be minimized; the opportunities should not be overlooked. If the class in occupations is to tour large local industries, it should tour small plants too. If personnel directors from large companies are invited to meet with the class to discuss employment opportunities in their companies, the proprietors of small businesses should be invited to discuss their occupations. If occupational pamphlets are to be displayed, the display should include pamphlets which describe the opportunities in self-employment.

Members of minority groups may sometimes circumvent discrimination by choosing an area in which they may be their own employers. So also may handicapped workers.

Helpful information is provided on request by the U.S. Small Business Administration, Washington, D.C. The Bank of America, P.O. Box 37000, San Francisco, California 94137, publishes the *Small Business Reporter,* each issue of which describes one kind of small business.

Teachers and counselors who wish to help students explore the possibilities of self-employment may write to Junior Achievement, 909 Third Ave., New York 10022, for information on a youth program in this area.

Some colleges now offer courses in how to get a job. Some instruction of this kind is included in many group guidance programs. More of it may be expected as more educators learn that most people do not get jobs through employment agencies.

Despite individual exceptions in the cases of some well-organized school and college placement services, many studies have shown that more than half of the people who get jobs obtain them through relatives and friends and by direct personal application to the employer. The effectiveness of these employment channels is due not so much to nepotism as to the fact that many small employers hire the first well-qualified applicant who applies and also show a distinct preference for applicants recommended by persons known to the employer. Relatives and friends can help the job applicant to learn about vacancies before they are advertised and can recommend him to employers who will place some confidence in the recommendation. The function of instruction in this area is to make students familiar with the more effective techniques of job hunting, including how to use relatives and friends ethically and effectively. These techniques are described in numerous books on the subject, available in most libraries.

Cuony [84] included job-finding techniques in a successful experimental course for high school seniors, which is described briefly in Chapter 25.

College courses in job-seeking techniques were briefly described by Calvert, Carter, and Murphy [40]. Lansner [230] described a short course in job-hunting techniques offered to college seniors by the college placement director. Keegan [216] described a similar course. Reeves [317] surveyed the ways in which job-getting techniques were presented to college students and reactions to these presentations. She found 60 colleges with courses in job finding, among 426 institutions which gave substantial assistance of some kind.

Other activities and other references designed to help students and adults to find jobs are described in Chapter 20; see the sections "Practice Job Interviews," "Job Clinics," and "Practice on Employment Application Blanks."

Special classes for children with retarded mental development often include instruction in the nature of the jobs open to them, how to get a job, and what to do when they lose their jobs.

In some states students who go to work before the age of eighteen are required to have working papers and should be familiar with some of the child labor laws. All students who are about to go to work should learn something about workmen's compensation, unemployment compensation, and social security. The education departments and the labor departments of several states have prepared bulletins for students and for counselors, summarizing essential information about employment certificates and related labor legislation. A letter to the state capital will bring samples. The U.S. Department of Labor also has published useful pamphlets on these subjects.

The Center for Vocational and Technical Education at Ohio State University is currently engaged in a project which is expected to produce curricular units and/or guidance methods designed to facilitate the student's resourcefulness and adaptability in coping with the problems encountered in the transition from school to work, including aspirations and expectations, attitudes and values, layoffs and rejections, alienation and communication, new roles, and behavior on the job.

Ross [325] reported the concepts of occupational information, essential in the general education of secondary school students, selected by a jury of educators from an original list of 720 items.

Darcy [88] described a course designed to "explain jobs in terms of social and psychological impact on the worker . . . ways in which employment influences a worker's life style."

There is still some difference of opinion among the textbook writers as to whether the major emphasis of the course or unit in occupations should be on current facts about jobs or on the technique of discovering such facts. Some writers have maintained that it is more important to teach the technique than to teach the facts, because the facts will go out of date while the technique will remain effective and because it is impossible to teach all facts about all occupations in any reasonable time. Certainly it is desirable for anyone to know where and how to get facts about jobs. But learning the sources of occupational information need not preclude learning immediately useful facts about current occupational opportunities. On the contrary, one of the best ways to learn the technique is to practice using it. The teacher who wishes to place the major emphasis upon sources of information and upon the methods of choosing an occupation will be particularly interested in Chapters 17, 18, and 19, "Case Conference," "Laboratory Study," and "Self-measurement," in this book. If any further argument is needed for including facts about jobs, the answer to their becoming obsolete is to teach them just before they are to be used, and the answer to the impossibility of teaching everything about all occupations is to do what we do in every other subject, namely, select the more important facts and teach them.

Whether we place major emphasis upon facts about jobs or upon how to get the facts, any course or unit in occupations should include somewhere some consideration of common errors in choosing an occupation, such as hero worship, overestimation of one's abilities or of employment opportunity, misconception regarding the nature of the work, other misinformation or lack of information about the occupation, and reliance upon recruiting literature and other biased sources of information.

Williamson [415] noted several errors of thinking which may lead to unwise occupational choices. Borow [25], in a thoughtful article, suggested conditions under which college courses in vocational planning function most effectively.

Redefer and Reeves [315] included an excellent chapter on how to teach college courses in career planning in their book on *Careers in Education.*

For additional suggestions on what to include in a course in occupations the reader may wish to review Chapters 2 and 3.

WHO SHOULD TEACH IT?

As with any other subject, the teacher should be a person who wants to teach it and who is already, or is eager to become, thoroughly competent in both the subject matter and the methods of teaching it. Potentially good prospects are:

Full-time teachers of this subject, who can give as much time to it as teachers of other subjects give to theirs.

Placement officers whose major task is helping their clients to choose and find jobs.

Career information consultants and directors of career resource centers who work full time compiling, evaluating, and using occupational information. See Chapter 23.

Counselors who work with students and clients on problems of career planning.

Teachers of related subjects, such as business education, industrial arts, and occupational education.

Other teachers who have demonstrated their interest in the subject by already doing something about it on their own time, perhaps as part of a career education program, or by voluntarily introducing units on occupations into their own courses.

In the best schools courses and units in occupations are taught by persons as well trained for this job as the teachers of chemistry, geometry, and French are for theirs. Once in a while a superior English teacher or social studies teacher does a brilliant job of teaching occupations—as the same superior teacher might do a brilliant job if assigned to trigonometry. But the miserably dull courses in school after school have long since demonstrated the futility of trying to get good instruction in occupations from teachers who have not been specifically trained for this work.

Some schools ask all teachers of other subjects to include in their courses some consideration of occupations in which these courses are useful. When well done by a teacher who wants to do it, this kind of teaching may have real value. At best, however, it is only a supplement to, and never an adequate substitute for, a course in occupations. Too many important occupations are not clearly connected with any academic subject. For more on this topic see the section "Presenting Occupational Information through Other Subjects" in Chapter 20.

On a college campus the best person to teach occupations is likely to be the college placement officer or someone on the college placement staff who is in daily contact with both job seekers and employers.

In high school the counselor is the logical choice, if he or she is eager to accept the assignment and willing to work on it. Individual counseling interviews reveal the problems which are common to the group. Class discussions lead some students to seek individual interviews. When these students come for interviews, the counselor has already had some acquaintance with them. Thus each part of the job reinforces the other.

Lapidos [231] has observed that ". . . from the point of view of the counselor, this approach enables one to observe the individual in a group setting, to evaluate his social responses, and ability to function in the interpersonal relations area. This opportunity for observation is rarely available to the individual counselor."

Christensen [59] described the course in self-appraisal and careers offered in the high schools of Worcester, Massachusetts, which was taught only by professionally trained counselors. Each teacher of the course served also as the counselor for the students in his or her section and had released time for individual counseling with each student.

Fox [129], Kenyon [217], and Sutherland [386] have described other high school and college courses taught by counselors. Unfortunately some counselors will never teach occupations, because their major interests are in other aspects of guidance. Where this is the case, occupations may be better taught by a classroom teacher who wants to teach it and who will take the trouble to learn how to teach it.

A counselor can always find plenty of excuses for not keeping his or her own occupational information up to date. When one fails to do this and makes no provision for anyone else to do it, students frequently receive misinformation, based on what the counselor thinks is true or what was true three years ago or what the student or client can dig out from a file which is always partly obsolete.

Students would get much better occupational information if there were one person in each school and college whose major job were to be an expert on the major occupations which the school's alumni usually enter—specifically, a fulltime teacher of occupations, hired and retained and promoted mainly because of his or her knowledge of the subject and skill in teaching it, or an occupational information consultant as described in Chapter 23. Candidates for either of these assignments may sometimes be found among teachers of business education, industrial arts, and vocational education.

With such a person on the faculty, a student could get as good information about jobs as he or she can now get about chemistry.

Somehow, if we are ever to do a good job of career guidance, we must provide in every high school and college an elective course in occupations taught by a teacher or counselor who is as competent in this area as the teacher of science is in his.

Throughout the remainder of this book it is assumed that the school counselor will be the teacher of occupations, and the words "teacher" and "counselor" are used interchangeably.

PROTECT TIME ASSIGNED FOR COUNSELING

When the teaching of occupations is assigned to counselors, the administrator must be careful to see to it that the total hours available for individual counseling are not thereby reduced. Every hour that the counselor spends in class releases for one hour a teacher who would otherwise be instructing the same students in some other subject. The hours thus saved should be reserved to replace the counseling time which the counselor now devotes to teaching.

To illustrate how this may be done, imagine the following: In a high school five periods of classroom teaching per day constitute a normal load. The school has had two full-time counselors and no group guidance. The school now proposes to introduce three elective sections of a course in educational planning for freshmen and two elective sections of a course in occupations for seniors. The total of five sections will be divided among the counselors. These five sections will replace five sections of other courses that were formerly taught by other teachers. The teaching time thus released is five periods, the equivalent of a full load for one person. This released time is used to add a third counselor to the guidance staff. These three counselors now divide the five group guidance sections among them.

The net effect of this arrangement is that five periods of group guidance have now replaced five periods of other subjects, three persons are assigned to guidance instead of two, these three persons now divide the responsibility for individual counseling and for group guidance, the hours available for individual counseling remain unchanged, and the budget has not been affected at all.

For another illustration, imagine a small high school which has had one part-time counselor giving three periods a day to counseling and two periods to teaching English. Two periods of group guidance are introduced to replace two discontinued sections of some other subject. Teaching assignments are shifted so that the counselor now teaches the two sections of group guidance while someone else teaches the two sections of English. The counselor can now devote full attention to guidance and gradually become as competent in guidance as he formerly was in English. The time available for individual counseling is unchanged, and the budget is not affected.

The school which is too small to have even one full-time guidance person will have to struggle along with part-time service. Expected results should be cut about 50 percent. A teacher who has to keep up to date in two fields obviously can do only about half as much in each as the full-time specialist. Virginia Hartman has well expressed the difficulties.

> I find that being a teacher-counselor creates more necessity for added preparation even though my class load is lessened, because essentially the same procedures must be followed to do an effective job of teaching and in addition and at the same time I have to learn and assimilate all the information and techniques I can to do an effective job of counseling. I desperately need more time for organization and overall planning for both jobs, and the days just aren't long enough.

METHODS OF TEACHING OCCUPATIONS

Teaching the textbook is the natural resort of teachers who have been trained in other subjects and assigned to teach occupations without training. It is one of the quickest ways to destroy student interest unless the teaching is superb. There are some good teaching ideas in textbooks. Judiciously used, they can be helpful. But to be effective the teaching of occupations must be related to local problems. To be interesting the course must be taught by methods adapted to its peculiar purposes. It cannot be taught by the traditional method of chapter assignment, reading, and recitation.

No two teachers can teach equally well by the same method. Every good teacher must experiment until he finds which techniques work best for him. Techniques which various teachers of occupations have tried and liked are described in the next several chapters. Most of these techniques can be used in any course or unit on occupations. Some can be used for one day and repeated or not. Some require continuity over a longer period. Some can be and have been used for a full-semester course. Some can be used as separate projects, not connected with any course.

The beginner is perhaps more likely to try too many methods than too few. He is advised, therefore, to select one method which appeals to him, to plan the first course largely around this method, and to introduce other methods during the first term only to provide variety when it is felt that variety is needed. The teacher should keep all plans flexible and have a second and a third method ready to substitute if the first proves unsatisfactory.

REVIEW QUESTIONS

1 Do you think career education will achieve its purposes? Why? Why not?
2 Do you think career education will compete with or support academic education and vocational education?
3 How do you feel about the Urban League's concerns about career education?
4 Of the reasons offered for the teaching of occupations, which do you find most convincing? About which are you skeptical? Why?
5 Do you think courses in occupations should be required or elective? Why?
6 Are courses in occupations ever accepted for college entrance credit? Do you think they should be? Why? Why not?
7 What basic principle should determine when the course in occupations will be taught?
8 Is there a place for a course in occupations in a vocational or professional school? Why or why not?
9 In what order of importance should occupations be selected for study?
10 Why should attention be focused on entry jobs?
11 What large category of employment is frequently omitted from courses in occupations?
12 Through what media do most people get jobs? What are the implications of this fact for the teaching of occupations?
13 Do you agree or disagree with the author's position on the teaching of facts about jobs versus teaching how to get the facts? Why?
14 Who should teach the course in occupations? Why?
15 Will anything in this chapter affect your future thoughts and actions? What? How?

Chapter 13

Students Follow Up Alumni

Anyone who hopes to do any effective career counseling must first find out what kinds of jobs previous students or clients of the school, college, or agency were able to get in the open competition of the employment market. This knowledge is indispensable. No kind of occupational information is more important or more useful. With this information the counselor can help the client to make plans that have some prospect of effective implementation. Without this information both counselor and client may be dealing in fantasy. This does not mean that one should never try to do anything that has not been done before, but that both client and counselor should know whether or not others *have* tried it before, and what happened when they did. Such information may be either encouraging or discouraging.

PURPOSE

Follow-up studies are made by many persons for many purposes. In this chapter we are concerned mainly with the follow-up study as a means of enhancing the career awareness and the career orientation of students, and as a means of giving them a more realistic picture of their probable employment opportunities, by helping them to find out what has happened to those who have preceded them.

Two persistent problems of the counselor are the discouraged, minority-group student who is convinced that nobody wants him, and the naïvely optimistic student who confidently anticipates success where few ever attain it.

By participating in a follow-up study, and by examining the results of previous studies, the discouraged student or the disabled adult who believes there are no opportunities for him may discover an encouraging variety of desirable jobs in which former students or clients like him or her are already employed. Thus some much-needed role models may be found. On the other hand, the student whose present plans have little chance of being realized may discover what happened to other students with similar plans, and may then add to his or her plans a second-choice occupation in case it is needed.

Many other high school and college students have disturbingly limited knowledge of the employment opportunities which they may expect to find when they are ready to look for a job. As a result their plans are often vague, unrealistic, and restricted to the few occupations with which they are familiar. Their concepts of entry jobs are reflected in the popular caricatures of the college student who wants to start as an executive. Their salary expectations are based on rumors they have heard about the fabulous earnings of an atypical few. Regrettably, in the area of occupational opportunities, some counselors are almost as naïve as their clients. For counselors a follow-up study can be an enjoyable experience in self-education.

PROCEDURE

A follow-up study may be made at surprisingly little cost when it becomes the project of an interested group of students or clients. As a teaching device it has the advantages of human interest, live material, and direct contact with original sources. It has been used by the author with both high school and college students; both groups have been enthusiastic about it. It may be used for an entire course, for a part of a course or unit, for a career awareness project in elementary school, or for a club program independent of any course. It may even be made by a small committee assembled for this purpose alone. A similar procedure was used by Ruderman [330] with a group of federal prisoners who followed up the "alumni" of their institution. Other variations of the technique are described near the end of this chapter.

Any project of this kind, which involves public relations, should first be discussed with, and approved by, the counselor's immediate superior. There are many different ways to conduct a follow-up study and to use the results. For the sake of simplicity, one method will be suggested; the reader should not hesitate to vary the procedure in order to suit his or her own and the students' purposes and preferences.

In the remainder of this chapter the word "teacher" may be interpreted to include counselor and group leader, and the word "student" to include client and group member.

Preparing the Questions The teacher, counselor, or group leader describes the project to the group and invites them to suggest questions which they would like to ask former students about their present jobs. As questions are suggested, they are written on the blackboard *in the words of the students* who suggest them. If a student has trouble in wording a question, the teacher may help. If the student's words are hopelessly ambiguous or confusing, the teacher may try to frame the question in simpler form and ask the student if this expresses the idea. But so far as possible, editing of questions by the teacher should be avoided at this point. There will be plenty of opportunity to edit the questions later. The task now is to encourage the students to think about what they want to know and to formulate their own questions. Public correction of a student's errors in composition may discourage other students from offering their own contributions lest they be similarly corrected.

Each question is numbered as it is written on the board. When the students exhaust their ideas or the teacher feels that enough time has been spent on them, the suggestions are stopped and the students are invited to consider which of the questions are most important to them. The teacher explains that too many questions will reduce the number of persons who will respond. Each student is asked to select the five questions which are most important to him and to write the numbers of these questions on a piece of paper.

The teacher announces that he reserves the right to add a few questions of his own and to edit the questions selected, but he assures the students that their preferences will be considered in the final choice of questions to be asked. Students usually do not mind a little teacher participation in the class if they are permitted to make some of the decisions themselves.

The teacher then asks how many students chose question number one. A student counts the raised hands; another student writes the total on the board beside the question. The teacher repeats this process with each question. Each student has chosen five questions, so each student may raise his hand five times, but not more than five. Some students like the idea of having five "votes."

When the votes for all the questions have been tabulated, the teacher announces that the five most popular questions will be included in the study and repeats that he will add a few of his own. If the teacher sees that the sixth and seventh most popular questions are ones which he would include as his own, he may accept them in lieu of some that he would ask.

The teacher announces that these questions will be incorporated in a letter which will be sent to all of last year's graduates and dropouts. Two or more of the best students are asked to copy the names and addresses of these former students from the school records. Each name and address should be put on a separate card. When some current addresses are unknown, they can sometimes be found by asking students, teachers, and respondents if they know how to reach the missing persons.

Preparing the Letter The teacher drafts a letter including the students' questions and his own. The following form is suggested as a guide:

Dear _____

Our class is writing to former students in order to learn something about the kinds of jobs that may be open to us when we finish school. I am a member of the class, and I am writing to ask if you will be kind enough to tell us something about your own experience.

What we would like best would be a letter, telling us as much as your time permits about the answers to these questions:

What is your present job?

Just what do you do?

How did you get your job?

How much do you earn? Or what do jobs like yours usually pay?

What do you like about your job?

What do you dislike about it?

What advice would you give to one of us who wants to do what you are doing?

If the answers to any of these questions are confidential, will you please tell me how far I may go in reporting them to the other members of the class? Replies which are not confidential will be shown to other students in this and in future classes.

I am sure you know how grateful we will be for any information you may send us. We do want to know what we are getting into. You who have gone before are the ones who can tell us best.

Sincerely yours, . . .

Mailing the Letters   The letters are duplicated and brought to class, along with the cards containing the names and addresses of the former students and an adequate supply of envelopes and stamps. The names, the letters, and the envelopes are evenly divided among the students. Students who wish may be permitted to choose the names of their friends from those on the cards. Each student takes the first of his cards, addresses an envelope to this person, fills in the salutation on one of the duplicated letters, signs it, and puts the letter in the addressed envelope. He does not seal the envelope yet. He repeats this process with each name. He puts his own name and the date on the back of each address card to provide a record of who wrote to whom. Then he addresses an equal number of return envelopes to himself, in care of the teacher, at the school. When all the student's letters and envelopes are ready, he shows them to the teacher, receives the necessary stamps, puts one stamp on each return envelope, inserts it with the letter in an envelope addressed to a former student, seals and stamps this envelope. When all his letters are ready to be mailed, he returns them to the teacher, who sees that they are mailed. A committee of dependable students may be assigned to mail the letters.

It is important that the letters be addressed in class and mailed at once. Experience indicates that when this task is assigned as homework too many students postpone it too long. It is also important that the return envelopes be addressed to the student in care of the teacher at the school; if they are addressed to the student at his home, too many students forget to bring the replies to school.

Discussing the Replies   Replies will not arrive the day after the letters are mailed. For five or ten days the teacher must plan interim activities for the class. Sometime in the second week there will usually be enough responses to provide material for a class session.

When the replies do come in, the teacher takes them to class, unopened, and gives them to the students, who immediately open and read them. The teacher then invites one student at a time to read his letter to the group, omitting any parts that are confidential. The students are invited to interrupt at any time they wish to raise a question or to make a comment. The teacher takes the real responsibility for selecting statements in the replies that are worth discussion. Whenever such a statement appears, the teacher interrupts and raises a question for discussion, emphasizes the importance of the statement just read, or, possibly, disagrees with it. When the letter is completed, the teacher inquires if anyone wishes to raise any question or make any comment, then calls on someone in another part of the room to read one of his replies. Sometimes two or three letters are read with no questions and no comments. At other times an entire period may be devoted to discussing one or two letters.

Some of the author's students have suggested that the discussion periods might be more profitable if the instructor would begin each period by inquiring what jobs were represented in the letters at hand and then selecting the letters to be read so that a good sampling of jobs would be presented.

Students have suggested also that the instructor be alert to opportunities to draw all the students into the class discussion. For example, when salaries are mentioned, the instructor may interrupt to inquire how many others have letters from persons in similar jobs, what they earn, how many have letters from people earning more money, what jobs they have, etc.

At the end of the class period all letters are returned to the teacher, who may collect separately those which have been discussed and those which have not. The discussion continues for as many days as letters are available or until the class or the teacher decides that further discussion would not be beneficial.

After the letters are discussed, they may be given to a class secretary or a committee who will compile a statistical summary. At the end of the course each student receives a copy of the summary.

In most of the discussions the teacher seeks first to draw comments from the class. After giving them ample opportunity to state their own ideas, the teacher contributes additional comments, sometimes agreeing with and emphasizing a point made by one of the students, sometimes gently disagreeing, and sometimes adding information. The teacher may be surprised and encouraged by the frequency with which the students themselves will draw from the letters the very inferences and conclusions which the teacher would otherwise call to their attention. The advantage of this procedure as a teaching technique is, of course, that the student having thought of an idea, having publicly expressed it, and having heard it publicly approved is more likely to value it and to remember it than if it had been presented in lecture form. In a lecture, if he were a bit inattentive, he might not even hear it. In the rapid-fire conversation of a class discussion it is difficult not to pay attention.

The alert teacher can find in the responses of former students live human-interest material on which to base discussions of many kinds. The arrangement of topics discussed will follow no nicely logical syllabus, but what is lost in continuity may be more than made up in the use of material that is interesting and vital to the students because they can see it functioning in the lives of former students who are doing now what the present students hope to be doing the following year. Beginners who have had little experience in leading discussion groups may find helpful suggestions in Appendix B.

The request for a response in letter form is imperative if the teacher plans to use the responses as a basis for class discussion. Respondents who write letters express opinions and relate experiences which invite discussion, as the brief responses to printed questionnaires do not. The number of responses will be smaller when a letter is requested, but the quality will more than compensate. One study of this kind at the college level brought responses from 32 percent of the former students. This is 8 percent less than the national average return for questionnaire studies using only one request. A higher percentage response can be obtained by sending additional letters at intervals of two weeks to the persons who have not responded. If the follow-up study is made in order to collect statistical data rather than to provide provocative material for class discussion, the conventional questionnaire will probably bring a larger proportion of returns, with the data in more convenient form for tabulation.

The eagerness with which students open and read the replies will convince any teacher that it really is important to have the letters addressed to them. This procedure and the active part which the students have in determining what questions will be asked give them the feeling that this is really their project. Natural human interest is reinforced by the fact that some of the respondents are close personal friends of the students, and they mix highly personal communications with replies to the questions. In such cases, the students may be permitted to withhold the personal parts and to copy on a separate sheet the replies to the questions. This sheet may be given to the teacher instead of the entire letter.

Teachers sometimes ask, "What's the use of trying to follow up students when they are in the army? How are you going to reach them? And if you do, what good will the information be?" An actual reply from an alumnus will indicate the material that can be obtained for use in orientation of students about to enter the service:

> **Question:** What advice would you give to this year's seniors who will be in the service next year?
>
> **Answer:** Prepare yourself for a terrific physical and mental readjustment!!! Forget right now all the movies you've seen, all the story book glamour you've heard about the army—the air force in particular. There is no glamour other than that of damn hard teamwork. You must learn to live, eat, and drink with all kinds and conditions of men and to get along with them all. You must be prepared to lead a life in which you as an individual will cease to exist save as a number on a filing card.

Summarizing the Data   The students should have a part in deciding which items will be included in the statistical summary. Among the items which they may wish to consider are the following:

A list of employers who hired dropouts and graduates, with each employer's address, the jobs for which former students were hired, and the number of persons hired for each job category.

A list of occupations in which the former students are now employed, the number employed in each, and the range of beginning wages, with the occupations arranged in descending order of numbers employed.

A similar list of occupations in which the respondents are employed, with their employers listed under each occupation. Employers and wages should not be shown in the same table unless the counselor first verifies the data. A few unfortunate errors may antagonize employers whose goodwill the counselor wants.

A list of the available high school curricula or college majors, showing the present occupations of the alumni from each curriculum or major.

Expressed likes and dislikes of workers in different occupations.

Suggestions made by dropouts and graduates, which the class has discussed and which a majority of the class considered to be sound.

Methods by which former students got their jobs, with the number who reported each method.

When the statistical summary has been completed, some of the interesting discoveries may be selected from it and included in a news release prepared by the class, by a committee, or by the teacher. This release should be submitted to the principal for approval and then sent to the local newspapers, including the school or college paper and the alumni news.

Bias of Incomplete Returns　　Baer and Roeber [13] in their second edition reviewed several researches on bias in follow-up returns. These researches suggest that incomplete returns are likely to be weighted with proportionately more replies from certain groups which tend to respond more readily than their opposites. The groups which tend to respond in larger proportions are graduates as opposed to dropouts, recent graduates as opposed to older graduates, girls as opposed to boys, and students near the top of their class in school grades as opposed to students near the bottom.

Because of these biases, careful research workers try to get as nearly complete returns as possible.

Mooren and Rothney [267] achieved a 100 percent return. Ganley [133] and Christensen [57] got 98 percent. Many persons have reached 90 percent or better. To get better than 90 percent may require telephone calls or visits to homes and places of employment, although Mooren and Rothney got 95 percent with four successive letters.

Jackson and Rothney [200] compared responses given by the same fifty persons to the same questions asked on a questionnaire and in a recorded interview five years after graduation from high school. They found that

> For every dollar spent for the mailed questionnaire study, approximately $60 was spent on the interview procedure. . . .
> Interviews elicited significantly more complete answers. . . .
> Each . . . procedure elicited evidence . . . which did not appear on the other.

The counselor whose time and facilities do not permit such persistent research should not be deterred from getting such data as he can. Despite all the inaccuracies that may creep into the results, even a small response will bring useful, interesting, and sometimes surprising information.

Postcards or envelopes for the future follow-up may be addressed by seniors to themselves just before graduation. The seniors may also be invited to suggest questions for inclusion in the questionnaire which they will receive; the more they participate in preparing for the follow-up, the more likely they may be to respond when the time comes to do so. An offer to send a summary of the results to those who respond, with present addresses of all who reply, may help to increase the number who respond.

Many years ago 200 schools cooperated with the National Association of Secondary School Principals in testing a variety of procedures for conducting follow-up studies. Forty of the schools were visited by members of the project staff. What was learned from this experiment has been ably reported by Beery, Hayes, and Landy [17]. Their report is still one of the best of all references on follow-up work.

Business firms experienced in direct-mail advertising have found that they can profitably use as many as ten or more different letters in series on the same prospects. From carefully controlled tests these firms have found that return envelopes of pink or goldenrod paper produce slightly more returns than those of white, blue, or green. A letter enclosing a return envelope brings more replies than one without it.

Other Considerations   When accurate data are imperative, the questionnaire must be carefully prepared to avoid ambiguity. When earnings are to be reported, the question should indicate whether hourly, weekly, monthly, or annual earnings are to be recorded and whether take-home pay or earnings before deductions are desired. Part-time work should be distinguished from full-time by some clear definition; full-time has sometimes been defined as employment for more than twenty hours a week.

The graduates and dropouts to be approached in any follow-up study should include those whose separation from the school occurred approximately a year earlier. Some schools also include graduates and dropouts of former years. Some follow up all former students each year for five years, some at intervals of one, three, and five years; some at intervals of one, four, and seven years; some at intervals of one, five, and ten years. The East Side Union High School District, San Jose, California, has followed up its students for fifteen years. One of the most extensive follow-ups yet undertaken is that of Project Talent, the reports of which may be obtained from the American Institutes for Research, Palo Alto, California 94302. Some placement officers follow up the persons whom they have placed at intervals of three, six, and twelve months. As noted in Chapter 2, high schools need to follow up their alumni after they have completed college and military or alternate service in order to find out where these former students got their first jobs. Without this information the vocational and educational guidance of prospective college students can be sadly unrealistic.

Seven of the author's graduate students have tried follow-up projects with their own students, following the procedure described in this chapter. Four reported enthusiastic reaction from the students; two had only average success; one tried harder than all the others but never quite managed to put it across. The kind of impromptu discussion described above requires a teacher who is a good discussion leader and who is alert and skillful enough to recognize and select good topics for discussion from the letters as they are read to the class. Such a teacher can do a superb job with surprisingly little effort.

The teacher who has misgivings about being able to lead this kind of discussion need not forgo the follow-up study as a class activity. With no discussion at all, the students can learn much if the responses from alumni are passed around the class so that each student is permitted to read each response. On one occasion the author used this procedure with his own students, and all the students in the class said that they had learned something worth the time devoted to reading the replies.

Another procedure is to divide the class into groups of five or six and invite the students in each group to tell each other what they learned from the letters they received. This plan requires some care in arranging the groups so that each will have some letters to discuss.

VARIATIONS

The possible applications and variations of the follow-up technique are innumerable. Any kind of organization that offers career guidance may follow up its former members, find out what has happened to them, and make their experiences available to present members as a glimpse into their own future. Alumni in military service may be followed up for a report on their experiences, which may include some items not mentioned in military recruiting literature. Alumni in college may be asked about things not mentioned in the college catalogs.

The follow-up may go to all alumni or to a small sample; it may be detailed or brief; it may ask for statistical data or for personal experiences and comments. Alumni may be reached by letter, by telephone, or by personal interview, or they may be invited to return to the school to meet with present students. The study may be conducted by counselors, students, an office staff, or the alumni themselves. The results may be reported orally, in mimeographed or printed form, on tape, or in films showing alumni at work and describing what they do.

Results may be presented also in a series of newspaper articles and bulletin board posters, each on one former student, with his photograph and a description of his job; on maps showing present work locations of alumni; in a series of weekly group conferences in each of which interested students and counselors ask one alumnus or alumna about his or her job. The results may be discussed in class, distributed to students, staff, and parents, and used in individual counseling. When the original questionnaires contain job descriptions, students in school and college have welcomed the opportunity to examine them.

Some state departments of education follow up the alumni of all vocational schools in the state.

Some require all high schools to report annually to the state deaprtment on the current activity of their most recent graduates. Regrettably, some schools never give these data to their students.

One state employment service made a follow-up of all high school dropouts and graduates who had registered with the service under the cooperative high school program. The results were reported to each high school in the program. Some employers sent information on selected employees back to the schools from which the employees came, as a means of recruiting more applicants.

An occupational therapist in a hospital got former patients to return and tell others of their experiences in achieving successful vocational rehabilitation. The patients asked questions eagerly.

A judge brought successfully rehabilitated former probationers to court to meet and talk with first offenders currently on probation [Sondern, 366].

Bowling Green University's Office of Career Planning and Placement Service organized a network of 200 alumni in various cities who were willing to help seniors and alumni who wanted information about local communities for use either in making decisions on job offers or in getting quickly and comfortably settled when they moved [Kuhlin, 228].

Christensen and Donovan [60] described how one school system compiled a useful list of local job opportunities for dropouts by keeping a record of the jobs already obtained by pupils who applied for work permits. "Contrary to the notion that dropouts enter blind alley jobs, several boys and girls entered such occupations as dental technician trainee, office clerk, spot welder, upholsterer."

Among the excellent reports of follow-up studies, for use in career planning, are those of the placement offices of the Fashion Institute of Technology, New York, New York 10001; the Hawkeye Institute of Technology, Waterloo, Iowa 50704; Wellesley College, Wellesley, Massachusetts; the counseling center at St. Peter's College, Jersey City, New Jersey; the College of Engineering, University of Illinois, Urbana; those in the catalog of the Southern Technical Institute, Marietta, Georgia; those of the Senior High School, Spring Valley, New York 10977; and those of the divisions of vocational education in the state departments of education of Connecticut, Georgia, and Pennsylvania.

If all colleges would make their own follow-up reports on their own alumni available to prospective students and their counselors, the problem of choosing a college would be simplified for some students, and some of the poorer colleges would receive fewer applications.

A major breakthrough in this direction has been achieved by Hoyt [191]. Based upon data collected from students and graduates of more than 400 different training programs in community colleges and in trade, technical, and business schools, his reports reveal the proportion of former students who found jobs directly related to their training, where the jobs were located, what they paid, and many other facts of interest to prospective students. The data are presented in easy-to-read charts, amusingly illustrated.

Perhaps it is time for counselors, students, and parents to begin asking colleges for information of this kind.

Descriptions of other ways in which follow-up data have been collected and presented appear in the following references: Davenel [89], Nolfo [284], Moyer [271], and Sutherland [386]. A comprehensive, critical review of follow-up studies may be found in Little [245].

The counselor or teacher who can do none of the things suggested in this chapter but who wants to get some of the benefits from follow-up returns can begin by writing informal personal letters to former clients or students at the rate of one a week, just to inquire about what they are doing now. If some of the alumni are in the same town as the institution, the counselor can make the same kind of inquiry by telephone or in person and learn much more. Anyone can do this, and anyone who will do it regularly for a few months will be impressed by what can be learned from the replies.

COMMENT

As noted above, the primary purpose of the follow-up technique described in this chapter is to give the students a more realistic picture of what is ahead of them. Other methods of occupational research show what jobs are available to all the workers in a given geographical area; from these data the jobs that will be available for the present seniors can only be inferred. A survey of local employers may reveal what jobs the employers think they will have available for young graduates, but no employer can be blamed for hiring the best-qualified applicant, and when the time comes to do the hiring, there may be experienced workers available. Only the follow-up study has these two advantages: (1) It has no geographical limits; it goes wherever the alumni go, and it maps the true geography of the employment market for this group; (2) it reveals the kinds of jobs that the alumni have been able to get in the open competition of the employment market. In addition, the follow-up study provides current occupational information on the student's own level of understanding and interest, obtained directly from original sources by means of student activity. It dignifies the student who is conducting one segment of the survey, the respondent who is being interrogated as an adult worker, and entry jobs, which no matter how unimpressive become the subject of group analysis and discussion. If well done, the project may help to build good alumni relations. Incidentally, the results may facilitate curriculum revision.

As a technique of teaching occupations, the student-made follow-up is not perfect. It is not foolproof. Employment conditions change from year to year; there may be desirable opportunities not discovered by former students; a single former class may be too small to provide an adequate sample of available employment opportunity; the information supplied by alumni may be inadequate or inaccurate because of ambiguous questions, omissions, errors in recall, or intentionally false replies. The class discussion is almost wholly dependent upon the returns and what the teacher can make out of them. However, no technique known to this author does a better job of bringing down to earth the naïve and unrealistic occupational expectations of the average group of high school and college students.

Most of this chapter has been devoted to the follow-up study as a technique of teaching a unit or a course in occupations. Follow-up data, of course, have other uses.

The good counselor follows up clients to the point of job placement and beyond, in order to learn what happened as these clients tried to follow the plans which the counselor helped them to make. The counselor thus learns how realistic or naïve he was in what he tried to do with and for the clients.

The counselor who does not do this kind of follow-up never knows how much he helped or hindered the clients who sought his aid in choosing or in reaching their occupational objectives. In ignorance of the results of his work, this counselor may go on confidently making the same mistakes for the remainder of his professional life.

The counselor who is planning career conferences, or buying occupational books, or arranging plant tours, or interpreting vocational interest inventories needs to know not only what occupations are of interest to his clients. He needs even more to know what kinds of jobs his former clients have been able to get, and what kinds they did not get despite his counsel and their persistent efforts.

Perhaps the greatest weakness in career counseling today is the widespread counselor ignorance of what has happened to former clients' and the consequent repetition by counselors of their own mistakes.

REVIEW QUESTIONS

1 What is the major purpose of the follow-up study in a course in occupations?
2 Why should the teacher accept suggested questions in the words of the student?
3 Why should letters be addressed in the classroom rather than at home?
4 Why should the class not use a long questionnaire?
5 Why should the replies be addressed to, and opened by, the students?
6 What are some of the topics suggested for the statistical summary?
7 What is the highest percentage return that others have obtained on follow-up studies?
8 Of the various kinds of follow-up projects described, which most appeals to you? Why?
9 What two advantages are peculiar to the follow-up study?
10 What technique of teaching does the best job of bringing unrealistic vocational expectations down to earth?
11 You have just been hired as a counselor in the high school or college that you attended. There have been no follow-up studies. Your boss asks you to make one. How will you proceed?
12 Is there anything in this chapter that you can use to improve your work? What? How?

Chapter 14

Plant Tours

The plant tour provides a painless way of getting students and clients to absorb information about occupations other than the ones they currently expect to enter—an important objective with those whose ambitions exceed their abilities. This method comes nearest of all to the author's definition of perfect teaching: a situation in which everyone learns, everyone enjoys learning, and no one feels overworked. An entire course or unit may be taught by this technique alone, it may be used to add variety to a course taught by other methods, or it may be used independently of any course.

In the remainder of this chapter the word "teacher" may be interpreted to include counselor and group leader, and the word "student" to include client and group member.

PURPOSES

The purposes of the plant tour are (1) to increase the career awareness of the participants by letting them see people at work in occupations of which the observers were unaware, and (2) to let the participants also see, hear, feel, and smell the environment in which they may work if they choose any of the occupations observed. Additional information will be picked up en route; it should be welcomed, but the teacher should not be too eager to teach every possible fact. Again, don't try to do too much. Enjoy the trip. Let your students enjoy it.

PROCEDURE

Because schools, colleges, and agencies have different policies regarding tours, the counselor's or teacher's first step should be to discuss policy with his or her immediate superior.

Where to Go   The first places selected for visits should be those in which large numbers of former students or clients are employed. These are most likely to be the places where the present students and clients ultimately will work, regardless of where they now think they will work. When these tours have been completed, the less important places may be visited as time permits.

If no follow-up studies have been made and the teacher has no information about the present employment of former students, the following potential sources of employment should be considered.

Retail stores
Restaurants and hotels
Telephone company
Transportation companies
Garages and service stations
Electric light and gas companies
Cleaning and dyeing firms
Building and general contractors

These businesses are usually found even in small communities, and they frequently account for a substantial proportion of entry jobs.

Many small communities also have one or more factories that are well known to everyone. The new teacher or counselor, coming in from another community, may quickly learn about them at the local bank, chamber of commerce, or library. The local office of the state employment service could be the best source of information about potential employers, but it is sometimes reluctant to release employers' names. The teacher should, nevertheless, visit the local employment office and get all the information possible. The employment services have a great deal of information on related topics which they are usually eager to share with school counselors.

How to Get In   After an industrial plant tour the author's students often ask, "How do you make arrangements for these tours? How do you get the companies to let us come?" Actually most employers need no persuading. In general, they are as willing to do another person a favor as are other human beings. Most employers are parents; they are interested in their children and in what the schools are trying to do for them. Many of them recognize that effective career guidance may help to reduce labor turnover, which is one of their persistent problems. Some employers welcome the opportunity to show what they have to offer to prospective employees. Others see potential future customers in any tour group. And nearly all of them have had twelve years of indoctrination in which to form the habit of doing anything that a teacher asked them to do.

For the reader who wants specific directions, the author's usual procedure is to telephone the company office and say to the person who answers, "Could you tell me the name and the exact title of your personnel director? . . . Will you connect me with him, please?" And when the personnel director answers,

> Good morning. This is Robert Hoppock. You don't know me. I'm a professor at New York University and I'm calling to see if you would like to do us a favor. May I tell you what we want? . . . We are trying to do a job here that may have some long-range effect upon the kind of people who come to you to apply for work. My part of this is in helping to train the school and college counselors to whom students go when they want help in deciding where they will look for a job. As a part of this training, we try to get them out of the classroom and into industry where they can see what a job looks like. I'm calling to inquire whether or not we could arrange sometime to take this group on a tour of your plant.

Usually, there follows a short conversation in which the personnel director inquires about the size of the group, what we wish to see, and when.

Sometimes a little preliminary conversation with the telephone operator or with the president's secretary is necessary when the company has no person whose title is similar to personnel director, and we have to identify the person who does the hiring. Sometimes the personnel director's secretary asks who is calling and about what. In rare cases, the secretary will handle all arrangements. An occasional employer finds it impossible or inconvenient to arrange a tour; most employers have responded favorably; many of them cordially.

If the reader wishes to arrange tours for high school students, the approach may be revised as follows:

> Good morning. This is Fred Lange. You don't know me. I'm a teacher at the high school, and I'm calling to see if you would like to do us a favor. May I tell you what we want? . . . We are trying to do a job here that may have some long-range effect upon the kinds of people who come to you to apply for work. We are trying to help our students to learn a little more about the kinds of jobs that may be open to them when they finish high school. In order to make this part of their education more realistic, we want to take them on some plant tours. I'm calling to inquire whether or not we could arrange sometime to take them on a tour of your plant.

Some teachers hesitate to ask for permission to tour a plant, because they fear their presence will distract the workers, lower production, and thus increase the employer's costs. The author has found no evidence on the effect of student tours, but Wright [419] reported that when the Rockbestos Products Corporation set aside a Family Day for their workers' relatives to tour the plant, " . . . production went up 15 per cent."

Preliminary Arrangements   It is desirable for the teacher to make a preliminary visit in order to determine whether the trip will be profitable, to explain to the host just what he or she hopes to accomplish, and to select important points for emphasis. In practice some busy teachers omit this step. It is perhaps better to omit it than not to take the class on any trips.

In making the preliminary arrangements, whether by visit, letter, or telephone, the teacher should do the following.

Explain clearly the purpose of the trip.

Determine into how many groups of what size the class will be divided and thus how many guides and assistant teachers will be needed. Try to keep the groups small enough for everyone to hear what the guide says during the tour of the plant; the ideal number probably is between five and ten students in each group. Do not insist on small groups if the host finds it difficult to provide for them. In the author's experience, hosts have often preferred to divide the class into small groups and to provide a guide for each group. On one trip to a hospital, each student in the class was provided with a nurse as a guide. On other occasions, a class of seventy-five has had to get along with one guide.

Fix the starting and closing time.

Find out where the group should report and to whom.

If possible, arrange for a question period in a quiet room before or after the tour; in large groups only a few students may hear what the guide says during the trip. If a question period can be arranged, see Chapter 15 of this book for suggestions on how to conduct it. Inquire whether or not it will be feasible to include a representative of the union or one or two young employees as resource persons in the question period.

Provide a sufficient number of assistant teachers to keep the groups together and in order; these assistants may be recruited from parents or older students or from the class itself.

Arrange transportation.

Secure the parents' consent if necessary.

If company literature is available for distribution, try to distribute it to the class a day or two before the tour. There is likely to be more student interest in reading it before the trip than after. The impending visit provides motivation for prompt reading plus an opportunity to ask questions which may be provoked by the publications.

The experience of the author and his students suggests that if the question period comes after the tour, the students will have more questions to ask and less time in which to ask them than if the question period precedes the tour. Few guides seem to be able to stick to a time schedule. If the tour comes last and the guides know that the class will depart at a certain time, they cover more ground in less time. Most plants of moderate size can be *seen* in forty-five minutes or less. They could not be fully explained in forty-five days. The major purposes of the tour are to see people engaged in a variety of activities, and to see, hear, feel, and smell the environment in which the work is done; these purposes can be accomplished on a fairly rapid tour. The author suggests that the teacher try arranging tours both ways until experience indicates which arrangement is better for his or her group. Sometimes the question period cannot be provided, because the host has no conference room large enough to seat the class.

Preparing the Students The students may be told that the trip has two major purposes. For those who think they may someday like to work in the place visited, the trip will provide an opportunity to see the surroundings in which they may work and the kinds of jobs to which they may be assigned. For the others, it will provide an unusual and a pleasant opportunity to learn something about how other people make a living—an important part of anyone's cultural education. The students may be invited to suggest other purposes which the trip may serve.

How to Behave Before the first trip the group should be told explicitly how to behave during the visit. Even well-bred children are often thoughtless. Even thoughtful, conscientious children may not realize the importance of not doing in a factory things which are permissible, perhaps even encouraged, in the classroom. Emphasis should be placed upon the status of the group as guests and upon the importance of acting like guests.

Reed [316] suggested several do's and don't's for counselors who visit industry. The following items have been selected from her list. Some of these suggestions apply mainly to counselors and to teachers; others apply equally to students and should be discussed with them.

Be appreciative. It costs time and money to entertain you.

Observe absolutely any safety precautions relative to dress, handling material, touching machinery, etc.

Don't act like a censor of business ethics or a labor inspector.

Don't ask impertinent questions.

Don't betray confidences. It is an unpardonable sin.

Don't introduce unpleasant or controversial topics.

Don't comment on what you have observed in other plants. Most of all, avoid comparisons.

Don't take along uninvited guests. It is bad manners and bad policy.

Don't try to educate or socialize employers.

Don't argue. It will not help in attaining your objective.

To Reed's suggestions may be added:

Don't smoke on tours without first asking if smoking is permitted.

Don't talk with employees without first asking the permission of your host. You may cause accidents, interrupt production, or lower piece-rate wages.

Don't lag behind the group. You may lose them or you may be suspected of pilfering.

Suggestions for acceptable behavior should be reviewed briefly before each subsequent trip until they become habitual practice with the students.

Further discussion of plant visitation may be found in Reed's book on pages 122 to 125 and 242 to 244.

What to Observe Perhaps the most important caution of all is to keep attention focused on the workers and *what they do.* Otherwise, the class may learn much about the manufacture of vacuum cleaners but relatively little about the workers who make them. The students should be asked to look at every worker and every job with these questions in mind: If I wanted to do that job, would I have what it takes? Would that job meet my needs? Would I enjoy doing it? Would I want to work here?

They may be asked, instead or also, to select the one job they see which they think they could do best and the one they could do least well.

Class Discussion after the Tour   At the next class session these points may be discussed and a blackboard or notebook list made of the abilities the students think would be required in the jobs they observed and the things they think they would like or dislike about such jobs. These lists should give the alert teacher an opportunity to correct misunderstandings and to initiate discussion of abilities, aptitudes, interests, and job satisfaction. The beginner who feels lost in exploring these topics need not abandon trips on this account; all this information is sur-plus value, incidental to the main purpose of giving the students the opportunity to see, hear, feel, and smell.

If the class saw too many jobs to discuss all of them, preference should be given to those which offer the largest number of opportunities to entry workers.

If time permits, the class may be taken to visit two or more places of employ-ment in the same line of business. In this way they may learn more effectively than from any lecture that opportunities, requirements, working conditions, etc., vary from employer to employer and that what one person says about an occupa-tion should never be considered final until it has been compared with what others have to say. Classroom discussion on the day following such visits may focus on which company the students would prefer to work for if they were offered jobs by both, and why.

Before and after each trip, news releases regarding it may be prepared by the class, by a committee, or by the teacher, submitted to the host for correction, approved by the principal, and sent to the local newspapers. A letter of thanks should go from the class or the teacher to the host.

VARIATIONS

Plant tours have been arranged and conducted *for* students and clients, counsel-ors and teachers, *by* teachers and counselors at all levels, by counselor educators and counselor associations, by placement officers in schools, colleges, and com-munity agencies, by group workers in social agencies, by other leaders of youth groups, and by employers.

Tours have been arranged for just one or two persons, and for hundreds of persons in one day. Small numbers permit more conversations with individual workers, but even the largest groups learn something about the kinds of jobs available and the environment in which the work is done.

Student teams have visited plants, interviewed employers and employees, tape-recorded their interviews, photographed and videotaped workers at work, made slides, presented the results to classes, and answered the questions of other students.

Tours for small groups have sometimes included hands-on activity, providing a mini-tryout for the participants.

Arrangements have been made for individual students to spend a day or more with one worker, observing every activity and performing some of the simpler tasks. Sometimes the workers were the children's relatives.

Similar arrangements have been made for individual students to have tryout experiences, working at one job for one or more days or weeks, and for cooperative work experience programs for one or more semesters.

"In Sweden . . . eighth-grade students . . . spend two periods of three weeks in different on-the-job work orientations. . . . In Denmark, basically the same program is offered in grade 7" [Cote, 76].

One college arranged an annual program, cosponsored by the local Rotary Club, in which 350 seniors visited thirty local firms, inspected operations, and talked with managers and supervisors.

Colleges have arranged for individual students to spend their spring vacations with alumni engaged in occupations which the students were considering [Katz, 214].

Employers have cooperated with, and sometimes initiated summer workshops and work experience programs for, teachers, counselors, and placement officers and discussion seminars for prospective dropouts.

Schools, employers, and parent associations have prepared, for teachers and counselors, directories of employers who were willing to cooperate in arranging plant tours and in other career guidance activities. Such directories sometimes include services available, persons to contact, and telephone numbers.

Canceling all classes for a period of one week, the McTigue School in Toledo, Ohio, provided 212 field trips to 117 different places of employment and brought 203 guest speakers to the school to discuss their occupations with the students. This kind of "Career Week" was repeated in each trimester under the direction of Jama Doenges, Career Coordinator. The McTigue School enrollment was about 1,300 students in grades six, seven, and eight.

Tours for Counselors, Teachers, and Placement Officers   For several years the Dutchess County Guidance Association in New York [198] scheduled one day a year on which teams of two or three counselors visited different plants. The captain of each team prepared a written report. All reports were edited, then duplicated on loose-leaf paper and distributed to each member school for insertion in a reference notebook.

Believing that the "more complex the local industrial community, the bigger the counselor's job," counselors in the suburban area of Philadelphia, Pennsylvania, applied "the principle of college visitation . . . to the area of vocational guidance." To learn at first-hand about working conditions, placement procedures and personnel, job requirements, salaries, and opportunities, the Montgomery County Personnel and Guidance Association dropped its after-school meetings in school buildings. With the help of the Manufacturers Association of Montgomery County, luncheon meetings were arranged at nine different industrial establishments. After each meeting, the host company provided a guided tour of the plant. Tour leaders were "asked to emphasize such things as jobs, opportunity, training, and placement practices rather than to focus on the product." Summary data on the company were mailed to all members of the counselors' association [Hughes, 195].

The six counselors of one junior high school took turns making weekly visits to local shops, offices, and industries, and sharing their information with each other.

Clark [62], McGuire [256], and other counselors and college placement officers have made their own plant visits in order to learn more about local jobs for their students and alumni.

Sinick [346] gave graduate students in counseling "An Outline for Reporting Observable Aspects of a Business or Industrial Firm."

"Business-Industry-Education (BIE) Day" has now become a popular annual activity in many communities. It has been widely sponsored by local industries. On one day the schools are closed, and all the teachers tour local industries as guests of the management. Each teacher chooses a company to visit. Each company arranges the day's program for its own guests.

"Structured field visits to private sector work sites" got half of the time of participants in the Career Guidance Institutes, financed by the U.S. Department of Labor through the National Alliance of Business Men "to upgrade existing career guidance programs so that teachers, counselors and administrators" might better help economically disadvantaged junior and senior high school students to "embark upon a realistic career goal-setting process." For further information write the Alliance at 1730 K Street N.W., Washington, D.C. 20006.

Sabbaticals for Counselors Some school systems have arranged for one or more of their counselors each semester to spend a "sabbatical" working in the state employment service. The employment service, in turn, sent one or more of its interviewers to serve as school counselors. The counselors learned more about jobs open to their students; the interviewers learned more about the kind of information they could get from the school. Valdez [396] described a program of this kind conducted in San Francisco. School counselors have been hired also as temporary employees during the summer when "the close of school brings thousands of youthful job seekers crowding into local employment service offices" [Sudweeks, 377].

COMMENT

No amount of reading and talking about jobs in a chemical laboratory will leave the lasting impression of one whiff of hydrogen sulfide. No amount of discussion in a comfortable classroom will give one the sticky feeling of the high humidity in the rooms in which certain industrial processes must be completed. The noise of a boiler factory, the heat of a hotel kitchen, the cool comfort of an air-conditioned retail store—these are important considerations to some persons in the choice of an occupation. The plant tour provides one means of finding out about them in such a way that they are not likely to be overlooked or forgotten.

One of the author's students has commented on this point as follows:

> During my first years in public health nursing, I had to visit a button factory and look for health hazards. I was amazed to learn the conditions under which people worked and to smell a terrible odor coming from a place where cows' hoofs were being processed for the making of the buttons. The smell was awful, but the visit educational and memories of it will remain with me for the rest of my life.

After a class tour of a garment factory a counselor wrote:

> What hit me was the speed at which most of the women and men worked. I had heard and read of piece work but I had never seen it. . . . Not ever for me, I thought.

After taking a class of high school seniors to tour two insurance offices, one teacher of secretarial subjects reported their reactions in these words:

> They noticed that one of the firms has a very lovely building with a spacious green lawn that looks like a velvet carpet. However, on the inside, the offices are generally dark and gloomy. There is no cafeteria; all the firm has for eating facilities are sandwich machines. People ate and smoked at their desks; the place was blue with smoke. The atmosphere was, on the whole, quite depressing. At the other firm, which does not boast of such an impressive exterior, the offices are cheerful, with plenty of light. There is a cafeteria where one may buy a hot lunch at a nominal fee. No one is allowed to smoke or eat at his desk. The atmosphere was efficient and businesslike, but at the same time, one of harmony and cordiality.

One high school junior commented:

> I always wanted to be a fireman. In fact it was one idea I had since I was a kid. Our social studies class took a trip to the New York Fireman's School. After I saw what went on I changed my mind.

One can read about working conditions; one can talk about working conditions; one can recognize and acknowledge them intellectually; one can even memorize them and retain them long enough to pass an examination. But the visitor who has seen them and heard them, felt them and smelled them, has learned them emotionally as well as intellectually, and rarely forgets them.

The conducted tour to observe occupations presents important, factual information in a way that is easy and pleasant to absorb. The trip adds zest to any class that is getting tired of the traditional classroom. It provides excellent motivation for later study and discussion. It gets the teacher or counselor out into the community and brings his or her own occupational information up to date. The information is obtained from primary sources and is presented to students simultaneously; errors due to intermediate communication and to obsolescence are thus reduced to a minimum. The information is more likely to be accurate, up to date, and pertinent to local conditions than is information obtained from most other sources. The visit also establishes and maintains employer contacts which may be useful in counseling, in placement, and in public relations.

Problems of Time and Transportation Like all techniques the tour has its disadvantages, too. If the trip is made on school time, students may miss classes in other subjects; if it is made after school, it may conflict with extracurricular activities or other responsibilities of the students. Sometimes there are transportation difficulties and expenses. These problems of conflict and of transportation are probably best solved as two high schools have solved them. In these schools the course in occupations was scheduled to meet for two or three consecutive periods two or three days a week. Nothing else except a study period was scheduled for these students in the afternoon session of the days on which the class met. School buses were not in use at this time and were used to transport students to and from the plants. The class returned to school by the end of the last period. The buses were then available for their usual duty and the students were free for their after-school activities. Using this plan, the class in occupations from one school toured thirty different plants in one year. At the end of the year the students and the teacher really knew something about the world outside the classroom.

In large cities with thousands of seniors and potential dropouts, popular employers may be reluctant to receive so many visitors, but in Detroit, Michigan, the Institute for Economic Education over a twenty-one-year period arranged plant tours for 58,196 teachers and 259,691 students.

The places visited may not be typical. Superficial impressions may be mistaken by teacher and student for adequate knowledge of opportunities and requirements. If the group is large, only a few students may hear what the guide tells them. Hosts may conceal facts that they prefer not to have widely known.

Though the tour is fun for the students, it is work for the teacher. Making advance arrangements takes more time and trouble than assigning another chapter in a familiar textbook. Occasionally, the tour is not welcomed by the prospective host, though this is unusual.

The most serious disadvantage is the danger of physical injury to a student and a subsequent suit for damages. In some states teachers are protected by law from such suits; in other states, insurance protection is available. The cautious teacher will discuss this aspect with the proper school authorities before arranging the first trip.

The teacher who has a public liability insurance policy on his home may be able to add protection against damage suits by students for a small additional charge.

Kearney [215] reported:

Most attempts to collect damages from teachers do not fare well in court. . . . The courts are inclined to hold that if teachers exhibit the kind of care and concern that would normally be used by prudent parents, they are not negligent and hence not liable for damages. . . .

So far as the author knows, there have been no lawsuits based upon things that have occurred on field trips.

Despite these disadvantages the author used tours when he taught his first high school class in occupations and later to give counselors in training realistic, up-to-date facts about occupational and educational opportunities and requirements. A class of his own graduate students who were taught mainly by tours and group conferences (see Chapter 15) voted overwhelmingly in favor of tours, even when they had to spend three extra hours in traveling and saw nothing more than the general offices of an advertising agency. They said that the tour gave them the "feel" of the organization and that employers talked more freely on their own premises than when they were guests at the school.

Comparison with the Group Conference   To compare the tour and the group conference techniques, the author invited the director of nurses of a nearby hospital to attend his class for a group conference. The instructor and the students spent an hour and a half asking the guest questions about nursing as a vocation. The following week the class toured the hospital. In a third session they listed things they had learned from the tour which they had not learned from the group conference. Some of the items listed were:

Institutional nurses may spend considerable time supervising student nurses.
Philosophical attitude of nurses toward their hours of work.
Opportunities for part-time work for high school students as nurses' aides.
Opportunity to choose specialization within the hospital after some experience.
Enthusiasm of student nurses.
Hazards: anesthetics are explosive.
Duties of nurse in operating room.
Duties with child patients.
Student nurses must make up time lost because of illness.
How troublesome patients can be.
Physical surroundings.
Odors.
Importance of habitual routine in emergency cases.
Need for good feet.
Nursing is not a glamorous occupation.
Nurses say the work is not hard.
Opportunity to teach student nurses.
Mental strain.
Difficulty of required studies.
The caste system and the way it is changing.

Some of the facts listed above could have been learned in the group conference, but they were not learned in the group conference despite the fact that everyone had ample opportunity to ask questions and most of the questions usually recommended for occupational studies were asked. Apparently, there are some questions one doesn't think of asking. Apparently, also, there are some things one can learn in no way except by firsthand observation.

Conceivably a group conference, following a tour, might produce a similar list of things not learned from the tour.

REVIEW QUESTIONS

1 What are the purposes of the plant tour?
2 What are the first places to be selected for plant tours? Why?
3 How would *you* arrange a plant tour for a group of your students or clients?
4 What valid reason may be given to students for touring plants in which they never expect to work?
5 What are some of the suggestions that may be made to students regarding their behavior on plant tours?
6 What questions should students be asked to think about as they look at each job?
7 Could *you* use the day-in-industry idea? Where? How? Why not?
8 If you were a director of guidance, would you try to arrange "sabbaticals" for your counselors? Why? Why not?
9 What does a plant tour do for the teacher?
10 How can you avoid the difficulties that arise when students have to miss other classes in order to go on tours?
11 Can plant tours be arranged in large cities?

Chapter 15

Group Conferences

The group conference resembles a press conference. In place of reporters there are students or clients seeking information for their own guidance. Their questions are answered by one or more resource persons who have the information desired.

This technique may be used to get information about occupations, employers, unions, schools, colleges, and other subjects. The group conference may be combined with a plant tour or conducted independently. It may be used in community agencies to get information for a small group of clients with common interests. It may be used in schools and colleges for a single class, club, or assembly, for a series of weekly career conferences, or for an entire unit or course in occupations. It has been used in second grade and in graduate school and at many points between.

In the remainder of this chapter the word "teacher" may be interpreted to include counselor and group leader, and the word "student" to include client and group member.

PURPOSE

The purpose of the group conference is to provide students and clients with information which the teacher or counselor may or may not possess, to get this information from primary sources, to deliver it to the participants before it becomes obsolete, and to do this in a way that will arouse and maintain student interest and attention and not require the resource person to prepare or to make a speech.

PROCEDURE: OCCUPATIONAL CONFERENCES

The procedure described below includes steps to be taken when one or more group conferences are to be arranged as independent projects. Some of these steps may be omitted when the group conferences are included in the course or unit in occupations. For example, if conferences are to be held after school hours and attendance is to be voluntary, it is imperative that the counselor first learn how many students plan to attend; otherwise he or she may be left embarrassed with a guest and no audience. If conferences are to be included as part of a course and held during the regular class session, the teacher will still wish to consider the interests of the students, but guests can be selected without fear of losing the audience.

Tabulating Student Interests   The present interests of the students are ascertained from a mimeographed or dictated questionnaire which includes such items as the following:

> Considering what you now know of your own abilities, interests, and opportunities, what occupations do you think you are most likely to enter when you finish school?
> What other occupations are you seriously considering?
> What others would you like to enter if you could?
> Would you like to have more information about any of these occupations? Which ones?
> Would you attend, after school hours, group conferences with persons employed in these occupations?

When the interests have been tabulated, the teacher examines the list. If important occupations or institutions have been omitted, the students may be asked how many would attend conferences on these subjects.

When the final list has been determined, a tentative schedule is prepared. Every conference is held on a different day in order that any student may attend as many as he or she wishes and the counselor or teacher may attend all.

Selecting Resource Persons   The teacher or counselor then looks for good representatives of the most popular occupations, who may be invited to confer with the interested students. A good representative will state frankly both the advantages and the disadvantages of the occupation. He or she is preferably not a recruiting officer. Employment managers and personnel directors usually have more of the desired information at their fingertips than do general managers and corporation presidents.

As noted in Chapter 5, employers and employees do not always agree about the advantages and disadvantages of employment in certain occupations, companies, and industries. It is, therefore, desirable to hear from both. Separate conferences may be arranged, or two guest experts may be invited to the same conference. If both are to participate in the same meeting, they should be so informed when they are invited.

If the same occupation is well represented locally in both large and small companies, both should be represented. In one community the small employers were neglected and resented it.

Good resource persons may be found among former students and clients; teachers, counselors, and other staff members; parents and other relatives; employers and employees; officers and members of unions, professional and trade associations, and local service clubs.

Alumni as Resource Persons   Schools and colleges frequently use their own graduates and dropouts as resource persons. Community agencies use former clients. Present students and clients may identify with, and find role models among, former students and clients and be more interested in their experiences than in those of other persons.

One graduate school offered a course on employment opportunities in guidance and personnel work in which every class session consisted of a group conference with from one to four alumni or students who were currently employed in the field. At one session three high school counselors answered questions about their jobs, at another three college counselors, then four counselors from community agencies, three placement officers, three industrial personnel officers, three personnel officers in government service, an assistant superintendent in charge of guidance, and two city directors of guidance. The students were enthusiastic about the results, and the instructor learned some things he had not known.

Forte [127] reported a high school assembly program in which five recent graduates and their employers answered questions asked by a panel of students. After the assembly the guests visited senior classrooms, where they met the students in smaller groups and where anyone might ask questions. The students asked to have the program repeated with additional former students and their employers.

Alumni selected as resource persons should, preferably, have terminated their full-time education within the past five years, be employed in an occupation of interest to the group, have been in their current jobs for at least a month, and have completed a level of education approximating that which the students expect to attain. Employed alumni who have gone to college have been enthusiastically welcomed by high school seniors who expect to go to college.

Students, Clients, and Staff as Resource Persons   In a survey of work experience among 721 high school seniors in Oakland, California, Marion Brown found 102 different occupations in which one or more students were experienced. Johnson and Briggs [209] found that 41 teachers in one rural consolidated school in Maine had worked in a total of 118 different occupations. When their experience is recent, such persons may make excellent resource persons. Too frequently we overlook the extent to which students can educate one another and sometimes can even teach us a few things we do not know. Little and Chapman [246] suggested that ". . . taken together, pupils in almost any secondary school probably know more about the work and the workers of that community than even the best informed teacher or counselor." One substitute teacher, assigned for one day to teach a subject he knew nothing about, substituted short group conferences on part-time jobs held by students in the class.

School employees may be valuable and handy resource persons. The secretaries and other clerical workers in the school offices, the maintenance personnel, the cafeteria staff, and the administrative officers may answer questions about their own occupations. In one school, the janitor was also part owner of a radio store and supplied students with firsthand information on radio repair work.

In cooperation with the heads of academic departments, Dittersdorf [109] arranged a series of group meetings between interested students and workers in occupations related to different school subjects. The meetings were held during the last period of the school day. Attendance was voluntary. One result was improved relations between counselors and faculty.

Parents and Others   Similarly, counselors and teachers may well catalog and utilize the occupational experience of the parents and other close relatives of students, most of whom welcome an invitation to help the school.

Rauschkolb [313] described a group conference arranged by a student club with the father of one of the members. The guest "was delighted to know that it would not be necessary to prepare a speech." A checklist of suggested questions was given to some of the students, who were instructed to cross off each question as it was asked and to ask the other questions whenever there was a lag in the discussion. The club members asked questions for forty minutes. At the conclusion the guest invited the students to apply to him for summer employment after they started college. On anonymous appraisals of the conference, some of the students' comments were "Great! On any industry"; "Much more beneficial than a prepared speech"; "I want more!!!"

Resource persons sometimes come in their work clothes, bring tools and materials, demonstrate their work activities, and let the students try simple tasks and ask questions.

Minimum Attendance   While a counselor may ask a resource person to meet just one or two students *and the counselor* in a conference at the resource person's home or work site, no resource person should be asked to come to the school or agency unless the counselor or teacher is certain of a minimum attendance of five students or clients. To assure this minimum there should be promises of attendance from ten to fifteen persons; experience will indicate the proper ratio. Twenty or twenty-five is probably a desirable maximum; if the group is larger, there may not be opportunity for all of them to ask as many questions as they wish. Except for this limitation the technique can be used with groups as large as the teacher can manage. The author has held group conferences frequently in college classes of fifty and seventy-five. Working with high school students, Rubinfeld [329] ". . . discovered that a group of over a hundred could be handled without any difficulty and with the informal atmosphere still maintained."

Inviting the Guests   The teacher or counselor telephones or writes to the representative, extends the invitation, explains the purpose of the conference, and says in effect, "Please don't bother to prepare a speech. We prefer an informal conversation. The students and I will have plenty of questions to ask you. The purpose of the conference is not to recruit students for this field nor to discourage their entering it but to provide them with some of the facts they should have before they decide either way."

Many guests are more willing to come when informed that a speech is not desired. At the conclusion of several conferences, I have asked the guests if they would have preferred to make a speech. Almost invariably, they have expressed a preference for the group conference. They like to know that they are talking about something that is of interest to the audience.

One school has reported considerable difficulty in getting guests for conferences which were held during the first period of the school day. I have encountered reluctance of some guests to leave their suburban homes and come to New York for Saturday morning conferences but have had no trouble getting guests for conferences at 4:15 and 6:15 p.m.

Guests from large organizations sometimes bring free literature for distribution. If this can be obtained and distributed a day or two before the conference, some students will read it in advance and ask questions about it during the conference. Employers, if asked, will sometimes supply copies of their employment application forms.

What to Ask   If the students are meeting periodically as a class, they may be given a part in suggesting and selecting the basic list of questions to be asked. Otherwise the teacher prepares the list. In either case the list should be long enough to utilize the time available.

In Chapter 3 appears a detailed list of possible questions, based upon the basic outline for occupational studies prepared by the National Vocational Guidance Association. In group conferences, the author uses a much shorter list, which is reproduced below:

Do you employ dropouts? High school graduates? College graduates?
    Do they all start in the same job?
    Do you have any part-time or summer jobs?
    What are the principal job categories in which beginners start? About how many beginners did you hire last year for each of these major job categories? Do you expect to hire more or fewer next year?

(From here on most of the questions are focused on the one or two categories which take the largest numbers of beginners.)

What are the starting salaries? About how much may the average worker expect to earn after five years? After ten years?
    What does a person do in this job? What is a typical day's work?

What are the minimum qualifications for getting a beginner's job? Minimum and maximum age, height, weight? Sex? (Although discrimination on the basis of sex and marital status is being vigorously and successfully opposed, it still exists and the fact will sometimes be admitted.) Other physical requirements? Do you require a physical examination? On what physical deficiencies would an applicant be rejected? How important is appearance, for example: dress, cleanliness, long hair, beards? Do you hire married women? Do you fire single women if they marry? Does the worker have to have a license? Where does he get it? What are the requirements for getting it? Must he supply his own tools? What do they cost? What aptitudes do you look for in new applicants? Do you give aptitude tests?

Must the beginner belong to a union? What are the chances of getting in?

Must the worker be a citizen? Must he live in the city or state in which he works?

Do you have any members of minority groups working for you now? Do you give preference to veterans? What chance does a nonveteran have?

Does a beginner need capital? How much? [This question is used only when the guest is self-employed.]

What preparation is required? What is the minimum you would accept? What do you prefer? How much time is required to get it? What does it cost? What subjects are included? Can you tell us where to get a list of approved schools? What subjects do you prefer to have an applicant study in high school or in college?

How does the beginner get a job? To whom does he apply? Where? When?

What are the opportunities for advancement?

What are the future prospects? Is the occupation or the business expanding or contracting? How does the current number of applicants compare with the number of vacancies?

Does the job affect the worker's family? His life-style?

What are the hours? Are they regular or irregular? Is overtime required? Optional? Do you work Sundays? Holidays? Evening?

Is the job steady or seasonal? What happened to the workers during the last depression? Does advancing age make the worker more or less valuable? What is the retirement age? Are pensions provided?

Do you ever have any accidents? What kind? What are the hazards?

Is the marriage rate among your employees higher or lower than average?

What three things do you think the workers like most about their jobs? What three things do they like least?

Do people generally have any mistaken ideas about this occupation?

Is there anything else we should have asked you?

Is there anything you would like to ask us?

For classroom use, even this list may be abbreviated to a few key words which serve to remind the teacher of the questions to be asked. This abbreviated form may be mimeographed as a checklist and each item crossed off as a student or the teacher inquires about it. In this way the teacher can keep track of the questions which have been asked even though they did not come up in the order listed. The key-word-reminder form follows:

Explain purpose and method.

Do you employ dropouts, H.S. grads., college grads.?

Start in same jobs? Summer or part-time? Principal job categories? How many hired last year? Next year?

Starting salaries? 5 years? 10?

Nature of work?

Qualifications? Age? Sex? Height? Weight? Other physical? Appearance? Marital status? Tools? License? Aptitudes? Unions? Citizen? Residence? Discrimination? Veterans? Capital?

Preparation? Minimum? Desirable? Time? Cost? Content? Approved schools? Preferred subjects?

Entrance? Advancement? Future prospects? Supply and demand?

Affect family? Life-style?

Hours? Regular? Overtime? Sunday and holiday? Evening?

Steady or seasonal? Effect of depressions? Advancing age? Retirement age? Pensions?

Hazards? Marriage rate?

What workers like most? Least?

Mistaken ideas

Anything we should have asked? You ask us?

Thanks.

Although the word "discrimination" appears on the key-word-reminder form above, the question is always asked in the words which appear in the longer form. By asking whether or not the employees include any members of minority groups and how many, the counselor can get at the same topic with less embarrassment to the guest and therefore with a better chance of getting a truthful answer. The same approach may be used with labor unions by asking how many union members are from minority groups.

When the resource person is being asked about his own job, questions about the nature of the work may be extended as follows:

Would you mind telling us what time you came to work this morning?
What was the first thing you did?
How long did that take?
What did you do next?
How long did that take?
What did you do next?
How long did that take?
[These questions are repeated as often as necessary to cover the entire day.]
What time did you quit?
Did you do anything yesterday that was different from what you did today?
How about the day before yesterday? Last week? Last month?
What else do you do on your job?
Of all these various duties, which ones occupy the largest share of your time?

The author's experience indicates that these questions often elicit important information that would otherwise be missed. They consume considerable time, sometimes to the exclusion of some of the other questions, but what they reveal is frequently so surprising as to be well worth the time. The reader is urged to try these questions a few times and draw his or her own conclusions.

With appropriate revision the same list of questions may be used when the guest is a student currently or recently employed in a part-time or summer job.

When the resource person is a former student being asked about his or her own job, the following questions may be added:

What schools did you attend?

Did you graduate? Drop out? When?

What problems did you meet in making the move from school to work?

Have you any suggestions for anyone in this group who would like to have a job like yours?

If I could ask any person only three questions about his or her job, I would ask those which have most often produced surprising responses. These are:

What are *all* the things you do on your job?

What are the three things you like most about it?

What are the three things you like least about it?

Physical Arrangements   The teacher or counselor arranges a comfortable place for the meeting. Small groups may meet in a conference room, in the counselor's office, in the living room of the home economics practice house, or in the career resources center; largers ones will meet in the library or in another room of appropriate size. If possible, the group is seated around one large table or several tables pushed together to give a round-table effect.

The teacher notifies the interested students several days ahead and reminds them on the day of the meeting.

Arrangements are made to have the guest graciously received and taken to the meeting place. The guest is seated at one end of the conference table, the teacher at the other. If it is necessary to use a classroom, the guest may be seated at the teacher's desk, and the teacher may sit in the rear of the room. The important point here is to make the physical arrangements suggest an informal conference rather than a lecture. It is desirable that all students be between the teacher and the guest, so that as they talk to each other they have to speak loud enough for all to hear. After the conference is well under way, the teacher may move about the room.

If a classroom is used, the teacher writes the guest's name, title, and business address on the board. If there is to be more than one guest, the names are placed on the board so that each guest's name appears above the chair which that guest will occupy. Students then find it easier to direct their questions to individual guests and to call them by name.

Encouraging Student Questions   Well in advance of the group conference the teacher or counselor duplicates the list of questions to be asked, and on one copy marks the questions that he or she wishes to ask if no one else does. The teacher or counselor opens the conference by stating the purpose of the meeting and introducing the resource person who is to answer the questions. Each student is given a fresh copy of the list of questions, asked to take a minute or two to read it, and to mark the questions he or she would like to ask. The teacher announces two ground rules for the conference: (1) the students may ask any questions they wish to ask, whether on the list or not, and (2) the guest does not have to answer.

To the resource person he says, in the presence of the group, "If we ask you any question you prefer not to answer, please just smile and say, 'Next question?' "

The teacher then turns to the group and says, "Who is ready to ask the first question?" What will happen next is unpredictable. There may be several students eager to be first, or there may be dead silence. If no one responds at once, the teacher waits, and waits, and waits. If the silence becomes unbearable, the teacher quietly announces that he will ask a question or two, and he invites the students to interrupt or raise their hands whenever they are ready.

On rare occasions the teacher may have to ask all the questions; he should be prepared to do so if necessary. Usually the group will begin to participate in a few minutes. Thereafter the teacher should be ready to ask another question whenever there is a lull in the conversation.

The teacher is also alert to facilitate communication if it appears that either the student or the resource person does not understand what the other has said. The teacher asks additional questions to clarify answers, and repeats questions which may not have been heard by everyone. He interrupts with a new question whenever this is necessary to keep the guest and the students reasonably on the subject.

Near the end of the conference, if any very important questions have not been asked, the teacher tells the group that only a few minutes remain and he would like now to ask a few questions. He does so, thanks the resource person, and adjourns the meeting. Sometimes it may be desirable to close the formal part of the meeting a few minutes early in order that shy persons may come forward and ask questions less conspicuously. After a series of weekly group conferences with high school students Rubinfeld [329] reported, "One of the things observed at later conferences was that students who had attended earlier had developed a framework of questions which they could fire in rapid succession without going off on tangents."

Student questions can be stimulated by a preliminary meeting, in which each student is given a question to ask, but this is likely to make the conference less spontaneous, the meeting more formal, and the students more reticent about injecting very important questions which arise in their minds during the conference.

During a high school career day at Port Jervis, New York, H. Townsend Carpenter gave a list of suggested questions to students in some of the group conferences and not to those in the others. The questions were not assigned to individuals. The students who received the suggested questions appeared to be more interested in the discussion and kept their guests longer than did the students who received no suggestions.

Questions can also be stimulated by asking the audience to divide themselves into groups of three, to take three minutes to prepare one question, and to assign someone to ask it.

The teacher should be alert for any sign that the guest is about to launch a speech and should intervene. If the guest brings notes and suggests that he open the meeting with a few remarks, the teacher may ask if he is willing to delay the speech until the teacher and students have had a chance to ask their questions. Then, if the questions have not brought out all the things that the guest thinks important, the group will be glad to have him make whatever additional comments he considers appropriate. To cover this, one of the teacher's last questions should be, "Is there anything else we should have asked you?"

An occasional guest will insist on making his preliminary speech, even if he has to do it in response to the first question. When this happens there is little the teacher can do without being rude. Fortunately, it does not happen too often to be tolerated.

Follow-up   On the day following the conference there should be opportunity for the students and teacher to discuss any further questions that either may wish to raise. If necessary, the teacher may stimulate discussion with such questions as, "How many would like to enter that occupation? How many would not? Why? Why not?" "How many think you have what it takes? How many do not? Why? Why not?" Or the teacher may give a short test on the information brought out during the conference, let the students correct their own papers, and then discuss differences of opinion regarding correct answers.

After each group conference a news release may be prepared by the class, by a committee, or by the teacher. It should include the name and position of the guest and some of the interesting things said. It should be submitted to the guest for correction and to the principal for approval, then sent to the local newspapers. A letter of thanks should go from the class or the teacher to the guest.

PROCEDURE: CONFERENCES WITH UNION OFFICERS

In some communities labor unions control admission to certain occupations. Union contracts affect promotion, tenure, and other conditions of employment. Even where unions are not in control, they are often excellent sources of information. Union officers and employers sometimes see things differently, and each may contribute information which the other would not volunteer. It is therefore often desirable to arrange group conferences with local representatives of the major unions—at their headquarters if convenient; otherwise, at the school.

After a group conference with James Clark, an officer of the Building Employees International Union, the author's students were asked what they had learned that they did not know before and how they felt about the conference. Among their responses were the following:

> I never realized that there *was* a union or that salaries for these jobs were so high. The time was certainly worthwhile!
> The building service trades are relatively stable sources of employment.
> The best time to get a job in the building service industry is during April, May, June.
> I learned the difference between a closed shop and a union shop. I learned that the union expects the employee to do his work, and may even agree to the firing of a shirker.
> I learned what a "union book" is.

Unions are another source of information about jobs which I had not given much consideration to.

Excellent source of employment for dropouts.

Education is *not* prerequisite for a job in the building service field.

Extremely interesting and informative.

Mr. Clark was "down-to-earth" in the answers he gave.

One of the most interesting sessions of the semester.

The most impressive material we have had from a guest speaker.

Enjoyed the class! *Do it again.*

What to Ask   The following questions will help to start the conversation.

With which occupations or industries is this union concerned?

In which of these are the largest numbers of union members employed?

In these occupations or industries, what proportion of the employees are union members?

Must a person be a union member in order to get a job?

If not, must he join the union in order to keep his job?

Is there any limit on the number of new members who will be admitted to the union? If so, who gets in?

How does one become a member? What does it cost?

Is there an apprenticeship program? How long is it? What does it include?

What other advantages are there in belonging to the union?

Are there any disadvantages?

Is there anything else we should have asked you?

Is there anything you would like to ask us?

To these questions may be added most of the questions suggested above for occupational conferences.

PROCEDURE: CONFERENCES WITH PLACEMENT OFFICERS

Some of the most realistic, most interesting, and most compelling information about occupations can be obtained from school and college placement offices, from the state employment services, and from commercial employment agencies. If visits to these offices can be arranged, the students may enjoy seeing what such places look like. Students who have been there once may feel less uneasy when they come later to register for placement or to be interviewed for a job. If visits cannot be arranged, group conferences with placement officers may be held in the classroom.

What to Ask   At either location, such questions as the following may bring out the desired information.

Which occupations account for most of your placements? What other kinds of job orders do you handle?

Where are beginning workers most in demand today? In which occupations is it hard for a beginner to find a job?

Where are experienced workers in demand? In surplus?

Among the occupations and industries with which you work, which provide the steadiest jobs? Which are least stable?

Can you venture any guess as to the occupations in which beginning workers will be in demand four years from now? In surplus?

What are some of the mistakes that people make when they are looking for a job?

Can you tell us about any successful applicants and what they did when they were looking for work?

Who may use your service? When? How? What does it cost the applicant?

Is there anything else we should have asked?

Is there anything you would like to ask us?

VARIATIONS

Some colleges have put resource persons at separate tables in one large room or dining hall and invited students to come and talk with them [Hughbanks, 194]. Some have invited students from neighboring high schools, and interesting local residents, to join their own students in questioning the resource persons.

The National Urban League sponsored a Black Executives Exchange Program to bring black executives to college campuses for two-day periods. The purposes included providing students with role models and informing students and faculty about job opportunities.

A school superintendent in Oregon found that the counselors knew little about occupations and arranged with local service clubs to send two members each week to spend an afternoon with the counselors.

If desired, interested parents may be invited to join the students in questioning the guests.

Beverley Lipschitz compiled a list of occupations on which parents expressed a desire for more information. She then recruited alumni employed in these occupations and arranged a group conference at which the parents queried the alumni. The parents asked that a similar program be arranged for their children.

One high school set aside one full day a week for special activities. During this time, forty groups of students, interested in different occupations, held conferences with workers in the fields of their interest.

Some schools and colleges have used telephone amplifiers to enable a group of students at school to talk to a resource person at work.

If there is a good stenographer or note taker in the group, a summary of the information presented may be prepared, submitted to the speaker for correction, distributed to interested students, and placed in the library for future reference. Business education students in a Connecticut high school took notes on occupational talks given by local businessmen. At three o'clock of the same day each speaker received a copy for correction. The speakers were pleased.

Tape Recordings   Some schools have made tape recordings of their group conferences and filed them for later use. One guidance director found that student interest was much lower when the class could only listen to a tape than when they were actively participating as questioners of a live guest. Tapes can better be used to provide information to individual students who are curious about a specific occupation or company.

COMMENT

Every career counselor, every teacher of career education, needs accurate, up-to-date information on the occupations most likely to be entered by the students and clients. Few counselors and teachers ever find time to visit and observe workers in these occupations, and much of the needed information cannot be found in print. But many students, alumni, and staff members have had recent work experience in some of these occupations. They are better equipped than many counselors to describe the nature of the work. They know what they liked and disliked about it. To ignore this convenient source of useful occupational information is to discard one of our valuable resources.

The group conference provides direct contact with these and other primary sources.

Like the tour, it helps to bring the teacher's information up to date, it establishes and maintains contacts which may lead to placement, and it may help shy students to overcome their fear of employers by getting to know a few. Most students find it more interesting than reading a book or listening to a lecture.

The informal, conversational question-and-answer technique can keep a wandering speaker on the subject. Every change of voice wakes up the student who would otherwise be asleep if the speaker were dull. Every student has the opportunity to participate in class activity. The question-and-answer technique also reduces the danger that teacher and guest both may guess wrong about what will interest the group. The author has used the group conference repeatedly in college and graduate courses, and in demonstrations with high school seniors, and is enthusiastic about the results; the students seem to like it, too.

The advantages of the group conference, as here described, over the common career conference and college night are discussed in Chapter 20.

The group conference has its disadvantages also. The guest may be dull or poorly informed; may be biased by limited experience, prejudice, age, success, or failure; may oversell or undersell the field. If he has a charming personality he may quite unintentionally recruit poorly qualified students who want to be like him and who think they will be if they follow his occupation. If he is offensive, he may repel even those who should enter the field.

Students will always be subject to influences of this kind as they meet workers from various fields and talk with them. Such workers turn up as relatives and friends, family doctors, etc. *There is no educational isolation from facts about jobs.* The group conference provides an opportunity to extend these casual conversations into systematic interviews in the presence of a trained counselor who can clear up misunderstandings, counteract bias, and follow through later with individual interviews.

The biases and the personality influences may be to some extent canceled by arranging subsequent conferences with two or three other persons in the same field, with employees and union representatives as well as with employers, with young workers, and with persons of only average success as well as with the distinguished. The author has tried having two or more guests from the same occupation in the same session; it can be done, but it requires skillful handling and extra time. Such guests have occasionally challenged and disagreed with each other, but they have invariably done so good-naturedly. Perhaps this is because no sharp clash of personal interest has yet arisen. Beginners may be safer starting with one guest at a time.

Fortunately, most of the guests who have appeared in the author's classes have been willing to cooperate in any way that promised to help the students. One, but only one, insisted upon making the ten-minute speech he had prepared despite instructions not to do so. On a few occasions, with two or more resource persons, one has been more eager to talk than the others and has threatened to consume much more than his share of the time. When this happens, the counselor who is running the conference can direct more questions to the other resource persons, who will often say what the loquacious one was about to say. The eager one can usually be depended upon to interrupt if there is anything important to add.

Another disadvantage, if the conference is part of a course, is that some students will not be interested in the occupation discussed. The conversational method, however, makes it less difficult for the students not personally concerned to accept the information presented as part of their cultural background.

The group conference will not do the whole job of guidance any more than any other technique. It will not always bring out all the desired information. In Chapter 14 reference was made to one of the author's graduate classes which participated in a group conference on nursing and later visited a hospital. Following both these experiences, four members of the group interviewed four nurses from other hospitals and reported that they learned the following things which had not come up in either the group conference or the visit:

Contrary to statements made in the group conference, some private-duty nurses will go into homes even when a shortage of nurses makes it easy for them to get hospital cases.

The nurse has more responsibility in home nursing than in the hospital, and must decide whether or not to call the physician and the family.

Some families turn off the heat at night and leave the nurse to sit up in a cold house.

Some hospitals exploit student nurses. It is imperative to choose an accredited school.

Nurses dislike giving baths, changing beds, arranging flowers, waiting on convalescents. They regard these activities as maid service and are eager to turn them over to others.

Many have overcome an initial fear of gore.

A head nurse needs some teaching skill.

No matter where you train, you must take state board examinations which are "three days of hell."

Small schools sometimes provide inadequate instruction.

Nurses in training resent being treated like children.

The overambitious teacher who hopes to present a complete picture of an occupation in one group conference will nearly always be disappointed. The teacher who seeks only to add something to the students' store of information will often be gratified with the results. Despite its imperfections the group conference does provide a means of obtaining some information which students and counselors badly need and would otherwise lack.

REVIEW QUESTIONS

1 What are the characteristics of a good guest expert?
2 How large a group can be handled in a group conference?
3 What is the best way to ask about discrimination?
4 By what series of questions can you get the best description of the nature of the work?
5 Where should the guest and the teacher be seated?
6 How did Carpenter increase student interest?
7 What should be one of the teacher's last questions?
8 Which of the following should be used as guest experts: personnel directors, union officers, placement officers, alumni, students?
9 What are some of the advantages of the group conference?
10 How can guest bias be counteracted?
11 How can you use what you have learned from this chapter?

Chapter 16

Students Survey Entry Jobs

Most high school graduates and dropouts get their first jobs near home. This happens even in many suburban communities, despite popular impressions to the contrary. Follow-up studies reveal the same to be true for the dropouts and graduates of some community colleges and urban universities and for the "alumni" of some community agencies. In such institutions it is imperative that the counselor and clients be familiar with the major employment opportunities of their community.

Try browsing through your classified telephone directory. After this experience one of the author's students commented, "It surprised me to find out how little I knew of the small community I was born in and lived in for twenty-one years. I never realized that there are so many places of employment in our community. . . . This report opened my eyes to something I was completely unaware of." Follow-up studies, plant tours, and group conferences compile and convey information about only those occupations which are known to alumni, students, or teachers. Good employment opportunities may be overlooked by students and clients because they and their counselors are unaware of the possibilities.

Planning, conducting, and reporting the results of a survey are more than a one-day job. This project is appropriate for a unit or a course in occupations, and for an interested homeroom or social studies class; some social workers have adapted it for use in community agencies.

In the remainder of this chapter the word "teacher" may be interpreted to include counselor and group leader, and the word "student" to include client and group member.

PURPOSE

The purpose of the student survey is primarily to help prospective graduates and dropouts to find jobs, and incidentally to facilitate career planning. To this end the survey is designed to inform the students and the counselor about employment opportunities which they might otherwise overlook, to reveal where most of the local job opportunities are likely to be found, to provide each student with a list of employers who may have vacancies for which he could qualify, to make the student a little more realistic in his expectations about the kind of job he may hope to get and how much he may hope to earn, to provide some training and experience in interviewing employers, and to relieve some of the apprehension which some students feel about approaching employers.

PROCEDURE

The teacher and students together discuss and select the territory to be covered. In a small community this may be the whole town; in a large city it may be the school district. It should be within the employment market area for the school and should not be too large to be covered thoroughly by the class.

A local street map is purchased from the city offices, or a committee of students may prepare one. The teacher and the class discuss and decide whether the students are to work individually or in teams. The map is divided into a number of sections equal to the number of individuals or teams. Allowance must be made for the greater concentration of employers in business and industrial zones, and the size of the sections adjusted accordingly. Each section is numbered and assigned to one student or one team. The map and the list of assignments are posted on the bulletin board.

If the city is too large to be covered by the available students, the survey may be restricted to one part of the city.

In a discussion session the students suggest the questions that they wish to ask employers. The final list is decided by vote, subject to approval by the teacher, who may wish to add to it. The list should be brief and the questions simple. Ten questions are probably enough for the first attempt; five might be better. Among the final questions may be such as these:

Do you expect to have any jobs open for our graduates this June?
What will the jobs be?
What will they pay?
What qualifications would we have to have to get one of them?
Will they be permanent or temporary, steady or seasonal?

An interview blank is prepared and duplicated with space for the name and address of the employer, the nature of the business, the person interviewed, the interviewers, the date, and each of the questions to be asked. Ample space is left for replies. This form is not given to the employer to fill in but is used by the students to guide the interview and to record their notes.

Practice Interviews   Several class sessions are spent in teaching the students how to approach the employer and how to conduct the interview, what to do and what not to do to secure the facts pleasantly.

As a part of this preparation several practice interviews are staged in the classroom with the teacher or a student acting the role of the employer. At the conclusion of each practice interview the other students and the teacher discuss two questions: What did the interviewer do well? What would you have done differently? For the first practice interview, one student may be asked to do everything wrong. This sometimes produces a hilarious session which dramatically emphasizes mistakes to be avoided. It serves also to give the other students a little confidence—surely they can do better than this. After a few practice interviews it may be possible to find an employer who will attend the class and participate in some final practice interviews, and add comments to those of the class and the teacher.

Letter to Employers   While this preliminary training is going on, the employers are approached by letter. The purpose of the project is explained, and their cooperation is solicited. Service clubs and chambers of commerce may help by sponsoring the project.

A sample letter follows.

Some of the students in our senior class will be looking for jobs within a few months. They are eager now to learn something about the kinds of jobs that may be open to them when they graduate. The purpose of this letter is to inquire if you would be willing to help them.

Specifically, would you be willing to have one or two of our students call on you sometime to ask you some questions about employment opportunities and requirements in your organization? Will you please indicate your reply in the space provided below and return this letter in the enclosed envelope?

Would you be willing to have a student call?   _____
What time of day is most likely to be convenient
for you?   _____
Would you like us to telephone in advance for an
appointment?   _____

Public Relations   Depending upon the extent of the teacher's interest in public relations, he may or may not wish to approach employers in other ways. Public acceptance and interest in the survey may be increased by appropriate publicity and by inviting a sponsoring committee to help plan the study. Potential sponsors may be invited to a few preliminary meetings for the exchange of ideas; the committee members may then be chosen from those who show the most helpful interest at the preliminary meetings. Potential sponsors include the board of education, the superintendent of schools, the state supervisor of guidance services, the state employment service, the state board for vocational education, the chamber of commerce, civic clubs, businessmen and women, labor unions, teachers, student-body officers, student groups, parent-teacher organizations, newspapers, and radio and television stations. As noted before, any extensive public relations activity should first be discussed with the teacher's immediate superior. Many successful surveys have been made without publicity or sponsorship of this kind.

If the territory to be covered includes any establishments which the teacher or the community consider hazardous to young persons, these places may be omitted from the survey. When in doubt the teacher may find it wise to discuss such problems with his supervisor. One blast of righteous indignation from a powerful community leader could wreck a community survey.

When the teacher is satisfied that the students will be a credit to the school, that they will be courteous, tactful, and appreciative, the actual interviews begin. A few of the more tactful students may be sent out first and then asked to tell the class about their experiences. After this each student or team calls on all the employers in the section assigned. Each day the students report results orally to the class and file their interview records with the class secretary for the final composite report. Interesting points are discussed informally in the classroom as they come up.

Discussion of Results   Discussion procedures may be varied to suit the preferences of the students and the teacher. The author's students have enjoyed the following: At the beginning of the period the class is divided into buzz groups of four to six students. Each group chooses its own chairman. Each person reports to the group the most interesting thing that he or she has learned about entry jobs since the last report. The group selects the three most interesting items to report to the class, and the persons to report them. The small-group discussion is allotted five to fifteen minutes, depending on the teacher's judgment of how much time seems to be needed. Then each group is asked to report one of the three items it has selected. After each report the teacher invites questions and comments. If time permits, each group is asked to report a second item and then a third.

Final Report   When all the returns are in, the class secretary or a committee prepares a composite report, listing the places where jobs are expected to be available and such additional data regarding them as may have been collected. This report is duplicated and given to each student as an aid to job hunting. Copies also may be placed in the school library for reference by future classes undertaking similar projects. If there are other prospective graduates or dropouts who were not enrolled in this class, copies may be offered to them or the composite report may be posted on homeroom bulletin boards or published in the school paper.

Surveys by College Students   Fick [122] described how 700 teachers and 500 junior college students canvassed all homes and businesses of one school district in a single day and recorded the collected data about occupational pursuits and opportunities.

Leis [238] used 84 students in a college psychology class to interview 210 local manufacturers. Devoting to the project an average of less than six hours per student the class obtained a 70 percent response, after which Leis took over and got reports from all but two of the remainder.

Surveys by Community Agencies   Social agencies and civic clubs have canvassed local employers to find part-time and vacation jobs for students.

Vincent J. Russo, a group worker, used six adolescent members of the Hudson Guild to survey entry jobs in the Chelsea area of New York City. As a result, two of the boys were hired for part-time jobs and three employers promised to call the Guild when they needed help.

VARIATIONS

The teacher who wants to get a little information in a short time can do so by asking each student to interview the members of his family regarding jobs for beginners at the places where they work.

Some schools have asked local employers to supply lists of jobs for which they have hired school dropouts and graduates without experience. These lists have then been duplicated and distributed to students.

Some counselors survey local employers in the spring of each year to discover summer job opportunities. Some counselors and teachers have spent summer vacations surveying local employment opportunities for their students. In one city nineteen counselors produced a handbook describing 175 local entry jobs.

In one school students selected help-wanted advertisements from the local newspapers and wrote to the employers, explaining that they were students who were not applying for the jobs but who would like to have more information about the jobs to supplement their study of occupations. Many personnel directors answered their letters fully.

Roxanne Zimet, a physical education teacher, reports: "I have . . . had my classes fill out index cards . . . about any jobs they have had. I have also asked them to have their parents and other members of their immediate family do the same. With surprising ease I already have a file of over 200 cards with firsthand information about local occupations."

In a summer program at Empire Junior High School in Cleveland, Ohio, six students interviewed successful black business men and women, wrote seven brief biographies, and published them in a pamphlet [Cager and others, 38].

Thirty counselors from out of town, who were attending a conference, surveyed all employers in Charles Town, West Virginia, in one afternoon. They found forty-four employers who received them well and were willing to talk; five were unwilling and five were absent.

De Haan and Kough [93] suggested:

Ask the dropout if he knows where to start looking for a job. Ask him if jobs are currently available. Ask him how much he thinks he will make the first weeks, by the end of the first year, and in the future. . . . You might even suggest that he scout around for a job a month or two before he drops out. Youngsters have been known to hurry back to the classroom for more education after getting the brush-off from several prospective employers.

For other descriptions of this technique in practice and for other variations of it, see Ames [10], Clark [62], Dempsey and Begnoche [94], Dresden [111], Engen [117], Janney [203], and Williams [414].

For more extended discussion of community surveys and job analysis see Chapter 8 in Norris, Zeran, Hatch, and Engelkes [286] and the *Handbook for Analyzing Jobs* [155].

COMMENT

Students whose plans are based upon starry-eyed visions of glamorous careers, in fields about which they know very little, sometimes need an opportunity to look at the realities of the employment market. Participation in a survey of entry jobs will not correct all the unrealistic dreams, but it may help a few students who want to be realistic to find out what the realities are.

This technique provides a quick way of covering considerable territory. It may reveal some employment possibilities previously unsuspected. It may injure public relations if poorly done or improve them if well done. From the results of the survey the more promising opportunities may be selected for further study by visit or group conference.

REVIEW QUESTIONS

1 What is the purpose of the student survey of entry jobs?
2 How are students prepared for interviews?
3 What are the guidance values of the survey?
4 You are teaching a twelfth-grade course or unit in occupations. You have time to do either a follow-up study or a survey of entry jobs, but not both. Which will you do? Why?
5 How would you conduct a survey if you were a counselor in the high school that you attended?
6 You are a counselor in a settlement house in a poor section of a large city. Your club members need and want part-time jobs. How will you organize a survey of entry jobs to help them?
7 You are a graduate student in a course for counselors. You and the other students in your class want to know more about jobs for counselors. How will you organize and conduct a survey?

Chapter 17

Case Conference — An Exercise in Decision Making

The case conference has long been used as a device for training counselors and for pooling information and judgment on difficult problems. It is here adapted to another purpose. It may be used for any length of time from one period to an entire unit or course.

PURPOSE

The purpose is the old, old ideal of education, so frequently sought, so seldom achieved—to teach students and clients how to think. But this time they are not to learn how to think in the abstract in any and all situations by some irrelevant exercise in mental calisthenics. Instead they practice thinking about problems of career planning by discussing actual or hypothetical cases. In this way, we hope, they become more aware of the many things they should know about themselves and about jobs when they are making career plans. We hope they may also begin to see how some of these facts relate to each other.

In the remainder of this chapter the word "teacher" may be interpreted to include counselor and group leader, and the word "student" to include client and group member.

PROCEDURE

Selecting the Cases The counselor or teacher selects from past experience the case of some student who faced a fairly common problem. He changes enough unimportant facts to disguise identities and then presents the case to the class. He says in effect, "If you faced this problem, what would you do? What do you think this person should have done?" For example:

Julia is a sophomore in high school. Her brother, who has been supporting the family, is to be married in April. Julia's mother has just told her that she will have to quit school in April and go to work. Julia wants to be a stenographer and has made a brilliant start in the commercial course. What can she do?

Tony has been offered two jobs. He can be a telephone lineman, or he can be assistant to the superintendent of a small manufacturing plant, which may not survive a severe depression. Which job should he take? Why?

Sheila is about to graduate from a secretarial course. She is wondering whether to look for a job in the small town where she and her parents live, or in the large city which is 100 miles away. Where should she look for work? Why?

Martin is shy, awkward, and uneasy in the company of strangers. He greatly admires his uncle who seems to be confident, poised, and cordial to everyone. The uncle is a traveling salesman. Martin thinks that if he becomes a traveling salesman, he will become more like his uncle. What do you think?

The beginning counselor, who has no cases of his own, may find case material in the recollection of problems that he or she or friends have faced, or may invent a case and tell the students that the case is hypothetical. Students also may be invited to invent and submit typical cases; some students may seize this opportunity to submit their own problems in disguise.

Excellent case conference materials on behavorial problems of young workers, and directions for using them with high school students, may be found in Meyer and Anderson [260] and in the Multi Media Training Package [272] developed by the Houston Vocational Guidance Service—Group Guidance Program under the direction of Keith Turkington and Carol Anderson.

Leading the Discussion   While the students discuss the problem, the teacher or counselor acts as moderator. Difference of opinion is encouraged. Students are assured that it is all right for them to change their minds during the discussion, to favor one approach at one time and later to favor a different approach, because we are all searching for the best approach, we are all trying to help one another to think logically about the problem, and we should all be as willing to receive new ideas as to contribute them. This cooperative approach to a problem may be at first a little strange to some students; if so, it is perhaps time they become acquainted with it.

During the discussion the moderator expresses no opinions, answers all questions regarding the person and the job, improvising answers if necessary, and injects pertinent questions if the students do not think of them. As the discussion of various possibilities is completed, the class may vote on them or not, as the moderator thinks wise. If they do vote, the moderator points out that a majority judgment is not necessarily a correct judgment and that the vote is taken merely as a matter of human interest and as a further means of comparing ideas.

When the discussion ends, the moderator reports what the former student actually did and mentions that this was not necessarily the best solution. The class may or may not wish to comment upon the decision. When they finish, the moderator makes any comments that seem appropriate and then goes on to the next case.

In presenting the case, the moderator gives just enough facts to start discussion. His entire presentation takes only a few seconds. Obviously, in this time he cannot present all the information that one should have before making an important decision. The presentation is inadequate; the inadequacy is intentional. The purpose of this intentional inadequacy is to give the students practice in thinking for themselves about what additional information they should have before they reach a decision. They may go a long way toward one decision before someone asks for information on a relevant point, and when this information is presented, they may see at once that they were on the wrong track. After a few experiences of this kind they begin to ask pertinent questions before they try to make decisions. This habit of inquiry is exactly what this technique is intended to develop.

Live Cases   After some experience on disguised cases the teacher may invite members of the class to submit problems of their own on which they would like to have the help of the class. From the problems submitted the teacher may select those which can be discussed with profit to the class and without injury to the individual who submitted the problem. The experienced teacher-counselor who knows the class will quickly recognize some problems that should be discussed only in private, lest the blunt comments of tactless youth crush the feelings of the subject. Other problems are so relatively free of emotional context that they can be discussed with little danger. When the students know that they are discussing a real problem and that what they say may affect someone's decision, class interest approaches a new high. The person whose problem is discussed sometimes gets help, too. After such a discussion one of the author's students, who had offered her own problem for demonstration use, wrote, "I can't express in words how grateful I am . . . for the help that you have given me. Thanks a million."

In a college course on choosing your vocation, Hewer [164] devoted each of several class meetings

> . . . to the discussion of the vocational problem of a different member of the group. The name of the member under discussion was not divulged to the group, but the member himself had been informed that he would be the one discussed. His test results, personal data and grades were available for the discussion.
>
> Observations of the groups indicated that the students became increasingly adept at requesting and utilizing data relevant to a vocational choice. The students also demonstrated the ability to acquire and use educational and occupational information in the small class setting. As a result of their discussion, the group generally arrived at several useful vocational suggestions for the person whose problem was under discussion.

Kagan [213] has observed that "resistive clients who tend to fear or distrust school personnel often become very communicative in group counseling situations. . . . There is a certain security in observing that the counselor is outnumbered. . . . "

The counselor who has had little experience in leading informal discussions may find helpful suggestions in Appendix B.

What Students Learn   To demonstrate this technique in a graduate course the author asked two classes to discuss the case of an experienced counselor who had been offered two jobs, one as a city director of guidance, the other as a college professor of counselor education. The question posed was which job she should take. Both classes were asked at the end of the discussion to list what they had learned from it. Their answers included the following:

> Probationary period in college teaching.
> Retirement provisions for college teachers.
> I'm sure I never realized that there were so many things to consider and weigh when making such a choice.
> A person must make the decision himself, but before doing so, he should consult with others for the purpose of completely evaluating each alternative.
> Because of college enrollment slump, professors may be discharged.
> I personally find I get too confused talking it over too much.
> Heretofore completely ignorant of university tenure.
> College professors have more freedom with regard to how they use their time and plan their work.
> Didn't know that some private colleges do not have legal tenure.
> Didn't think of the internal politics that the director might have to cope with.
> Discuss with others the pros and cons of the position—a larger number of people than I would have consulted before having learned of this technique.
> All I learned that would be of value to me is how very complex such a problem is. It teaches me fully to explore the issues. This problem is presenting itself to me within a month.
> I did not learn anything I did not know before I came to this class.
> Need for thoroughly investigating the pros and cons of each situation in every respect for present and future possibilities.
> Freedom in the classroom for college professors.
> I also found out what the expression "retiring on the job" means with regard to college professors.

VARIATIONS

Fink [123] invited students to submit their own problems for class discussion and reported:

> I have used a variation of the case conference and this has been so successful it has become a Friday morning feature of every week. We discuss problems of the kids in the class. At first it was slow getting started and the problems were of a minor nature or were about "friends of mine." Since then it has become a real problem solving period and the class is not at all reluctant about admitting the problems are personal. The only part I play is to decide whether the problem could be best demonstrated by

role-playing or discussion and from then on the class takes over. No attempt is made to try to reach an answer or to solve the problem; I only want the problem brought out and want the class to see that all problems have some degree of universality and that there are many possible solutions.

Greenberg [144] used flash cards to impress students with the desirability of getting all the pertinent facts before selecting an occupational objective.

To try it out on an average ability seventh grade class, I prepared the following five flash cards:

1   $110.00 salary per week
2   outdoor work
3   physical work
4   college is not required
5   most people in this field are employed by the city

After showing each card I asked how many would accept the job knowing only what was on the card. Five out of thirty wanted the job upon seeing card #1, seven more joined in upon seeing card #2 and by the time I got to card #5 twenty students had accepted the job. I then informed the 20 that they were all hired as garbagemen. . . . By the time we had played the game several times, most of the students had formulated a series of very sophisticated questions which they wanted answered before committing themselves to a job.

A technique similar to the case conference has been used in several group efforts to teach job-hunting techniques. Individual students have presented to a group their own statements of qualifications, their letters of application, etc., for suggestion and criticism. Case histories revealing how other persons chose jobs, planned campaigns to get them, and got them have been discussed.

Other job-hunting courses have included practice job interviews before a class, followed by class discussion of good and bad practices displayed. This variation will be discussed further in Chapter 20. `

Life Career Games are exercises in simulated career planning, consequences of decisions, and factors affecting personal life satisfaction. Teams of students compete in planning the most satisfying life of a "profile" person by deciding how the person will spend a typical week representing a year in that person's life. Counselors can choose profiles ranging in age from junior high through high school and beyond. Consequences of decisions are given after each "year," including unplanned events affecting future plans. As students plan for education and careers they use occupational information which can be expanded by supplemental materials as the counselor desires. See Boocock [22] and Varenhorst [398, 399].

COMMENT

An alert group that likes to argue will bring out many of the important elements in any case. They will quickly catch the fallacies in each other's thinking and will improve as they go along. A slow class or one accustomed to docile acceptance of whatever teacher says may require more help and a longer time to get under way. Some cases readily provoke profitable discussion. Others do not. The teacher must expect considerable variation in the quality of class sessions until experience indicates which are the most stimulating cases.

The teacher who likes to encourage students to think for themselves, who enjoys provoking discussion, and who has had some success at it will do better with this method than the teacher who prefers to tell them how to do things, though the latter teacher, if able to keep reasonably quiet while the students are discussing, may find the audience more attentive than usual when he or she starts to lecture.

The author's experience seems to indicate that the technique does result in making students more conscious of the variety of considerations that should influence career decisions.

The technique of the case conference is developed in more detail in two books by Richard D. Allen, *Case-conference Problems in Group Guidance* [4] and *Common Problems in Group Guidance* [6]. Although both books are now out of print, they are still excellent, and are still available in some libraries. Other excellent materials on decision making may be found in Gelatt, Varenhorst, and Carey [136, 137], and in Gelatt, Varenhorst, Carey, and Miller [138, 139].

REVIEW QUESTIONS

1 What is the purpose of the case conference, and how is this purpose achieved?
2 In opening the case conference, how much information does the moderator offer? Why?
3 Does the moderator express his or her own opinions?
4 Does the moderator raise questions?
5 What are the values and the dangers in using live cases from the class?
6 In what ways is the case conference superior to instruction on the same topics? In what ways inferior?
7 Where and how could you use the case conference in your present or future work? For what purposes? What would be its values and limitations in this situation?

Chapter 18

Laboratory Study

The techniques previously described require all the students to study substantially the same thing at the same time. The laboratory study undertakes to provide for individual differences.

Though developed and used primarily for career planning, this technique could be used for educational planning by the substitution of a different set of questions. The method may be used in either a unit or a course in occupations.

PURPOSE

The purpose is to give each individual an opportunity to study intensively one or more occupations of particular interest to the person, to compare the requirements of these with what he already knows about himself, to prepare a summary of his present thinking that may facilitate profitable discussion in the counseling interview, and incidentally to learn where and how to get facts about jobs whenever they are needed in the future.

In the remainder of this chapter the word "teacher" may be interpreted to include counselor and group leader, and the word "student" to include client and group member.

PROCEDURE

Students Select Occupations   Each student selects one or more occupations that he or she would like to study. The student or client who has no preference may be given a list of occupations from which to choose, or may have an occupation assigned. Lists of possible occupations may be found in the reports of local follow-up studies which reveal the jobs most frequently obtained by former students, in the classified telephone directory, in the table of contents of the *Occupational Outlook Handbook* [292], and in the *Dictionary of Occupational Titles* [98]. At this point the teacher or counselor may wish to review the section "The Client with No Preferences" in Chapter 10.

Resources Are Provided   Books, pamphlets, magazines, and newspaper clippings on various occupations are moved from the career resources center or from the school library to the classroom, or arrangements are made to conduct the laboratory study in the center or the library itself. The students are asked not to deface library materials.

Each student is given one or more copies of an outline for the study of an occupation such as the one in Chapter 3 or the one in Appendix C.

The students are taught how to find and use the sources of information available to them: indexes, bibliographies, publications, and people. Most available printed material may be located through the indexes described in Chapter 4. The librarian may be asked to show the class what other indexes and materials are available locally and how to use them. The class may also visit the nearest public library for the same purpose.

The teacher gives a few simple suggestions on how to compare and appraise materials from different sources by noting copyright dates, authors' related experience and qualifications, biases to be expected in recruiting literature, etc. These suggestions are repeated later at appropriate times as the teacher helps individual students with the problems they present. For more on this see Chapter 5.

Students may be encouraged also to visit the local office of the state employment service and to call on local workers and employers for information. Suggestions regarding visits will be found in Chapter 14. Additional suggestions regarding sources of occupational information may be found in Chapters 4 and 5.

The students next proceed to work individually on the occupations they have chosen. Each class period is used for independent study. The teacher is present as a consultant, to answer questions, and to be generally helpful, but each student plans his own work and proceeds at his own pace.

Students Report Frequently and Briefly   Occasionally the teacher calls the group together to compare experiences and to tell one another very briefly and informally, never in more than a few sentences, where they have found the most interesting and useful information. At these times each student is given an opportunity to ask the others if they know where he can find something that he has had trouble locating. The skillful teacher can use these sessions to develop a mutually helpful attitude that will make the class profitable and pleasant for all. A few minutes also may be devoted to exchanging interesting bits of occupational information that the students have picked up. These reports should be brief, never longer than a few sentences per student; they can become insufferably boring if each student is asked to tell all that he has learned. The author has obtained the best results by asking each person in turn two questions: What is the most interesting thing you have learned since your last report? Is there anything on which you want our help? Students who talk too long should be gently interrupted. For suggestions on how to do this see Appendix B.

The reporting procedure may be varied by asking each student to write one sentence stating the most interesting thing he has learned about any occupation or about sources of occupational information since his last report. The teacher may collect the papers and read each sentence to the class, pausing after each one to inquire, "Does anyone want more information on this?"

For further variety, the class may be divided into small buzz groups and asked to exchange with one another the most interesting things they have learned. Each group may also be asked to choose its own moderator who will report to the total group on the one most interesting item reported to the buzz group. Time for questions may be allowed after each report.

Students who complete the study of their preferred occupation before the rest of the class may be assigned to help others who are having trouble, or they may begin the study of a second field.

The project terminates when the teacher feels that the students have spent as much time on it as will be profitable. This may be at the end of a few weeks or at the close of a semester.

There should be no final symposium in which each student has to suffer through long oral reports on occupations in which he or she is not interested. If some kind of final review is desired, it can be arranged by announcing all the occupations that are being investigated and then inviting the students to ask each other any questions they wish.

VARIATIONS

One high school used substantially this technique, but with a shorter outline, in the occupational part of its course in self-appraisal and careers. The author never saw a better laboratory session than one conducted by this method in a class of general-course seniors. The room was equipped with a small library of occupational pamphlets. Books describing several occupations had been taken apart and the individual chapters separately rebound as pamphlets in order that several students could use the books at once. Each student had a folder containing his own outline and notes. Each came into the room quietly, went to his desk, opened his folder, went to the library, selected his materials, brought them back to his desk, and sat down to read and take notes. During the entire period the teacher talked with her two visitors; only two or three students came to ask for help. At the close of the period each student took his materials back to the library, put away his folder, and went on to his next class. As here described this procedure could suggest a lazy teacher, but the quiet, competent, interested students convincingly reflected the effective teaching that had gone before. Here were students, by no means above average in ability, who had learned and were learning to get what they wanted with a minimum of outside help. One could easily anticipate their continued use of similar techniques in adult life.

A high school in Wisconsin used a similar technique with younger students. A classroom was equipped like a library with bookshelves, tables, and movable chairs. The school collection of occupational books and pamphlets was moved in. Each student chose six occupations and arranged them in order of preference. Then each began with the occupation at the foot of the list and worked up.

At one small New England high school, the five teachers invited the eighty students to state their vocational preferences. The teachers divided the more popular occupations among themselves, got all the information they could on these occupations, and made periodic oral reports to the students. Attendance at the report sessions was voluntary and close to 100 percent. In one year the five teachers reported on a total of thirty occupations.

At another school each teacher undertook to become an authority on one occupation and to report to the students on it. Each Tuesday the seventh period of the school day was reserved for these reports. Classes were rotated so that each teacher got a different class each week until all the students had heard all the teachers.

In many schools, students have been asked to interview members of their families about their occupations and to make brief reports to the class.

Natalie Brody, when teaching general sciences in junior high school, reported: "Each period starts with two reports given by students on their interviews of persons who are making careers in science. This has created a feeling of practical reality and usefulness as a background to the work covered in our course, namely, physics, chemistry, biology, geology and astronomy."

After trying the laboratory study method in two group guidance classes, Adalinda Rodrigues reported that "the brighter group was able to work independently, enjoyed it more and seemed to benefit from the experience. . . . For the other group whose reading level is very low, the reading material was too difficult and they did not know how to use the sources of information . . . they rapidly lost interest."

COMMENT

Hutson [196] has criticized the laboratory study:

> Instead of having the pupil become acquainted with the whole array of occupations so that he will have a basis for choice, it serves to concentrate his attention on a narrow sector of the vocational horizon. It is true that he will make a report to the class and that he will listen to their reports, but the learning acquired from such experience is of doubtful quantity and quality.

The author has seen some of the best and some of the worst teaching of occupations done by this method. In the hands of a lazy teacher it can be a quick way of killing all interest. Under a good one it can be a stimulating experience in independent research.

Arutunian [11] described a one-semester Life Decision Making Course, open to all eleventh- and twelfth-grade students and reported to be "the most popular elective on campus." The course met in the Career Development Center where both teachers had their offices. Each student selected his or her own learning activity packages. Each package took two weeks to complete.

Some students will do a superficial job of research, but even this can be helpful to the counselor, for the report will quickly reveal the nature and extent of the information upon which the student's occupational preferences are based; in two minutes a skilled counselor can learn from a completed outline what might easily require twenty minutes to draw out by oral questioning.

Students will pick up some misinformation; they will do this in any case. Some of it will be corrected by contradiction from other sources. Some will remain to be corrected as the teacher reviews the outline, some will be corrected in the counseling interview, and some will get by. Nothing we do is perfect.

But students under a good teacher will learn by this method where and how to find the most reliable facts about jobs—a useful part of anyone's education. They will accumulate pertinent occupational information from a variety of sources. They can hardly escape comparing sources. They will have, in the blank form constantly before them, a reminder of the important kinds of information to be sought and considered. They may also have the experience of thinking somewhat systematically about the relation of occupational facts to their own needs, abilities, limitations, ambitions, and interests before they come to the counselor to discuss them.

REVIEW QUESTIONS

1 What are the purposes of the laboratory study? How is it conducted?
2 What are some of the methods that may be used to exchange information? Which do you prefer? Why?
3 Should each student report the results of his or her research to the group? How?
4 What are some of the advantages and disadvantages of the laboratory study?
5 If you were teaching a course in occupations, would you use this method? Why? Why not?
6 If you had to choose between the laboratory study and the case conference, which would you choose? Why?
7 What do you like or dislike about the outline for the study of an occupation which appears in Appendix C?

Chapter 19

Self-measurement

Most counselors and teachers of occupations have tried in some way to help their students to consider their own fitness for the occupations in which they were interested. Many teachers and counselors have hesitated to give students the results of psychological tests, perhaps rightly fearing that these would be misinterpreted and misused and that bitter protests might follow from parents of children with low intelligence quotients.

Some years ago the late Richard D. Allen boldly proposed to surmount these difficulties by teaching students what tests do and do not mean, how to take them, how to score them, and how to interpret and use the results. The implied assumption was that teachers, counselors, and psychologists are not the only ones who can learn such things. He wrote a book called *Self-measurement Projects in Group Guidance* [5], in which his proposals were implemented with suggested teaching techniques. A number of schools have since put Allen's ideas into practice in their courses in self-appraisal and careers. Some colleges have included discussion of test scores in career planning courses.

The technique may be used within a course or a unit, or as an entire course in itself.

In the remainder of this chapter the word "teacher" may be interpreted to include counselor and group leader, and the word "student" to include client and group member.

PURPOSE

The purpose is to help students learn whatever tests and inventories may reveal about their needs, values, interests, abilities, and limitations and to teach them how to interpret and use the results of such tests.

PROCEDURE

The students are given an elementary course in psychological testing, not unlike the training courses offered to future school psychologists and counselors in colleges and universities but adapted to the level of the students.

In this course they study the nature of individual differences, the theories of testing, the concepts of reliability and validity, the meaning of percentile ranks, the use of norms, and the interpretation and use of test scores in making career plans.

The students then take a wide variety of tests and inventories; they discuss in turn what each one measures and fails to measure, what the results mean and do not mean. The students get their own scores; no one else sees them except the teacher. The students are not compared with one another, but they are encouraged individually and helped to compare their scores on one test with their scores on other tests of similar and different characteristics in order to learn all they can about their own strengths and weaknesses. Each student has a folder in which to keep a profile sheet. On this sheet the student records graphically his or her percentile rank on each test, in order to be able to see at a glance those areas in which he or she is relatively strong and weak.

Class discussions of test results are always in terms of hypothetical rather than actual cases. The teacher never says, "John has a P.R. of 17; what does this mean?" but rather, "If you had a P.R. of 17, what would it mean?" Each student has a chance to hear his or her own score or one near it discussed as a hypothetical case and to ask any questions desired without revealing her or his own score.

VARIATIONS

College preparatory students at a university high school, in a course called "Vocations and College Life," visited several local places of employment, then took a battery of aptitude tests and compared their measured abilities with the requirements of the occupations they had seen.

One liberal arts college included a unit on self-measurement in its required course in freshman orientation. Whenever possible the students scored their own tests. All test scores, including intelligence quotients, were released to the students. The course was taught by a professor from the department of psychology to sections of twenty to twenty-five students each.

Other self-appraisal units in college courses in vocational planning are described in Chapters 13 and 16 of Morse and Dressel [269].

Van Dusen [397] described an evening course offered to adults by an urban university:

It is scheduled for a one-hour and forty-minute meeting weekly. . . . The enrollment is limited to about fifty students each semester. . . .

The Counselors who serve these adult students are graduate students. . . . There are thirteen such Counselors, each serving four or five clients. . . .

The battery includes two intelligence tests, two interest inventories, and two personality inventories. . . . After the group finishes each test they again "buzz" in the smaller groups on the issue of what kinds of questions, pertinent to the counseling situation, the test they have just completed could possibly answer. . . . And we feel that having the clients explore, with each other in their small sub-groups and then with the discussion leader, the limitations of test scores, erroneous ideas concerning the usefulness of tests more quickly dissipate than is ordinarily accomplished through the counseling interview alone. At least it seems that in most instances, the client has a large headstart on understanding the tests when such issues arise in the interview.

Morelli [268] described how the Utah State Employment Service experimented with one, two, and three sessions of group counseling with the "hard core unemployed" from several occupational groups and with "high school seniors who had participated in the school counseling and testing program."

From two years of experimentation the following tentative conclusions were drawn:

Each group should consist of not less than 7 nor more than 12 individuals. Sessions should be scheduled for 2-hour periods.

Individuals appear to gain more insight into their problems through personal interaction with the group than they do through an individual interview with the counselor.

Jolles [210] reported another variation of this technique as follows:

A formal course in Industrial Psychology was given to 10 prison inmates of at least above average mentality. During the course the students became interested in learning about their own vocational aptitudes, and they profited from a class discussion of their test results. At the end of the course the entire group had lost their hostile attitudes toward Psychology and the prison classification system. Many of the group wished to continue guidance on an individual basis. Finally, the technique is not only time saving but also makes it easier for inmates to seek help by enabling them to escape ridicule from fellow prisoners.

Slotkin [360] described a method of teaching high school students to understand test norms.

Froehlich [131] and Hoyt [190] reported experiments in which group discussion of test scores produced as good results as individual counseling.

COMMENT

Many tests are good enough to be used in the rough screening of applicants for employment, but they are not good enough to predict the success or failure of any one individual.

Test scores may be spuriously high or low because of individual differences in cultural background and in previous education or because of errors in test administration.

Before any test score is given to any student, the teacher should be as certain as possible that the score is as accurate as can be obtained, and that both he and the student fully appreciate the possible errors of measurement.

But once the teacher and the student are satisfied that a specific test score will add useful information to the student's self-knowledge, there is no more reason for concealing low scores on aptitude or intelligence tests than there is for concealing defective eyesight, poor hearing, or a weak heart. Sooner or later every human being must learn and accept his own limitations. One of the counselor's responsibilities is to help the student to discover both his assets and his liabilities, to accept those which cannot be changed, and to make wholesome emotional, educational, and vocational adjustments to them. The longer we delay revealing them, the more difficult the adjustments may become.

Warters [404] noted:

> Because teachers of classes in group guidance fail to make clear the basic concept of the limitations of human capacity, students often gain wrong conceptions of their individual possibilities. . . . Students should not be led to believe that endless opportunities are awaiting them in adult life and that these possibilities are open to all who are ambitious and willing to work hard enough to attain them. . . . Making clear the basic concept of limitations helps to decrease neurotic tendencies, whereas failing to make clear this concept helps to increase them.

Emotional Turmoil   Unquestionably, there will be emotional turmoil when some students discover their limitations, but emotional turmoil is not necessarily undesirable. Skillfully handled, it may even facilitate improved adjustment. The effective teacher will not ignore it nor minimize it; he will face it squarely as one of life's common occurrences. He will arrange counseling interviews whenever the need for them is indicated.

There is no simple formula for helping people to adjust to their newly discovered limitations. Sometimes group discussion will help. Sometimes individual counseling will succeed. Sometimes nothing seems to work. However, the inability of some individuals to face reality with equanimity is no reason for denying to others the opportunity to plan their own futures on fact rather than on fancy. The bluntness of this argument for giving students the truth is not intended to imply that the counselor should be blunt when he presents the facts. Indeed, there will be few times when the counselor will have more need for all the kindness, consideration, and tact at his command.

Although some students are disturbed when they learn of their limitations, others are relieved. To a frustrated student, the most welcome news in the world may be the discovery that his intellectual capacity is not equal to that of his competitors and that neither he nor his teacher nor his parents should expect his achievement to meet the standard previously set.

The teaching of occupations has been criticized on the ground that students learned about occupations beyond their own range of ability and thus acquired unrealizable ambitions. If the criticism is justified, the remedy is not to abandon the course in occupations. The remedy is to teach students all we can about the nature of individual differences in vocational aptitude—how to discover them and how to make appropriate vocational adjustments in the light of them. And we must stop being secretive about test results, which are more vital to the student than to anyone else who uses them. Not every test reveals a limitation. Students sometimes discover aptitudes and abilities of which they were unaware. The desirability of this revelation is seldom questioned.

One of the limitations of aptitude testing has been the general lack of cutting scores, without which the counselor cannot tell whether a mediocre score is too low for satisfactory work performance or high enough to permit the client to hold a steady job if he has the other essential qualifications. Christensen [56] reported a promising attack on this problem. A large manufacturer and a carpenters' union used the General Aptitude Test Battery for selection purposes and established their own cutting scores. High school seniors were " . . . referred for GATB testing early in their senior year. . . . Counselors may help . . . a . . . senior to estimate his chances . . . as a carpenter's apprentice since they know from past experience the approximate cut-off scores used for selection."

The author does not recommend that every beginning counselor rush out and buy the first tests to be found, administer them carelessly, have them scored without rescoring to check accuracy, and interpret them without reading the manual of directions! Certainly anyone who is to use tests and teach students to use them must be adequately trained in test administration and interpretation. The necessity of such training already is recognized in some state certification requirements for school counselors. If the beginning teacher of occupations has not had such training, he or she should get it as promptly as possible.

Although the self-measurement technique gets pretty close to individual differences, it is still not intended to substitute for individual counseling. It is intended to facilitate counseling by enabling student and counselor to discuss test results without the counselor's having to teach a thumbnail course on test interpretation in one interview.

Witnessing one of these courses in action, the author was amazed to hear general-course seniors discussing test interpretation with far more understanding than one finds in many meetings of beginning counselors and in most meetings of school teachers. High school students can learn psychology; it is high time we taught them some.

Public Relations   Because some schools have established policies regarding the release of test scores, the teacher should inquire about such policies before undertaking a unit on self-measurement. The possible effect of the unit on public relations should be discussed in advance with the teacher's immediate superior.

The beginning counselor, who is using this technique of group guidance for the first time, may be wise to begin with tests that will create a minimum of disturbance, for example, tests of musical aptitude, spatial relations, vocational interest, clerical aptitude, etc., rather than tests of intelligence. Personality tests, if used at all, probably should be introduced last, and only when the counselor has time and skill to counsel individually and immediately those who may be greatly disturbed by their extreme scores.

Rothney [328] found that counselors who reported and interpreted test scores to 869 high school sophomores noted obvious disappointment in "only 3 per cent of the cases."

REVIEW QUESTIONS

1 Do you agree that test scores should be released to students? Why? Why not? Under what circumstances?
2 If you were to conduct a self-measurement project, would you change the procedure described in the text? How? Why?
3 Do you agree with the author's comments on emotional turmoil?
4 Are students always disturbed by learning of their limitations? What did Rothney find on this topic?
5 If you were teaching a course in occupations, would you include self-appraisal in some form? In what form? Why? Why not?
6 Has anything in this chapter surprised, provoked, or challenged you? What? How?

Chapter 20

Computers and Other Methods of Getting and Using Occupational Information

The methods of getting and using occupational information already described are not the only good ones, nor are they the only ones that have been widely used. This chapter contains brief descriptions of, and comments upon, some other techniques which appear to have merit and some which the author questions but which require comment because of their common use.

As in other chapters, the word "teacher" may be interpreted to include "counselor" and "group leader," and the word "student" to include "client" and group member."

Computers, VIEW Decks, etc. The use of mechanical and electronic equipment to store and retrieve occupational information has grown rapidly in recent years. Most of the current uses of this equipment fall roughly into three categories: VIEW decks, job banks, and interactive computers.

VIEW decks are sets of IBM or similar punched cards. In an aperture in each card is a small piece of microfilm which carries a description of one occupation. The cards may be punched according to any desired code that will facilitate the mechanical extraction of cards describing occupations which fit any desired set of specifications. Selected cards may be placed in a microfilm reader and read at once, or in a reader-printer from which the user may get a full-size printed copy of the microfilmed material to take with him. Some later decks include microfiche and casettes.

VIEW decks have been created and maintained by state, county, and city school systems to serve both school and college students. Information on local employment and training opportunities usually has been included. Once prepared, VIEW decks are easier and cheaper to revise than printed materials. In at least one county all of the VIEW decks are collected at the end of each school year, revised during the summer, and returned to the schools in the fall.

The reprints produced by the reader-printers are inexpensive and are produced only as needed. There are never any surplus copies to be thrown away, hence there is no temptation to keep them and use them when they should be discarded.

Job banks are computers used for one specific purpose, and frequently restricted to it. They have been created and maintained by the U.S. Employment Service and its affiliated state services, by school and college placement offices, and by private employment agencies. Brief information on unfilled job orders from any number of employers, received by any number of placement offices and agencies, in any number of locations, can be fed into a single computerized job bank, and a complete computer printout can be produced each morning at as many terminals as desired. The input may also include data on any number of job applicants. It is thus possible for all the public and private employment services in a city, state, or nation to pool and to exchange as much information as they wish. A placement interviewer, a counselor, or a job applicant may have instant access to all job orders. A branch employment office can then be established anywhere, with no more equipment than a computer terminal and the usual office furniture.

Interactive computerized career information and guidance services have been created and maintained by schools, colleges, and other agencies, operating individually or in consortia, and by commercial organizations which sell their products and services to such institutions and organizations. Equipment may be purchased and a computerized service developed locally; or the service can be purchased, and delivered via telephone lines, from an organization which has developed a centralized computer system to serve a wider area.

The input to the data bank of a computerized guidance system may include information of any kind about educational and occupational opportunities, in any desired length, in words or pictures; it may include the academic records, test scores, expressed interests, preferences, values, and other data about the students and others who will use the equipment, and records of previous interactions between the user and the computer.

The output may be in the form of words typed on a typewriter terminal and in color film images on a cathode-ray tube. Some systems will provide a paper copy of anything which appears on the terminal screen.

A computer may be programed to ask the user a series of questions similar to some of those asked in counseling interviews, and thus to guide the user in exploring what the computer has to offer. A student's "conversation" with the computer may be reproduced for the counselor, or such conversations may be made confidential. The computer may also be programed to provide the counselor, at the end of each day, with a list of all the persons who have used the computer during the day. The occupational information on computer tapes can be revised as frequently as desired, in less time and at less expense than similar information in printed form.

The interactive computer can do one thing faster and better than any counselor or client. It can compare almost any amount of information about an individual user with almost any amount of information on almost any number of occupations. It can then quickly produce a list of occupations for possible exploration, or a report on the appropriateness of any occupation for any student, in terms of the data already fed into the computer. Thus the computer may tell a student that his or her academic record, measured interests, and expressed values all resemble those of successful persons in a specified occupation or differ from them in stated ways.

Such reports may be produced for any one individual at any time, or for a large number of individuals at a time of day when the computer is not in demand; the latter use is called "batch processing."

VIEW decks and computers have one important characteristic seldom shared by the usual school, college, or agency collection of occupational information: one person, with or without assistants, must be designated to prepare the occupational information input and to keep it up to date. If the input is inaccurate or biased, or if it is allowed to become obsolete, the responsible person can be readily identified. If the designated person gives his or her entire time to this job, as many do, that individual can become far more competent in occupational research than are most counselors. Some systems already have five or more full-time persons continually preparing and revising the occupational information input. One staff reviews and revises its occupational descriptions every six to eight months.

To date, most of the VIEW decks and computer systems have been produced with substantial project grants from government funds, or from the research and development budgets of commercial producers. Some of the VIEW decks and some of the simpler computer systems are now operating with only local support. Two of the more complex computer systems have been abandoned by their original sponsors because they were too expensive to find a market. One conclusion appears to be justified from experience to date: a computer system which is compatible with the computer hardware used by a school system for other purposes has a much better chance of survival than one which is not compatible.

One of the early expectations of the producers of VIEW decks and computer systems was that they would be more attractive to students than the familiar and sometimes forbidding printed materials. Everyone was encouraged when students, counselors, and teachers all responded to invitations to use the new equipment. While the systems were new and novel and were actively promoted by their sponsors, use was widespread. But when the promotional efforts were discontinued, the use of the equipment in some places declined alarmingly. The decline was not universal, but some VIEW deck and computer sponsors now say that some kind of continual promotional effort is necessary if student, teacher, and even counselor use of the system is to be maintained at a level sufficient to justify the cost. In one school every student is notified, at least once a year, that a computer terminal has been reserved for his or her exclusive use at a specified day and hour, and the student is asked to notify the office if he or she does not intend to use it. Apparently there are places where students do not use these new resources any more than they previously used the occupational pamphlet collections unless someone in some way prods them to do so, and where counselors do not prod students unless someone prods the counselors.

Computers can also be used in occupational research. Christal [55] described computer programs that will answer a great variety of detailed questions about the specific tasks performed by almost any group of Air Force workers in any occupation at any location, who have been working for any specified length of time, who have any stated interests, level of job satisfaction, and educational background.

New job banks and computer systems are still being developed, and VIEW decks are being expanded and refined.

The U.S. Department of Labor has sponsored one and is currently considering other statewide experiments in assembling, processing, distributing, and revising, every six months, existing occupational information which does not currently reach counselors.

For further information write to the U.S. Employment Service and to the National Occupational Information Service, at the Department of Labor, Washington, D.C., and ask for their latest reports on job banks and other labor market information systems. Write to the National Center for Career Information Services, University of Indiana, Bloomington, Indiana, for current information about VIEW decks. Write to the National Vocational Guidance Association, 1607 New Hampshire Avenue, N.W., Washington, D.C., for its latest report on computer-assisted guidance systems. Write to the ERIC Clearinghouse on Counseling and Personnel Services at the University of Michigan, Ann Arbor, Michigan; to the ERIC Clearinghouse on Career Education at Northern Illinois University, De-Kalb, Illinois; and to the U.S. Office of Education, Washington, D.C.; ask how you can use their resources to learn more about job banks, VIEW decks, and computerized career guidance systems. See Harris [159] and McKinlay [257].

Career Resource Centers   These have been created by schools, colleges, and community agencies. Some are part of a learning resource center; some are separate. Some are fully equipped with computer terminals, VIEW deck reader-printers, occupational films, filmstrips, slides and projectors, audio and video tapes, and collections of the best available occupational books and pamphlets. Some centers are staffed by competent professional counselors who continually compile local occupational information by means of follow-up studies and community surveys, publish brief, readable reports and newsletters, arrange plant tours, find resource people for group conferences, provide job placement services for work experience programs and other part-time, summer, and full-time jobs, and help students, alumni, teachers, and counselors to find out whatever they want to know about occupations and help them to distinguish good information from bad. Some center directors periodically interview recent graduates and their employers in order to facilitate the transition from school to work with a minimum of friction and frustration. Some provide a bilingual telephone service for anyone in the community.

At the other extreme, some centers are no more than a new name for the familiar file of obsolete pamphlets in the counselor's waiting room. In between are community agencies specializing in career counseling and placement which have their own occupational libraries staffed by trained special librarians, and smaller centers in schools and colleges staffed by paraprofessionals who do little more than order and file anything they can find, with no competent critical review of the content. Supervision of paraprofessionals appears to be minimal.

Where one competent professional can give full time to the center, I think it may prove to be one of the most effective means we have of improving the quality of the occupational information we give to our students and clients. Without such professional responsibility the center may just multiply the amount of misinformation dispensed.

For more on these centers see Jacobson [201, 202] and Breckenridge [29].

Mobile Units   Some states and counties have supplemented existing occupational information services by equipping a truck trailer as a career resource center, and sending it, with a counselor, to spend several days at each of several schools, where students, teachers, and local counselors visit it individually or in small groups. Some units also visit shopping centers to make their services available to adults.

Audiovisual Media   Slides, films, audio and video tapes, and phonograph records have been produced and used by counselors, teachers, students, and others in schools, colleges, and community agencies, and by employers, associations, and commercial publishers. Among their purposes are:

To arouse interest, stimulate discussion, change attitudes, and motivate further inquiry.

To increase awareness of occupations previously unknown to the student or client, by brief exposure to many jobs. Some students who resist reading will look at pictures.

To do the same with jobs in a single company, industry, or occupational category.

To show in more detail the work activities in a single job, the abilities required, and the environment in which the work is performed.

To show the life-style of one or more workers in one occupation by including pictures and descriptions of the worker's home, family, recreations, and other activities before and after work.

To provide role models by including photographs of persons with whom the viewer can identify, such as graduates or dropouts from the school or college the viewer is attending, and workers of the same race or sex or near the viewer's age.

The utility of audiovisual means of presenting occupational information obviously depends upon the accuracy and the appropriateness of the material presented. Some industrial films are prepared for purposes other than guidance; they show processes and products but reveal little about the worker and the job. Some recruiting booklets from colleges, industries, and military services are lavishly illustrated with photographs that show only those facilities and activities which are most attractive; they give biased impressions that the counselor may find difficult to correct. All guidance materials should be critically previewed before they are exhibited to students.

Tapes and discs   With the help of audiovisual directors, audio and video tapes can be prepared, reviewed, and edited on location. Conversations and group conferences with employed alumni, other workers, and employers have been recorded on both tapes and discs. Some teachers have used such tapes as much as the counselors. Discs have been placed in juke boxes available to students and others.

Kenyon [217] has reported how one high school and its staff and students, a radio station, and local industries cooperated to prepare recorded descriptions of local employment opportunities and requirements. All recordings were made at the factories and included the normal factory noises as sound effects. The expense was underwritten by the companies. The recordings were used in the course in occupations.

Laramore and Thompson [236] described a one-week workshop in which counselors taped interviews with workers.

One community collects employers' job orders and records them on tapes to which applicants may listen by dialing a telephone number.

Student use of and enthusiasm for tapes and discs has varied. Group conferences with a live resource person and a live audience usually capture more student attention than do recordings of the same conferences when replayed for other groups. Recordings are therefore not recommended as substitutes for plant tours and group conferences except when equally good live performances cannot be provided.

Some schools that have produced their own tapes will make duplicates for other schools that supply them blank tapes. Tapes and discs are also available from the commercial publishers who advertise in professional journals.

The picture story   Some of the best visual aids are homemade. These show former students, both dropouts and alumni, engaged in their present activities at work. There should be several pictures of each person in order to portray adequately all activities. Emphasis should be on photographs of the worker at work in the work environment rather than on industrial processes and equipment. Students whose hobby is photography can produce surprisingly good studies of local jobs. All that is necessary is to explain clearly the results desired and leave the rest to them.

The author once required a college class to present a photographic term paper, showing one worker performing all the duties of his job, with explanatory captions. Some of the results were mediocre, of course, but all were at least acceptable, and a few were really superb. One student presented the work of a barber, including everything from honing a razor to sweeping the floor, in thirty-three photographs so clear and simple that no captions were needed. Another did an illustrated study of a medical laboratory technologist with a half-page of explanation under each picture. Both were far superior to most of the textbook descriptions of these two occupations. The technique is good for what it teaches the person who makes the pictures, and it is helpful in presenting facts to other students. The teacher who is a photographer and who wishes to do a superior job will find helpful suggestions in *The Technique of the Picture Story* by Mich and Eberman [261]. *Ebony* magazine has published a series of picture stories on successful black workers.

Many schools have had students prepare "career books," in which they pasted clippings and pictures related to the occupations of their choice and in which they sometimes recorded whatever they learned about the occupations. The laboratory study method described in Chapter 18 is a refinement of this early technique; the picture-and-clipping notebook may still be used to supplement the laboratory study. Students should be instructed to give preference to pictures that show the worker at work. They should be urged not to cut clippings from library references.

One fourth-grade teacher asked parents who could do so to have pictures taken of themselves at work, and to let their children bring these pictures to school. The children told each other what work their parents did. Many were suprised at the range of occupations.

A teacher of retarded children clipped newspaper and magazine pictures of workers doing their jobs. Each picture was then mounted on a piece of cardboard. A few interesting facts about the work depicted were typewritten and pasted on the reverse side. Then the card was covered with cellophane. Sets of these completed picture cards were passed around the class. Considerable interest was reported.

Job fairs and exhibits Schools, colleges, chambers of commerce, and others have produced employment days, job fairs, career expositions, and opportunity exhibits which resemble the commercial exhibits at national meetings of professional and trade associations. When business is booming and labor is scarce, employers are often willing at their own expense to prepare exhibits, set them up, and provide their own recruiters to answer questions.

Such exhibits have remained open from one evening to ten days for students, parents, and others, from one or more schools, colleges, or other organizations. As many as 40,000 persons from 140 schools have attended a single exhibition. (See Souther [367], Wilstach [416], and Musselman [278].)

Exhibits add some of the values of visual education to other methods of presenting occupational information. They may expose students to a wide variety of occupations in a short time. When the exhibits are all shown on the same day and for one day only, they have many of the disadvantages of the career day, which is discussed later in this chapter. The counselor cannot be present in every booth to hear what goes on, so the student is dependent upon the ethics and integrity of the company representative. In a period of acute labor shortage, recruiters may be tempted to omit facts that might discourage prospective applicants.

Bulletin boards These are used to display photographs of former students at work, with descriptions of their jobs, announcements of future events, jackets from new occupational books, and occupational news and posters from many sources.

Counselors who plan to use bulletin boards to display occupational information may find the following suggestions helpful: Place the board where it will be seen and passed frequently by large numbers of students. Post only one item at a time. Change items frequently, at least once a week. Use short captions in big letters that can be read from a distance. Occasionally post something amusing—a cartoon, a joke, or an anecdote.

Slides The Waukegan Township High School [410] in cooperation with the American Steel and Wire Company prepared a series of forty-eight slides from photographs taken in the Waukegan Works. One purpose of the slide series was "to present visually . . . the occupational opportunities of local industry." The slides were used in orientation, shop, commercial geography, and general English classes in the high school and also in training programs at the mill. Included in the series were pictures of recent high school graduates at work in the plant.

Educational films and filmstrips—homemade Motion pictures of former students at work have been mentioned already in the chapter on follow-up. One school also made a film on entry jobs and one on how to hunt a job. Students and teachers who have 8- or 16-millimeter motion-picture cameras may do likewise in their own communities. For helpful suggestions see the N.V.G.A. *Guidelines* [152], Laramore [233, 234], *Movies with a Purpose* [270], and Peters and Brown [303].

The Urban League in PIttsburgh, Pennsylvania, once prepared a motion-picture film showing Pittsburgh blacks at work in more than thirty occupations, including the professions, business, industry, and personal service.

Cleland [64] described how three amateur photographers were temporarily released from teaching in order to produce a film showing twenty-three alumni at work in twenty-three occupations. Only one graduate and one employer declined to cooperate.

Quick results have been known to follow the showing of some films. After seeing a motion picture about job opportunities in the telephone company " . . . many girls who were not particularly good in secretarial work, but were alert and with pleasing personalities, applied immediately for part-time operator jobs, and were accepted."

Educational films and filmstrips—commercial Reviews of new films and filmstrips on occupations are prepared by the Career Film Evaluation Committee of the National Vocational Guidance Association and published from time to time in the *Vocational Guidance Quarterly* [401]. Some state departments of education have published lists of recommended films on occupations. The National Information Center for Educational Media at the University of Southern California maintains a data bank in which occupational information materials are listed under "Personnel and Industrial—Vocational Choice and Guidance" in the biennial *Index to Psychology*. New productions are listed periodically in the *Blue Book of Audiovisual Materials* [21] and also in the *A V Quick List* on career education [12].

For several years Saterstrom and Steph [337] have prepared an annual *Educators Guide to Free Guidance Materials.* This is a bibliography of films, filmstrips, and other materials, many obviously produced for recruiting or public relations purposes. A bibliography of "General Guides to Media" may be obtained from the Association for Educational Communications and Technology, 1201 16 St. N.W., Washington, D.C. 20036.

Because films are expensive to buy, there may be difficulty replacing them when they become obsolete. For this reason, rental is usually preferable to purchase. Film and tape libraries are maintained by some universities and by many city, county, state, and provincial departments of education in the United States and Canada.

Educational television   In cooperation with local broadcasting companies, several schools and colleges have experimented with television programs. Interviews between a moderator and one or more guests have followed the general outline proposed for group conferences in Chapter 15. Some programs have been filmed at, or telecast direct from, places of employment in an attempt to provide some of the values of the plant tour discussed in Chapter 14.

How the Atlanta schools produced and used thirty-nine television programs, describing local employment opportunities, is described in *Occupational Information Via TV* [289].

Some state employment services have used television to announce local job openings. In less than three months 1,700 persons found jobs through one such program at CBS's TV Station WBBM in Chicago [395].

To date it appears that the principal advantage of educational television is in reaching a larger audience than can go on a plant tour or participate in a group conference. The larger audience may permit the expenditure of more time and money on preparation, and hence, potentially a better production. The principal disadvantage appears to be the lack of active pupil participation and the inability of the audience to ask questions of those who appear on the screen. The possibilities of this medium have not yet been fully explored.

Entertainment films and television programs   No one will ever know how many persons have based the choice of an occupation in part upon some bit of fact or fallacy picked up from a commercial motion-picture or television program. A substantial proportion of these programs portray occupational conditions, activities, requirements, advantages, and disadvantages. The portrayal is often accurate so far as it goes but is frequently inaccurate in its effect because of the necessary emphasis upon dramatic situations. The effect upon emotional attitudes toward the occupation is frequently undesirable because the occupation is made to appear much more or less attractive than it is in fact.

Just as students need to be inoculated against biased information in recruiting literature, so they need to be warned about the danger of accepting the impressions they receive from entertainment programs on television and in the motion-picture theater. In some way we must develop in young people the habit of looking critically at all excessively glamorous and incomplete occupational presentations.

The teacher of occupations may do something about this by occasionally assigning students to see a particular motion-picture or television program and then to discuss such questions as, "What occupations were shown?" "What impressions did you get regarding these occupations?" "Do these impressions truly represent the facts?" "What other facts would you want before choosing one of these occupations?" For students who do not have access to television sets and who cannot afford a trip to the movies, alternate assignments should be provided.

Museums   Trips to museums have been suggested for classes in occupations. The author cannot work up much enthusiasm for them. Even commercial and industrial museums show mainly industrial processes and products; they show very little about the worker and his work. A museum trip may not "do the students any harm," but it does consume time that might better be spent on a tour of some place where the students might later find a job. These comments, of course, would not apply if the purpose of the visit were to learn about opportunities for employment on the staff of the museum itself.

Dramatization   Several schools have had students write and produce one-act plays designed to teach something about occupations. The author has seen some very good dramatizations of the right and wrong ways to apply for a job. Both the performers and the audience appeared to enjoy the productions and to learn from them.

Martha Watkins, a former speech teacher, and Glynda Cryer, a former English teacher, both counselors at Northside High School in Memphis, Tennessee, produced a puppet show in which Nellie Nervous, Carl Confident, and John Jobgetter all applied for jobs to the same employer.

Other dramatic programs in guidance are frequently duds. Elaine Stearn Carrington did a good one on plumbing once for the National Vocational Guidance Associaton and the American School of the Air over CBS [50]. Commercial script writers like Carrington are paid several hundred dollars per script. Those who do guidance programs usually get much less. The results reflect the difference.

Except for the kinds of productions described above, most of the guidance dramatizations that the author has seen have been embarrassingly undramatic. Doubtless they provided motivation for the authors and performers to learn related facts, but they have not appeared effective as media of instruction or entertainment for the audiences. Some of the author's students insist that the dramatic medium has possibilities not yet realized.

Role Playing Role playing is a kind of dramatization without a script, sometimes without an audience. Each actor is told to pretend that he or she is a certain character with certain problems, interests, motives, needs, or other characteristics and is to act as he or she thinks such a person would act in real life or as he or she would act if in such a situation. Each actor improvises conversation as the action proceeds.

Role playing is often an effective way of arousing interest and starting discussion on any topic that can be dramatized. The action may take the form of an interview between a client and a counselor, a student and a parent, or a student and an employer or employee. Small-group discussions, such as a family conference, a teachers' meeting, an industrial staff conference, or a meeting of union officers, can be dramatized in the same way.

Role playing is sometimes used to help an individual to understand the thoughts and feelings of another person by asking him or her to assume the role of the other person in an appropriate situation.

Job Attitudes Beginning workers who want to do a good job are sometimes confused by the differences between education and industry. Students may be helped to anticipate some of these differences. As part of a survey of entry jobs or as a separate assignment, students may ask employers for some of the reasons why they have promoted some workers and discharged others. On the basis of the answers received, selected students may role-play an employer promoting one employee and dicharging another, in both cases explaining the reasons. Or an employee may ask for an increase in salary, and the role-playing employer may explain why the employee will or will not get it.

Employers who come to the school, college, or agency to participate in group conferences or practice job interviews may be asked about the effect of job attitudes on employee acceptance and promotion. Some excellent examples may be found in *Why Young People Fail to Get and Hold Jobs* [412].

Practice Job Interviews Role playing is often used to give students classroom practice in applying for a job, the teacher or another student playing the role of employer. At the conclusion of each interview the students and teacher discuss: "What did the student do well? What would you have done differently?" Both interview behavior and job attitudes may be explored in the discussion. Interest and humor may be added to the practice sessions by having one student intentionally do everything wrong.

Some teachers have invited employers to participate in the practice interviews and then to tell the students which applicants they would hire and why if the applications and the vacancies were real. Some employers have subsequently hired students whom they discovered in such practice sessions. This technique was used and evaluated by Cuony [84] in a course which produced encouraging results in subsequent occupational adjustment. For more on Cuony's research see Chapter 25.

The author and his students have observed that in a period of labor shortage, employers are frequently less critical than members of the class. One employer even said she would hire the girl who had tried to do everything wrong. The employers' comments have been enlightening and helpful on many items about which the students were in doubt.

Some employers have held practice interviews in their own offices and then come to the classroom to comment on the good approaches and to suggest improvements in the poorer ones.

Role-playing interviews may be taped for immediate playback and discussion in individual or group sessions. For discussions of this see Chervenik [53], Kenyon [218], Prazak [310], and Soltys [365].

Berkowitz [20] has noted the ways in which the middle-class background of the average counselor may lead into error in teaching some students how to apply for a job. The student who does not own a business suit, who does not want a white-collar job, or who has a long experience of failure in paper-and-pencil activities may need a different kind of instruction from the prospective stenographer.

In a sixth-grade class, Carol Ann Fox got the school custodian to interview "applicants" for a job as his helper.

Peagler [301] used the practice job interview with a group of seventeen retarded adults, few of whom had ever been gainfully employed.

Patricia Hartwig, working with unemployed adults, found one woman who

> . . . was blowing interview after interview because of her interview techniques. Finally I had her interview me and I played her the way she had been coming across with employers. Suddenly halfway through the interview, her eyes lit up, a big smile of realization came across her face and she exclaimed, "That's me!!" We then reversed roles and she handled the interview perfectly. The following week she got a job and is doing well.

Prazak [310] described how a model job interview was constructed, videotaped, and used in teaching rehabilitation clients to improve their job-seeking behavior.

Job Clinics   Observing that colleges spend much time in preparing students for their careers but little time in teaching them where and how to get jobs, one college [118] held annual job clinics attended by 450 seniors. Employers were invited to the campus for a full day of open-panel discussions on how to get a job. Questions submitted in writing by students in the audience were discussed extemporaneously by the employers. At the end of the day, students and employers met in the college cafeteria for coffee and doughnuts while the students circulated from employer to employer and asked additional questions. The questions dealt mainly with where to look for a job, how to write a letter of application, and how to dress properly for and what to say during the employment interview.

The sponsors of these clinics reported enthusiastic response from both students and employers. They noted two problems which the clinics did not solve: how to locate employers who have vacancies and how to prepare the college senior to answer effectively when asked what specific job he wants. "Certainly throughout the entire college training a more intensive effort must be made to familiarize the student with those businesses which may become prospective employers." The sponsors observed also that the success of a clinic of this kind is affected considerably by the skill of the moderator who conducts the panel discussion.

Various community agencies have organized group activities to help adults improve their job-hunting methods. Among these is the Man Marketing Council sponsored by the Sales Executives Club of New York.

How to use directories and other references to compile a list of prospective employers is explained well in Wasserman and Mason [405].

Sinick [346] offered some excellent "Suggestions to Clients Seeking Jobs." Several books on this subject can be found in most libraries.

See Chapter 25 for the results of experiments in teaching applicants how to find jobs. See also *Handbook: A Guide for Group Training in Job Finding* [156].

Practice on Employment Application Blanks   Some teachers have asked local employers for copies of their employment application forms and for permission to duplicate them. The students in class have filled in the blanks, compared the completed forms, and submitted them to the teacher for criticism. Some employers have consented to review the blanks and then come to school and tell the students which applicants they would have selected to interview if the applications had been genuine and why they would have selected them. Teachers reported that they found plenty of room for improvement in the blanks submitted by students at the beginning of projects of this kind and substantial improvement later.

Coaching on how to apply for a job should not become too standardized. As an employer, the author has received identical letters of application from several seniors about to graduate from the same school.

Work Experience   This is sometimes arranged by schools and colleges, and accompanied by group discussions in which the students exchange experiences. Such exposure gives the student a realistic view of what at least one job involves and an opportunity to learn what kinds of attitudes and behavior are acceptable at work and what kinds are not. Work experience may also provide an opportunity for the beginners to test their abilities on the job and to discover whether or not they like the work and the environment.

The following are excerpts from the reports of students who have participated in such programs:

> I found out that this is the type of work I would like.
> Even though the buildings are old, the staff and employees were wonderful. I learned that a good place to work does not always include new and expensive buildings.
> This type of work is not for me.
> This is a job that I have never considered before and now that I have had a preview of what it would be like, I want to learn more about it.

Norris and others [286] noted some of the potential disadvantages and limitations of work-experience programs.

> Work hours keep students from participating in various school activities both during and after school hours. Jobs often are routine in nature and provide limited occupational experience. Full supervision cannot be provided on the job by many employers. With a limited number of staff assigned as coordinators, on-going class instruction is not tied together adequately with the job experience.
>
> Too much emphasis is placed upon the remunerative values of the experience rather than the life adjustment values. School and work hours prove to be too heavy a schedule for some students and the health of students is endangered. Some students may be too immature to gain the benefits which should accrue from work experience. Teachers report that students use work as an excuse for not attending school or not performing certain duties. The program causes too many interruptions in an organized and smoothly operated school schedule.

Youngberg [421] found that fewer life insurance agents quit their jobs in the first six months if—before they were hired—they had some actual contacts with prospective purchasers of life insurance, either by telephone or in joint calls with an assistant manager.

Job Experience Kits   These have been developed by Krumboltz [223, 226] and provide an opportunity for students and adults to perform tasks selected to sample those required in twenty occupations.

Work Experiences for Counselors   Fountain House, a center for the rehabilitation of former mental patients in New York City, provided for the gradual introduction of patients into employment in carefully selected jobs. Before any patient was placed in a job, the counselor worked in the job for a day or longer in order to be sure just what the worker would have to do and under what conditions.

Some universities and industries have cooperated in arranging summer work experience programs for counselors and for placement officers.

School and Agency Publications   Among the most useful publications are those prepared locally, by counselors and by students under counselor supervision, to describe local employment opportunities.

One of the best of these is Johnson's [206] series of briefs on entry jobs in Atlanta. In addition to the usual occupational information, each brief includes the street address and telephone number of the employment office, when and how interviews are arranged, and what bus to take to reach the plant. Also unusual is the frank and persuasive information on the work attitudes essential to getting and holding a job in each company and the reasons the attitudes are valued.

Moore [266] described how a university used a career planning newsletter to present occupational information to students.

The *Modesto Bee,* a newspaper in Modesto, California, ran a weekly series of twenty-seven articles entitled "The Vocational Corner." Each article described the present job of one former student of the local schools. A photo of the worker accompanied each article. The twenty-seven articles were reproduced in a bound volume for distribution to students and counselors in the public schools of Stanislaus County.

The Pupil Personnel Services Section of the Minnesota Department of Education publishes *The Minnesota Senior,* a newsletter of occupational information distributed to all eleventh- and twelfth-grade students through the school counselors.

Library Tour   Students may be more likely to use a library if they know that it contains something they want and if they are acquainted with the personnel and with the procedure for using the library's resources. It is, therefore, not uncommon for teachers to take students on library tours.

Brooks [32] described how one high school set aside one week for special emphasis on the use of the library in vocational guidance. The guidance director spoke to the senior class, reviewed library materials on occupations, and told the students how to use them. Books and pamphlets on occupations were placed on browsing tables at one end of the school library, with a different counselor in attendance each period and after school. Parents were invited. The senior guidance classes contributed a display of their notebooks containing surveys of local industries. Teachers cooperated by making related assignments. Average daily visitors to the exhibit numbered 141.

Evelyn B. Hunt, a high school teacher of reading, displayed thirty-three books on careers, on the ledges of classroom blackboards, and invited her students to use them to practice skimming to find the answers to eight specific questions.

Writing the Gyps   Counselors in training, who are struggling through three years of graduate work to earn an Ed.D. or a Ph.D. at a cost of several thousand dollars, will be pleased to learn that there is one "university" which, upon payment of $100 and the completion of one correspondence " . . . course in Counseling . . . grants the degree of Doctor of Psychology (Ps.D.) and wards [*sic*] a degree diploma (17 x 22 in.) which you will be proud to own and display as evidence of your study." The program " . . . consists of 29 fascinating assignments. . . . Text books, study assignments, testing material, lectures, etc., are included in the tuition fee without additional charge. . . . There are no hard and fast entrance requirements. High School, while helpful, is not required." The advertising circular does not mention that the institution is not accredited and that its degrees are not recognized by other institutions or by the legal agencies which certify counselors.

The activities of degree mills have been described by Porter [308].

Every year thousands of former public school students become the victims of gyp schools—unscrupulous institutions that misrepresent their offerings, proffer extravagant assurances of employment for their graduates, and entice students and their parents into signing contracts to pay exorbitant tuition fees. One of the important guidance responsibilities of the public school is to warn its students and their parents to beware of gyp schools. Community agencies have the same responsibility to their clients. Some schools have prepared and distributed bulletins on this subject.

How to identify the gyps is a difficult problem. Some are flagrant. Others are borderline. The least the counselor can do is to caution the students to beware of any institution that advertises in pulp magazines, promises employment at high wages after a short period of training, and employs high-pressure salespersons. The better correspondence schools have organized the Accrediting Commission of the National Home Study Council with offices in Washington to accredit schools that offer instruction by mail; it publishes a directory [104].

Information about schools that are suspect can sometimes be obtained from the state department of education and from the Better Business Bureau of the state and city in which the school is located. Local employers may be asked if they have ever hired graduates of the school. If a local lawyer will examine the cancellation clause in the school's contract, his interpretation of its meaning may sometimes differ from that implied by the school's salesperson.

The teacher or counselor who wants to inform students about gyp schools may answer a few of their advertisements in pulp magazines. He will soon be able to display some gaudy sales literature and to report some of the sales tactics to which students may be subjected if they answer similar advertisements. Another approach is to find a cooperative parent, preferably a lawyer, who will permit a son or daughter to answer a few such advertisements and who will then join the child in reporting their experiences to the class. The same experiences might also be reported to a parent-teacher meeting. *Caution:* Do not give this assignment to *your* students without first doing it yourself, then warning your students and their parents to expect to see some high-pressure salespersons and to sign nothing without first discussing it with you.

The American Personnel and Guidance Association has published *Looking at Private Trade and Correspondence Schools, A Guide for Students* [248], which offers suggestions on how to distinguish the good schools from the gyps.

There are unquestionably some excellent private schools that do a better job than some public schools. The best basis for identifying the good ones is the kind of follow-up done by Hoyt [191] and described in Chapter 13.

Presenting Occupational Information through Other Subjects   Some teachers try to show the occupational uses of their subjects to their students, some teachers refuse to do so, and some do so perfunctorily under compulsion. Some teachers know more about occupations in their own fields than do counselors, some teachers know less, and some know many things that are no longer true. Bedell and Nelson [16] found that less than 40 percent of 311 high school educators " . . . feel they are qualified to present occupational information in the subjects they teach."

The school that depends on the teachers of other subjects for the teaching of occupational information will get some very good information on some occupations and some very bad misinformation on others. Many occupations will not be described at all, because they are not obviously related to any one subject in the curriculum.

Should subject teachers then be excluded from the presentation of occupational information? Certainly not. The teacher who has or will get accurate information about employment opportunities in his own field can be a real asset to the ingenuous counselor, both in and out of the teacher's own classes. He can help to arrange and he can participate in tours and group conferences. He can give his own advanced students more detailed information than should be included in a group guidance program for all students. He can relieve the counselor of trying to keep up to date on details in the fields that the teacher can and will cover.

Students can and should have the benefits of all that the interested teacher will do for them. Students should not have to depend for occupational information upon teachers who will not undertake to keep their own information up to date. Subject teachers who are interested in guidance should be used to supplement the group guidance program but not to replace it.

A counselor can extend his service to his colleagues by informing teachers each time a new occupational book or pamphlet that is related to their fields is received. Some teachers will not be interested; others will be grateful and will help to call the publications to the attention of their students.

In New York State occupational information units were for several years included in the course of study approved for social studies classes. Here Hartley [160] reported:

> In most schools visited, the guidance units were left to the individual teachers and were taught according to their interest in the subject. In only a few cases, did counselors indicate that they ever visit these classes or work with the teachers concerned. . . . The question of how effective guidance units in social studies are was raised by a number of persons interviewed. One system had established guidance laboratories as a substitute for these units and another had established laboratories in addition to them. Many counselors were only partially satisfied with the occupations units in social studies and some of the teachers of the units indicated they passed over them as quickly as possible. In one system, the social studies supervisor was suggesting that teachers eliminate the unit.

How the teachers of these units feel about them is revealed in Hamel's study of 389 schools in New York State [154]. Although the teachers of these units felt that the subject of occupations was worthwhile, they were not satisfied with present arrangements for teaching it. They recommended that the time devoted to the teaching of occupations be extended up to twenty or forty weeks, that occupations be offered as a separate course in the eleventh or twelfth grade, and that it be taught either by the guidance counselor or by a teacher specially trained and hired to teach occupations.

Hansen [157] reported:

> A study done by Sanstead in 1966 reviewed 47 unit outlines in the United States and Canada and surveyed teachers of such units in small, medium, and large junior high schools. The questionnaire, sent to 40% of the junior high schools in Minnesota, produced a 91% return. The investigator attempted to ascertain both present practic-

es and ideal practices as perceived by teachers of such units. Among his findings were the following:

1 Many of the teachers expressed a feeling of inadequacy of lack of preparation for teaching the unit. About 75% expressed an interest in attending a summer workshop devoted to the teaching of an occupations unit.

2 Many wanted more help from state departments of education and from counselors. Only 13 of the state departments surveyed were able to provide unit outlines.

3 The larger the school the more time was spent on the unit and the more satisfaction was expressed with it.

4 There was a great discrepancy between the present practices and the "ideal" recommended by those teaching the unit. For example, only 15% had used field trips, but 87% recommended them for an ideal unit.

5 Most of the instructors seemed to have positive opinions regarding the study of occupational information units. They found it at least as interesting as other parts of the social studies course, and 43% found it to be more interesting. In larger schools, teachers reported a greater interest in the unit than in other parts of the course. About 95% felt that students need to study such a unit and could benefit from it.

Hoy [189] found that in schools where units on occupations were included in other subjects, 40 percent of the principals expressed satisfaction with the results; in schools that had separate courses in occupations, 76 percent of the principals were satisfied.

How to teach a unit on occupations The classroom teacher who has been asked to include a unit on occupations in his subject or who wishes to do so need not give up in despair. The poor results reported may be caused by lack of interest, which retards the teacher from doing the work required to produce better results. The really interested teacher who wants to do a good job may find some help in the following suggestions.

Do not try to do what you know you cannot do, even if the syllabus or the textbook seems to imply that you should.

Do not waste your time giving your students an overview of the world of work which is so superficial that it gives them nothing which they do not already know.

Scan Chapter 2 of this book, "What the Counselor Should Know about Occupations," and ask yourself "Are there things here that my students should know and that we could learn together? " Do the same with Chapter 3, "What the Client Should Know about Occupations."

Take your class to visit your school or college placement office or the nearest office of your state employment service, or ask the placement officer to visit your class. At either place, conduct a group conference as described in Chapter 15, using the questions suggested there for conferences with placement officers.

If your school has made a recent follow-up study of the occupations of former students, present the results to your students. Let your students select the jobs they would like to know more about. Bring in former students as guest experts for group conferences on their occupations. See Chapter 15.

If your school has not made a recent follow-up study, consider whether or not you and your students will have time to make one and to discuss the results.

You might wish to follow up just the students who majored in your subject. See Chapter 13.

With the help of your students, do a quick tabulation of the present jobs of the members of their families and of the students who have part-time jobs. Let your students select the jobs they would like to know more about. Bring in students and parents as guest experts for group conferences on their occupations. See Chapter 15.

With or without your students' help, examine your local classified telephone directory. Select some of the major businesses and companies of your community. Take your class on plant tours or arrange group conferences with representatives of these companies. See Chapters 14 and 15.

As a class project make a quick survey of entry jobs. See Chapter 16.

Ask some local employers to help you, and run several sessions of practice job interviews as described above.

For additional suggestions see DuBato [112], Munson [275], and Chapter 22 of this book.

Career Clubs   Most high schools and colleges have student clubs. Some club programs include a career club, which is, in effect, a course in occupations on an extracurricular basis. Under favorable circumstances, with a superior club leader, a career club can be good. As a permanent substitute for a course in occupations, it is about as effective as an algebra club would be if it were substituted for an algebra class.

Several of the teaching techniques described in this book can be used in career clubs and in other clubs that wish to devote one or more club meetings to occupational opportunities. Particularly appropriate are the tour and the group conference.

The Explorer program of the Boy Scouts of America organizes young people with common career interests into groups which make plant tours, talk with workers, and engage in other projects designed to extend their knowledge of related occupations. For a related program, with emphasis on learning how to run a business and with tryout experiences in a variety of activities, write to Junior Achievement, 909 Third Ave., New York 10022.

Career Day   The career day is a variation of the group conference described in Chapter 15. Twenty or more guest speakers are invited for the same day and assigned to as many classrooms. Each guest makes a speech and then answers questions about his occupation. Students choose which meetings they will attend.

Excellent suggestions on how to plan a career day for a community agency may be found in Feingold [121].

For schools and colleges, I think the single career day is probably less desirable than a series of group conferences, spread over several weeks and months, because:

Students can attend only one or two meetings in one day. They may be interested in more. They can attend any number of group conferences held on different days.

The counselor can be present in only one meeting at a time. What goes on in the others is either unsupervised or supervised by teachers who are mostly amateurs in career guidance. In a series of group conferences the counselor can attend all, can clear up on the spot any statement which may be misunderstood, can learn things about his or her students from the questions they ask, and can subsequently go to the counseling interview with the same background of information as the student. Incidentally, the counselor may have his or her own occupational information brought up to date.

The career day must be held on the day announced. It is always difficult to get twenty good speakers who are all free on the same day. If one speaker withdraws, a substitute must be found quickly. Too frequently these problems result in the counselor turning to a vocational training school which has a selfish interest in recruiting students and which will gladly send a speaker. Some of the worst guidance is done by such recruiting officers. The group conference can be postponed if the scheduled speaker cannot come.

The career day creates a bulge in the demand for individual counseling that is greater than most counseling staffs can meet before student interest has been attracted elsewhere. A series of periodic group conferences spreads the demand for counseling and permits the staff to see the students promptly.

After experience with both the single career day and a series of group conferences, Rubinfeld [329] reported:

> Students . . . who had previously undergone . . . a regular career day were emphatic in their praise and appreciation of the informal group technique as opposed to the regular career day program. Speakers . . . invariably stated that they would welcome the opportunity to return. . . .
>
> There was no longer question of lack of control over the conferences, since some member of the guidance council was in charge and could detect any flagrant mistakes in the talks—in one instance we called in students who had attended a conference, in order to correct an erroneous idea implanted by one of our guests.
>
> Speakers found it a pleasant experience, and willingly consented to come again. Sometimes after a regular career day in the past, speakers who were personal acquaintances had candidly begged us not to call on them again because of the obvious lack of interest on the part of some students in attendance at the conference.
>
> From a public relations standpoint our individual conferences proved far superior to the standard career day. There was now ample time to meet with each speaker . . . answer any questions . . . and extend the many courtesies that are almost impossible during the hustle and bustle of a regular career day program. . . .
>
> ' . . . Some interested students . . . have attended as many as 15 conferences, and many of our students have participated in at least 10.

Employment Day   This is similar to career day, except that the emphasis is on imminent job placement and that the resource persons all represent employers who presumably are looking for good applicants.

Both high schools and colleges have cooperated in arranging a common employment day at a central location.

The area vocational-technical schools of Georgia arranged a series of Techdays. Each school had one day on which Georgia employers were invited to visit the campus for group and individual conferences with interested students.

Employment days have one advantage over career days: they do focus attention on the realities of the employment market. They are difficult to arrange, and not very popular, when employers have no jobs to offer.

Citizen Counselors, Dutch Uncles, etc.   Many counselors have arranged for students or clients who were curious about specific occupations to interview persons engaged in these occupations. Organized programs of such interviews are sometimes arranged in cooperation with local service clubs.

There are obvious values in getting up-to-date information from a primary source. There are less obvious dangers in getting such important information from only one person, whose experience may be limited or atypical and who may function as a very biased but very persuasive amateur counselor.

The author recalls a school superintendent who had wanted to be a physician, until he discussed the profession with a physician who was very unhappy in his work and who persuaded the boy to change his goal. Not until he had gone too far to turn back did the boy discover that he had been given a grossly distorted view of the medical profession. In middle age he still regretted that unfortunate interview.

An overly enthusiastic person, on the other hand, may recruit for his occupation many persons who would be better placed elsewhere.

Some counselors try to prevent such unfortunate results by careful selection of their resource persons and by urging them to present a balanced picture of advantages and disadvantages of the occupation. The reader may judge how effective such admonitions may be.

Youngberg [421] found that prospective life insurance agents who discussed the job with other agents before deciding to undertake it were just about as likely to quit their jobs in the first six months as were agents who did not have such preliminary conversations. A taste of work experience, as noted earlier in this chapter, did reduce the termination rate.

The author and a few of his counselors-in-training have tried three-way interviews, in which the counselor and client together went to interview the resource person. Reports from those who have tried this have been encouraging. The counselor has an opportunity to see if an obviously biased picture is presented. He can help the client to get information by rephrasing ambiguous questions, by asking for clarification of answers, and by injecting important related questions not asked by the client. He can help the client to learn how to conduct such interviews. Incidentally the counselor has some of his own occupational information brought up to date and some of his misinformation corrected. This, of course, takes time. But it is time well invested.

In some communities a local company has "adopted" a school and designated one of its employees to help the school to arrange plant tours, to provide teachers with information about the industrial applications of their subjects, and to help in other ways on request.

Industry-Education Councils in many states and cities welcome requests from teachers and counselors who want help in getting information from local companies. A list of local councils may be obtained from the National Association for Industry-Education Cooperation, 235 Hendricks Boulevard, Buffalo, N. Y. 14226.

Career Development Groups   The University Counseling Center at Colorado State University arranged for groups of six to eight students to meet with a counselor and/or a paraprofessional in three one-hour weekly sessions. Participants discussed their test scores, sought occupational information from campus and community resources, shared the information obtained, and heard a Career Services officer discuss where Colorado graduates got jobs. I have some reservations about paraprofessionals. See Chapter 23.

College Night   This is another variation of the group conference in which college recruiting officers describe their institutions and answer questions. It is even less desirable than the career conference, because every speaker has a selfish interest in the outcome. Even when colleges are crowded, every institution is looking for more students of the type it prefers, and some recruiting officers are paid in proportion to the number of acceptable students whom they recruit.

Honest college representatives do have a place in high school guidance programs. The good ones are really helpful. But they can meet students and parents just as well in a series of group conferences at which the counselor can be present to see what goes on.

Ross [326] suggested that "If the college-day type of activity is to be held in the school, it should be broadened to the extent that all types of training situations should be included. Students should learn about trade training, apprenticeships, and business schools as well as about colleges and universities." The same suggestion should be followed in arranging a series of group conferences.

The admissions and recruiting officers who usually represent the colleges may know what occupations the college purports to prepare its students *for;* but they rarely know what kinds of jobs its graduates *get.* Students might make better college choices if high school counselors would ask the colleges to send their directors of career placement along with the admissions officers.

Assembly Speakers   Assembly speakers are sometimes used to present information about schools, colleges, and occupations. This technique requires too many students to sit through lectures in which they are not interested. It allows the counselor no opportunity to interrupt if the speaker gets off the subject. If the speaker is dull, the students become restless.

Some schools have kept more of the students interested by turning the assembly program into a massive group conference, with one or more young alumni as resource persons.

Debates   The teacher who likes to promote debates or informal arguments will find plenty of controversial issues in the area of occupations. The relative desirability of two occupations for a person equally qualified for both can be discussed repeatedly by changing the occupations. Students may be assigned in advance to one side of the argument or assigned to one side for half of the class period and then reassigned to the other. Some students will study much more enthusiastically in preparation for a debate than for other purposes. Contrasting points of view may serve to emphasize individual differences in values and help the students to see the desirability of making their own choices in terms of their own values.

Cooperation with Employment Services   School and college placement offices and local offices of the state employment service are among the best sources of up-to-date occupational information. As such they have been mentioned frequently in this book.

Many college counselors and faculty advisers are unaware of the resources available in the better college placement offices. The *College Placement Annual* [68] is given free to college seniors who seek the services of their college placement offices, if the offices are members of their regional associations. The *Annual* is a directory of employers who recruit on college campuses. It indicates the jobs for which these employers expect to hire college graduates during the year ahead. The companies are arranged alphabetically and indexed geographically and by major job categories. Also indexed are companies that recruit for foreign employment, those that offer summer jobs, and those that recruit holders of doctoral degrees and experienced college alumni.

The occupational listing of employers can open the eyes of the college student who has no idea of what he wants to do. In addition to suggesting many jobs that may not have occurred to the student, this list also indicates how many employers are recruiting for each occupation and thus gives some indication of the probable demand for workers. One issue, for example, listed only two employers who planned to hire interior decorators but sixty-five who would be recruiting dietitians and home economists. Engineers were sought by twenty-five times the number of companies that wanted liberal arts graduates. The companies recruiting mechanical engineers were ten times as many as those recruiting mining engineers. There were twenty companies recruiting salesmen for every one company hiring public relations personnel.

Also available for students and faculty to consult at college placement offices are periodic salary surveys [334] prepared by the College Placement Council. These surveys report the monthly salaries currently being offered to college seniors in different curricula by various types of employers.

In Canada the *Employment Opportunities Handbook* [115] is published by the University and College Placement Association and distributed to all universities and community colleges and to one counselor in each high school. It consists mainly of descriptions of opportunities for college graduates in various companies, prepared by the companies themselves. It is published in both French and English.

In several communities cooperative arrangements have been developed between the state employment service and the public schools. These arrangements vary greatly. They have included the following:

Lists of typical entry jobs and wages for high school dropouts and graduates have been prepared by the employment service for duplication and distribution by the schools.

Employment-service representatives have met with classes in occupations and with other student groups for group conferences on employment opportunities, supply and demand for workers in different fields, and related topics. Conferences have been held at the school and at the employment service.

Employment-service interviewers have gone to the schools to interview and register students who were about to graduate and look for work.

Employment-service counselors have become job counselors to prospective graduates, at the request of the school, long before graduation.

An employment-service counselor has been assigned to work full time in a high school, registering all seniors, placing them in part-time jobs during the school year and in full-time jobs thereafter. Follow-up visits to employers have been made by teachers under the direction of the employment-service counselor.

The employment service has administered its General Aptitude Test Battery to high school students, scored the tests, and reported the results to students and counselors. Tests have been administered individually at the employment service and to groups of students at the schools.

School counselors have made available to employment-service counselors the cumulative records of students who were applying for work.

Employment-service counselors and school counselors have exchanged jobs for a semester, each remaining on his own payroll and each learning much that would increase his understanding of future clients and their problems.

The counselor who wishes to make some similar arrangement should discuss possibilities with the placement officer of the school or college or agency in which he works and with the manager of the nearest local office of the state employment service. Most managers welcome such inquiries.

In one community, the social agencies, schools, and state employment service jointly arranged and sponsored two meetings for young people who wanted summer jobs. At the first meeting, a personnel director discussed how to get a job and how to hold it. At the end of this session 349 attendants registered on the spot with the state employment service. At the second meeting the participants were divided into ten groups to meet with speakers who discussed opportunities for summer employment in various fields such as construction, restaurants, service stations, hospitals, baby sitting, and lawn care. The joint committee solicited job orders from employers; letters were mimeographed by the state employment service and mailed by the community chest. Of the 349 participants in the project, 267 found summer jobs.

Other Methods Other ways of getting and using occupational information are described in excellent reviews by Budke [35], Campbell and others [41], and Hansen [157] and in *Vocational Education: Innovations Revolutionize Career Training* [400].

REVIEW QUESTIONS

1 Of the methods described in this chapter, which would you most like to try? Where? With whom? Why?

2 What possibilities do you see in the use of tape-recorded television programs?

3 How may entertainment films and television programs be used in teaching occupations?

4   What kind of dramatization has proved effective?

5   Do employers appear to be willing or reluctant to help schools and colleges to present occupational information?

6   What can *you* do to protect your students or clients from gyp schools?

7   Would you build your first course in occupations around a good textbook? Why? Why not?

8   To what extent and in what ways should subject teachers participate in presenting occupational information? What are the limitations of this approach to the teaching of occupations?

9   Do you think Hartley's report on occupations units reveals any neglect on the part of counselors? If you were a high school counselor, what would you do about it?

10 If you were a classroom teacher of your favorite subject and were asked to include a six-week unit on occupations in your course, what would you do?

11 What are the disadvantages of career days and college nights?

12 How do career days affect the demand for counseling?

13 Did Rubinfeld's students perfer the career day or the weekly group conference?

14 Did Rubinfeld find any need to correct misinformation presented by guest experts?

15 Did Rubinfeld find the career day or the weekly group conference better for public relations?

16 What are some of the ways in which state employment services and other placement offices cooperated in presenting occupational information to students?

Chapter 21

Occupational Information in the Elementary School

Between the ages of five and ten, many children spontaneously announce occupational choices. Adults correctly expect many of these choices to change as the children mature. No one wants to urge or even to encourage children to make decisive choices before such choices must or should be made, but this does not mean that occupational choices in early childhood should be ignored. Occupational choices and the interests that they reflect provide teaching opportunities the alert teacher will be quick to utilize.

How the teacher responds to the child's announced "decision" may help to determine whether the child will come to regard the choice of an occupation as important or unimportant, as something that one may properly discuss with a teacher or as something in which the teacher is not interested, as something that the child should investigate and think about realistically or as something just to dream about in fantasy.

The teacher's response to the child's expressed occupational choice may help to determine the child's attitude toward different occupations. If the teacher regards some occupations as preferable to others, he will probably be unable completely to conceal his own feelings. He should, however, be acutely aware of the fact that whenever he does reveal his feelings, he thereby risks substituting his own values for the values of the child. The substitution may not always be desirable. The teacher who has never thought much about his own attitudes toward different occupations may do well to examine himself with care to see how frequently his prejudices are showing and whether or not any of them should be revised.

The teacher's response to the child's early occupational choice may affect also the child's attitude toward himself. Many other influences come to bear here, of course, but it is always possible that the teacher's attitude toward the child's choice will be interpreted by the child as an indication of the teacher's attitude toward the child himself, and that this, in turn, will affect the child's own attitude toward himself.

As the child approaches the end of the elementary school program, his current occupational choices become more likely to affect his future. If he will go on to high school, he may have to make an immediate choice among various vocational and academic high school courses, and these educational choices will often be influenced by his occupational objective. If he will not continue his formal education, he faces the immediate problem of where to look for work.

The time for concentrated doses of occupational information and for formal courses in occupations has already been suggested in Chapter 12. Except in rare cases, this is not in the early years of the elementary school. However, regardless of our plans and intentions, children do pick up a great deal of occupational information and misinformation during their years in the early grades. They become aware of many occupations which were unknown to them before. They acquire impressions of the work people do in these occupations, of the kinds of people who do it, of the compensations it offers, of the abilities that are required for acceptable performance, and of its social acceptability. On the basis of these impressions they enthusiastically embrace some occupations as possible careers for themselves, and they firmly reject others from either present or future consideration.

Hill [166] has reviewed some impressive evidence:

Awareness of adult occupations and their status emerges at least by the mid-elementary school grades among boys, and perhaps a little earlier among girls, according to Simmons. Davis found that status attitudes regarding occupations were well under way in their formation among third graders. . . .

Nelson has demonstrated that children as low as grade three have well-formulated status attitudes regarding occupations and level of education. His finding that children start as young as eight and nine to reject some occupations as of no interest to them is especially significant since this rejection tends to harden as age increases. He concluded that "the process of narrowing the range of occupations considered favorably by children was definitely begun prior to third grade." . . .

Earlier characterizations of the vocational thinking of younger children as largely in the realm of "fantasy" no longer seem defensible. If "realism" is the quality of occupational planning that brings plans into harmony with abilities, values, and opportunities, the occupational thinking of children by grade six has been shown to be surprisingly realistic. . . .

Units of instruction on education and work should be planned and taught beginning no later than the third grade.

How much these early impressions affect later occupational decisions we do not yet know, but the potential effect appears to be considerable. To the extent that the information which children receive is accurate, the probability of good choice increases. The elementary teacher has as great an obligation as the counselor to see that the occupational information incidentally presented in his classroom is accurate information.

The occupations to which elementary school children are most frequently exposed are not the occupations that they are most likely to enter. Lifton [243]

> . . . requested cooperation from some 400 teachers at all grade levels. Each teacher was asked to consider which occupations they could use as illustrative of classroom concepts. To insure real occupational sophistication on their part, they were restricted to only those jobs for which they knew training requirements, salary levels, and job opportunities. . . . As a group, teachers knew most about professions. This was followed by sales and clerical jobs, with skilled trades barely being mentioned. This proportionate distribution of jobs, representing teachers' knowledge about occupations was *in almost exact reverse* to the distribution of jobs resulting from census data.
>
> Using another approach, teachers were asked to go through all the books they used in their classes and to make a list of occupations used for illustrative purposes in the texts. . . . In the primary grades there was a heavy emphasis on service occupations—firemen, policemen, and so on. There was then a rapid shift in the upper grades to the professions, with the skilled trades again being barely represented. In other words, from both their teachers and their texts, youngsters were receiving a distorted picture of the importance and types of jobs available. . . .

The counselor or teacher who wants teaching materials and ideas for using them will find a wealth of resources in Peterson's [304] annotated bibliography of curriculum guides, projects, units, textbooks and other books, films, filmstrips, film loops, tapes, records, etc.

New teaching materials for career education in the elementary school now appear so frequently that any list of them is soon obsolete. One way to find the newest ones is to read the book reviews and the advertisements in the professional journals, for example, *Elementary School Guidance and Counseling, The School Counselor,* and *The Vocational Guidance Quarterly,* all published by the American Personnel and Guidance Association, Washington, D.C. 20009.

Of course, all that has been said above applies not only to teachers, but also to counselors in elementary schools which have counselors.

PURPOSES

Among the specific purposes in presenting occupational information to elementary school children are:

To Increase the Child's Feeling of Security in the Strange New World Outside the Home by Increasing His Familiarity with It   To timid children, the unknown is always fearful. As they become better acquainted with their communities and the people in them and find these people friendly, their fears tend to decrease.

To Encourage the Natural Curiosity of Young Children by Helping Them to Learn the Things They Want to Learn—and to Enjoy Learning Them

To Encourage Wholesome Attitudes toward All Useful Work   Both very rich and very poor children may come from families in which nobody works. Inheritance or welfare supports them. So why work? Some people do so because they enjoy it; work meets some of their emotional needs (see Chapter 8). Some work because they want to help other people or because they feel an obligation to contribute something to the society in which they live. My own favorite way of presenting this concept is, "For the rest of your life you will probably be eating food that someone else produced, wearing clothes that someone else made, and living in a house that someone else built. Will you be doing something equally useful in return?"

To Provide Needed Role Models   Some children from minority groups enter the kindergarten already convinced that nobody wants them, that they will never find a desirable job. So why try? Why study? Why go to school even? Some girls still think only in terms of traditionally "female" occupations. By enabling these children to see, meet, and talk with young men and women just like themselves, who now hold jobs which the children do perceive as desirable, we may give them new hope and new motivation.

To Extend the Occupational Horizons of the Child, So That He May Begin to Think in Terms of a Wider Range of Possible Future Occupations

To Begin Developing a Desirable Approach to the Process of Career Planning   By appropriate suggestion as opportunities arise, the alert teacher can gradually help students to become more aware of the personal needs that they are seeking to meet through their occupational choices and of the desirability of considering their abilities and their employment opportunities as well as their interests when they are thinking about what they will do for a living. As in other subjects, so in the area of occupational information, children can be taught where and how to get facts and what biases to beware of. Final choices, of course, will come later, but they may be better choices if the children's early attention has been directed to reality as well as to fancy, and if they can be persuaded to keep all their options open until they learn more about them.

One of the painful experiences of many young persons comes when they find that no employer is prepared to hire them at the lucrative salaries they expect or for the kind of work they wish to do. The elementary teacher can help students to face reality before it becomes painful to do so by letting students see the kinds of jobs that beginners get and by answering students' questions with accurate information about beginning salaries and the median salaries of experienced workers. To explore the need for such information, one eighth-grade teacher asked students what occupations they expected to enter and what they expected to earn at the start and after ten years. He found that most of them expected "fabulous salaries."

To Help Students Who Are Dropping out of School and Going to Work There are still some elementary schools from which overage graduates go to work. Most school systems have at least a few retarded children who never reach the high school. These students need occupational information on which to base their immediate decisions about where to look for work, just as do high school and college seniors who will not continue their education.

To Help Students Who Face a Choice between Different High Schools or High School Programs   Some large cities have a bewildering variety of specialized vocational high schools that some students must choose from at the end of the eighth grade. Other communities have only one high school but a variety of curricula. If the student faces a choice of this kind, if the choice will be based in part upon his occupational objective, he may need occupational information. If he needs it, his school has an obligation to help him to get it.

To Show Children Who Really Need Money How They Can Get It without Stealing   In the poorer sections of some cities this is a real problem, and teachers make it their business to help their students to get and to exchange information about part-time jobs.

ACTIVITIES

Most of the methods of presenting occupational information that have been described in this book have been used in elementary schools.

Among the most frequently mentioned are class tours of local places of employment. These may begin as early as the kindergarten. They are frequently included in the social studies program as a part of learning about the community and about how people in an organized society help each other. The first places visited may be within the school. In the words of one first-grade teacher,

> We visit school helpers. We watch the school fireman shovel coal into the furnace and haul away barrels of ashes. We watch the clerk use the typewriter and the adding machine. We watch the dental hygienist sterilize instruments. We watch the lunchroom helper cut sandwiches and portion out soup. We watch how Bill cleans the windows, his body secured by a safety strap.

Other places frequently visited include firehouses, police stations, post offices, public libraries, banks, restaurants, newspaper plants, dairies, bakeries, retail stores, garages, and local industries. One group of students who were about to drop out of school made regular visits to a neighborhood employment agency to study the kinds of jobs available. Some teachers have taken their classes on "walking tours" to observe several kinds of outdoor workers at work.

To broaden the occupational horizons of prekindergarten children, Fedele [120] took her class on several neighborhood trips to see how many different types of jobs they could find. They found nine in a supermarket, thirty-two at a dockyard, and eighteen in their own school. The children were "fascinated."

Another frequent activity is some kind of survey of the occupations of the children's parents, other relatives, and friends. Sometimes the children are asked to interview their parents and report to the class. Sometimes parents come to the classroom to describe their occupations and to answer questions. Sometimes the class visits the parent at the work site. One fifth-grade teacher reported that her children "fight to have their fathers come in to tell us about their work." On this subject, Colin S. Baron has suggested:

An understanding teacher would employ tact and show respect for the child's feelings when setting out to do this. He would not rush into this but prepare the ground by finding out first: What do most fathers work at? Or brothers, mothers, sisters? What issues have to be handled carefully to avoid embarrassment to children—who hasn't got a father or whose dad is unemployed, etc? What are the local resources of the community which can be utilized by the children themselves to find out about a particular job? To be more positive, how can the child be made to feel good about some of the jobs in which members of his family are engaged, even if they lack "prestige value" from a middle-class point of view? After studying a particular job, can people—fathers, etc.—who actually do this be brought into the study and be questioned by the class?

To avoid embarrassing the child whose parents are dead or unemployed, the teacher may refer instead to "some member of your family, some other relative, or a neighbor or friend."

To avoid embarrassing yourself, do not issue open invitations to all parents to come and describe their occupations. What would you do with a topless dancer?

One elementary teacher got a shoemaker, a cabinetmaker, and a watchmaker to visit her class, bring their tools, and show the children what they did in their work. She found the students keenly interested.

Whenever possible, teachers and counselors try to provide some kind of "hands on" experience, permitting the pupils to use some of the tools and materials frequently used in the occupation being observed.

Children have collected pictures of workers at their work and displayed them on bulletin boards or in scrapbooks. Some pupils have taken their own photographs of workers at their jobs. All the usual visual aids have been employed.

Stories of workers are frequently included in the reading program. Children sometimes role-play workers in different occupations performing their usual duties. One class played a game in which one student pretended to be engaged in a certain occupation and described the duties while the class tried to guess the occupation.

Instruction about working papers and child-labor legislation is given to prospective dropouts. One school provided tryout experiences within the school for any of its fifth- and sixth-grade students whose occupational interests made this possible; participants included prospective librarians and secretaries.

One eighth-grade teacher of mentally retarded children spent almost the entire year on occupational information. For most of the pupils this was to be their last year in school. Because of their low reading level the teacher presented much of the information orally. Attention was focused on the kinds of jobs these students could get, the nature of the work, earnings, deductions, how to find vacancies, and how to dress for and how to behave during a job interview.

"It is not unusual to find toddling young Czechs learning to read from books about workers in the morning and in the afternoon performing minor assembly tasks on actual mechanical components provided by a local branch of a state industry" [Cote, 76].

The following provocative questions for group discussion with elementary school children are among those suggested in *Career Development* [45]. Some of them might well be used also with older persons.

What kind of work would you like to do? Why?
What kind of work would you like to avoid? Why?
What would you need to learn in order to do your work?
Where could you learn it?
How long would it take?
What jobs can you prepare for in your own high school?
Why do people work?
Must everyone work?
Should everyone work?
What are some of the things you should know about a job before you take it?
What are some of the things you should know about an occupation before you decide to prepare for it?
How can you learn more about any occupation?
Are some jobs more important than others? Which ones? Why?
Is security important? To you? To anyone else? Why? To whom? Which jobs are most secure? Why? Which jobs are not secure? Why?
Will your job help you to live the kind of life you want to live? How?
How does work fulfill needs? What needs?
Is your attitude toward work important? To you? Why? To anyone else? Why?
What attitudes toward work would you want
    Your father to have?
    Your employees to have?
    Your employer to have?
    Your children to have?
    Your husband to have?
    Your wife to have?
What do you think your attitudes should be?

Shirley H. Brown conducted very brief group conferences in grade two, using only the following five questions, which were hand-printed on a large wall chart:

1   What do you LIKE about your job?
2   What DON'T you like about your job?
3   How did you get your job?
4   What do you do on your job?
5   What is the name of your job?

The children enjoyed guessing the answer to question 5 from the answers to the other questions. Any adult who entered the room was invited to remain long enough to let the class ask the five questions [Hoppock and Brown, 181].

Susan Elman used a similar list of questions when her third-grade class asked their older siblings about their part-time and summer jobs. "Leaving the name of the job till the end [made the pupils] very excited to try and guess what each job was."

To broaden occupational horizons and improve reading skills, Marguerite Pope Thompson designed and directed an "Elementary Occupations Workshop" for children in grades three, four, and five. The group met for six weeks in the summer. Activities included bus tours, walking tours, seeing filmstrips, talking with visitors, and finding and clipping pictures of people at work. With only a week and a half in which to publicize the project, Mrs. Thompson recruited fifty-five pupils, of whom ten never appeared and thirty-five attended frequently. Daily attendance ranged from twenty to thirty. Many pupils went on short vacations and then returned to the class. Pupils, parents, teachers, and the Community Resource Team evaluated the course favorably. Thirteen mothers baked cakes for a final party.

Leonard and Stephens [242] described an elementary school employment service established in Detroit to give fourth-, fifth-, and sixth-grade children early exposure to the process of applying for a job.

> The jobs were those that are available in almost any elementary school: senior and junior safety squad boys, audio-visual aides, library helpers, service squad helpers, auditorium assistants, office helpers, etc.
>
> A representative from the Michigan Employment Security Commission . . . conducted an in-service training session [for student interviewers, who then designed a job application blank and interviewed student applicants].

Ninety percent of the faculty "felt the service was worthwhile," and 258 of 278 students said the service had helped them.

For grades four to six DiMinico [100] developed a self-administered slide-and-tape presentation using 600 cartoon drawings showing workers performing typical tasks.

For teachers in grades four to seven of an all-black, inner-city school Dodson [110] got successful, respected young blacks with disadvantaged backgrounds to spend an afternoon with five classroom groups, giving a five-minute talk and answering questions for ten minutes in each room.

In cooperation with a social studies teacher, Parker developed an occupational unit which was taught to a fifth-grade class for eighteen days. Learning activities and materials included an interview with a state employment service representative, practice interviews with workers, field trips, filmstrips, library research, attempting to plan an ideal community from the students' chosen occupations, and discussions of:

> How does one get a job?
> What does a good worker do?
> What do you have to know?
> What former jobs no longer exist?
> What new jobs have appeared in the past ten years?
> What new jobs do you expect to appear in the future?
> What jobs have women entered only recently?

Students in a control group "demanded to be given the same unit. . . . Several teachers . . . contacted the counselor for assistance in planning similar units for their classes, which were subsequently taught to three classes in the seventh grade and three in the second" [Thompson and Parker, 389].

Lila Breiter discussed with her fifth-grade class the possibility of interviewing some workers and arranging some group conferences. The children suggested and voted on the questions they would like to ask. One girl who was about to go to Bermuda for a spring vacation volunteered to interview an airline stewardess. Two boys called on the veterinarian who was treating their dogs. One girl telephoned a laboratory and arranged to interview a bacteriologist. Group conferences were arranged with a pediatrician, a school nurse, a lawyer, and a chemist. Among the things the pupils said they learned were these:

> I found out that some branches of medicine require longer working hours than others.
> Television glamorizes the doctor's job. It is not realistic.
> I have learned that a doctor needs more preparation in school than many other jobs do.
> I never knew that nurses could work in industry as well as in doctor's offices, hospitals and schools.
> I have learned about bacteriologists and what they do. I never even heard of one before.

Kathleen Herzog invited her sixth-grade pupils to tell each other about the part-time and vacation jobs which they had held. One or more of the pupils delivered newspapers, groceries, and pictures for a camera store; sold greeting cards and bleach from door to door; sold frankfurters, candy, ice cream, and other things at a country club, from a truck, and in retail stores; carried bags at a supermarket for tips; washed cars, shoveled snow, swept floors and steps, picked up ashes, and took out garbage pails. There was one baby-sitter, one pet-sitter, one errand boy, one gardener, and one shopper. In some states, child-labor laws may impose heavy penalties on anyone who hires young children for some of these jobs. The teacher may therefore not wish to encourage children to apply for such work. But this kind of classroom activity may provide just the motivation needed for a lesson on child labor, working certificates, and the kinds of jobs at which children may be employed lawfully.

Jesmur [205] asked her sixth-grade pupils what occupations they thought they would be most likely to enter when they were ready to start working and whether they would like to learn more about any of these occupations. All but one said yes. The class decided they would interview relatives, friends, and neighbors about their occupations. Together they prepared the questions they would ask. Later the students were asked what they had learned from the interviews. Among their responses were:

> You need to be good in math.
> You need three years of apprenticeship.
> I was surprised at the many different things he did.
> He made more money than I thought.
> The job is more dangerous than I thought.
> It takes more education than I thought.
> You have to live in or near a large city.
> You need to travel a great deal.

Of twenty-eight pupils, twenty-three thought they learned something from the experience; ten thought they had what it takes to do the job they investigated, and eight thought they had not; thirteen thought the job would meet their needs, and ten thought it might not.

Field trips were arranged for the class to observe four of their resource persons at work. Several of the informants came to class for group conferences.

A county judge came to the class and also arranged for the pupils to see a trial and to tour the county courthouse. After these experiences, the class discussed the jobs they had seen. Three thought they would like to be judges, twenty-seven thought they would not. Eighteen were interested in some kind of work they had seen, and twelve saw no job that interested them. Everyone thought the trip was worthwhile. Everyone discovered some occupation of which he was unaware before the trip.

The New Jersey State Department of Education developed and supported a program of Technology for Children, which included hands-on experience with the tools used in several occupations.

Pierce Palmer reported his experiences in taking his students on tours as follows:

> My section of the sixth grade is made up of sixteen students with an IQ range of 46 to 92. Two are Puerto Rican children who entered this country in October and know very little English.
>
> The first visit was to the telephone office. I called the manager on Monday and made arrangements to visit on Wednesday. My first mistake: that was my only contact; I made no further arrangements. I explained to the class that the visit was being made to acquaint them with possible future jobs. I told them to watch for anything that interested them.
>
> When we arrived at the office we were met by the manager (a personal friend), who immediately broke the group in half, put each half in charge of a conductor, and hustled me off to a midmorning snack. The groups were halfway through their tour before I got back to them. The children were asking questions and receiving good answers—but mostly on operating procedures, not about jobs. The tour consisted of the switchboard room and the cable-contact room—no outside work. As soon as the tour was over, we left. One point to the good here: all concerned told me how well behaved and polite the class was. The manager gave each child a little book for phone numbers.
>
> We arrived back at school just at lunchtime, so discussion had to wait until after lunch. I then asked what anyone had gained from the visit. One girl said that she had asked the operator supervisor how to get a job in the office and was told that a high school diploma was almost a necessity. "I'll never get that," she said. A chorus of "me either" followed, and I knew it to be only too true. As far as occupational opportunities are concerned the visit was an utter failure. . . .
>
> I felt I had only one way to go: I couldn't do any worse. You had mentioned in class that the reason for visits was not to understand the process involved but to learn about jobs. This was my goal.
>
> I visited the manager of the local knife factory and asked a few questions. I learned they employed 173 women and 76 men. There are jobs available for all levels of ability. He would be pleased to show the class around, as it would be good public relations and it might help him out in the future.

I explained that I was not interested in the class learning how knives are made. I wanted jobs explained, wanted to let the class find out what is expected of each worker. I also asked him to please concentrate on beginning jobs. We then made a rapid tour of the plant, and he pointed out the beginning jobs and explained a few of the simpler machines.

The next day I asked the class what they would be most interested in if looking for a job. Pay, time off, and liking the work were most often mentioned. I explained our next visit and briefed them on what they would see. I cautioned them to examine what each job entailed, not just watch how the knives progressed.

The class was divided into three groups, each to be shown the same things. This time I spent one-third of my time with each group. The conductors had been well coached by the manager. The plant is divided into departments, and the groups were started on the beginning job in each and worked on up, with the main emphasis on beginning work. (I had asked for office and administrative positions to be omitted.) The plant tour was very successful, and in about two hours we gathered outside and walked back to school. During the walk back, I realized a big omission: no session with the manager after the tour.

We had time to talk before lunch, and what I expected happened. We didn't know anything about pay scales, and I also pointed out fringe benefits. During the noon hour I called the manager and got this information. But there were still other questions brought up the answers to which I did not know.

We wrote a letter of thanks to the manager, including the conductors and workers in our thanks. The mother of one of my boys works in the plant. She told him the letter was posted on the employees' bulletin board for all to see. We had a return letter of favorable comment on the behavior of the class and the interest shown.

I believe that this was a very successful visit in spite of my omission. The class was enthusiastic. Nearly all had seen at least one beginning job he liked. My 46 IQ boy had seen a man pushing a cart around picking up waste material to be reused and thought that job to be ideal—incidentally, it would be for him.

The Wood Novelty Works came next. I used the same procedure for this visit as for the knife factory but added one step: the owner agreed to answer questions after the tour. The day before the visit the class formulated a list of questions to be asked.

The plant setup was different, and the class was divided into only two groups, but results were still good. The class asked good questions, adding many not on our list.

It has occurred to me that perhaps a first visit without questioning at the plant may be advisable with a class such as mine. I can then help them formulate better questions with more class participation.

My supervisor has received favorable comments (unsolicited) from all three of the places concerned, and the two weekly newspapers have printed notices of the visits.

I have planned several more visits. . . .

Palmer took another sixth-grade class to visit a television-antenna plant employing about 500 men and women. This class had IQs ranging from 114 to 142, with an average of 121. After the tour, he asked the students to write their answers to these questions: "What did this trip do for you as far as helping you decide what you want to be? Did it help you in any way?" Among the students' replies were the following:

I thought most of the jobs were very boring, because you do the same thing all the time. . . . When we took a trip to the Telephone Company I saw the job I wanted.

One thing I didn't like about it was the noise. I don't think I could ever stand it. When I grow up I want a cleaner job.

One thing I didn't know was that women worked in a factory like this one.

I would like to work in the cafeteria. . . .

One thing did hold my interest. I liked the cafeteria. I wouldn't mind working there. . . .

I don't think I would like to work on a machine because of the monotony and noise.

The trip . . . really did give me something . . . it showed me what I didn't want to do.

If you're not careful, you can easily get hurt.

It made me even surer that I wouldn't want to work in a factory. I think I would find the work monotonous.

I enjoyed the offices, because I want to be a private secretary.

I wouldn't like welding, because if you weren't careful you could get pieces of things in your eyes. . . . I would like a much cleaner job.

The reader may observe here the contrast between the reactions of children with low and high IQs. When the class with IQs of 46 to 92 visited the knife factory, nearly everyone saw at least one beginning job that he liked. When the class with IQs of 114 to 142 visited the antenna plant, several pupils "wouldn't like to do that kind of work because it must get very monotonous." Many counselors, teachers, and other people of above-average intelligence dislike repetitive work and mistakenly assume that everyone else feels as they do about it. But many persons do not find such work monotonous or boring or distasteful. This fact has been known to industrial psychologists at least as far back as 1913. See Münsterberg [276].

Information about other ways in which occupational information has been compiled and presented to pupils in elementary schools may be found in Bank [15], Campbell and others [41], Dunn and Payne [113], Hansen [158], Kaback [212], Jefferies [204], Laramore and Thompson [235], Munson [274], and Norris [285].

The reader who likes a historical perspective may enjoy examining one of the earliest books, *Occupational Information in the Elementary School,* by McCracken and Lamb [255].

WHAT TO DO

You cannot do everything at once, so where should you start? What are the things that every teacher can and should do?

Listen   When a child wants to talk about his occupational interests, let him. And listen attentively. Let your attention indicate that this is important, that you think the discussion is worth your time and his, and that you are glad that he feels like telling you about it.

From kindergarten to about third grade, let the children dream. The child-development people tell us that these are the ages during which fantasy is a good thing, when many children do not clearly distinguish between fantasy and reality.

Somewhere around the fourth grade many children learn to make this distinction, and they reject fantasy. This is the time to start facing the realities of supply and demand, suggesting that children consider not only, "Would I like this occupation and would it meet my needs" but also, "Do I have what it takes and can I earn my living at it?" This is the time to encourage children to investigate every occupation that interests them, to keep their plans flexible, and always to have alternate plans in case the preferred plan proves later to be less attractive or feasible than it now appears.

If Children Want Information, Help Them to Get It   Use your own professional skills to find the best information available. Use the sources described in Chapter 4. Help the child to learn where and how to look for facts about jobs. Appraise what you find as suggested in Chapter 5.

Critically Examine Your Own Comments on Occupations   Do they reflect the values of your social class? Are you saying things that will make it harder for your students to feel satisfied with honest work in occupations which you consider menial? Are you tossing out bits of misinformation about occupations because you have not bothered to verify your casual impressions or to bring up to date the information you acquired some time ago?

Check Your Facts   Introduce occupational information into your teaching only to the extent that you consider appropriate. When you do introduce it, be sure it is as accurate as you can make it. Give a reasonable portion of the time to local occupations and to the entry jobs in which young beginners start. Help them to learn about jobs you know they can get as well as about the glamorous ones that have caught their attention.

Take Your Pupils on Tours of Places Where Some of the Workers are Former Pupils of Your School   The more trips we can provide, the more jobs children will see and the broader will be the base from which they start to think about what they will do when they go to work. See Chapter 14.

Arrange Group Conferences with Dropouts and Graduates of Your School Who Are Now Employed   The inclusion of former students is important for several reasons. It increases the probability that your pupils will be exposed to occupations in which they *can* get jobs. It reassures some pupils that there really are jobs for people like them, which can be especially important for children who face the discouraging prospect of racial discrimination.

If your school includes grades seven and eight, if your students must choose between specialized high schools or curricula or elective subjects before they leave you, or if some of them reach the age at which they can and do drop out, review Chapter 12.

Review the teaching methods described above and in Chapters 13 to 20. Use the methods which seem most appropriate to your group, which you and they will enjoy.

REVIEW QUESTIONS

1 How may the elementary teacher unintentionally influence the pupil's future occupational choice?

2 What are some of the purposes of presenting occupational information to elementary school children? Which of these make most sense to you? Why?

3 What workers in *your* school or college or organization could profitably be visited and observed by your students or clients?

4 Of the other methods described in this chapter, which do you like best? About which are you skeptical? Why?

5 What are four things that every elementary teacher can and should do? Should *you* do them, too?

Chapter 22

Suggestions for Beginners

If you are not sure where to begin or what to do, perhaps some of the following suggestions will help you.

PURPOSES

If you have not done so already, find out why you were hired and what your employer expects to get in exchange for your salary. If you do not do this, you may be fired some day, not for doing a poor job, but for doing the wrong one.

Identify the group to be served. What is their present grade level? How much longer will they be likely to continue their education?

Identify the major purpose of the work you are about to undertake. Is it to help students to find jobs, to select tentative career objectives, to prepare for objectives already chosen, or is it something else?

Prepare a written list of the problems that you think are common to most of the students in this group, and that you think you might help them to solve. Arrange these problems in order of importance.

Decide which you think are the one or two or three most important problems that you can really do something about.

For your first year, concentrate on these and ignore the others. Don't try to do too much. What you do, do well.

For your own guidance, put down in writing exactly what you really expect to accomplish and when. Keep it modest. State it in terms of things that you know you can do. You can provide an opportunity for your students or clients to learn certain things. You cannot be sure they will learn them. On the contrary, you can be pretty sure some of them will not. Hold yourself responsible only for what you know you can accomplish.

Prepare a second statement of additional things you *hope* to accomplish. Do all you can to accomplish them, but do not consider yourself a failure if your first attempt falls short of all you wish.

Discuss all of the above with as many persons as you feel might help you—your family, your friends, your colleagues, your students, your alumni.

Ask for comments and suggestions on what to delete, what to retain, what to change, and what to add.

Take all the advice that is offered; then act on your own judgment.

Finally, discuss all of this with your supervisor. Be certain that you both clearly understand and agree upon what you are going to try to accomplish.

In the remainder of this chapter the word "teacher" may be interpreted to include counselor and group leader, and the word "student" to include client and group member.

ACTIVITIES

Provide a reasonable balance between individual counseling and group activities. For a start, try giving equal time to both. For your individual counseling, review Chapters 9 to 11. For your group activities, see below.

Because most counselors have had much more training in individual counseling than in group work, and still less in the teaching of units or courses in occupations, the next part of this chapter is devoted to helping you to prepare to teach your first course or unit.

Review Chapter 12 of this book. See if you have overlooked anything that you think you ought to consider. Revise your plans if necessary.

Review Chapters 13 to 20, and select the method of teaching that you think will be of most help in achieving the goals you have set yourself. Consider your own emotional response as well as your intellectual judgment. If you enjoy your teaching, the students will be more likely to enjoy their learning. Choose the technique you think you could use most easily and effectively.

Select two alternate techniques that you can introduce for variety when you feel that variety is needed and that you could turn to for the whole course if the first one should prove a failure.

If you feel a bit overwhelmed by the problem of choosing from techniques of teaching that you have never tried, if you would feel more comfortable following another teacher's choices on your first attempt, then try the following. These suggestions may be used for courses or units in occupations in school or college, or for a series of group sessions with clients in a rehabilitation or other community agency.

Begin with a simple follow-up study. Explain to the group that the purpose of this is to help them to discover what happened to former students when they went out to look for a job, what obstacles they encountered, how they surmounted the obstacles or modified their plans, and what kinds of jobs they got and have now. With the help of the group, compile names and addresses of former students or clients of the same institution. Develop with the group a project designed to get the information you and they want. Do as much as possible of this by personal interview between present and former student or client. As replies are obtained, discuss them in class. For more detailed suggestions see Chapter 13.

After the follow-up is under way, get as many former students or clients as you can get to meet with your group as resource persons in group conferences. Invite only one resource person to each class session. Inquire in detail about the nature of his job. Ask also what three things he likes best and what three things he likes least about his work. Ask how he got the job, and what advice he would give to a present or former student or client who wants to get a job like his. Invite the members of the class to ask any questions they wish. Provide them with a suggested list of questions, or help them to develop such a list in preparation for the first group conference. For more detailed suggestions see Chapter 15.

Provide practice in applying for a job. Ask local employers for sample copies of their job application forms. Ask permission to duplicate these for class use, unless the employer will provide enough copies for the whole class. Have the students fill in one of these application forms in class. Invite the students to raise for immediate discussion whatever questions arise in their minds while they are filling in the forms. Ask the employer to review the completed forms, then to visit the class and suggest how the students can do a better job. If you cannot get the employer to do this, do it yourself. Repeat with the application form of another company. Stage a series of practice job interviews. At first, let the students role-play both employer and applicant. Later ask local employers to role-play themselves as interviewers. Ask the student applicants to come to class dressed as they would dress to apply for a job. Ask the employer to comment on each interview after the class has discussed it. For more detailed suggestions see the section "Practice Job Interviews" in Chapter 20.

To supplement the three major activities described above, or to provide additional variety, consider one or more of the following:

A survey of entry jobs. See Chapter 16.
Group conferences with employers and unions. See Chapter 15.
Plant tours. See Chapter 14.
Practice in writing letters of application. This may be a joint project with the teacher of English composition.

Invite your supervisor to comment on the methods you have selected. One counselor developed a follow-up project with her junior high school class after obtaining her principal's permission. When the class was about to mail the letters, the superintendent of schools stepped in and forbade the whole project on the ground that only the senior high school principal should authorize a follow-up of graduates. Hence it may be well to ask your supervisor whether or not any other person's approval is either necessary or desirable.

Tell your students in general terms what you are going to do and why. Let them participate as much as you think wise in making the final plans. Keep perfectly clear in your mind and theirs that you are teaching the course and making the final decisions. You are inviting them to help by contributing ideas and suggestions, but if you and they disagree, you will still be carrying the responsibility for the course, and you will have to make the final decisions. Do not apologize for this attitude. Do not be officious about it. The students will respect you as long as you do your job conscientiously and considerately, even if they disagree with you. They will not respect you if you are afraid of them.

Adapt the suggestions in Chapters 13 to 20 to fit your own local needs and purposes. Do not think that because you are new, you cannot improve on them. Think always about what your students need and want and how you can give it to them in ways that will be profitable and enjoyable for all of you.

Halfway through the course ask the students to write for you the answers to these two questions: "What have you liked about this course so far? How do you think we might improve it?" Repeat these questions at the end of the course.

WHEN YOU AND YOUR SUPERVISOR DISAGREE

Remember that one sign of maturity is the ability to disagree without being disagreeable. Expect to make some compromises. Expect to do some things you would prefer not to do. Would you hire a person who would do only what he wanted to do?

If you and your boss are to work together comfortably and effectively, you must somehow reach an understanding on how you will share the responsibility for deciding what you will do. You may have a supervisor who wants you to assume responsibility for results and make your own decisions about methods. You may have a supervisor who wants you to make tentative decisions, subject to his or her approval. Or you may have a supervisor who wants to make most of the decisions alone. You may wish to work in whichever relationship the supervisor prefers, or you may wish the supervisor to adjust his or her methods to your preferences. If you are aggressive, you may wish to make your own decisions without consulting anyone and take the risk of being reprimanded or discharged. Some ambitious persons do extend their authority by assuming responsibilities without authorization; some get away with it, some do not.

As a beginner you may be more comfortable if you adjust to your supervisor's wishes. Because of the superior's greater knowledge of the organization and its problems, he may have very good reasons for wanting you to do things his way. When you have done what he wants, and done it so well that he is pleased with your work, he may be much more willing to let you do some of the things you want to do.

If you are asked to do something that you consider unethical or unprofessional, quietly explain your concern and ask how your employer feels about it. You may have misunderstood him, or he may not have thought of all the ethical implications of some proposed activity. If you decide that he is basically unethical, start looking for another job. But don't be hasty about this. Take a few days to cool off. Discuss the problem with your family and friends. Make sure the real issue is ethical, and not just a matter of your own disappointment or hurt feelings.

Except where confidences of your students or clients are concerned—and you should have an agreement about these—never conceal from your employer what you are doing on your job. He has bought your services, he has a right to know what you are delivering, and in simple honesty you have an obligation to let him know.

You may avoid some conflicts and disappointments if, after you have been offered a job and before you have accepted the offer, you inquire about what your prospective employer will expect from you. If you are unwilling to deliver what he thinks he is buying, this is the time to say so.

WHEN YOU GET DISCOURAGED

Remember that even you can:

1 Show the *Dictionary of Occupational Titles* [98] to the client.

1.1 Explain that it provides brief descriptions of thousands of occupations.

1.2 Explain that it also provides a list of thousands of occupations with related occupations grouped together.

2 Show the *Occupational Outlook Handbook* [292] to the client, and suggest that the client examine it whenever he or she wants information on any of the occupations which are described in it.

3 Warn the client to beware of recruiters and recruiting literature, from schools and from employers, because they often emphasize the attractions but say little about the disadvantages of what they are trying to sell.

4 Warn the client to look for the copyright date on any piece of occupational literature before reading it.

5 Urge the client who contemplates preparing for any occupation to ask not only, "Would I like it?" but also, "Do I have what it takes?" and "Are average workers in demand or in surplus?"

6 Give the client a copy of "A Checklist of Facts About Jobs for Use in Career Guidance" (see Chapter 3). Urge him or her to read it and to seek the answers to any of the questions that seem pertinent to a decision.

7 However limited your competence, *use it* to help your client to get the information he wants. Don't just refer the client to an occupational file or pass the buck to someone else.

8 Always remember that is just as easy to misinterpret occupational information as it is to misinterpret scores on a psychological test, and just as dangerous. Use whatever professional knowledge you have to find the best information available for your client, and to help the client to understand it.

9 Learn all you can about what happened to former students of your school, or former clients of your agency, when they went to look for work. Did they get the kinds of jobs for which they had prepared? If not, what kinds of jobs did they get? Where are the jobs in your area? Share this information with your students or clients whenever the information is pertinent.

10 For as long as you live, keep looking for better sources of more accurate information of the kind your clients want. Never forget that some of the best information is not to be found in any printed publication.

If there is no one to help you, do what *you* can. Over 6,000 mental retardates became federal employees because counselors studied federal employment needs, learned the techniques of filling federal jobs, and provided follow-up services after placement.

WHEN YOU NEED MORE HELP

Write to your state supervisor of career guidance. He is there to help you.

If you think the author of this book can help you, write to him.

If you use any of the information or ideas in this book, the author will be grateful for a brief report of your experience and your own judgment of the results. If you have any suggestions for the next revision of this book, they will be welcomed. Revisions always raise questions about what should be retained, deleted, or added.

REVIEW QUESTIONS

1 Summarize the most important points in this chapter. Try to do it in not more than five sentences.
2 What might be the different purposes for teaching occupations to different groups?
3 Select the group of students or clients of most interest to you. What would be your purposes in teaching occupations to them? Be as specific as you can. What are you sure you could do for them? What teaching methods would you use?
4 Would you discuss your plans with your supervisor as the author suggests? Why? Why not?
5 To what extent would you let your students participate in deciding what the class will do? Just how would you provide for this participation?

Chapter 23

Suggestions for School and College Administrators

While this chapter obviously is written for administrators in schools and colleges, some parts of it may interest administrators in other agencies. For example, the isolation of counseling and placement from each other may be as undesirable in a community agency as on a college campus.

Most school and college administrators now feel reasonably convinced that a good program of education must include some provision for guidance, but they are not at all certain just what that provision should be. They have heard enough extravagant claims of guidance enthusiasts to be wholesomely skeptical. They have seen enough failures to make them uneasy.

The administrator who examines this book will do so, presumably, in the hope of finding some acceptable answer to the question, "What should I be doing about occupational information?"

Here is a suggested minimum program:

A MINIMUM PROGRAM OF OCCUPATIONAL INFORMATION
SERVICES FOR AN ACCREDITED SCHOOL OR COLLEGE

An annual follow-up of the dropouts and graduates of the preceding twelve months, and of others who have been gone long enough to have completed their higher education and to have obtained full-time employment. Tabulation of the present occupations and employers of all respondents. Distribution of this tabulation to all students and staff. See Chapter 13.

An annual survey of entry jobs expected to be available to dropouts and graduates in the year ahead. Tabulation of job titles, employers, and employers' addresses. Distribution of this tabulation to all students and staff. See Chapter 16.

Plant tours to principal sources of employment as revealed by follow-up studies and surveys of entry jobs. At least one tour a month, arranged and conducted by the school counselor, the college placement officer, the teacher of occupations, or the occupational information consultant. See Chapter 14.

Group conferences with employed alumni in a wide range of occupations. Admission open to all interested students, staff, and parents. At least one such conference a week, arranged and conducted by the school counselor, the college placement officer, the teacher of occupations, or the occupational information consultant. See Chapter 15.

Tape recordings of all group conferences, indexed by occupation, industry, and employer, with the date of the conference recorded on the tape itself and clearly labeled on the container. Tapes filed with occupational books and used as a source of occupational information in counseling. All tapes removed from current use when five years old.

An occupational information file in which no publication is more than five years old and all publications have been reviewed and approved by someone employed in the occupation. All recruiting materials labeled as such. See Chapters 4 to 6.

An elective course in occupations for terminal students and prospective dropouts, taught by a person who has been adequately trained to teach this subject. See Chapter 12.

Appointment of an Occupational Information Consultant, with a roving commission to do everything possible to improve the accuracy and adequacy of the occupational information made available to students by counselors, teachers, librarians, placement officers, psychologists, social workers, and all other members of the school or college staff. In school systems that are large enough to have full-time supervisors of other subjects, such as music, the occupational information consultant should have no other responsibilities. He should do no individual counseling with students, because if he does he will soon have no time left to do anything else. Federal vocational education funds may be used by states to help reimburse local schools for the salaries of occupational information consultants.

Occupational Information Services Are Frequently Poor   This is often the case because the demands for other services are more insistent. Most students, parents, and counselors do not know the difference between good and bad occupational information; so no one urges anyone to provide anything better than the misinformation currently distributed.

A few attempts have been made to provide better service.

Occupational information consultants have been appointed by state, county, and city school systems, by universities and community colleges, and by state employment services. They appear with a variety of titles, e.g., Director or Coordinator of Career Center, Career Development Center, Career Guidance Resource Center, Career Information Center, Career Information Service, Occupational Information Center, Occupational Information Center for Education-Industry, Career Resources Center, Occupational Resource Center; Supervisor of Occupational Research and Information; Career Education Specialist, Career Information Specialist, Certified Vocational Counselor, Occupational Analyst, Occupational Information Consultant, and Vocational Information Coordinator.

More detailed descriptions of the work of occupational information consultants may be found in Hoppock and Novick [186], Johnson [207, 208], and Laramore [232].

As indicated by the titles above, several schools have established career resource centers, to serve students, teachers, and counselors. The resources include the usual printed materials, audiovisual equipment and supplies, and sometimes computer terminals to provide occupational information and related services.

Most state employment services have one or more occupational analysts. One state reimbursed thirty school stystems for the salaries of "career education specialists," on four-year contracts which reduced the subsidy to zero in the fourth year.

In one city six counselors were assigned to six elementary and secondary schools as "Developmental Career Guidance Consultants" to inner-city youth, parents, and teachers. Activities included industrial field trips for 7,000 pupils, group conferences with fifty business experts, work-study programs, etc. Aspiration levels of pupils in experimental schools went up while those of controls went down [Leonard, 241].

One large city university employed a full-time occupational trends analyst to make follow-up studies, report the percentage of alumni who said their first job was related to their training, and in other ways to help administrators, professors, and counselors keep abreast of the changing supply and demand for workers in the occupations for which they prepared their students [Davison, 90].

One county school system employed an itinerant occupational consultant, who spent four days a week in the schools and one day visiting area business and industry.

Baker and Jensen [14] followed up Mexican-American, black, and other graduates and dropouts of San Jose schools for fifteen years to provide a better base for curriculum revision and career guidance.

Some schools and colleges have assigned one or more interested counselors to work exclusively with students who expect to go to work upon graduation, or sooner. Some have hired counselors whose qualifications seem particularly appropriate for working with such students. The persons so employed have been designated "vocational counselors" or "career counselors." Their activities have included:

Conducting group counseling sessions and teaching courses or units on problems of career planning, job finding, and how the problems of behavior at work differ from those at school.

Teaching courses or units on occupations or helping teachers with such units.

Establishing, maintaining, and utilizing contacts with employers, unions, and community agencies such as the state employment service.

Helping students to find part-time and full-time jobs.

Conducting follow-up studies of graduates and dropouts. Presenting the results of such studies to staff, students, and parents in attractive, readable form.

Developing and administering a career resources center.

> In the State of Washington . . . certified vocational counselors . . . serve as resource personnel to the general counselors and teachers. . . . They also are in charge of career conferences, group guidance activities dealing with vocational choice . . . field trips . . . talks from business, industry and labor . . . placement services in cooperation with the Washington State Employment Service and local placement firms, help . . . in the State Follow-up program, and do individual counseling with students [Wagaman, 402].

Smith and Lindberg [362] reported how one school system, on a rotating cycle, each year gave to one-fifth of the counseling staff the opportunity and the time to conduct follow-up studies of dropouts and graduates, interview employers of former students, counsel out-of-school youth, and lead seminars for teachers on the relation of their subjects to local job opportunities.

One administrator arranged an in-service course in which counselors visited local industries and received credit toward salary increases.

In a series of workshops for teachers in each major subject, one school brought in people from industry to describe the competencies they look for in new employees.

On some college campuses the counseling center and the placement office have developed independently, and the administrator faces the problem of getting them to work together. If career counseling is restricted to either office, the students may miss the rich resources of the other. Typically, counseling centers are staffed by psychologists who know little about employment opportunities, while placement officers know little about counseling on emotional problems. Somehow the administrator must find a way to get the two offices to cooperate in serving students rather than to compete for jurisdiction and funds. For more on this topic see the section "Fantasy in Counseling" near the end of Chapter 7.

Scherini and Kirk [339] described provisions made by the University of California Counseling Center at Berkeley to keep counselors informed of changing occupational opportunities and requirements. One full-time specialist in occupational information maintained a library, visited public and private employment agencies, and reported at weekly staff meetings on new opportunities and trends. Counselors went on plant tours, met with the staff of the University Placement Center, served internships in the Placement Center, and had weekly seminars with specialists in different occupations.

The Commission on Post-Secondary Education in Ontario proposed the creation of a national and a provincial Human Development Commission which

> . . . should have the important responsibility of establishing and coordinating a system of education and career information services. These should be made widely

available through offices located variously in shopping plazas, store fronts, other public places, and libraries. Libraries can perhaps be recommended as the most logical, convenient, and manageable [237].

Paraprofessionals   Some schools and colleges have employed untrained paraprofessionals to help counselors. Paraprofessionals can and do perform a variety of clerical tasks as well as or better than counselors. But the untrained paraprofessional is no more competent to perform the functions of an occupational information consultant than to assume the full responsibilities of the professional counselor. An intelligent paraprofessional might be trained to do both of these jobs, but *he would need as much training for one as for the other.*

A paraprofessional who thinks that all occupational information is found in books and pamphlets; who does not know how to identify inaccurate and biased materials; who does not comprehend the significance of follow-up studies, nor know how to make one; who compares salary and other data from different sources without considering size and nature of samples, date of collection, and differences between seasonal and stable jobs; who encourages students and teachers to rely on recruiters and recruiting literature as disinterested sources of accurate information; who refers students to a collection of occupational pamphlets that is contaminated by obsolescence; or who does not know the difference between a copyright date and a publication date is as dangerous to students as would be an equally ignorant counselor.

Again, it is just as easy to misinterpret occupational information as it is to misinterpret the results of a psychological test, and *it is just as dangerous.* Assigning occupational information to an untrained paraprofessional is not wholly unlike assigning surgery to a nurse.

Certified Occupational Specialists   Recognizing the need for training, and observing that "there is built-in academic bias in the counselor education system, and the typical graduate [of it] has little, if any, firsthand exposure to or experience with the world of work," the Legislature of the State of Florida provided for the certification of occupational specialists who would be at least twenty years old, have "two cumulative years of successful full-time gainful work experience; . . . provide written evidence supporting [their] ability to relate to young people; . . . have a minimum of clerical responsibilities." The responsibilities of the occupational specialist

. . . may include—but are not limited to—compiling and disseminating occupational and vocational information and assisting in orientation to vocational programs, job placement, and follow-up. . . . counseling students, teachers, and school administrators about job opportunities . . . and evaluating career guidance programs. . . . The proposed training generally involves on-the-job preparation with course work at junior colleges.

Although the specialists are to work "under the direct supervision of a certified counselor," some counselors fear "that occupational specialists may be employed in lieu of available certified counselors" [Panther, 299].

Such a certified occupational specialist should be able to provide better occupational information services than an untrained paraprofessional, perhaps even better than a counselor who feels that other things are more important. I have more hope of getting good occupational information to students where there is an independent occupational information consultant who can neither supervise nor be supervised by counselors, a consultant who is an experienced counselor, who will be recognized and accepted by teachers as an equal, and who sees occupational information as being just as important as any other part of the counselor's job.

What to Do   The college or school administrator who wants to improve the occupational information available to students can probably make his greatest contribution in five minutes—by designating one competent person to make occupational information his or her major responsibility. If finances preclude the creation of a new position, a realignment of the present staff may serve. What is imperative is that one person clearly understand that his or her worth to the institution is henceforth to be judged by the accuracy and the adequacy of the occupational information that the students receive.

Someday, perhaps, we shall see occupational information as a field of specialization for experienced counselors who have demonstrated both interest and competence in this area, who will be certified for this work at an advanced level as are specialists in other professions, and who will be paid accordingly.

REVIEW QUESTIONS

1   Summarize the minimum program in fifty words or less.
2   If you were free to do whatever you thought wise, which parts of the recommended minimum program would you introduce and in what order? Why?

Chapter 24

Suggestions for College Teachers

This chapter is for the instructor in a counselor education program who intends to use this book as a text. The chapter reflects the author's philosophy of education and describes the procedures that he has found useful in teaching a graduate course in occupations to counselors in training. The description of the author's practices is not intended to imply that he has found the only or the best way to teach a course of this kind. He has never taught the course twice in exactly the same way. This chapter is intended only to provoke in the mind of the beginning instructor some ideas of his or her own for doing something better than conducting recitations and examinations.

Teacher Education   The purpose of teacher education is not to indoctrinate willing or resistant students with the contentions of the author or the convictions of the instructor. It is not to turn out teachers who will be uniform, interchangeable units, stamped with the brand of the institution from which they come. It is, rather,

> To orient beginners in a new field
> To tell them what we think the purposes of our work should be
> To acquaint them with past and present practices and ideas and research
> To encourage them to try their own ideas whenever they think they see a way to do things better than we have done them

To encourage them to challenge our thinking at every point and to evaluate the results of their own activities

We have had very little research on the uses of occupational information in counseling or in teaching. None of us really knows very much about it. If we are to develop and improve our service, we must be modest about our own limited knowledge and never lose our respect for the student now in our own classes who will someday show us how to do a better job. Although this book can be used in the conventional manner of assignment, recitation, and examination, the author does not recommend such use. At our present stage of development, it is more important to start students thinking than to have them memorize what someone else has thought or done.

Teaching Methods   The author has used in his own college classes a variety of methods which may be employed independently or in combination. On page 313 will be found a series of lesson plans, some of which may be helpful to the instructor who is teaching this course for the first time. At least one plan is provided for each chapter in the text. Additional assignments will be found starting on page 336. The author does not suggest that every student be asked to do everything suggested in these appendixes but that the instructor select the projects that appeal to him, add his own ideas, and try them. If he will invite his students to help him evaluate his work as suggested below, he will soon find which projects work well for him and his students and which do not.

The methods which the author has used most frequently are demonstration and discussion. The Lesson Plans call for demonstration counseling interviews by students and demonstrations by the instructor of the techniques of teaching occupations. In practice the instructor has done some demonstration interviews, and the students have demonstrated some of the teaching techniques. Some student demonstrations have been brilliant; some were excellent examples of what not to do. There is real value even in poor demonstrations; in addition to providing material for discussion, they may encourage timid members of the class to say to themselves, "I could do better than that."

Experiments in the author's classes have indicated that demonstrations produced better results than class discussions based upon questions brought in by students, that demonstrations by the instructor produced better results than demonstrations by the students, and the students preferred to have some demonstrations done by the instructor and some by students rather than to have all done by either. For more on these experiments see Hoppock [178, 179]. For other methods of teaching occupations to counselors see Goldman [143], Hoppock [175, 176], Rundquist [331], and Wellman [409].

Discussion of Student Demonstrations   After student demonstrations of interviews and of teaching techniques the author frequently asks the class to discuss two questions: "What did the demonstrator do well? What would you have done differently?" The author's students have never been asked nor permitted to say that what another student did was "wrong." The reason for this distinction is the author's desire to build in the class a spirit of mutual helpfulness which may permit a student to accept new ideas rather than a competitive atmosphere of captious criticism which threatens the demonstrator with loss of status and puts him on the defensive. What the demonstrator did well is always discussed first in order to assure him that he can do some things well and that his achievements are recognized and accepted before any changes are suggested.

How to Lead Discussions   Several of the lesson plans provide for class discussions. When the topic is one of great interest to the group, a student leader may preside and conduct what looks like a good session. Actually it may be only a session in which a few aggressive students stage a hot argument. Leading and developing a good discussion, extracting from it the maximum value for the group, is a job for a skilled professional. It is in this kind of class leadership that the instructor earns his or her salary. Students may be invited to lead discussions when the instructor wishes to demonstrate what an amateur can do with a technique that is being studied or when the instructor is willing to sacrifice the welfare of the class in order to provide practice for the one leader; but the instructor who wants class discussion to contribute maximum learning to the total group will develop his or her own skill as a discussion leader, and will use it. The beginner will find some suggestions for discussion leaders in Appendix B.

Buzz Groups   Several of the lesson plans mention buzz groups. These are small groups of four to six students each, into which a larger class may be divided for various purposes. The group is usually asked to select its own moderator and secretary. The function of the moderator is to see that everyone in the group gets a chance to talk. The secretary takes notes and makes the kind of report requested by the instructor. The groups usually remain in or near their usual seats in the classroom.

Buzz groups are used to give the timid student an opportunity to speak in circumstances that may be found less threatening than the usual class discussion, to arouse interest in a topic which the instructor wishes the entire class to discuss later, to exchange more information than can be reported to the whole class, to summarize quickly data collected by the class or the ideas of all the students.

Buzz-group discussion may continue as long as the groups are interested and the instructor considers desirable. Usually the discussion is terminated after five or ten minutes. If brief reports are desired, it is imperative that the instructor word the question for discussion so that it can be answered in one or two sentences, for example, "What is the *one* most interesting item reported in your group? What does your group consider to be the *one* strongest argument on either side of this question?"

External Motivation   The author has taught in some universities in which he was warned to be careful how much work he assigned, because the students would do it all. In such institutions no external compulsion to work may be either necessary or desirable. In other institutions, students are subject to so many demands on their time that even the better ones are tempted to neglect work which is entirely voluntary. Most students who enroll for courses want to learn something and intend to do a reasonable amount of work outside class, but many of them need a little external motivation to get them started and to prevent them from postponing much of their reading until just before the final examination. Several of the author's students have confirmed these impressions and thanked the instructor for providing the motivation.

As a further check on these impressions the author once compared two sections of the same course. In one section the final examination was given in weekly quizzes on each week's assignment. The other section, which met later in the week, was given identical quizzes but assured that the results would not affect their grades. The percentage of correct responses in the first group was substantially higher, and more of the students in the first group said they had done each assignment.

It is the present opinion of the author that some kind of frequent quiz or written report is a necessary evil for many students and that it should be designed to direct the attention of the student to those of his or her own needs which may be met by the work assigned. Examinations on useless trivia are often convenient to score but frustrating to students. They may be used occasionally if the instructor explains that their sole purpose is to determine whether or not the student has done the work and if the question is one that every conscientious student should be able to answer easily. But significant questions that reinforce the purpose of the assignment are certainly preferable to the memorizing of details that serve no purpose of the student.

The author has no objective evidence but has seen many indications that some students will work more industriously if they are assured that quiz questions will be taken from a list provided in advance. The review questions at the end of each chapter have been used in this way by the author and others.

Student Reports   In lieu of quizzes the author has from time to time asked his students to report orally or in writing on how they proposed to use what they were learning in the course. Some students have stated bluntly that they could see no use for it in their jobs. Others have been surprisingly ingenious in applying the principles and techniques to a great variety of situations in and out of school. Excerpts from a few of the better reports follow:

> My class for expectant mothers continues to benefit from this course. . . . A review of . . . techniques decided us on a planned visit to the home of a former student, now mother of twin girls. The students were oriented as to purpose, future possibilities for discussion and need for cooperation.
>
> The alumna demonstrated care of the infants (handling, bathing, dressing, feeding, etc.) and explained methods and even need for improvising in the home. The students asked practical questions. The next class showed the benefits of the visit in increased questions, enthusiasm and optimism in their own ability.

> This course has given me the courage to put on a marionette show called "Who Gets the Job?" It is simple enough to bring out the proper and improper way of applying for a job and since the mentally retarded must have everything presented to

them in an objective manner, I believe I have succeeded in arousing their interest in occupational education and vocational guidance.

The material in the text . . . was used in planning a more effective visit to a hospital recently made by a small group of seniors. An informal experiment was carried out by discussing with half of the group such things as the purpose of the trip, what questions should be asked, etc. The group which discussed these items was more interested, asked more intelligent questions, and in general appeared to profit more from the visit.

The discussion and demonstration of . . . techniques . . . has now opened up for me some excellent possibilities for group guidance in my homeroom period. This past Tuesday I used the "resource visitor" technique in the homeroom period by inviting the custodial engineer of the school to talk on the possibilities of employment in his field. The students and the visitor had an informative and stimulating discussion that ran well into the next regular period. Since the beginning of the course, I have also taken my students to the local fire station, both as a lesson in civics and with a view to questioning the fireman assigned to us on employment possibilities in the department. This was followed by two periods of evaluation of the visit when the class met the following day.

Student Comments   As a quick, rough means of evaluating his own teaching, the author frequently asks his students to use the last two or three minutes of the class period to write one sentence of comment on the session just ending and not to put their names on the papers. The papers are collected by a student at the door and given to the instructor.

In Conclusion   The instructor who believes that students cannot tell good teaching from bad, who thinks that they do not want to learn the things they should, who is convinced that he or she can teach better without their help than with it will have little interest in student comments on the teaching, and in many of the teaching methods described in this book. There is room for difference of opinion in education and for a variety of teaching methods. Any of us could be wrong, and we may be grateful that our colleagues who disagree with us provide some insurance for the student against our mistakes.

The evidence to date seems to this author to suggest that most students do want to learn, that they welcome the teacher who will show them what they need to know, help them to learn it, provide a moderate amount of external motivation when they need it, consider their wishes and their preferences when it is feasible to do so, adapt course content and methods to their needs, and try to make learning a pleasant experience. Educational institutions exist primarily to find out what students want to learn and to help them learn it, effectively and enjoyably. Education should be fun. Education should leave the students with the feeling that what they got was worth the effort.

An Invitation   If you teach a course in which you use this book as a text, and if you would like to talk with the author or have him visit your class, when and if he is ever in or near your community, please write to him at 104 Webster Ave., Manhasset, New York.

REVIEW QUESTIONS

1 Why does the author suggest discussing what the students would have done differently rather than what the demonstrator did wrong? Do you agree?
2 Do you agree or disagree with the author's views on student discussion leaders?
3 What is a buzz group, and what purposes does it serve?
4 How can the instructor encourage brief reports from buzz-group secretaries?
5 To what extent do you agree or disagree with the author on external motivations?

Chapter 25

Evaluation

Up to the present time most of what has been done in counseling and guidance has been done because it seemed like a good idea. Only in rare instances has anyone attempted to find out whether or not the anticipated ultimate results were in fact achieved. A few of the rare attempts to evaluate the formal and informal presentation of occupational information are reported in this chapter. The results are summarized under two headings: "General Conclusions" and "Specific Results."

This summary includes only those evaluations in which ultimate rather than intermediate criteria were used. The limitations of intermediate criteria are discussed later in this chapter. Other studies have been reported in Budke [35], and in a series of articles by Sinick and others [347–357].

In the remainder of this chapter the word "teacher" may be interpreted to include counselor and group leader, and the word "student" to include client and group member.

General Counclusions Sweeping generalizations based upon a few research studies frequently are upset by later research. The reader is urged to regard the following conclusions as tentative. They *appear* to be justified by the research to date, but any or all of them may have to be revised if future evidence contradicts rather than confirms the pioneer studies. From the research which the author has found to date, the following inferences appear to be reasonable:

Courses in occupations measurably increased the subsequent job satisfaction and earning power of the students who went to work.

Courses in occupations reduced unemployment among both graduates and dropouts.

Individual counseling, group counseling, and a combination of both had about the same effect upon subsequent salary and job satisfaction.

Intensive instruction in how to find a job produced quick results.

Turnover among new employees was reduced by improving the accuracy of the job description given to applicants for employment.

Conflicting results from different studies indicated encouraging success in some cases and dismal failure in others. Apparently the success or failure of a course in occupations depends upon one or more factors about which at present we can only speculate. Presumably these factors include the competence of the instructor, the appropriateness and accuracy of the instructional materials, and the interest and ability of the students.

Specific Results   The conclusions stated above were drawn by the author of this book from the results of research by several different investigators. The specific results which led to these conclusions are summarized below.

Research results frequently are qualified. These qualifications may be indispensable to accurate understanding and interpretation of the investigator's report. In the brief paragraphs that follow, qualifications have been omitted in order to make the summaries concise and intelligible to the beginner. The reader again is urged to read with caution and to base no important decision upon any of these results without first reading the complete report of the original research. Names and numbers in brackets indicate the references in the Bibliography in which the complete reports may be found.

Cuony taught a course in job finding and job orientation to an experimental group of thirty-five high school seniors in Geneva, New York. One year after graduation he compared them with an equated control group from the same class of the same school. The students who had had the course were better satisfied with their jobs than those who had not had the course. The combined annual earnings of the experimental group exceeded those of the control group by $7,719; the course cost $1,542 [Cuony, 84].

Five years after graduation Cuony again compared the two groups. During the fifth year the students who had had the course were still better satisfied with their jobs, were unemployed less frequently, and again earned more money than those who had not had the course. All differences were greater at the end of the fifth year than at the end of the first. During the fifth year the combined annual earnings of the experimental group exceeded those of the control group by $14,226 [Cuony and Hoppock, 85].

Rosengarten followed up two groups of graduates of the high school at Roslyn, New York, over a four-year period. The experimental group had had a course in occupations in their senior year; the control group had not. Differences in time employed, in job satisfaction, in merit ratings by employers, and in earnings favored the experimental group; but only the difference in earnings was statistically significant. Average weekly earnings of the experimental group exceeded those of the control group by $7.75. Total earnings of the experimental group exceeded those of the control group by $23,992. The cost of the course was $6,274 [Rosengarten, 324].

Kutner took one experimental group of seniors at the Technical and Vocational High School in Paterson, New Jersey, on a series of eight plant tours. Another experimental group took ten tours. One year after graduation both groups were compared with equated control groups on job satisfaction, weekly wages, number of jobs held, number of weeks employed, and employer ratings. Although most of the differences favored the experimental groups, the differences were not statistically significant [Kutner, 229].

Toporowski selected three experienced social studies teachers who agreed to add eleven weekly lessons on occupational planning and job finding to their twelfth-grade course of study for one-half of their pupils. Six months after graduation he compared these pupils with a control group taught by the same three teachers. The students who had had this unit on occupations were better satisfied with their jobs, earned more money, and suffered less unemployment than the students who had not had the unit [Toporowski, 391].

Boys who had had courses in occupational information while in high school excelled, in percentage of time employed after they left school, boys who had not had such courses. Girls who had had similar courses did not show similar superiority [Long, 247].

When a list of employers " . . . who needed students for part-time and eventually full-time employment" was given to all teachers in a high school, dropouts caused by financial difficulties declined 97 percent [Cox, 79].

When the Illinois State Employment Service announced job vacancies over TV Station WBBM in Chicago, 1700 persons found work in less than three months [395].

A one-month course for prospective dropouts in several New York City schools emphasized job-finding techniques, minimum skills, and realistic goals. The unemployment rate of the "graduates" was checked on four occasions. At its highest, the unemployment rate was less than half that of all sixteen-year-old dropouts [Slotkin, 359].

After five years, boys who had received a variety of guidance services, including group guidance, through the Worcester Boys' Club were superior to boys who did not receive the services, in the proportion of those still attending school or college, in the percentage of out-of-school youth employed, in stability of employment, in average earnings, and in job satisfaction. The proportion of adjudicated delinquents was smaller in the experimental group [Cole, 66].

The Houston, Texas, Vocational Guidance Service conducted a pre-employment group guidance program of twelve to fourteen one-hour sessions for economically disadvantaged high school students. Followed up one year after graduation from two high schools, and compared with graduates who had not participated, 7 percent more participants were employed full time [Mellon and Champagne, 258].

Daane [86] trained 10 public employment service employees, who in turn trained 156 other employees in eight states, to conduct three-hour Vocational Exploration Group sessions for 850 employment service applicants. The applicants thus trained obtained twice as many jobs as the applicants in a comparable control group.

Ziegler taught job-search techniques to 673 unemployed adults in small groups, each of which met for two sessions of one and one-half hours each. Of the 673 participants, 424 found jobs within four weeks—267 of these within one week [Miller, 265; Ziegler, 424, 425].

Weitz compared two groups of life insurance agents to see if the percentage who terminated their jobs within the first six months could be reduced. Before they were hired, the experimental group received an illustrated booklet that described the typical activities of an agent and the time spent in each activity. The control group did not receive the booklet. Turnover within the experimental group was 30 percent lower than in the control group [Weitz, 408].

In a similar experiment in another company, the experimental group received a recruiting booklet that presented both the advantages and the disadvantages of becoming a life insurance agent. The booklet clearly and candidly stated the disappointments and frustrations an agent faces and asked, "How would you react to problems like these? Could you take them in stride?" The control group in this experiment received the usual type of recruiting literature that emphasized the positive aspects of the agent's job. Turnover in the first six months was 33 percent lower in the experimental group [Youngberg, 421]. Subsequent follow-up at six-month intervals revealed that the experimental group continued to show fewer terminations over a total period of two years [Youngberg, 422].

Actual contacts with prospective purchasers of life insurance—either by telephone or in joint calls with an assistant manager—also increased the probability of survival, but conversations with life insurance personnel were of doubtful value [Youngberg, 421].

At the University of Minnesota, in a seven- to eight-year follow-up of students who had been enrolled for one quarter in a course called "Choosing Your Vocation," Hewer found no differences in salary or in job satisfaction "among those receiving individual, group, or a combination of individual and group counseling" [Hewer, 162].

Brief Comments on Selected Studies   Readers who want to read some of the original research may be interested in the following additional comments.

Cole [66] used more ultimate criteria than anyone else to date. His is the only one of the researches here reviewed that included delinquency as a criterion. In the unguided group, 11 percent became delinquent; in the guided group, only 1 percent. The guided group was self-selected.

Cuony [84] offers one of the best examples of careful equating by alphabetic sampling, extensively pretested. It is one of the few studies to demonstrate the financial profit that may accrue to a community and its workers from effective work in career guidance. The full report includes a fairly detailed description of the course in job finding and job orientation which produced the impressive results in job satisfaction and in earnings.

Cole [66], Cuony [84], Daane [86], Long [247], Mellon and Champagne [258], Slotkin [359], Toporowski [391], Weitz [408], Youngberg [421], and Ziegler [265, 424, 425] all reported less unemployment or longer duration of employment following the presentation of more or better information on jobs or how to get them. When and if we have another severe economic depression, we may have more research using these criteria.

Weitz [408] and Youngberg [421] produced some of the most impressive evidence of the direct effect of occupational information alone on subsequent job satisfaction. With no difference between experimental and control groups except in the nature of the printed recruiting brochure, both found that turnover among new workers could be reduced by 30 percent when the accuracy and adequacy of the job description were improved. We do not yet know whether the better job description led different persons to accept or reject employment, or whether it simply led to more realistic expectations and hence fewer disappointments and frustrations. But either way, the better job description did produce better job satisfaction for the worker and impressively lower turnover costs for the employer.

With respect to the Weitz and Youngberg studies, one of my students has asked, "What should the schools do about this?" I think we should do all we can to help the student or client who is making plans based in part upon his or her perception of a job or an occupation to learn all that is possible about what people in that occupation actually do, and what they like and dislike about it.

Daane [86] and Ziegler [265, 424, 425] demonstrated how much can be done in a very short time when a skillful teacher meets people who really want to learn how to get a job. Many teachers and counselors would dismiss as superficial any attempt to produce impressive results in only three hours, but few teachers and counselors have ever equaled these results even in thirty hours. One is reminded of Parkinson's Law: work expands to fill the time available for its completion.

How to Tell How Well You Are Doing Teachers often fear evaluation, sometimes with good reason, because the results may be influenced more by the prejudices of the evaluator than by the quality of the teaching. No one, however, need fear his own evaluation of his own work if he begins it quietly, in a small way, for his own information, and without the publicity which might encourage unfriendly critics to demand the results.

There are several different ways in which a teacher may seek to learn whether or not his work is producing the results that he hopes it is. The beginner may start with the simplest and easiest methods and progress to the more complex as his own interest and competence grow. Every professional worker owes it to himself and to those he serves to try at regular intervals to learn as much as he can about how well he is doing.

Described below are some of the ways in which teachers try to evaluate their results. Some of these methods are used also to evaluate the results of individual counseling and of other activities in guidance, in education, and in other kinds of work with people.

Teacher opinion   Perhaps the most elementary method of evaluation is for the teacher frequently to ask himself, "How am I doing? Do I seem to be getting the results I expected?" Every good teacher does this almost automatically. Every good teacher should do it. And every good teacher should recognize that this kind of evaluation can be far from accurate. The research worker calls this kind of evaluation highly "subjective," because the results depend so much upon the judgment of the person who makes the evaluation.

Student appraisal   A slightly higher level of evaluation is reached when the teacher asks the students to express their opinions of the program. The expression may be oral or written, formal or informal, anonymous or not. This method also is subjective, because it depends so much upon the judgment of the persons who evaluate the program. It is perhaps less fallible than the teacher's judgment, because the number of judges is increased and the personal welfare of the judges is less affected by the outcome. The teacher who asks students for really candid comments on anonymous reports will sometimes get surprisingly frank appraisals. One second-grade child said, "I hate arithmetic and you can't teach it." One ninth-grade student, when asked why he took a course, replied, "So you wonder too!"

Measurement   Another type of evaluation may be employed when the objectives of instruction can be measured. For example, if one objective is to reduce failures or dropouts, the number of failures or dropouts can be counted. If one objective is to increase the average earnings of the participants, the average earnings can be computed. Similarly amenable to quantitative treatment are such criteria as lapse of time between school leaving and employment, percentage of time employed, scores on tests, and rating scales.

Pretest and retest   There are various ways of using measurements in evaluating any course. One may be called "pretest and retest." For example, a test of information about occupations may be prepared and given to the participants before and after the course. If there is a marked increase in scores on the test, one may conclude that the course produced the increase. This kind of evaluation is called "objective" because the results depend very little upon the judgment of the person making the evaluation. Two different evaluators could give the same tests to the same groups at the same time, and they would presumably get the same results. But even this kind of evaluation may produce erroneous conclusions. For example, any person's knowledge about occupations is continually increased by everyday conversations, reading, and observations. The pretest-retest technique provides no way of determining whether the measured increase was caused by the course in occupations or would have occurred from other causes if there had been no course.

Control group Another way of using quantitative data is often called the "control-group experiment." This requires the use of two groups of people, groups which are as nearly identical as the evaluator can make them. One group is called the "experimental" group; the other group is called the "control" group.

A test of occupational information is given to both groups at the beginning of the experiment. Then the experimental group is exposed to the course in occupations while the control group is not. At the end of the experiment both groups are measured again; if the experimental group has shown a greater gain than the control group, we may conclude that the difference was caused by the course. We may still be wrong if the two groups were not truly equated in the beginning or if the experimental group had superior opportunities to learn about occupations aside from the course. But there is less danger of error in the carefully controlled experiment of this kind than in the kinds of evaluation previously described.

In the same way, experimental and control groups may be compared on average earnings one year after graduation, on percentage of time unemployed, on self-estimates of job satisfaction, etc.

Criteria The basis on which we finally compare experimental and control groups, in order to determine the success or failure of an experiment, is called the "criterion." No evaluation experiment is better than the criterion or criteria employed.

Intermediate criteria One of the weaknesses in several evaluations of counseling and guidance has been the use of an intermediate rather than an ultimate criterion. For example, one of the ultimate aims of counseling is to help people find their way into jobs in which they will be reasonably successful and reasonably satisfied. We think that they will be more likely to reach this objective if they are well informed about occupational opportunities and requirements. Hence we teach facts about jobs, and the acquisition of such facts becomes an intermediate objective on the way to the ultimate objectives. Because the acquisition of facts can be measured more readily than subsequent success and satisfaction, some investigators have used this intermediate criterion to evaluate courses in occupations. The use of this intermediate criterion makes the entire evaluation dependent upon the truth or falsity of the original assumption that people who acquire a knowledge of occupations will subsequently achieve more vocational success and job satisfaction than those who do not acquire such information. If this assumption is true, the evaluation may be a good one. If the assumption is false, the evaluation may be misleading.

Intermediate criteria that have been used include the number of occupations a student can name; the range of career preferences within a group; the frequency of job changes; the duration of floundering among jobs; satisfaction with career development to date; changes in tentative occupational choices and the reasons therefore; changes in scores on tests of occupational information and career maturity; changes in desire to learn more about occupations, in information-seeking behavior, in level of aspiration, in attitudes toward work and toward employers, in perception of reasons why people work and of the relation between school subjects and occupations; changes in the percentage of students or clients who say they were helped, who would recommend a course in occupations to others, who express occupational preferences, who transfer from one curriculum to another, who fail in school or drop out of school; ratings of students' career plans as good or poor in relation to what the rater knows about the clients' ability or about employment opportunities. There is some evidence that the last item bears little relationship to subsequent success [Hewer, 163].

Ultimate criteria for counselors and clients include the amount of time that former students or clients are involuntarily unemployed, average earnings, and job satisfaction. Ultimate criteria for the employer may include employee turnover, production, and other measures of the employee's value to the employer. Ultimate criteria for the society may include what the worker contributes to the welfare of the total group in relation to what he or she takes from it.

Some of the research on vocational maturity has indicated a positive relationship between some measures of it and some ultimate criteria. To the extent that such relationships are demonstrated, our confidence in the intermediate criteria may increase and we may feel more confident in using them when it is not possible to use the ultimate criteria themselves. Because correlations as high as .70 still leave more than half of the variance unaccounted for, ultimate criteria are preferred whenever it is possible to use them.

The use of intermediate criteria does not necessarily invalidate an evaluation, but it does make the experiment dependent upon the truth or falsity of the assumed relationship between the intermediate criterion and the ultimate objective.

Equating experimental and control groups   If valid conclusions are to be drawn from control-group experiments, the two groups should be similar in all respects at the time the experiment begins. They should remain similar throughout the experiment, in all respects, except that one group is exposed to the experimental variable while the other group is excluded from it.

For example, in Cuony's research the persons who had had the course in job finding and job orientation were found to be better satisfied with their jobs than the persons who had not had the course. If most of the persons in Cuony's experimental group before the experiment were cheerful, happy, and easily satisfied with life in general, and if most of the persons in his control group before the experiment were morose, anxious, and hard to please, then we might expect the persons in the experimental group to be better satisfied with their jobs even if they had not had the course. Under these circumstances we could not tell whether the course did or did not contribute to their job satisfaction.

In order to have a valid experiment, Cuony had to be reasonably sure that his groups were equated on all the things that might affect their job satisfaction. Since he also wanted to measure the effect of his course on earnings, he had to be reasonably sure that his groups were equated on all the things that might affect their earnings. Job satisfaction and earnings might be affected substantially by mental health, motivation, work habits, and personality; these are extremely difficult to measure.

The best way that we know to equate groups on characteristics that we cannot measure is to choose both groups from the same population by means of sampling. This may be done by taking names at regular intervals from an alphabetic list, or it may be done by using a table of random numbers.

For most experiments in counseling and guidance, it is better to use alphabetic or random sampling than to equate the groups on such things as age, intelligence, achievement, and other characteristics which can be measured. To equate groups adequately on specific variables we must assume that we know all the variables which might affect our criteria and that we can equate on all of them. Since we can seldom make this assumption, we can seldom feel confident that our groups are properly equated. The inherent weaknesses in this kind of equating have been well stated by Travers [392].

We do know, however, that if we use large enough samples, we can equate on practically anything by means of alphabetic or random sampling. We can also pretest our equating procedures to see if they do produce equated groups. Cuony's experience in pretesting suggests that random groups may not have to be prohibitively large in order to serve our purposes.

Pretesting equated groups A method of pretesting equated groups in order to see if they are free of contaminating differences has been described by Hoppock and Cuony [182].

How Statisticians Can Help The careful research worker wants to be as sure as possible that the results of an experiment mean what they appear to mean. The careless investigator can deceive himself or herself as well as others. Statisticians have devised ways of helping the research worker to determine whether the results of an experiment might have been caused by certain errors of chance.

The counselor or the teacher of occupations who wants to do precise research will take a good course in educational statistics as soon as possible. The counselor or teacher who does not expect to do statistical research should nevertheless study statistics in order to understand the reports of research which appear in professional literature and to be able to judge their importance. The reader who has not yet had a course in statistics may find some help in the following brief explanation of some statistical terms and concepts frequently used in evaluation studies.

Errors of sampling Experimental and control groups are frequently samples of a larger group. Because human beings differ from one another in many ways, no sample composed of human beings is ever a perfect sample of the total group from which it was drawn. The careful research worker tries to select experimental and control groups so that they will both be representative of the larger group from which they were drawn and therefore also similar in all characteristics which might affect the outcome of the experiment. However, the researcher should realize that there will always be small differences between any two samples even before the experiment begins.

Conceivably a difference observed between the experimental and control groups at the end of an experiment could have been caused by these original differences between the groups rather than by the experiment itself. We would then say that this observed difference was due to errors of sampling.

The research worker who finds a difference between groups at the end of an experiment naturally wants to know whether the difference is so small that it might have been caused by these errors of sampling or so large that it can be reasonably explained only by concluding that the experiment caused it. There is no known way of computing the probability that a difference observed at the end of an experiment was caused by the experiment. There is a way of computing the probability that errors of sampling might produce a difference as large as that observed by the research worker at the end of the experiment. How this probability is computed is too involved to explain here, except as follows:

The first result of the computation is a figure which is called "the standard error of the difference." The research worker divides the observed difference by the standard error of the difference. The result of this division is another figure, with which the research worker then refers to a statistical table. From this table he learns what is the probability that errors of sampling alone might produce a difference as large as the difference that he has observed.

If there is only 1 chance in 100 that errors of sampling might produce such a difference, the research worker has more confidence in the results than if there were 10 chances in 100 or 50 chances in 100.

In current research literature these probabilities are often reported in such phrases as "significant at the 1 percent level" or "significant at the 5 percent level." What these phrases mean is that there is only 1 chance in 100 or only 5 chances in 100 that errors of sampling might produce a difference of the size reported.

Errors of interpretation   Some research workers make mistakes in interpreting the results of their own research. One reason a good counselor learns statistics is to avoid being misled by such mistakes. For example:

Some research workers report as insignificant any difference which is not significant at the 5 percent level. They may say correctly that no statistically significant differences were found, but they go on to imply that the observed differences are trivial and unimportant. They may even go so far as to conclude that an experiment was a complete failure because there are 6 chances in 100 that errors of sampling might produce a difference as large as the difference observed.

Some research workers err in the opposite direction. Having concluded that their experiment made one group superior to another and that the difference between the groups is statistically significant, they assume that everyone should be greatly impressed and should immediately begin to reform education along the lines they suggest. They are bewildered and hurt to discover that weather-beaten superintendents of schools are still skeptical and even other research workers are annoyingly calm about the whole thing. The explanation is simple.

If an experiment involves enough persons, a difference as small as one or two points in average test scores can be statistically significant. It can indicate a genuine superiority, which almost certainly was not caused by errors of sampling, but most administrators would correctly regard such a small difference as educationally unimportant, however genuine it might be. In terms of the labor involved in any educational activity, such a small result would not be worth the effort. A difference of this kind might be called statistically significant but educationally insignificant.

The beginner should never forget that a single experiment proves only that in one situation certain results followed certain events. If we conclude from one experiment that a replication of the experiment in the same or a similar situation would produce similar results, we may be right, or we may be wrong. The conditions surrounding two experiments are never identical. If the replication is conducted in a different location, under a different teacher, by means of different teaching methods, or in different grades, the results may be entirely different. The fact that Cuony obtained a statistically significant result at Geneva does not prove that Rosengarten will be able to obtain a similar result at Roslyn, nor that Cuony will obtain a similar result at Geneva if Cuony repeats his experiment. In any replication, similar results may or may not be obtained. We never know until we try. Cuony's success gives us hope; it does not give us proof that we will be equally successful. This is why every teacher and every counselor should in some way continually evaluate the results of his or her own work.

Where Do We Go from Here?   In common with other aspects of guidance and in common with nearly all aspects of education, what the presentation of occupational information needs most is more and more evaluation of results. We have had enough research now to know that certain desirable results can be produced and measured if the conditions are right. We do not yet know what the right conditions are. In time we may find the right conditions if enough of us will do whatever we can to evaluate our work.

We need an almost infinite variety of studies to evaluate the teaching of occupations to different groups, for different purposes, at different age and grade levels. We need evaluations of courses taught by teachers with different kinds and degrees of preparation who use different methods under different conditions. Bit by bit we shall learn what we need to know until someday we can say with some assurance what are the essential conditions for the effective use of occupational information. Meanwhile we must find out empirically whether or not the methods that we use are producing the results that we anticipate.

This book was written for beginners. Therefore, what can the beginner do about evaluation? Here are a few suggestions:

Formulate a concise, written statement of your objectives. Whenever possible, state these objectives in terms which will permit you to find out whether or not the objectives have been achieved.

Whenever possible, use ultimate rather than intermediate criteria.

Let your students help you. At the end of each course ask them what they liked about it and how they think it could be improved.

Compare every class with itself before and after your course. If you are teaching facts, prepare an examination before you begin to teach. Give this examination at the beginning of the course; repeat it at the end.

Seize every opportunity to set up controlled experiments. Try one technique with one group, a different technique with another, and compare results. Make the two groups as much alike as possible in every respect except the one that you wish to investigate. If you cannot control the assignment of students or clients to your groups, but the method of assignment is likely to remain the same for two years, repeat your experiment the second year and exchange the methods used in the two groups.

Read one or more good books on how to do research.

Include in your professional preparation a course in educational statistics and a course in how to do research. Before you enroll for either course, ask the instructor if it will help you to evaluate your own work.

Why Do Research? If you follow these suggestions, you will do more work than the average teacher or counselor. Why bother? You will not be paid extra for it. You will not be given a lighter workload. You may even have to finance the research yourself. But if you are a real teacher, or a real counselor, you would not be in this business unless you had a little missionary zeal, a genuine desire to help the people you serve and to leave your small corner of the world a little better because you were here. If you are modest, you do not talk much about this. In some circles you may even hesitate to admit it. But at times you know that your greatest satisfaction comes from this kind of service.

You will, then, undertake research because it will help you to improve your own work and thereby to be of more service to those you are trying to help. You will undertake research because it will stop you if you are wasting your time on laborious procedures that do not produce results. You will undertake research because it will contribute to improving the techniques by which other teachers and counselors will help future students long after your work is done. Incidentally, your investment of time and money in research need not be wholly unselfish. If you have what it takes to become a leader in your profession, one of the quickest ways to establish your leadership is to do good research on significant problems and to publish your results in the better professional journals. You might try it once, just for fun. You might find a thrill in discovering something that no one in the world ever knew before.

REVIEW QUESTIONS

1 Of the various research results reported in this chapter, which did you find of most interest? Why?
2 How have courses in occupations affected job satisfaction, earning power, and success in college?
3 Was Cuony's course a good financial investment for his community? What was the yield on the investment?
4 What did Cole find about the relationship between guidance and delinquency?
5 Of the methods of evaluation described in this chapter, which could *you* use now to evaluate your work? Which would you like to use in the future? Why? How?
6 What is the difference between intermediate and ultimate criteria? Which is better? Why?

7 For experiments in guidance, why is sampling preferable to other methods of equating experimental and control groups?

8 What is the difference between "not significant" and "insignificant" ?

9 What are some of the errors of interpretation made by research workers?

10 Why should *you* do research?

Appendixes

Principal Publishers of Occupational Pamphlets

The following are the principal publishers of pamphlets containing information about different occupations, prepared specifically for purposes of career guidance. In general, the quality of their publications is at least as high as the average of occupational literature. This does not mean that all their publications are free from error or that each is the best publication on the occupation that it describes or that the pamphlets of any publisher are of uniform quality.

The reader is urgently advised not to order complete sets of any of these publications without first getting the copyright dates on all the publications in the set. Most publishers do not include copyright dates in their advertising. The prospective purchaser will have to request the information and insist upon getting it. The addresses given were correct at date of publication. Anyone using the list should check.

Arco Publishing Company, Inc., 219 Park Ave. So., New York, N.Y. 10003
Alumnae Advisory Center, 541 Madison Ave., New York, N.Y. 10022
Bellman Publishing Co., P. O. Box 172, Cambridge, Mass. 02138
B'nai B'rith Career and Counseling Service, 1640 Rhode Island Ave., N.W., Washington, D.C. 20036
Careers, Inc., P. O. Box 135, Largo, Fla. 33540
Catalyst, 6 E. 82 St., New York, N.Y. 10028
Chronicle Guidance Publications, Inc., Moravia, N.Y. 13118
Guidance Centre, University of Toronto, Toronto 289, Ontario, Canada
Institute for Research, 610 S. Federal St., Chicago, Ill. 60605

Julian Messner, 1 W. 39 St., New York, N.Y. 10018

National Career Information Center, APGA, 1607 New Hampshire Ave., N.W., Washington, D.C. 20009

Richards Rosen Press, 29 E. 21 St., New York, N.Y. 10010

Science Research Associates, Inc., 259 E. Erie St., Chicago, Ill. 60611

U.S. Bureau of Labor Statistics, Washington, D.C. 20212

U.S. Small Business Administration, Washington, D.C. 20416

U.S. Women's Bureau, Washington, D.C.

The list above includes only those publishers who produce pamphlets in series, with each new title covering a different occupation. On request, most of these publishers will add the counselor's name to their mailing lists to receive announcements of new publications as they appear. A longer list of pamphlet publishers, including many professional associations that cover only their own occupations, may be found in Forrester [126].

Suggestions for Discussion Leaders

Teachers who are just learning to lead student discussions may find the following suggestions helpful:

Select, for discussion, topics that you think are of vital interest to students, topics on which you think they are likely to disagree with one another and with adults.

Formulate provocative questions about these topics, questions that you think will draw an immediate response from someone in the class.

Whenever possible, prepare in advance twice as many topics and questions as you expect to need. Then if one fails to provoke discussion, drop it and go on to the next.

If the group seems unresponsive, give them a question, ask them to think about it for sixty seconds, then call on someone to express an opinion. Then call on another and another. When you find difference of opinion, ask the first speaker to respond to the challenge. Or divide the class into small groups of four, five, or six students. Ask them to discuss the question four, five, or six minutes among themselves. Ask each group to select one person to summarize its discussion for the class. After all reports have been heard, invite further comment. During the reports and the comments, look for supplementary questions that can be used for further discussion in the small groups.

When the members of the group start to talk, encourage them. Never express disapproval if you can avoid it; it will discourage the student from participating voluntarily again. If you feel that a contrasting point of view needs to be presented, ask, "Does anyone disagree?" or "What do you think of this idea? Some people think . . . "

When several persons raise their hands at once or when you are calling on individuals to report, start with a person in one corner of the room. When he finishes, select someone in the opposite corner, then someone in the middle, etc. If students in one part of the room seem to be monopolizing the discussion, students in other parts will feel left out.

If the group is really talkative, aggressive, and not easily discouraged, you may find it desirable sometimes to take the unpopular side of a debatable issue, be the devil's advocate, and invite the group to attack your position.

Welcome every bit of humor. A hearty laugh will wake up drowsy students and add zest to the whole discussion.

Occasionally summarize the discussion so far. Note points of agreement and disagreement. Thus help the group to see that they are making progress, if only in learning where they disagree.

Sometimes you can encourage further comment by summarizing what one student has just said, e.g., "You feel that . . . ," "It seems to you that . . . ," "You wonder if . . . " For more on this technique see Cantor [43].

When the discussion veers off the topic, let it go for a few minutes. Wait to see if one of the students will bring it back. If no one does and the diversion is not profitable, bring the group back to the topic, e.g., "I think we're getting a little off the subject. What do you think about . . . ?"

If you have to express disapproval, include yourself in the group disapproved, e.g., "*We* have talked long enough on that question. *We* are getting off the topic. *We* are forgetting our respect for individual differences." Do not do this when it does not seem natural; your students will soon recognize insincerity. But make yourself one of the group in every sincere and dignified way that you can.

If you have to restrain a student who talks too much, try to do so in ways that will not discourage others from participating. Conceal your annoyance. When you invite comments from volunteers, ask them to raise their hands; then call on the volunteers who have participated least. When the loquacious one gets the floor, watch for an opportunity to interrupt by agreeing or disagreeing with something; then, while you have the floor, invite someone else to comment on the same topic or introduce a new topic. If necessary, speak to the offender privately. Say that you appreciate his help in keeping discussion active, that recently he has contributed so much that some of the other students have not had time to make their contributions. Would he please try to limit himself to about the same amount of time that others use or raise his hand and let you decide whether or not it is his turn. If nothing else works, you may have to interrupt him in class and say, "Forgive me for interrupting you; I think it is time we heard from some of the others." You may not always feel like being so considerate of his feelings, but if you are less so, you will discourage some of the timid students from participating in the discussion. You can get maximum participation only when the most timid person feels safe to speak without fear of being either reprimanded or ridiculed.

You do not have to be excessively permissive. The author's favorite comment on his own teaching may not have been entirely complimentary but was certainly perceptive. It was, "In this class we could always say anything we wanted to say, and ask any question we wanted to ask, but there was never any doubt about who was teaching this course."

Do not expect inexperienced, untrained students to make good discussion leaders. Let them try occasionally, if you wish, for their sakes. But do not expect them to do your job for you.

Above all, maintain a friendly atmosphere. A good, lively discussion should be an enjoyable experience for everyone. Enjoy it yourself. Help your students to enjoy it.

Outline for the Study
of an Occupation[1]

1 Duties List here all the things you would have to do in this occupation that you think you could do well AND enjoy doing.

2 List here all the things you would have to do in this occupation that you think you could not do well OR that you would dislike doing.

_____

_____

_____

_____

_____

_____

_____

_____

_____

_____

_____

[1] For related discussion, see Chapter 18.

3 **Physical Requirements** List here any physical requirements that you must meet in order to enter this occupation, for example, height, weight, 20/20 vision, freedom from color blindness.

_____

_____

_____

_____

_____

_____

_____

_____

4 List here any of these requirements that you think you might find it hard to meet.

_____

_____

_____

_____

_____

_____

_____

_____

5 **Aptitudes** List here any aptitudes in which you must be better than average in order to do satisfactory work in this occupation or to get the training necessary to enter it, for example, mechanical aptitude, clerical aptitude, scholastic aptitude, finger dexterity, pitch discrimination, reaction time.

_____

_____

_____

_____

_____

6 List here the names of any tests you have taken to measure these aptitudes and the results of the tests and any other evidence of the aptitudes you possess. List also the results of any tests you have taken to measure your interest in this occupation and any other evidence of your interest in it.

_____

_____

_____

_____

_____

7 **Preparation** List here the number of years of high school and college training that you must have to enter this occupation.

High school_____College _____

9 **Earnings** List here how much money you think you could earn in this occupation.

First year $ _____

After five years $ _____

After ten years $ _____

8 List here the number of years of high school and college training that you think you have the ability, the money, and the desire to get.

High school_____College _____

10 List here how much money you think you would have to earn in order to feel that you were doing about as well as you have a right to expect.

First year $ _____

After five years $ _____

After ten years $ _____

11 Other Requirements List here any other requirements that you must meet in order to enter this occupation, for example, license requirements, examinations, union membership.

---

12 List here any of these requirements that you think you might find it hard to meet.

---

13 Number of Jobs List here how many persons are employed in this occupation in the community in which you wish to work.

---

14 List here the best estimate you can get of how many jobs in this occupation become vacant each year in the community in which you wish to work.

Job Satisfaction Ask several persons now working in this occupation what are the three things they like most and least about it.

15 List here the things that most of them say they like most.

---

16 List here the things that most of them say they like least.

---

17 Miscellaneous List here any other reasons why you think this would be a good occupation for you to enter.

_____
_____
_____
_____
_____
_____
_____
_____
_____

18 List here any other reasons why you think this would NOT be a good occupation for you to enter.

_____
_____
_____
_____
_____
_____
_____
_____

SUMMARY

Go back over the things you have written on the preceding pages and:

19 List here the most important reasons why you think this would be a good occupation for you to enter.

_____
_____
_____
_____
_____
_____
_____
_____
_____

20 List here the most important reasons why you think this would NOT be a good occupation for you to enter.

_____
_____
_____
_____
_____
_____
_____
_____
_____

21 Tentative Decision If you had to decide today whether or not to enter this occupation, what would you decide, and why?

Suggestions for Opening a Counseling Interview

1 Listen. Let the other person tell you whatever he (or she) wants to tell you. If he asked for the interview, let him open it. Let him direct the course of the conversation. At this point do *not* ask questions.

2 Try to understand how all this looks to him. In your own words, summarize what he has told you, including the feelings he has expressed. In this way help him to tell his story.

3 If he has a problem, restate the problem as he sees it.

4 If he wants help from you, restate in your own words what he has said he wants you to do.

5 Revise your restatements until he agrees that you now understand
His problem as he sees it
How he feels about it
What he wants you to do
At this point, ask questions if you need to.

6 Find out what he has done already in his own efforts to solve his own problem.

7 If you can do what he wants, and there is no good reason for not doing it, do it.

8 If you cannot do all that he wants, tell him what you can and cannot do.

9 Let him accept or reject your services.

10 Do what you can to help him in the way that he wants to be helped.

11 When you have done this, and not before, offer any additional services that you wish to offer, and let him accept or reject them.

Using Occupational Information with the Handicapped[1]

by Daniel Sinick

Knowledge of the world of work is often especially important for students and clients with disabilities. The mentally retarded, the blind and partially seeing, the deaf and hard-of-hearing, the orthopedic, and cardiac have typically been deprived of the fairly constant contact normally experienced with work and workers. This deprivation results from reduced mobility, sensory or mental impairment, or prolonged medical treatment. Specific ways teachers and counselors can enhance the handicapped's familiarity with occupational information are suggested in this article.

Two basic points should first be made. One is that occupational information is only in part occupational literature; the printed word must be transcended and supplemented in every way possible. The other point is that the same principles and practices generally employed with the nonhandicapped are applicable to the handicapped. Certain selected emphases on content, however, seem desirable, as well as selection or adaptation of particular methods.

Content emphases that apply broadly to variously disabled individuals—because of their circumscribed contact with life—include knowledge of work in general, of the workaday community (including transportation to places of employment), of job-finding techniques, and of job interview skills in particular.

[1] Revised and reprinted from the *Vocational Guidance Quarterly,* Summer, 1964, pages 275–277, by permission of the author and publisher.

Among methods of general value are those which provide personal knowledge of work and work situations: not only visits to places of work but actual employment, whether paid or unpaid, in the school or in the community. This can be accomplished through a work experience program or through part-time, temporary, or volunteer work. Methods that bring workers into the school are also useful: career speakers might include "handicapped" as well as nonhandicapped alumni, and educational television might be adapted to this general purpose. Toward job-hunt knowhow, practice is needed in obtaining and pursuing job leads, while role playing provides practice in the conduct of job interviews.

The Physically Handicapped For the physically handicapped, two additional emphases on content suggest themselves. One has to do with physical requirements of occupations. These must be regarded imaginatively, however, and not narrowly or superficially; strict adherence to the findings of job analysis would rule out occupations actually engaged in by severely disabled individuals. Another natural area of emphasis, because of hiring difficulties encountered, is that of self-employment opportunities. A teaching and counseling aid in the first area is the *Dictionary of Occupational Titles,* prepared by the United States Department of Labor; excellent self-employment information is available from the Small Business Administration, Washington, D.C.

Additional methods in using occupational information with the visually handicapped include records and tape recordings, optical aids, large-print materials, brailled materials, special chalk and chalkboards, and persons to serve as readers. Recordings and other materials may be either purchased or prepared.

Three general sources of materials and related information are: American Foundation for the Blind, 15 W. 16 St., New York; American Printing House for the Blind, 1839 Frankfort Ave., Louisville, Ky.; and National Society for the Prevention of Blindness, 79 Madison Ave., New York. Large-print materials are easily prepared with large-type typewriters, available from most manufacturers. An example of preparation of other materials is the taping of a suitable radio program for later playback.

For the hearing impaired, methods involving visual aids are especially appropriate. Such techniques as demonstrations, charts, pictures, and posters can achieve significance without sound. Also effective are *captioned* slides, filmstrips, and films. Captions can be separately prepared, then coordinated with the presentation, a procedure equally applicable to educational television. A useful device in dealing with the deaf or deafened is an overhead projector, which allows the teacher to present material visually while facing the class, thus maximizing the opportunity for lip-reading (better called speech-reading).

The orthopedic, the cardiac, and others with neuromuscular or circulatory limitations, can profit from teachers' or counselors' use of opaque projectors, adjustable reading stands, automatic page turners, and home-to-school telephone. Books, pamphlets, and magazines are inserted directly into an opaque projector for ready reading. Reading is facilitated as well by inexpensive stands that hold material in any position desired; electrically operated page turners, while rather expensive, serve to expedite reading. For the homebound, a telephonic system can be installed for the communication of occupational and other information.

The Mentally Retarded As for the mentally retarded, a number of content areas and methods need emphasis. Occupations requiring broadest coverage are at the service, semiskilled, and unskilled levels, where the retarded find most of their jobs. Toward finding jobs, these students and clients need practice in using the telephone and completing application blanks. Telephone use includes the directory, dialing, and the etiquette of telephone talk.

Application blanks obtainable from employers for practice are normally expected to be completed by job applicants themselves, whereas friends and relatives may help with letters of application. To hold their jobs, the retarded require particular attention to work attitudes, habits, and standards; they must recognize the importance of cooperativeness, persistence, punctuality, and work quality.

Methods with the mentally retarded, who have been characterized as "here-and-now persons," are best geared toward immediate and tangible learning outcomes. Concrete materials and activities, when accompanied by demonstration, extra repetition, and drill, can be effective. Special occupational materials are needed at a reduced reading level, in regard to both vocabulary and conceptual content.

A few such materials are currently available [1–4].[2] Pictures, slides, filmstrips, and films are useful, films more so when run at a slower pace. Of two suitable sets of filmstrips now available, one [6] was designed specifically for older mentally retarded pupils, and the other [5] for the upper elementary and junior high grades.

In summary, this article has suggested content areas and methods requiring emphasis in teachers' and counselors' use of occupational information with the physically handicapped and mentally retarded. These students and clients need added exposure to the realities of jobs and work situations, if their typical underexposure to such realities is not to develop into blurred vocational plans.

REFERENCES

1 Carson, Esther. *Teen-agers prepare for work.* Books I and II. Castro Valley, Calif. (18623 Lake Chabot Road): Author, 1960.

2 Goldberg, H. R., & Brumber, Winifred T. (Eds.) *Rochester occupational reading series.* Chicago: Science Research Associates, Inc., 1961.

3. *Handbook for the custodian's assistant.* Hayward, Calif. (224 West Winton Ave.): Hayward Union High School District, 1961.

4 Lifton, W. *What could I be?* Chicago: Science Research Associates, Inc., 1960.

5 Lifton, W. *Foundations for occupational planning.* Chicago (1345 Diversey Parkway): Society for Visual Education, no date.

6 *Occupational education.* Jamaica, New York (146–01 Archer Ave.): Eye Gate House, no date.

[2] Numbers in brackets refer to references at the end of this appendix.

Lesson Plans
and Assignments

Lesson Plans for a Graduate Course in Occupations for Counselors[1]

Most of the lesson plans in this section include assignments which are intended to be announced to the students in advance of the sessions in which the lesson plans are to be used.

In the lesson plans the assignments are first identified by numbers. The numbers refer to numbered items in the section "Assignments for Use in Counselor Education," in which all the assignments are reproduced. The purpose of this arrangement is to make it convenient for the instructor to make assignments by number and for the students to find the assignments easily by referring each time to the same section of the book.

In nearly all cases, the assignments are also printed in full with the lesson plans, so that the instructor need not refer to the Assignments section. There are a few exceptions in cases where the assignments are unusually long. Such exceptions are noted in the lesson plans.

[1] For related discussion, see Chapter 24.

313

LESSON PLAN 1   GETTING ACQUAINTED

Purpose   Even at colleges where it is traditional for everyone to speak to everyone else, there are shy students who will not go beyond a simple hello without some encouragement. In large summer sessions and in urban universities, students have been known to sit through an entire course without ever speaking to the students in adjoining seats. The timid souls sometimes welcome a little help in getting acquainted.

The students who do talk freely with everyone sometimes report that they learn as much from each other as from the instructor. Most instructors probably wish to encourage such learning. Helping students to become acquainted is one way of encouraging it. Students sometimes feel more comfortable with an instructor whom they know something about. The purpose of this plan is to help students to become better acquainted with one another and with the instructor.

Procedure   There are several ways of breaking the ice. The frequently employed practice of asking each student to introduce himself to the group is probably the least desirable. It embarrasses the shy student, and it does little to start conversation.

Perhaps the simplest and quickest way to start students talking is to say to the group, "Will you please reach over and shake hands with the persons on each side of you and in front and in back of you. Tell them your name, your nickname, where you come from, what you do, and why you are here." In the author's classes this usually starts the group buzzing even before the instructor finishes speaking. Conversation continues until interrupted by the instructor's calling the group to order and inquiring, "Does anyone object if I now pronounce you all properly introduced to everyone else in the class?" To date no one has objected.

Another method is to ask the class to suggest what they would like to know about each other, list the suggested items on the board, then ask them to converse until each person is prepared to introduce to the class the person in the next higher-numbered seat. When all are ready, the introductions are performed. Students seem to find it less embarrassing to introduce others than to introduce themselves. This method may consume too much time to permit its use in large classes; it has worked well in small ones.

Both the latter methods start students talking with each other immediately. Once started, they frequently continue.

Students are sometimes curious about the instructor but hesitant to ask personal questions. To overcome their reluctance they may be invited to form small groups of four to six students each and to formulate any questions they wish to ask the instructor about his or her education, experience, or anything else. By designating one of their group to ask all the questions, they can conceal the identity of the interested person and thus be relieved of any anxiety about the instructor's reaction to the question. Questions directed to the author have ranged all the way from "What other jobs have you held?" to "Are you married?"

LESSON PLAN 2   TEACHERS OBSERVE OWN COMMENTS ON OCCUPATIONS

Purpose   To make classroom teachers aware of the fact that they do influence the attitudes of their students toward occupations even if they do not intend to.

Assignment   Number 28.

For one week observe yourself. Notice every remark you make to anyone about any occupation. Observe the frequency and the content of your remarks, and ask yourself: What effect might these remarks have on the attitudes of these persons toward these occupations? How might these remarks influence the future occupational decisions of these persons? Are my remarks based upon accurate knowledge of the facts? Do I want to change what I have been doing? How?

Activities in Class   Divide the class into buzz groups of four to six students each. Ask each group to select a moderator and a secretary and to exchange their reactions to this assignment. After five or ten minutes ask each secretary for an oral summary of the discussion in his or her group. As each report is received, invite questions and comments from the class. Near the end of the period, summarize the discussion and add your own comments.

LESSON PLAN 3   HOW OCCUPATIONAL CHOICE AFFECTS LIFE OFF THE JOB

Purpose   To emphasize the importance of occupational choice.

Assignments   Numbers 1 and 29.
Read the Preface, Contents, and Chapter 1.
For one week, take a detached look at your life. Notice and list all the ways in which your job affects your family and your own life off the job. At the end of the week review your list and reflect on what it reveals about the importance of occupational choice.

Activities in Class   Divide the class into buzz groups of four to six students each. Ask each group to select a moderator and a secretary and to exchange information on ways in which they have seen the choice of an occupation affect the worker's life *off* the job. Ask each secretary to take notes and to select the three most interesting instances reported in his or her group.

After five or ten minutes, ask each secretary to report orally one of the interesting items selected. After each report, pause long enough to permit questions or comments. If time permits, continue with a second and then a third round of reports from each secretary. Interrupt the reports when the end of the period approaches or when the class appears to have heard enough.

Make any summary comments that you wish to make to emphasize the importance of occupational choice.

LESSON PLAN 4   GROUP CONFERENCE WITH ALUMNUS

Purpose   To show the students the kinds of information that can be obtained from alumni. To demonstrate one way of getting it. To add a little to the counselor's store of useful occupational information.

Assignment   Number 30.
Bring to class some questions that you would like to ask any young alumnus or alumna of any high school or college about his or her job.

Preparation   Arrange in advance for a young, employed alumnus or alumna from some high school or college to serve as guest expert in a group conference. In preparation for this, review Chapter 15.

Activities in Class   Explain the purpose of the session. Describe the procedure to be followed. Introduce the guest, and conduct the group conference as suggested in Chapter 15.

LESSON PLAN 5   GROUP CONFERENCE WITH PLACEMENT OFFICER

Purpose   To show to the students the kinds of information that can be obtained from placement officers. To demonstrate one way of getting it. To add a little to the counselor's store of useful occupational information.

Assignment   Number 2.
Read Chapter 2.

Preparation   Arrange in advance for a placement officer from a school or college or from a local office of the state employment service or from a private employment agency to serve as guest expert in a group conference. In preparation for this, review Chapter 15. The conference may be held at the placement office if space permits.

Activities in Class   Explain the purpose of the session. Describe the procedure to be followed. Introduce the guest, and conduct the group conference as suggested in Chapter 15.

LESSON PLAN 6   GROUP CONFERENCE WITH UNION OFFICER

Purpose   To show to the students the kinds of information that can be obtained from union officers. To demonstrate one way of getting it. To add a little to the counselor's store of useful occupational information.

Assignment   Number 3.
Read Chapter 3.

Preparation   Arrange in advance for an officer of a union local to serve as guest expert in a group conference. In preparation for this, review Chapter 15. The conference may be held at union headquarters if space permits.

Activities in Class   Explain the purpose of the session. Describe the procedure to be followed. Introduce the guest and conduct the group conference as suggested in Chapter 15.

LESSON PLAN 7   STUDENTS EXCHANGE OCCUPATIONAL EXPERIENCES

Purpose   To add a little to the students' store of useful occupational information by helping them to learn from one another's work experiences. To demonstrate a method which some of them can use to help their students to exchange information about their part-time and vacation work experiences.

Assignment   Number 4.
Read Chapter 4.

Activities in Class   Ask each student who has been employed in some occupation other than teaching, at any time during the past five years, to name one such occupation and to state one thing that he liked about it and one thing that he disliked. Then invite the other students to ask any questions they wish to ask about the occupation. For some occupations there will be no questions. For others there may be so many that a time limit will be desirable. Continue until all students have had an opportunity to report or until the end of the period approaches. Then mention to the students that one accessible source of occupational information is the students in their own classes who have had part-time or vacation work experience, and suggest that they try a class session like this one.

LESSON PLAN 8   STUDENTS PLAN OCCUPATIONAL LIBRARY

Purpose   To give students some practice in using what they have learned. Specifically, to help them to plan the beginning of an occupational library.

Assignments Numbers 5, 31, 32, and 33.

Because of the length of these assignments, they are not reproduced here in full. Briefly, they instruct the student to read Chapter 5, examine several references, then:

Assume that you have just been hired as the first counselor in a new high school. The principal tells you that you may order a reasonable number of books to begin the school's collection of occupational information. What will you order? Prepare a list of the first ten titles that you will order. Bring it to class.

Activities in Class Invite the students to report orally the titles they have selected. Ask one student to write the selections on the blackboard as they are reported and to leave a margin in which votes can be recorded later. Accept only one title from each student until all who volunteer to contribute have had an opportunity to do so; then invite further contributions from anyone.

When all or most of the selections have been reported, ask the class to look at the blackboard and to make any changes they may now wish to make in their own selections. Then read the first title from the board and ask all students who have this title on their revised lists to raise their hands. Have a student count the hands, and report the count to the blackboard secretary. Ask the secretary to record the count opposite each title. Repeat with all the titles. Then ask the secretary to draw a circle around the number of votes for the most popular titles until the number of the titles so designated comes to ten.

Invite the students to compare the titles so marked with the titles which they selected individually, and to tell each other what they would delete from the blackboard list and what they would substitute and why.

LESSON PLAN 9   COMPARISON OF FILING SYSTEMS

Purpose To give the students some practice in thinking about the advantages and disadvantages of different plans for filing occupational information. To provide an opportunity for them to submit their judgments to the appraisal of their colleagues and the instructor.

Assignment Number 6.
Read Chapter 6.

Activities in Class Select from Chapter 6 one of the review questions which asks the student to decide how occupational information will be filed in a specific situation. Divide the class into buzz groups of four to six students each, and ask them to compare their ideas on the question for five minutes. Then invite the class as a whole to discuss the same question. For suggestions on leading the discussion see Appendix B.

Take your own notes on the discussion. Summarize the discussion for the group. Add your own comments. Repeat with another question.

LESSON PLAN 10   COMPARISON OF THEORIES OF OCCUPATIONAL CHOICE AND CAREER DEVELOPMENT

Purpose To encourage the students to formulate their own theories and to compare and to revise them.

Assignments Numbers 7, 35, and 36.
Read Chapter 7.

Review the theories described in Chapter 7. Prepare to attack those with which you disagree and to defend the others.

From all the theories of occupational choice and career development with which you are now acquainted, select the parts that make sense to you, add your own ideas, and state your own theory in your own words. Compare your theory with the phenomena you have observed in your own life and in your own work with other persons, and see how well it serves to explain your actions and theirs.

Activities in Class   Invite the students to suggest and to vote on the theories they would most like to discuss and on how much time they wish to spend on each. Start with the theory that gets the most votes. Invite those who disagree to open the discussion by attacking this theory. Then invite its defenders to respond. Continue the discussion until the time limit has expired or until discussion lags. Summarize what has been said, add your own comments, and repeat with the next theory.

LESSON PLAN 11   STUDENTS EXAMINE OWN NEEDS

Purpose   To clarify the composite theory for counselors described in Chapter 8. To arouse the interest of the students by relating the theory to their own personal experiences. To increase their own understanding of themselves and others.

Assignments   Numbers 8 and 34.
Read Chapter 8.
Review the occupational choices that you have made in the past. Note particularly the decisions that you made when you had to take some action, such as accepting or declining a job offer. Try to identify the needs that influenced your decision. Consider how these needs have affected your own job satisfaction and job performance. Prepare to share some of your thoughts with the class.

Activities in Class   On the chalkboard write:

> Job Choice
> Job Satisfaction
> Job Performance

Divide the class into buzz groups of four to six students each. Ask each group to select a moderator.

Ask each person to recall, during one minute of silent meditation, how his own needs have affected his own job choices, his own job satisfaction, and his own performance in the jobs he has held, and ask him to select one such recollection that he will share with his group.

Ask each buzz group moderator to invite the members of his or her group to share their recollections with each other and to ask each other any questions they wish. Allow five to fifteen minutes for this, depending on how animated the discussion appears to be.

Terminate the group discussion. Provide another one minute of silent meditation; ask each person to formulate one question he or she would like to raise or one comment if desired.

Invite volunteers to ask their questions or make their comments. Add your own comments if you wish.

LESSON PLAN 12   DEMONSTRATION CLIENT-CENTERED INTERVIEWS

Purpose   To let the students see what can happen when a client seeks occupational information from a nondirective counselor. To provide an opportunity for the students to compare their ideas on the use of client-centered counseling in this kind of situation.

Assignment   Number 9.
Read Chapter 9.

Preparation   Ask two or three students to prepare to do demonstration interviews before the class and an equal number to act as clients seeking occupational information. Ask the counselors to be as nondirective as the circumstances permit.

Activities in Class   Have the first counselor and client conduct their interview before the class. If the interview runs too long, interrupt it when you think it has served its purpose. Then ask the class to discuss two questions: "What did the counselor do well? What would you have done differently?" Summarize the discussion, add your own comments, and repeat with the next interview.

LESSON PLAN 13   DISCUSSION OF THE USE OF OCCUPATIONAL INFORMATION IN COUNSELING

Purpose   To give the students an opportunity to compare and to revise their ideas about the proper use of occupational information in counseling.

Assignments   Numbers 10 and 26.
Read Chapter 10.
Bring to class one written question that you would like to have discussed in class.

Activities in Class   Invite the students to vote on which of the questions they would most like to discuss. Start with the question which gets the most votes.

Divide the class into buzz groups of four to six persons each. Ask each group to select a moderator and a secretary and to discuss the question for five minutes. Then ask each secretary to summarize in two or three sentences the remarks most likely to interest the class. After these reports, invite further comments from the class as a whole. Summarize the discussion, add your own comments, and repeat with the next question.

Or skip the buzz sessions, invite open class discussion of each question, summarize the discussion, add your own comments, and repeat with the next question.

LESSON PLAN 14   MORE DEMONSTRATION INTERVIEWS

Purpose   To give the students another opportunity to compare and to revise their ideas about the proper use of occupational information in counseling.

Assignment   Number 11.
Read Chapter 11.

Preparation   Assign two pairs of students to demonstrate counseling interviews on some of the kinds of problems described in this chapter. The assigned counselors may select their own problems, or the teacher may choose them. The interviews may be rehearsed or not.

This procedure may be varied by announcing only the nature of the client's problem and asking everyone to prepare to be either the counselor or the client if called upon.

Activities in Class   Have the first counselor and client conduct their interview before the class. If the interview runs too long, interrupt it when you think it has served its purpose. Then ask the class to discuss two questions: "What did the counselor do well? What would you have done differently?" Summarize the discussion, add your own comments, and repeat with the next interview.

LESSON PLAN 15   COUNSELING BY COLLEGE FACULTY ADVISERS

Purpose   To encourage students to think about the proper use of occupational information by amateur counselors. To give them an opportunity to compare and to revise their ideas.

Assignment   Number 37.

You have just been appointed as the first dean of students in a coeducational liberal arts college of 1,000 students. You have no assistants. There is no college placement office. During your first week on the campus you are asked to meet with a group of faculty advisers. One of them asks you how they should respond to student requests for occupational information. Write your reply on one page and bring it to class.

Activities in Class   Divide the class into buzz groups of four to six students each. Ask each group to choose a moderator and a secretary, to compare their answers to the assignment, and to select the one best answer from the group. If the group cannot agree, ask the secretary to make the choice.

Ask the persons chosen by the group to read their answers to the class. Ask the class to discuss which of these is the best answer and to choose one of them.

Encourage the expression of dissenting opinions. Help the class to express all their ideas and to compare them. Help them to see where they agree, where they disagree, and why.

Summarize the discussion, and add your own comments.

LESSON PLAN 16   COUNSELING BY TEACHERS

This plan is identical with the one preceding except for the assignment, which is number 38.

You have just been appointed as the first counselor in a new school of 500 students. You have no assistants. During the first month you are asked to meet with a group of teachers. One of them asks you how they should respond to student requests for occupational information. Write your reply on one page and bring it to class.

LESSON PLAN 17   COUNSELING BY GROUP WORKERS

This plan is identical with the one preceding except for the assignment, which is number 39.

You have just been employed by a national organization as its specialist in vocational guidance. At the annual convention you are asked to serve as the resource person in a section meeting of group workers. Most of them are paid professionals, with some training in social work but none in occupations. They are employed in boys' clubs, settlement houses, YWCAs, etc. The group asks you how they should respond to requests for occupational information. Write your reply on one page and bring it to class.

LESSON PLAN 18   DISCUSSION OF PLANS FOR THE TEACHING OF OCCUPATIONS

Purpose   To give the students an opportunity to compare and to revise their ideas about the teaching of occupations.

Assignments   Numbers 12 and 40.
Read Chapter 12.
You are a counselor in the high school or college that you attended or in another school that you know well. Your supervisor asks you to recommend when and where courses or units in occupations should be offered, what they should include, and who should teach them. What will you recommend? Write your reply on one page and bring it to class.

Activities in Class   Divide the class into buzz groups of four or five students each. Ask each group to choose its own moderator. Ask each moderator to invite each student to read his or her recommendations; then invite the group to ask questions about, and to comment on, each report as it is read. Divide the time so that every report can be presented and discussed.

If time permits, reassemble the students into one group and invite questions for the whole class to discuss. Or ask each group to select one of its reports to be read to and discussed by the entire class.

LESSON PLAN 19   DEMONSTRATION DISCUSSION OF FOLLOW-UP RETURNS

Purpose   To demonstrate one way in which the returns from a follow-up study may be used for class discussion. To show the class some of the things that can be learned from follow-up projects. To add a little to the counselor's store of useful occupational information.

Assignments   Numbers 13 and 41.
Read Chapter 13.
Prepare five or ten questions that you would like to ask the alumni and alumnae of some school or college, or the former clients of some counseling agency, or the former members of some club or other group. Find three such persons, ask your questions, and bring the replies to class.

Activities in Class   Invite volunteers to read some of their interesting responses. Invite the other students to ask questions or to comment on these reports. Comment on them yourself when you feel inclined to do so.

As the reports are made, suggest to the class, or ask them to suggest, ways in which the items reported could be used to develop useful discussions in high school or college classes, or in meetings of other groups.

Or divide the class into buzz groups of four to six persons each. Ask the students to tell each other what they learned from their inquiries and what they think we ought to do about it, and to invite questions and comments.

LESSON PLAN 20   DEMONSTRATION PLANT TOUR

Purpose   To demonstrate how to conduct a plant tour as described in Chapter 14. To show the class some of the things that can be learned on a tour. To add to the counselor's store of useful occupational information.

Assignments
For the first tour. Number 14.
Read Chapter 14.
For subsequent tours. Number 42.
You are soon to go on a plant tour. The instructor will tell you where. Go to as many libraries as you can, and read everything you can find on occupations in the industry to be visited. Review Chapter 4, "Sources of Occupational Information," and use any sources that might help you to learn more about these occupations.

Try to find someone who is now employed in the place we are to visit, or in similar work elsewhere. Ask the person what are the three things he or she likes most and least about the job. Ask what are *all* the things he or she does in the job.

Ask your students, family, and friends for any questions they would like you to ask on the day of the tour. Formulate the questions you wish to ask.

During the tour, assume that the jobs you see are the only jobs open to you and that you really need a job. Select the job for which you would apply. Consider your ability to do the job or to learn to do it. Consider how well the job would meet your most important needs.

Activities in Class   Conduct the tour as described in Chapter 14, with such modifications as may be necessary or desirable to fit local conditions.

At the next class session after the trip ask the class:

Has anyone ever worked at the place we visited? At any place like it?
Did you observe anything different from what we saw on our tour?
Does anyone have any questions or comments?

LESSON PLAN 21   DEMONSTRATION GROUP CONFERENCE

Purpose   To demonstrate how to conduct a group conference as described in Chapter 15. To show the students some of the things that can be learned in group conferences with guests of different kinds. To add to the counselor's store of useful occupational information.

Assignments   *For the first conference.* Number 15.
Read Chapter 15.
For subsequent conferences. Number 43.
Go to as many libraries as you can, and read everything you can find on the occupation or industry to be covered in the next group conference. Review Chapter 4, "Sources of Occupational Information," and use any sources that might help you to learn more. Bring to class any questions that you would like to ask the guest expert.

Activities in Class   Conduct a group conference as described in Chapter 15. If time permits, devote several class sessions to group conferences with different kinds of guests, including an employer, an employee, an apprentice, a self-employed proprietor, a parent, and a student. Group conferences with an alumnus, a placement officer, and a union officer have been provided in previous lesson plans. After some experience, try having two guests at one time, then three or four.

LESSON PLAN 22   DEMONSTRATION SURVEY OF ENTRY JOBS

Purpose   To demonstrate some of the ways in which the information collected by the students may be exchanged in class discussion. To give the students a few of the experiences that their students will have if they undertake a student survey as described in Chapter 16. To add a little more to the counselor's store of useful occupational information.

Assignments   Numbers 16 and 44.
Read Chapter 16.
Prepare five questions that you would like to ask employers if you were participating in a survey of the kind described in Chapter 16. Interview three employers, and ask them the questions you have prepared. Submit a one-page report that could be duplicated and given to the staff and students of a school or college, or to the staff and clients of an agency.

Activities in Class   Divide the class into buzz groups of four to six students each, and ask each group to choose a moderator and a secretary. Ask each person to tell the others in the group the one most interesting thing that he or she learned from the interviews. After five minutes or more of discussion in the small groups, ask each group secretary to report to the whole class the one most interesting discovery made by the group. Encourage any discussion that the report may inspire, but do not force it. Continue until each secretary has reported one item. Then ask each to report a second item. Continue until all the items have been reported and discussed or until the class period nears its end. Then ask each student in turn, "Would an assignment and a class session like this be of any value to the persons with whom you work, or hope to work? Would any variation of it help them? Tell us the kind of group you work with and how you would use or vary this technique with them." Again encourage questions and discussion if time permits. If much time remains for this part of the class session, ask the class to form buzz groups and to discuss this topic before they report to the whole class.

LESSON PLAN 23   DEMONSTRATION CASE CONFERENCE

Purpose   To demonstrate how to conduct a case conference as described in Chapter 17. To show the class some of the kinds of topics that come up for discussion during a case conference and how the conference may be used to give students practice in making career decisions.

Assignment   Number 17.
Read Chapter 17.

Activities in Class   Select from your own experience a case of career planning in which occupational information was important, or devise one or more hypothetical cases. Select two alternate cases to use if the first one fails to provoke discussion. Present the first case to the class, and conduct the case conference as described in Chapter 17. If time permits, repeat with additional cases.

Or explain to the class that you are about to demonstrate a case conference and ask: "Are any of you now facing a decision about whether or not to accept a job that you can have if you want it? Is there such a person who would not be embarrassed or hurt by the questions we might ask or the comments we might make if we used you and your problem for our demonstration case conference?" If you get any volunteers, choose one of them and let the class ask questions of him or her and then express their thoughts on whether or not the volunteer should take the job and why. If you get no acceptable volunteer, use one of the cases you brought to class.

LESSON PLAN 24   DEMONSTRATION LABORATORY STUDY

Purpose   To give the students some of the experiences that their students will have if they undertake the laboratory study of one or more occupations as described in Chapter 18. To demonstrate one way in which the information collected by the students may be exchanged without a series of boring oral reports. To add a little more to the counselor's store of useful occupational information.

Assignments   Numbers 18 and 45.
Read Chapter 18.
Select an occupation about which you know very little but that you might consider entering if you were to leave your own. Learn everything you can about this occupation, following the checklist in Chapter 3 and the suggestions in Chapter 4. Record what you have learned and your reaction to it by filling the blanks in the "Outline for the Study of an Occupation" which appears in Appendix C. Consider whether or not some experience of this kind would be helpful to your students or clients. Come to class prepared to exchange information on the two or three most interesting things that you have learned from this experience.

Assignment 45 may be made several weeks in advance. It may be used as a term project. It was once used by the author as the basis for an entire course in sources of occupational information; a report of this experience, with the students' evaluation of it, may be found in Hoppock [175].

Activities in Class   Ask each student to write one sentence stating the most interesting thing he has learned from this experience about any occupation or about sources of occupational information. Ask each student to read his one sentence to the group. After each sentence is read, ask the class, "Does anyone wish to ask Mr. Blank for any more information on this topic?" After a few times this query may be shortened to "Anyone want more information?" or "Any questions?" Do not be surprised if the first few sentences evoke no questions. Encourage discussion, but do not force it. Make any comments you wish to make on the information reported and on the class discussion. If time permits, call on each student for a second or third report.

Continue until the class period nears its end. Then invite the class to discuss "What seem to you to be the values and the limitations in this method of teaching occupations?"

LESSON PLAN 25   DEMONSTRATION SELF-MEASUREMENT

Purpose To demonstrate how aptitude tests may be administered, scored, and discussed in class.

Assignment Number 19.
Read Chapter 19.

Materials Needed Enough copies of one vocational aptitude test to supply all the students and the instructor. An equal number of test manuals and scoring keys. The test selected should be one that can be administered to a group and scored by the students. If the instructor wishes to devote only one period to this lesson, the test should be one that can be completed and scored in not more than half of the available time. For teaching purposes, the manual should include several validity coefficients, obtained against different criteria, and tables of norms for several different populations. The author has found the hand-scoring form of the Revised Minnesota Paper Form Board [244] convenient for demonstration purposes. ·

Activities in Class Explain the purpose of the demonstration. Distribute and administer the test, following the directions in the test manual. When the test is completed, distribute the scoring keys and have each student score his own test. Then distribute the test manuals. Invite the students to ask questions about the meaning of various scores for various purposes. In answering their questions, call attention to the validity coefficients for various criteria; invite the students to comment on, and to ask questions about, what these coefficients reveal about the validity of the test for various purposes. Call attention to the tables of norms, and ask the class to answer questions that you ask about how a person with a given score would compare with various groups and about which norms should be used for various purposes.

Suggest to the class hypothetical cases in career planning, and ask how certain scores on this test might affect such plans. Near the end of the period ask the class to discuss the values and the dangers of this kind of class session for high school and college students, assuming that several successive periods would be devoted to it and several tests taken and discussed.

If you wish to devote more than one period to self-measurement, the tests may be scored and the test manual studied between classes. Obviously, one cannot teach a semester or a year course in statistics, in test administration, and in test interpretation all in one class period. It is assumed that any counselor or teacher who proposes to use this technique will have had or will soon take adequate training in testing.

LESSON PLAN 26   GROUP CONFERENCE WITH A COUNSELOR OR TEACHER OF OCCUPATIONS

Purpose To inform the students about some activity that they may wish to adapt to their own purposes.

Assignment Number 20.
Read Chapter 20.

Preparation Invite to the class a counselor or teacher of occupations who is doing something that you believe will interest your students. Such a person will sometimes be found among the students in the class.

Activities in Class   Conduct a group conference as described in Chapter 15, but substitute such questions as the following:

What was your purpose in undertaking this project?
How did you proceed?
What results did you get?
What did it cost?
Did you make any mistakes?
If you were to do it again, would you change anything?
Have you any suggestions that might help us if we were to try something similar?
Is there anything else we should have asked you?
Is there anything you would like to ask us?

LESSON PLAN 27   OCCUPATIONAL FILMS

Purpose   To show the students the kind of occupational information that is available on film. To give them a little practice in appraising occupational films.

Assignment   Number 46.
Review the sections on films in Chapter 20.

Preparation   Select two or three occupational films from one of the film catalogs, rent them, and arrange to show them during the class period.

Activities in Class   Tell the class that they are about to see a film that contains some occupational information. Ask them to view it critically, to identify its good and bad points, and to decide whether or not they would show it to the students or clients with whom they work or hope to work. Explain that an occupational film is not intended to present a complete picture of an occupation; it is intended to extend the range of occupations of which the student is aware, to add something to his knowledge, and to arouse enough interest to start a profitable discussion.
Show the film.
Ask the class, "From this film, what did you learn that you did not know before?" Have a student write the answers on the blackboard, so the class can see how much new information the film did convey.
In buzz groups or in open class discussion ask the class to list the reasons why they would or would not use this film, and to suggest how it might be used to start discussion. Summarize their discussion and add your own comments. Repeat with another film.

LESSON PLAN 28   DEMONSTRATION PRACTICE JOB INTERVIEW

Purpose   To demonstrate one way in which students and clients may be prepared for employment interviews. To add a little to the counselor's knowledge of how people are hired.

Assignment Number 47.
Review the section "Practice Job Interviews" in Chapter 20.

Preparation Invite a local employer to attend the class, conduct the interviews, and participate in the discussion. Select three students and assign them to apply for the kind of job for which the selected employer hires workers. Ask one of the students to do everything wrong. If the classroom is large, provide a public address system with two microphones.

Activities in Class Introduce the guest, and explain that he or she will interview three students from the class just as would be done if they were genuine applicants for work. Ask the other students to focus their attention on the applicant and to take notes on what the applicant does well and on what they would do differently if they were being interviewed. Do not ask or permit the students to say that what the applicant did was "wrong." Urge them to try to help one another by comparing ideas of how to do things well, but not by sniping criticism.

Ask the guest not to be concerned about time limits. Say you will interrupt the interview after five or ten minutes, depending on the length of the class period. Seat the guest at a desk at the front of the room. Provide an extra chair for e the applicant. Ask the first applicant to leave the room and reenter as if the room were the employer's office. The interviewer greets the applicant, and the interview proceeds without previous rehearsal.

At the conclusion of the interview ask the class to comment on what the applicant did well. Ask this question first in order to bolster the applicant's morale before any changes are suggested. Encourage discussion. Add your own comments if you wish. Then ask the students what they would have done differently. If students start to criticize the interviewer, remind them that the purpose of this session is to help the applicant, who may expect to meet all kinds of interviewers, and ask the students to restrict their comments to the applicant. Encourage discussion as before. Assure the applicant that he need not defend what he did, that he is to accept only those suggestions which appeal to him and to ignore the others. He may ask questions if he wishes.

At the conclusion of the students' discussion, invite the applicant and the guest to comment on both the discussion and the interview.

Repeat the process with the two remaining applicants. Hold the one who does everything wrong until the end, as a relief from fatigue and repetition. His performance usually provokes much laughter; it serves to dramatize and reinforce some points by exaggeration.

LESSON PLAN 29 GYP SCHOOLS

Purpose To make the students aware of the kind of sales pressure to which their students and clients may be subjected when they respond to the advertisements of gyp schools.

Assignments Numbers 48 and 49.
Review the section "Writing the Gyps" in Chapter 20.

Buy the gaudiest pulp magazine you can find. Scan the advertisements, and answer three which seem to you to represent gyp schools. Bring to class some samples of the recruiting literature that you receive. *Caution:* Do not give this assignment to *your* students without first doing it yourself, then warning your students and their parents to expect to see some high-pressure salespeople but to sign nothing without first discussing it with you.

This assignment should be made at least two weeks in advance.

Activities in Class   Invite volunteers to report their experiences with school salespeople and to read excerpts from the sales literature.

Divide the class into buzz groups of four to six students each. Ask each group to choose a moderator and a secretary and to discuss what they should do to protect their students and clients from gyp schools. Ask each secretary to report the one best idea his or her group can devise.

As each report is received, invite the class to comment on the values and limitations of the action proposed and to offer suggestions for improvement. Summarize the discussion, and add your own comments.

Tell the class how to terminate the sales pressure to which they have been subjected by a school. No method is guaranteed to end it, but the following have helped: Write to the school, saying, "I have enrolled at [Blank University] and am no longer interested in your school. Will you please remove my name from your mailing list." Give the same message to salespeople who call or phone. If this fails, return all mail to the post office, unopened; on the face of the envelope write "Refused." It will then be returned to the senders at their expense.

LESSON PLAN 30   COURSE UNITS ON OCCUPATIONAL INFORMATION

Purpose   To encourage the students to think about a problem which some of them will face. To give them an opportunity to exchange and revise their ideas.

Assignments   Numbers 50 and 51.

Review the section "Presenting Occupational Information through Other Subjects" in Chapter 20.

You are the counselor in a small high school that has no course in occupations. The social studies teacher has offered to devote ten weeks of class time to a study of occupations if you think this desirable. The teacher asks you: "Should we do this? In what grade? What should we cover and by what methods of teaching? Who should teach it?"

Write your reply on one page and bring it to class.

Activities in Class   Present to the class, for open discussion, the questions in the assignment. Take one question at a time. Encourage expression and comparison of all shades of opinion. Divide class time so that all the questions can be discussed. As you approach the end of the time limit for each question, summarize the discussion and add your own comments.

LESSON PLAN 31   DISCUSSION OF OCCUPATIONAL INFORMATION IN THE ELEMENTARY SCHOOL

Purpose   To give the students an opportunity to compare and to revise their ideas about the use of occupational information in the elementary school.

Assignments   Numbers 21 and 52.
Read Chapter 21.

Interview three elementary school teachers. Ask what they do to make their students more familiar with the ways in which people earn their living. Bring to class a composite list of the things that these elementary teachers do.

Activities in Class   Divide the class into buzz groups of four to six students each. Ask each group to choose a moderator and a secretary and to tell each other what they learned from their interviews with elementary teachers. Ask each secretary to report the things which the group found elementary teachers to be doing. As these reports are made, ask a class secretary to compile on the blackboard a composite list of all activities reported.

Ask the students to imagine that they are members of an advisory committee of parents that has been asked to tell the teachers which of these activities they would prefer to have provided for their children if some have to be omitted. Ask each student to select the one activity that he considers most valuable and to argue for it as if he were in such a meeting. Near the end of the period, the students vote on which activities should be given priority.

LESSON PLAN 32   DISCUSSION OF PLANS FOR BEGINNINERS

Purpose   To give the students an opportunity to compare and to revise their plans for using what they have learned from this course.

Assignments   Numbers 22 and 53.
Read Chapter 22.
Quickly review the entire text to this point. Formulate a plan for one thing that you intend to do in your present or future job as a result of the things you have learned in this course. Prepare to describe your plan to the class if you are asked to do so.

Activities in Class   Ask for a volunteer, or select one of the better students, or appoint buzz groups and ask each of them to select one of their group to report his plan. Ask the selected student to take your place at the front of the class to describe briefly the plan he has prepared. Limit him to five or ten minutes. Then ask the class to comment on two questions: "What do you like about this proposal? What would you do differently?" When the discussion lags or you feel that it has served its purpose, interrupt it, summarize it, add your own comments, and repeat with another student.

If time permits, the answers to the assignment may be written and collected a week in advance. Then the best papers may be selected for class discussion and returned to their authors at the next meeting.

LESSON PLAN 33   DISCUSSION OF PLANS FOR ADMINISTRATORS

Purpose   To give the students an opportunity to look at guidance from the point of view of their supervisors and to begin thinking about what they will do when and if they become administrators.

Assignments   Numbers 23 and 54.
Read Chapter 23.
Imagine that you are the top administrative officer in the organization in which you now work or hope to work. Formulate a plan for one thing that you would do about

occupational information in your organization. Prepare to describe your plan to the class if you are asked to do so.

Activities in Class   Same as in Lesson Plan 32.

Because Chapters 22 and 23 are short, the lesson plans based on them may be combined, and the students may be given their choice of the two assignments.

LESSON PLAN 34   APPRAISING THE COURSE

Purpose   To give the students an opportunity to help improve the course, to compare and revise their ideas on how it should be taught. To help the instructor to learn more about the student response to his or her efforts.

Assignments   Numbers 24 and 121.
Read Chapter 24.
If you were to teach this course, what would you do differently? What would you retain from the content and methods of the course as it has been taught this year? If you prefer to make some comments anonymously, put them on a separate sheet without your name on it.

Activities in Class   Divide the class into buzz groups of four to six students each. Ask each group to select a moderator and a secretary and to select the one best suggestion for improvement that has been proposed by its members. Ask the secretaries to report these suggestions. As each proposal is reported, invite questions and comments from the class. Ask the class to vote on each suggestion. How many agree? How many disagree? How many did not vote either way?

Repeat with the things they would like to retain from the present course.

LESSON PLAN 35   FACULTY MEETING ON OCCUPATIONAL INFORMATION

Purpose   To encourage the students to think about how they can use what they have learned in this course or to arouse their interest at the beginning of the course.

Assignment   Number 56.
You are a teacher in a school that has never done much to inform its students about occupations. Your principal calls you to the office and says, "I think we ought to do something to make our students better informed about occupations. I'm looking for ideas. How do you think we ought to go about it?" Write your reply on one page and bring it to class.

Activities in Class   Divide the class into buzz groups of four to six students each. Ask each group to choose a moderator and a secretary and to decide what is the first step they would suggest to this principal. If time permits, ask them to list subsequent steps in sequential order.

After five or ten minutes, ask each secretary to report the first step suggested by the group. List these steps on the blackboard.

Ask the class to imagine that they are teachers in a faculty meeting and that the principal has asked them to decide which of these steps should be taken first. Invite discussion. Try to reach amicable agreement. When you think the discussion has continued long enough, take a vote.

Ask each secretary to report the second step suggested by the group. Add these to the list on the board. Ask the class to discuss and vote on what the second step should be.

Continue with subsequent steps until near the end of the class period. Then summarize the discussion and add your own comments.

LESSON PLAN 36   DISCUSSION OF PLANS FOR EVALUATION

Purpose   To encourage the students to think about evaluating their work. To give them an opportunity to compare and revise their plans for doing so.

Assignments   Numbers 25 and 57.
Read Chapter 25.
Formulate a plan for evaluating something that you now do or plan to do. Prepare to describe your plan to the class if you are asked to do so.

Activities in Class   Same as Lesson Plan 32. This plan may be combined with Lesson Plans 22 and 23, and the students may be given their choice of the three assignments.

LESSON PLAN 37   COMPARISON OF CURRENT ACTIVITIES

Purpose   To give the students a glimpse of the occupational information services provided by the schools and colleges represented in the class.

Assignment   Number 58. This assignment should be made at least two weeks in advance.
Prepare a one-page summary of the occupational information services provided in your school, college, or counseling agency. If you are not so employed, choose a school with which you are or can become familiar. Include the following information: name and address of institution; grades included; number of boys, girls, teachers; number and nature of guidance staff; past and present occupational information activities that you think (1) have worked well, (2) are of doubtful value.

Make enough copies of this report so that each member of the class may have one. Bring these to class on the date that this assignment is due.

Sample report
High School, Somewhere, New Jersey, Grades 9–12. 200 boys. 200 girls. 16 teachers. One full-time counselor who teaches courses in occupations.
Occupational information activities that have worked well:

1   Course in occupations for seniors
2   Form for requesting interviews
3   Bulletin board for new books

Occupational information activities of doubtful value:

1   Career day

Activities in Class   Give each person a complete set of the reports.
Invite the students to read the reports silently and to ask questions of one another when they want more information.

LESSON PLAN 38   DISCUSSION OF JOURNAL ARTICLES

Purpose   To encourage students to read professional journals and to look for information and ideas which they can use in their own work. To help them to improve the tentative plans that they formulate from such reading. Incidentally to help some of them to become acquainted with journals that they have not read before.

Assignment   Number 59.

Browse through the back issues of any of the journals listed below. Find and read five articles that discuss some aspect of occupational information. Look for ideas that you can use in your present or future work. Submit a report on two pages: (1) your plans for using anything that you learned from this assignment; (2) full bibliographic data on the articles that you read.

Start page 1 with the words "I intend to . . . " If you cannot get one good idea from the five articles, continue reading additional articles until you do get results.

Journals
Bulletin of the National Association of Secondary School Principals
Clearing House
Elementary School Guidance and Counseling
Journal of College Placement
Journal of College Student Personnel
Journal of Employment Counseling
Journal of Non-White Concerns in Personnel and Guidance
Personnel and Guidance Journal
Rehabilitation Counseling Bulletin
School Counselor
Vocational Guidance Quarterly

The journals in your own specialty, e.g., vocational rehabilitation, vocational education, industrial arts, nursing, social work, industrial personnel work.

Activities in Class   Collect the papers. Tell the class that you will read aloud the plans they have reported. Ask them to try to help one another by contributing additional information and ideas. Read the first paper. Invite discussion by asking such questions as, "Have any of you ever tried anything like this? Have you ever seen anyone else try it? How did it work? How many of you like this idea? What do you like about it? Does it have any disadvantages? Is there any way in which it might backfire? Can you suggest any improvements?"

Add your own comments to those of the students and go on to the next paper. Do not be surprised if the students have no comments on some of the papers. If you need help in encouraging discussion, see Appendix B.

LESSON PLAN 39   QUESTION, COMMENT, AND DISCUSSION

Purpose   To give the students an opportunity to ask questions about anything in their reading which puzzles them or arouses their interest. To let them express and compare their reactions to what they read.

Assignment   Number 60.

Any chapter in the text or any other reading the instructor may choose, accompanied by the following instructions:

Read the material assigned. As you read, note anything which is not entirely clear to you, anything you do not understand, anything that seems to you to be unsound or debatable, anything you would like to challenge, anything about which you would like to ask a question, or anything that you would like to have discussed in class. Note also any suggested activities that you have seen in operation, with which you have had experience that you could report to the class, or on which you would like to comment. Whenever you encounter anything of this kind, stop reading and write your question or comment. Put each question or comment on a separate sheet of 8 ½- by 11-inch paper. In the top left corner put the number of the page in the publication which provoked your response. In the top right corner put your name and seat number. Hand these sheets to the class secretary at the beginning of the class period.

Activities in Class   Select a student for class secretary, and seat him or her near the door of the classroom. As students arrive and hand in their papers, have the secretary sort them by page number. By the time you have completed announcements and other preliminaries, the secretary should have most of the papers sorted. If the sorting is not completed, start with the top paper and let the secretary finish the sorting during the early part of the class period. The sorting process is not imperative; it merely saves some time by grouping together the questions and comments which relate to the same topic.

Open the class session by asking the secretary to read the first paper. If this contains a question, answer it, or ask the class what they think about it, or both. If the paper contains a comment, express your agreement or disagreement, or ask the class to do likewise, or simply thank the contributor and go on to the next paper. If questions arise which you cannot answer, say simply, "I'm sorry, I don't know. Does anyone else?" If the question is important enough, take it home and try to find the answer before the next session. Some questions can be answered in a sentence. Some could be handled adequately only by writing a book. Appraise each one as it comes up, in terms of its probable interest to the class as a whole, and allocate time accordingly. If some papers have not been read by the end of the period, take them home, read them, select a few of common interest to be handled during the first few minutes of the next class period, and answer the others by writing comments on the papers and returning the papers to the students at the next class session. If all the papers are covered before the end of the period, ask the class, "Is there anything else you would like to discuss?" If there is no response, dismiss the class.

The procedure is informal. Your answers are extemporaneous. There is no preliminary selection of questions to be discussed and no advance preparation of replies except in the case of holdovers as noted above.

Questions could be collected at one session and discussed at the next. This procedure would permit more selection and preparation, but it would postpone the discussion until after the students had read another assignment and written another set of questions and comments. The author prefers to discuss the comments and answer the questions while the subject matter is as fresh as possible in the minds of the students, even at some sacrifice in selection and preparation. The obviously unrehearsed classroom procedure assures a spontaneity which the students seem to like, too.

LESSON PLAN 40   DISCUSSION BY INTEREST GROUPS

Purpose   To give students with common interests an opportunity to ask each other questions, to exchange information, ideas, and experiences.

Assignment Number 107.

Bring to class one or more questions that you would like to ask other members of the class whose present or future work is in some way similar to yours.

Activities in Class Divide the class into interest groups, e.g., elementary schools, junior high schools, senior high schools, colleges, rehabilitation, others. Send each group to another room. Instruct the students in each group to ask each other any questions they wish, continue as long as they feel the discussion is productive, then prepare one question they would like to ask the instructor or the class, and return to the main classroom. Use the remaining time, if any, to discuss the questions brought back.

LESSON PLAN 41   FILLERS FOR EMERGENCIES

Occasionally a teacher must conduct a class session for which he or she is wholly unprepared. An expected guest does not appear for a group conference. A well-planned lesson ends when the period is only half over. A colleague is taken ill, and someone must cover the class. In such situations the author has found the following procedures helpful, and the students have said they found them worth the time spent on them.

1 Ask each student to review what he or she has learned during the past few days or weeks from any source about any subject, to select one item that might interest this group, to state that item in one written sentence. When most of the students have written their sentences, invite volunteers to read theirs. If no one responds, call on them individually. After each item is read, invite the class to ask questions or to comment. Do so yourself, if inclined. Then go on to the next item.

In a large class this procedure may be varied by asking buzz groups to review the sentences that their members have written and to select the most interesting one to be read to the group.

Writing the items is not always necessary. It does, however, seem to produce results from some students who otherwise say they cannot think of anything to report.

2 Ask each student to write one question that he would like to have the class discuss for his benefit and to sign his name. Collect the questions; read them aloud. After reading each question, ask the class how many would like to discuss it, count the raised hands, record the number on the paper with the question. Assure the students that they may raise their hands as often as they wish.

Ask the class how much time they wish to give to each question, and let them decide.

Arrange the questions in order of popularity, and invite the class to discuss them in this order. Summarize the discussion on each question, and add your own comments.

Assignments for Use in Counselor Education[1]

Assignments can be given to students more accurately and in less time if they are printed or mimeographed and numbered. Then, instead of dictating a long paragraph to the class, the instructor can simply announce, "For the next session please prepare assignments 7 and 34."

The assignments below include all those which appear in the lesson plans in the preceding section, plus additional assignments for enriching the course. Some of the assignments require very little time; some are long enough to be used as term projects; some can be long or short as the student or the instructor may desire.

GROUP I   READING ASSIGNMENTS IN THIS BOOK

1	Read the Preface, Contents, and Chapter 1.					
2	Read Chapter 2.	**10**	Read Chapter 10.	**18**	Read Chapter 18.
3	Read Chapter 3.	**11**	Read Chapter 11.	**19**	Read Chapter 19.
4	Read Chapter 4.	**12**	Read Chapter 12.	**20**	Read Chapter 20.
5	Read Chapter 5.	**13**	Read Chapter 13.	**21**	Read Chapter 21.
6	Read Chapter 6.	**14**	Read Chapter 14.	**22**	Read Chapter 22.
7	Read Chapter 7.	**15**	Read Chapter 15.	**23**	Read Chapter 23.
8	Read Chapter 8.	**16**	Read Chapter 16.	**24**	Read Chapter 24.
9	Read Chapter 9.	**17**	Read Chapter 17.	**25**	Read Chapter 25.

[1] For related discussion, see Chapter 24.

GROUP II   OTHER ASSIGNMENTS

26 Bring to class one written question that you would like to have discussed in class.

27 Prepare and submit a one-page statement of how the work assigned for this session has affected your thoughts, your actions, and your plans for the future. How can you use what you have learned?

28 For one week observe yourself. Notice every remark you make to anyone about any occupation. Observe the frequency and the content of your remarks, and ask yourself: What effect might these remarks have on the attitudes of these persons toward these occupations? How might these remarks influence the future occupational decisions of these persons? Are my remarks based upon accurate knowledge of the facts? Do I want to change what I have been doing? How?

29 For one week, take a detached look at your life. Notice and list all the ways in which your job affects your family and your own life off the job. At the end of the week review your list and reflect on what it reveals about the importance of occupational choice.

30 Bring to class some questions that you would like to ask any young alumnus or alumna of any high school or college about his or her job.

31 Examine the issues for the past three years of the several indexes listed in Chapter 4 under "Publications." Select one occupation, and compare the indexes to see which would be of most help to you in finding information on this occupation. Repeat with two other occupations. Decide which of the indexes would best serve your needs as a guide to the purchase of occupational publications for your library. Select and write for ten or more of the free publications listed in recent issues of these indexes.

32 Examine any of the following that you have not previously examined. Spend enough time with each to be reasonably sure that you know whether or not it contains any information of value to you. Read what interests you; skip what does not. Consider which references may be of value to your future students or clients. Take appropriate notes on those you wish to remember.

Occupational Outlook Handbook, Superintendent of Documents, Washington (see latest edition).

Occupational Outlook Quarterly, Superintendent of Documents, Washington.

Dictionary of Occupational Titles, Superintendent of Documents, Washington.

National Trade and Professional Associations of the United States and Labor Unions, Columbia Books, Washington (see latest edition).

Encyclopedia of Associations, vol. I, *National Organizations of the U.S.,* Gale Research Co., Detroit, Mich. 48226 (see latest edition).

33 Assume that you have just been hired as the first counselor in a new high school. The principal tells you that you may order a reasonable number of books to begin the school's collection of occupational information. Prepare a list of the first ten titles that you will order. Bring it to class.

34 Review the occupational choices that you have made in the past. Note particularly the decisions that you made when you had to take some action, such as accepting or declining a job offer. Try to identify the needs that influenced your decision. Consider how these needs have affected your own job satisfaction and job performance. Prepare to share some of your thoughts with the class.

35 Review the theories described in Chapter 7. Prepare to attack those with which you disagree and to defend the others.

36 From all the theories of occupational choice and career development with which you are now acquainted, select the parts that make sense to you, add your own ideas, and state your own theory in your own words. Compare your theory with the phenomena you have observed in your own life and in your own work with other persons, and see how well it serves to explain your actions and theirs.

37 You have just been appointed as the first dean of students in a coeducational liberal arts college of 1,000 students. You have no assistants. There is no college placement office. During your first week on the campus you are asked to meet with a group of faculty advisers. One of them asks you how they should respond to student requests for occupational information. Write your reply on one page and bring it to class.

38 You have just been appointed as the first counselor in a new school of 500 students. You have no assistants. During the first month you are asked to meet with a group of teachers. One of them asks you how they should respond to student requests for occupational information. Write your reply on one page and bring it to class.

39 You have just been employed by a national organization as its specialist in vocational guidance. At the annual convention you are asked to serve as the resource person in a section meeting of group workers. Most of them are paid professionals, with some training in social work but none in occupations. They are employed in boys' clubs, settlement houses, YWCAs, etc. The group asks you how they should respond to requests for occupational information. Write your reply on one page and bring it to class.

40 You are a counselor in the high school or college that you attended or in another school that you know well. Your supervisor asks you to recommend when and where courses or units in occupations should be offered, what they should include, and who should teach them. What will you recommend? Write your reply on one page and bring it to class.

41 Prepare five or ten questions that you would like to ask the alumni and alumnae of some school or college, or the former clients of some counseling agency, or the former members of some club or other group. Find three such persons, ask your questions, and bring the replies to class.

42 You are soon to go on a plant tour. The instructor will tell you where. Go to as many libraries as you can, and read everything you can find on occupations in the industry to be visited. Review Chapter 4, "Sources of Occupational Information," and use any sources that might help you to learn more about these occupations.

Try to find someone who is now employed in the place you are to visit or in similar work elsewhere. Ask what are the three things he or she likes most and least about the job. Ask what are *all* the things the person does in the job.

Ask your students, family, and friends for any questions they would like you to ask on the day of the tour. Formulate the questions you wish to ask.

During the tour, assume that the jobs you see are the only jobs open to you and that you really need a job. Select the job for which you would apply. Consider your ability to do the job or to learn to do it. Consider how well the job would meet your most important needs.

43 Go to as many libraries as you can, and read everything you can find on the occupation or industry to be covered in the next group conference. Review Chapter 4, "Sources of Occupational Information," and use any sources that might help you to learn more. Bring to class any questions that you would like to ask the guest expert.

44 Prepare five questions that you would like to ask employers if you were participating in a survey of the kind described in Chapter 16. Interview three employers, and ask them the questions you have prepared. Submit a one-page report that could be duplicated and given to the staff and students of a school or college, or to the staff and clients of an agency.

45 Select an occupation about which you know very little but that you might consider entering if you were to leave your own. Learn everything you can about this occupation, following the checklist in Chapter 3 and the suggestions in Chapter 4. Record what you have learned and your reaction to it by filling the blanks in the "Outline for the Study of an Occupation" which appears in Appendix C. Consider whether or not some experience of this kind would be helpful to your students or clients. Come to class prepared to exchange information on the two or three most interesting things that you have learned from this experience.

46 Review the sections on films in Chapter 20.

47 Review the section, "Practice Job Interviews" in Chapter 20.

48 Review the section, "Writing the Gyps" in Chapter 20.

49 Buy the gaudiest pulp magazine you can find. Scan the advertisements, and answer three which seem to you to represent gyp schools. Bring to class some samples of the recruiting literature that you receive. *Caution:* Do not give this assignment to *your* students without first doing it yourself, then warning your students and their parents to expect to see some high-pressure salespeople but to sign nothing without first discussing it with you.

50 Review the section, "Presenting Occupational Information through Other Subjects" in Chapter 20.

51 You are the counselor in a small high school which has no course in occupations. The social studies teacher has offered to devote ten weeks of class time to a study of occupations if you think this desirable. The teacher asks you: "Should we do this? In what grade? What should we cover and by what methods of teaching? Who should teach it?"

Write your reply on one page and bring it to class.

52 Interview three elementary school teachers. Ask what they do to make their students more familiar with the ways in which people earn their living. Bring to class a composite list of the things that these elementary teachers do.

53 Quickly review the entire text to this point. Formulate a plan for one thing that you intend to do in your present or future job as a result of the things you have learned in this course. Prepare to describe your plan to the class if you are asked to do so.

54 Imagine that you are the top administrative officer in the organization in which you now work or hope to work. Formulate a plan for one thing that you would do about occupational information in your organization. Prepare to describe your plan to the class if you are asked to do so.

55 If you were to teach this course, what would you do differently? What would you retain from the content and methods of the course as it has been taught this year? If you prefer to make some comments anonymously, put them on a separate sheet without your name on it.

56 You are a teacher in a school which has never done much to inform its students about occupations. Your principal calls you to the office and says, "I think we ought to do something to make our students better informed about occupations. I'm looking for ideas. How do you think we ought to go about it?" Write your reply on one page and bring it to class.

57 Formulate a plan for evaluating something that you now do or plan to do. Prepare to describe your plan to the class if you are asked to do so.

58 Prepare a one-page summary of the occupational information services provided in your school, college, or counseling agency. If you are not so employed, choose a school with which you are or can become familiar. Include the following information: name and address of institution; grades included; number of boys, girls, and teachers; number and nature of guidance staff; past and present occupational information activities that you think (1) have worked well, (2) are of doubtful value.

Make enough copies of this report so that each member of the class may have one. Bring these to class on the date that this assignment is due.

Sample report
High School, Somewhere, New Jersey. Grades 9–12. 200 boys. 200 girls. 16 teachers. One full-time counselor who teaches courses in occupations.
Occupational information activities that have worked well:

1   Course in occupations for seniors
2   Form for requesting interviews
3   Bulletin board for new books

Occupational information activities of doubtful value:

1   Career day

59   Browse through the back issues of any of the journals listed below. Find and read five articles that discuss some aspect of occupational information. Look for ideas that you can use in your present or future work. Submit a report on two pages: (1) your plans for using anything that you learned from this assignment; (2) full bibliographic data on the articles that you read.

Start page 1 with the words "I intend to. . . ." If you cannot get one good idea from the five articles, continue reading additional articles until you do get results.

Journals
Bulletin of the National Association of Secondary School Principals
Clearing House
Elementary School Guidance and Counseling
Journal of College Placement
Journal of College Student Personnel
Journal of Employment Counseling
Journal of Non-White Concerns in Personnel and Guidance
Personnel and Guidance Journal
Rehabilitation Counseling Bulletin
School Counselor
Vocational Guidance Quarterly

The journals in your own speciality, e.g., rehabilitation, vocational education, industrial arts, nursing, social work, industrial personnel work.

60   Read the material assigned. As you read, note anything that is not entirely clear to you, anything you do not understand, anything that seems to you to be unsound or debatable, anything you would like to challenge, anything about which you would like to ask a question, or anything that you would like to have discussed in class. Note also any suggested activities that you have seen in operation or with which you have had experience that you could report to the class, or on which you would like to comment. Whenever you encounter anything of this kind, stop reading and write your question or comment. Put each question or comment on a separate sheet of 8½- by 11-inch paper. In the top left corner put the number of the page in the publication that provoked your response. In the top right corner put your name and seat number. Hand these sheets to the class secretary at the beginning of the class period.

61 For students whose major field is counselor education and who have not done this already in one of this instructor's classes: Prepare a brief autobiography covering anything that you think might help the instructor to be more helpful to you. What do you hope to get out of this course? Why? How do you hope to get it? If the instructor had unlimited time, how could he be of most help to you? If you have written a similar autobiography for another class and have a copy of it, this may be substituted.

62 Review the history of your own occupational preferences and of the information that influenced them. Recall the sources of this information. List all these sources, and compare them for probable accuracy and adequacy. Compare your own experience with what you know or can learn about the occupational preferences of the students or clients whom you serve and with what you know or can learn about the sources from which they get their information. Reflect upon what you might do to help them to get better information upon which to base their decisions.

63 Look back over your own educational and vocational experience, and try to recall any times when you were given vocational guidance by anyone. Select three of these occasions, recall the guidance you were given, and evaluate it in the light of your subsequent experience. Then consider how your experience as a client may help you to improve your service to your clients.

64 Sometimes we grow so accustomed to our work that we do not notice how much it affects our happiness. For twenty-four hours, observe and record every aspect of your daily work that brings you feelings of satisfaction, pleasure, frustration, annoyance, or any other emotion. Compile a list of all the emotions associated with your work during this time, and of what aroused these emotions. Browse through Hoppock [174], noting particularly Chapters 1, 2, and 3 and the epilogue. Reflect upon what you might do to increase your own job satisfaction.

65 For twenty-four hours, think about the occupation of every person you see at work and of the persons in every place of business that you pass. Ask yourself what you think would happen to employment in these occupations in the event of a severe economic depression. Select the occupations that you think would be most likely to offer steady employment in periods of depression. Learn anything you can about what happened to employment in these occupations during previous economic cycles.

66 Identify five occupations in which you feel reasonably sure you could perform as well as, or better than, the average worker and five other occupations in which you think your performance would be so far below average that you would find it difficult to hold a job. For each occupation find one item of evidence to support your conclusion.

67 Find ten persons employed in ten different occupations, or ten persons all in the same occupation, or both. Ask each one, "What three things do you like most about your job? What three things do you like least about it?" See how often the answers surprise you. Consider making these questions a part of your daily conversation with other persons in other occupations to add to your store of occupational information and to give your acquaintances the pleasure of talking about themselves.

68 Ask your students what occupations they expect to enter when they go to work. Tabulate their responses. Consider what your community would be like if all of its workers chose these same occupations in these same proportions.

69 List all of your past experiences that you can recall in which you enjoyed success and satisfaction. Consider all aspects of your life at all ages. Determine whether the activity was concerned primarily with *data, people, or things*. Record your decision by putting the letter *D, P,* or *T* after each activity. If two of these were equally predominant, use two letters; avoid using all three, if possible. When you have finished, count the number of times you used each letter. Consider whether or not this tells you anything about yourself that you want to consider in making your own career plans. If you have trouble distinguishing between *data* and *things,* think of "things" as material objects you can pick up and put down, like a monkey wrench, and "data" as words, figures, ideas, and anything else that is neither people nor things.

70   Appraise the adequacy of your own occupational information about the employment opportunities for the students or clients that you now serve or hope to serve. From the suggestions in Chapter 2, select some things that you can do to extend your own knowledge of these occupations and start doing them.

71   Select one occupation that you have sometimes thought you might like to enter but in which you have had no experience. Read the checklist in Chapter 3 with this occupation in mind. Consider what additional information you should have if you were seriously thinking of changing to this occupation.

72   Ask some of your students or clients to read the checklist in Chapter 3 and then to tell you what additional information they would like to have on the occupations they are considering.

73   Ask your students what they would like to know about occupations. Select several of their questions on which they need help that you would like to give them. Go and get the information. If you need help, ask for it in class.

74   Examine the books and pamphlets on occupations in your school, college, agency, or public library. Appraise some of them by the criteria suggested in Chapter 5.

75   Go to any library that has both a collection of occupational publications and the *Dictionary of Occupational Titles.* Select several books and pamphlets, each describing a different occupation or group of occupations. Select the *D.O.T.* classification number under which you would file each publication. Decide how you would cross-index those publications that describe more than one occupation.

76   Visit each of the following:

The libraries where you work
The public library nearest where you live or work
The manager of the nearest office of your state employment service

Explain that you are a teacher, a counselor, or a counselor in training, and that you want to learn more about sources of occupational information for your students or clients. Ask the persons in charge to tell you and show you what kinds of information about occupations and about schools and colleges you can obtain at each place. Ask how they file occupational information and what they have found to be the advantages and disadvantages of their filing plans.

77   If you are now employed as a teacher, ask your students these two questions: "If you could have your choice of all the jobs in the world, what would you choose? Considering your abilities and limitations and opportunities, what occupation do you think you are most likely to enter after you finish school?" Examine the responses, and see whether your students are more or less realistic than you expected. Consider whether or not you should do anything to make them more aware of reality, or to extend their occupational horizons.

78   In your next ten counseling interviews or in your casual conversations, be as nondirective as you know how to be and as the situation permits. See what happens.

79   Review your own counseling to see if you have been using occupational information in the ways that you now think you should. If you think changes are desirable, make the changes and observe the results as well as you can.

80   Ask all the students in your classes to answer this question: "If the elective courses in our school included a course on opportunities and requirements in different occupations and if you were free to take the course this year, would you take it?" See how much demand there is for a course in occupations in your school. Consider whether or not you should do anything about it. If you are not a teacher, omit this assignment.

81 Read "Training for Failure" in the March, 1938, issue of *Occupations,* pages 563 to 564.

Think about what *you* should do for those of your clients who might do well as proprietors of their own small businesses.

82 Find out whether your school or agency has ever made a follow-up study of its former students or clients. If it has, examine the results to see how many surprises you can find.

83 Using the procedures suggested in Chapter 13 and any others you can invent, learn as much as you can about the present occupations of the former students or clients of your school, college, or agency.

84 If possible take a group of your own students or clients on a plant tour. If this is not feasible, go on a plant tour yourself, and do the things you would ask your students to do if you were taking them.

85 Examine the classified section of your local telephone directory. Prepare a list of the larger business classifications that you think should be called to the attention of your students or clients as potential sources of employment. Add an appropriate title and introductory paragraph, so that your list could be duplicated and distributed to the persons you serve. Consider what else you could do to make your students or clients aware of the wide range of occupations in your community.

86 Go for a one-hour walk through the business section of the territory served by your school or agency. Observe the occupations that might be open to your students or clients. Bring to class a numbered list of all the occupations you found.

87 Each day for one week read carefully the business news in your daily newspaper, including the help-wanted and situation-wanted advertisements. See what you can learn about present and probable future employment opportunities for the students or clients you serve. Notice the kinds of jobs that are offered, what they pay, and what they require. Consider whether or not you should read such news regularly and whether or not an assignment like this would be of value to the persons with whom you work.

88 If you are a teacher, plan and conduct a lesson, a project, or other activity on employment opportunities in one or more occupations related to one or more of the subjects you teach. Use one or more of the teaching techniques described in Chapters 13 to 20. Repeat with other occupations and other techniques. Compare results, using one or more of the techniques of evaluation described in Chapter 25.

89 Attend meetings of the nearest local branch of the American Personnel and Guidance Association and related groups. Talk with the people you meet. Find out what they are doing. Look for ideas you can use.

90 Consult your local classified telephone directory and directory of social agencies. Find the organizations that have names like Career Clinic, Job Finding Forum, and Man Marketing Clinic. Visit one or more of them. See it in action. Learn what the sponsors are trying to do and why and how. Consider whether or not you should do something similar, now or in the future. This assignment may be repeated as many as five times if you wish to visit more than one of these.

91 Visit one or more employment agencies: public, private, school, or college. (See "Employment Agencies" in the classified telephone directory.) Explain that you are a present or future counselor or teacher and that you are trying to learn something about agencies to which you might refer applicants. Ask if they will tell you what kinds of applicants the agency registers, what kinds of jobs it handles, and what kinds of applicants are easiest and hardest to place. Inquire about fees. Ask for sample registration forms and contracts, and read them.

92   Find one way in which you can use something that you learned in this course. Use it. Evaluate the results. Submit a one-page report.

93   Write to all the organizations listed below, as indicated in these assignments. Examine the material that you receive. Write one page on your reactions to what you have received, in terms of its value to you and your students or clients and how you propose to use any of it. The addresses were correct at date of publication. Anyone using the list should check.

In these assignments, "P and L" means write to this organization as follows: "Please send a list of your publications on occupational information and career guidance to [your name and present address] and send announcements of future publications to [your name and future address]." Use your official letterhead if possible.

When you receive the list of publications, order any that interest you, and read them. Write to:

The principal publishers of occupational information listed in Appendix A, for P and L.

U.S. Employment Service, Washington, for P and L.

Your own state employment service and your own state department of labor for P and L.

U.S. Bureau of Apprenticeship and Training, Washington, for P and L.

Your own state apprenticeship council for P and L.

U.S. Bureau of Labor Statistics, Washington, for P and L. Ask also for the address of the nearest regional office of B.L.S. and write to it for P and L.

U.S. Civil Service Commission, Washington; the State Civil Service Commission in your home state; and the Civil Service Commission in your home town or county for announcements of all future examinations of interest to your students or clients.

U.S. Office of Education, Washington, for P and L.

Your own state department of education for P and L, and for any free publications which describe the employment certificates issued to minors and the responsibilities of the school counselor in connection therewith. Read enough of what they send you to become generally familiar with your responsibilities in this area.

U.S. Rehabilitation Services Administration, Washington 20201, for P and L.

U.S. Small Business Administration, Washington, for P and L.

Superintendent of Documents, Washington, for P and L.

The department of commerce of your own state, and your own city or county, for P and L.

The chamber of commerce of your own state and your own city or county for P and L.

American Personnel and Guidance Association, 1607 New Hampshire Ave., N.W., Washington, D.C. 20009, for P and L.

American Vocational Association, 1510 H St. N.W., Washington, D.C. 20005, for P and L.

College Placement Council, Box 2263, Bethlehem, Pa. 18001, for P and L.

American Federation of Labor and Congress of Industrial Organizations, 815 16 St., N.W., Washington, D.C. 20006, for P and L.

National Child Labor Committee, 145 E 32 St., New York, for P and L.

National Alliance of Businessmen, 1730 K St., N.W., Washington, D.C. 20006, for information on their Career Guidance Institutes.

National Urban League, 55 E. 52 St., New York 10022, for P and L.

Federal Extension Service, U.S. Department of Agriculture, Washington, for P and L.

American Nurses Association, Inc., 2420 Pershing Rd., Kansas City, Mo. 64108, for P and L.

Director of College Recruiting:

Armstrong Cork Co., Lancaster, Pa. 17604

E. I. du Pont de Nemours & Co., Wilmington, Del. 19898

General Foods Corp., White Plains, N.Y.

General Motors Corp., Detroit, Mich.

Texaco, Inc., P. O. Box 52332, Houston, Tex. 77052

Ask for brochures on employment opportunities for college graduates.

94 Find a client who needs and wants occupational information to help in planning a career and who can work with you all term. Get the facts for him, and deliver them to him. Do a thorough job, using everything appropriate that you learn in this course. Discuss with your client the probable accuracy and adequacy of the information you get and his feelings about it. If you lose one client during the term, get another. Keep a complete record of everything you do. Hand in a one-page summary of what you did and of your own and your client's evaluation of it.

Do *not* refer your client to other sources of information. *You* go to the sources. *You* read the references. *You* get the facts. *You* compare sources to verify the information. *You* present the information to your client only when *you* are sure it is the most accurate and the most adequate information that *you* can provide. *Never* forget that if *you* make a mistake, your client may suffer for it for years to come.

95 From your own follow-up reports or from your own community survey or from your classified telephone directory or from the most recent *Dictionary of Occupational Titles,* compile a list of occupations that you want to learn more about. Arrange the occupations in order of their interest to you. Study as many of these occupations as your time permits, as thoroughly as your interest indicates. See Chapter 4, "Sources of Occupational Information." Submit a one-page report, briefly describing what you did and listing some of the things you learned from this project.

96 Make a list of the occupations which appear in as many motion pictures or television programs or short stories or books of fiction as you have time to see or read before this assignment is due. Consider whether the nature of the occupation is presented accurately or not. Would a person get a correct or a false impression of the occupation from what you have seen? In your report, list the name of the picture or program or story and the occupations shown. Opposite each occupation write A, B, or C to indicate your rating of the accuracy of the impression conveyed.

97 Prepare a photographic follow-up report on the present jobs of ten or more of your former students or clients, with pictures of them at their work and a running commentary on what they do, what they earn, how they got their jobs, etc.

98 Do a photographic survey of ten or more jobs for beginners in the neighborhood of your school or agency. For each job, get pictures of workers at their work, showing their principal activities. Add such explanatory comments as you would want for your students or clients.

99 Visit ten or more placement offices or employment agencies—public, private, school, college, etc. To find them, look in your classified telephone directly under "Employment Agencies." Explain that you are a present or future counselor or teacher and that you may wish to refer applicants to the agency. Ask if they will tell you what kinds of jobs the agency handles and what kinds of applicants are easiest and hardest to place.

Submit a two-page report. On page one, list the agencies visited and star (*) those which were cordial and cooperative. On page two, summarize the most interesting things you learned.

100 Ask the instructor to assign you to a specific bibliography of occupational information. Write to all the publishers of free materials listed therein, as follows: "Gentlemen: Will you please send me any free publications of yours that contain facts about jobs for use in career guidance." Prepare and submit a list of the publishers who send you any free material that you think counselors would like to have, with the address of each publisher and the titles of the free occupational publications received from each.

101 From the *Occupational Outlook Handbook* prepare a list of occupations in which the employment outlook is favorable. From your list, select those that offer the most opportunities in your community. Check local sources of information, e.g., placement services, employers, unions, employees, regarding local opportunities. Compile a final list of occupations in which the outlook is good both locally and nationally. In not more than five pages, report what you did and what you learned and how this experience has affected your plans for the future. Give both reports to the instructor on the date assigned.

102 Examine all the books, pamphlets, and magazine articles you can find on elementary education published in the past two years. Select short quotations that summarize what these publications say about the use of occupational information in elementary schools. Put each quotation on a separate sheet of paper, and add full bibliographic data on the source. Bibliographic data for each reference should include authors' names and initials, title of book or article, copyright date, name of journal if an article, name and address of publisher if a book, page numbers from which you took quotations, the library call number, and the library in which you found the reference. On a separate sheet list the author and title of each book you examined that said nothing on this subject.

103 Same as assignment 102 but with books, pamphlets, and magazine articles on guidance, counseling, and interviewing, published in the past two years, to see what they say about the use of occupational information in counseling.

104 Interview the counselors and librarians of ten high schools or ten colleges. Get the best estimate you can of how much each school spent for occupational information during some recent period of twelve months and the best record you can get of what they spent it for. Find out how many students were enrolled in the school during the same period. Compute the expenditure per pupil per year for occupational information for each school and for the total group of schools. Submit a full report.

105 Using the *Education Index* as a guide, explore periodical literature on the uses of occupational information in counseling and in teaching. Look for ideas that you can use. Each time you get an idea, write a one-paragraph description of it. Add full bibliographic data on the source. Submit these notes as your report.

106 Find some way in which you can help some group of people who want occupational information to get what they want. The group may be a school or college class or club, a community youth group, a parents' association, or any other organized or unorganized group. You may use one or more of the methods of teaching occupations described in the text, or you may invent your own methods. Submit a one-page report summarizing what you did and your own and your group's evaluation of it.

107 Bring to class one or more questions that you would like to ask other members of the class whose present or future work is in some way similar to yours.

108 If you are a teacher, or counselor, ask the students or clients who are assigned to you: "In what occupations are you interested? What would you like to know about them?" Get the answers in writing. Read them. Select some of the questions raised, and help your students or clients to find the answers.

109 Take a group of your own students or clients on a plant tour.

110 Prepare a photographic report on *all* the duties of one person now employed *as a beginner* in any job that you might reasonably expect to be open to the persons with whom you now work or hope to work. If you are now employed in a school, college, or agency, use one of your former students or clients as a subject. Show the report to your present students or clients.

111 Using everything you now know about the sources of occupational information, find the best answers you can to the question or questions assigned.

112 Examine one or more of the following. Quickly scan the preface, table of contents, and index to see if the book contains anything of interest to you. Read as much or as little as you like. If you learn nothing useful in the first fifteen to thirty minutes, try another book.

Baer, M. F., and E. C. Roeber: *Occupational Information.* [13]
Borow, H. (ed.): *Career Guidance for a New Age.* [24]
Borow, H. (ed.): *Man in a World at Work.* [26]
Isaacson, L. E.: *Career Information in Counseling and Teaching.* [199]
Norris, W.: *Occupational Information in the Elementary School.* [285]
Norris, W., and others: *The Information Service in Guidance.* [286]
Shartle, C. L.: *Occupational Information.* [343]

113 A girl was always collecting and caring for animals of all kinds. At age 16 she was tested by a university psychologist who reported that the girl had high-level aptitudes in English and in science. Her high school average was 96.

She went to a liberal arts college, majored in science, and became editor of the college newspaper. She spent each summer in camp, continuing her interest in animals.

In her senior year of college, she applied for admission to colleges of veterinary medicine. She was denied admission because she was currently failing in organic chemistry.

She asks you, "What other occupations are there for a person like me?"

Consult the *Dictionary of Occupational Titles.* Bring to class a list of possible occupations for this student to consider. Include the *D.O.T.* code number and title of each occupation. Arrange and number the occupations in order of their probable appropriateness for this student. Keep your list for use in class and for possible future reference.

114 If you work in a high school or college, find out if a unit or a course in occupations is taught there. Talk with the teacher, ask if you may visit and observe the class. If the teacher is cooperative, ask if you may take over one or more sessions and try your hand at a case conference, a group conference, a practice job interview, or a plant tour.

115 Arrange to spend all or part of one day talking with a person and observing his or her work in some job that you would like to have some day, or in some occupation that seems likely to be open to your students or clients, or in some other occupation that interests you.

116 Find one former student of your school or college, or one former client of your agency, who fits the following description:

He has completed his formal education.

He has completed his military or alternate service, or has not yet been called.

He is now employed.

He has been employed not more than five years since he left your school, college, or agency.

Arrange for a leisurely personal interview with him. In this interview, learn all that he is willing to tell you about:

His present job:
   What are *all* the things he has to do?
   What three things does he like most about it?
   What three things does he like least about it?
   How did he get it?
   What suggestions would he offer to *your* students or clients if they wanted to get a job like his?
His vocational development:
   What were his vocational choices at different times?
   When did he change them and why?

Before the interview, get all the information you can about him from the records of your school, college, or agency and from counselors and teachers who knew him.

Look for records of any discussion of vocational preferences in any counseling interviews and for records of any vocational aptitude tests or interest inventories.

Submit a summary of the most interesting things you learned from this experience. Maximum length, one page.

On the reverse side of the page, report how this experience has affected your thoughts, your actions, and *your plans for the future.*

117   Visit five, ten, or fifteen factories, stores, offices, and other places of employment where your students or clients might find jobs. See, hear, feel, and smell the environment in which people work. Observe what they do. Take your students or clients with you if you wish.

Interview the employer about opportunities and requirements in the jobs for which your students or clients might be hired. Interview union representatives or other employees if possible.

Try to include some places in which your former students or clients have found jobs, and interview them as well as the employer. You may find some interesting differences in the answers you get—not because either one is trying to deceive you, but because they see things from different points of view.

Before each visit, read any parts of the *Occupational Outlook Handbook* that cover occupations or industries that you might expect to see. You may then ask better questions and learn more of what you want to know.

Prepare a reference notebook that you will want to keep on your desk for your own use in teaching and counseling. If you type, please make a carbon copy that we may keep to show future students here.

118   From the assigned reading, copy and bring to class one or more of these:

1.   One sentence with which you heartily agree
2.   One sentence with which you disagree
3.   One question you would like to raise for discussion

Hold your paper until the end of the period. Then give it to the class secretary.

119 Find one occupational information pamphlet file not in this university. You may find it in the library or in the counselor's office of a high school or college, in the office of a vocational counseling service in a community agency, or in a public library. Ask permission to look at the file.

Examine the first twenty-five pamphlets in the file. Make a list of the copyright dates of these twenty-five pamphlets. You will find the date in small type, preceded by the word "copyright" or the letter "c" with a circle around it, usually near the front or the back of the pamphlet. If you can find no copyright date, but you do find another date which clearly indicates the age of the pamphlet, copy this date. If you can find no dependable date, put on your list the words "no date."

For every pamphlet that is more than five years old, copy also the title and the publisher.

If the person whom you ask to let you use the file questions your purpose, show him these instructions and assure him that you will not report the name of the organization. You will indicate only that the file was in a school, a college, or a community agency. Do report this much, and your list of dates.

Add one paragraph on what you would do with this file if you were responsible for keeping it up to date.

120 Ask the students in your classes, "In what occupations are you interested? What would you like to know about them?" Get the answers in writing. Read them. Select some of the questions raised, and help your students to find the answers. In one paragraph answer this question: How has this experience affected your thoughts, your actions, and your plans for the future?

121 If you were to teach this course, what would you do differently? What would you retain from the content and methods of the course as it has been taught this year? If you prefer to make some comments anonymously, put them on a separate sheet without your name on it.

Bibliography

1 *Accredited Institutions of Higher Education,* American Council on Education, Washington (see latest edition).
2 *Accredited Post Secondary Institutions and Programs,* Government Printing Office, Washington (see latest edition).
3 *Action and Careers in a New Age,* APGA Peace Commission, 1607 New Hampshire Ave., N.W., Washington, 1972.
4 Allen, R. D.: *Case-Conference Problems in Group Guidance,* Inor Publishing Company, New York, 1933.
5 Allen, R. D.: *Self-measurement Projects in Group Guidance,* Inor Publishing Company, New York, 1934.
6 Allen, R. D., F. J. Stewart, and L. J. Schloerb: *Common Problems in Group Guidance,* Inor Publishing Company, New York, 1933.
7 *American Junior Colleges,* American Council on Education, Washington (see latest edition).
8 *American Universities and Colleges,* American Council on Education, Washington (see latest edition).
9 *American Vocational Journal,* American Vocational Association, Washington.
10 Ames, D. A.: "Toms River Surveys Its Needs," *Personnel and Guidance Journal,* January 1953, p. 227.
11 Arutunian, C. A.: "Career Development Center, Troy High School, Fullerton, Calif.," *Case Studies in Practical Career Guidance,* no. 2, American Institutes for Research, Palo Alto, Calif., 1973.

12 *AV Quick-List,* Career Education, The Baker & Taylor Company, Box 230, Momence, Ill. (see latest edition).

13 Baer, M. F., and E. C. Roeber: *Occupational Information,* Science Research Associates, Inc., Chicago; 2d ed., 1958, 3d ed., 1964.

14 Baker, W. P., and H. C. Jensen: *Mexican American, Black and Other Graduates and Dropouts,* East Side Union High School District, San Jose, Calif., 1973.

15 Bank, I. M.: "Children Explore Careerland through Vocational Role-Models," *Vocational Guidance Quarterly,* June 1969, p. 284.

16 Bedell, R., and W. H. Nelson: "Educators' Opinions on Occupational Information Use in Rural High Schools," *Occupations,* December 1950, p. 205.

17 Beery, J. R., B. C. Hayes, and E. Landy: *The School Follows Through,* National Association of Secondary School Principals, Washington, 1941.

18 Bennett, W.: *Occupations Filing Plan and Bibliography,* The Interstate Printers & Publishers, Inc., Danville, Ill. (see latest edition).

19 Bergstresser, J. L.: "Counseling and the Changing Secondary-school Curriculum," *Bulletin of the National Association of Secondary School Principals,* May 1940, p. 67.

20 Berkowitz, B.: "The 'Leftys' Make You Stop and Think," *Vocational Guidance Quarterly,* Autumn 1955, p. 16.

21 "Blue Book of Audiovisual Materials," published annually in *AV Guide: The Learning Media Magazine,* 434 S. Wabash Av., Chicago.

22 Boocock, S. S.: *Life Career Game,* The Bobbs-Merrill Company, Inc., Indianapolis, Ind. (see latest edition).

23 Borgen, F. H., D. J. Weiss, H. E. A. Tinsley, R. V. Dawis, and L. H. Lofquist; *Occupational Reinforcer Patterns* (1st vol.), Industrial Relations Center, University of Minnesota, Minneapolis, 1968.

24 Borow, H. (ed.): *Career Guidance for a New Age,* Houghton Mifflin Company, Boston, Mass., 1973.

25 Borow, H.: "College Courses in Vocational Planning," *Vocational Guidance Quarterly,* Winter 1960–1961, p. 75.

26 Borow, H. (ed.): *Man in a World at Work,* Houghton Mifflin Company, Boston, 1964.

27 Brayfield, A. H., and G. T. Mickelson: "Disparities in Occupational Information Coverage," *Occupations,* April 1951, p. 506.

28 Brayfield, A. H., and P. A. Reed: "How Readable Are Occupational Information Booklets?" *Journal of Applied Psychology,* October 1950, p. 325.

29 Breckenridge, A. L.: "Multi-media Guidance Center—a Reality," *Pupil Personnel Services Journal,* State Department of Education, St.Paul, Minn, January 1973, p. 28.

30 Brewer, J. M.: *History of Vocational Guidance,* Harper & Row, Publishers, Inc., New York, 1942.

31 Brill, A. A.: *Basic Principles of Psychoanalysis,* Doubleday & Company, Inc., Garden City, N.Y., 1949.

32 Brooks, A. B.: "Occupations Week," *Wilson Library Bulletin,* January 1942, p. 364.

33 Brown, N.: *After College . . . Junior College . . . Military Service . . . What?* rev. ed., Grosset & Dunlap, Inc., New York, 1971.

34 Brown, N.: *Are You an Occupational Ignoramus?* College Placement Council, Inc., Bethlehem, Pa., 1971.

35 Budke, W. E.: *Review and Synthesis of Information on Occupational Exploration,* Publication no. 0-420-463, Government Printing Office, Washington, 1971.

36 Burianek, B., and W. Tennyson: "File It for Display Use," *Vocational Guidance Quarterly,* Winter 1955–1956, p. 51.

37 Byrn, D. K.: *Career Decisions,* National Vocational Guidance Association, Washington, 1969.

38 Cager, W., B. Eatman, H. Jones, D. Mackey, E. Paul, and V. Tidwell: *Cleveland Blacks Moving Up: The Lives of Cleveland's Black Businessmen,* Empire Junior High School, Cleveland, Ohio, 1970.

39 Calvert, R., Jr.: *Your Future in International Service,* Richards Rosen Press, New York, 1969.

40 Calvert, R., Jr., E. M. Carter, and I. Murphy: "College Courses in Occupational Adjustment," *Personnel and Guidance Journal,* March 1964, p. 680.

41 Campbell, R. E., G. R. Walz, J. V. Miller, and S. F. Kriger: *Career Guidance: A Handbook of Methods,* Charles E. Merrill Books, Inc., Columbus, Ohio, 1973.

42 *Canadian Classification and Dictionary of Occupations,* Information Canada, Publishing Division, Ottawa, KIA OS9, Ontario, Canada (see latest edition).

43 Cantor, N.: *Dynamics of Learning,* Henry Stewart, Incorporated, Buffalo, N.Y., 1946.

44 Caplow, T.: *The Sociology of Work,* The University of Minnesota Press, Minneapolis, 1954.

45 *Career Development, Increasing the Vocational Awareness of Elementary School Children: A Guidebook for Teachers,* Division of Vocational Education, N.J. State Department of Education, 1969. Order from Curriculum Laboratory, Department of Vocational-Technical Education, Rutgers University, New Brunswick, N.J., or from ERIC.

46 *Career Guidance Index,* published periodically by Careers, Inc., P.O. Box 135, Largo, Fla.

47 *Career Index,* published periodically by Chronicle Guidance Publications, Inc., Moravia, N.Y.

48 *Career Information Kit,* Science Research Associates, Inc., Chicago (see latest edition).

49 *Career World,* Curriculum Innovations, Inc., 501 Lake Forest Ave., Highwood, Ill.

50 Carrington, E.S.: "Working with Hands and Brains," *Occupations,* May 1935, p. 694.

51 Carter, E. M., and R. Hoppock: "College Courses in Careers—1952," *Personnel and Guidance Journal,* February 1953, p. 315.

52 Carter, E. M., and R. Hoppock: "College Courses in Careers," *Personnel and Guidance Journal,* January 1961, p. 373.

53 Chervenik, E.: "Demonstration Employment Interviews," *Occupations,* April 1950, p. 433.

54 Chervenik, E.: "Tempting Students to Sample Occupational Information," *Vocational Guidance Quarterly,* Winter 1953, p. 39.

55 Christal, R. E.: "Occupational Research Inputs to Vocational-Technical Education," *Vocational Guidance Quarterly,* June 1970, p. 253.

56 Christensen, T. E.: "Helping Students Enter Industry," *Vocational Guidance Quarterly,* Autumn 1954, p. 24.

57 Christensen, T. E.: Letter to R. Hoppock, Nov. 29, 1961.

58 Christensen, T. E.: *Resource Units for Junior High School Orientation Classes,* Public Schools, Worcester, Mass., 1961.

59 Christensen, T. E.: *The Self-appraisal and Careers Course Helps Seniors Achieve Educational, Vocational, Personal Maturity,* Superintendent of Schools, Worcester, Mass., 1953.

60 Christensen, T. E., and C. M. Donovan: *A Report on Counseling Pupils Who Secure Work Permits,* Public Schools, Worcester, Mass., 1967.

61 Clark, H. F.: *Economic Theory and Correct Occupational Distribution,* Teachers College Press, Columbia University, New York, 1931.

62 Clark, V. M.: "A Local Occupational Survey," *Vocational Guidance Quarterly,* Winter 1962, p. 115.

63 Clary, J. R., and H. E. Beam: "Realistic Vocational Education for Ninth Graders," *American Vocational Journal,* May 1965, p. 16.

64 Cleland, H. L.: "A Follow-up Survey through Visual Aids," *Occupations,* February 1941, p. 331.

65 Clifton, R. S.: "Counseling Youth for Military Service," *Personnel and Guidance Journal,* December 1955, p. 202.

66 Cole, R. C.: *An Evaluation of the Vocational Guidance Program in the Worcester Boys' Club,* Boys' Club, Worcester, Mass., 1939. (Out of print.)

67 *College Guide for Jewish Youth,* B'nai B'rith Career and Counseling Services, Washington (see latest edition).

68 *College Placement Annual,* College Placement Council, Inc., P.O. Box 2263, Bethlehem, Pa. (see latest edition).

69 *Colleges Classified: A Guide for Counselors, Parents and Students,* Chronicle Guidance Publications, Inc., Moravia, N.Y. (see latest edition).

70 Comfort, A.: *Authority and Delinquency in the Modern State: A Criminological Approach to the Problem of Power,* Routledge & Kegan Paul, Ltd., London, 1950.

71 Conant, J. B.; *Slumns and Suburbs,* McGraw-Hill Book Company, New York, 1961.

72 *Conscientious Objectors,* Selective Service System, Washington (see latest edition).

73 "Conversion Table of Code and Title Changes," *Dictionary of Occupational Titles,* Government Printing Office, Washington (see latest edition).

74 Cooley, W. W.: "The Classification of Career Plans," *Proceedings of the 73d Annual Convention,* American Psychological Association, Inc., Washington, 1965.

75 Corre, M. P.: "Filing Occupational Information," *Occupations,* November 1943, p. 122.

76 Cote, T. J.: "Vocational Guidance European Style," *American Vocational Journal,* May 1970, p. 24.

77 *Counselor's Information Service,* published quarterly by B'nai B'rith Career and Counseling Services, Washington.

78 *A Counselor's Professional File,* Chronicle Guidance Publications, Inc., Moravia, N. Y., 1964.

79 Cox, C. L.: Memorandum to R. Hoppock, October 1952.

80 *The Crisis of Career Education,* EPIC, National Urban League, New York, Summer 1972.

81 Crites, J. O.: *Vocational Psychology: The Study of Vocational Behavior and Development,* McGraw-Hill Book Company, New York, 1969.

82 Cronin, A.: "Reclaimed Housewives," *Women's Education,* September 1964, p. 5.

83 Crosby, M. J.: "Planning Vocationally and Finding a Job," in E. Lloyd-Jones and M. R. Smith, *Student Personnel Work as Deeper Teaching,* Harper & Row, Publishers, Inc., New York, 1954.

84 Cuony, E. R.: "An Evaluation of Teaching Job Finding and Job Orientation," doctoral thesis, New York University School of Education, New York, 1953, summarized in E. R. Cuony and R. Hoppock, "Job Course Pays Off," *Personnel and Guidance Journal,* March 1954, p. 389.

85 Cuony, E. R., and R. Hoppock: "Job Course Pays Off Again," *Personnel and Guidance Journal,* October 1957, p. 116.

86 Daane, C. J.: *Vocational Exploration Group: Theory and Research,* Manpower Administration, U.S. Department of Labor, Washington, February 1972. (Limited copies available from the author at P.O. Box 1039, Tempe, Ariz.)

87 Dale, R. V. H.: "To Youth Who Choose Blindly," *Occupations,* April 1948, p. 419.

88 Darcy, R. L.: "A Classroom Introduction to the World of Work," *Occupational Outlook Quarterly,* Winter 1971, p. 23.

89 Davenel, G.: "Retooling for the Space Age," *Journal of College Placement,* December 1959, p. 21.

90 Davison, M.: *Career Graduates: A Profile of Job Experience and Further Study of Students with A.A.S. Degrees,* City University of New York, Office of Community College Affairs, New York, 1971.

91 Dawis, R. V., L. H. Lofquist, and D. J. Weiss: "A Theory of Work Adjustment (A Revision)," *Minnesota Studies in Vocational Rehabilitation,* 23, Industrial Relations Center, University of Minnesota, Minneapolis, April 1968.

92 "A Day with a Social Worker," *Glamour,* November 1953, p. 142.

93 DeHaan, R. F., and I. Kough: *Teachers Guidance Handbook,* Part II, "Helping Children with Special Needs," Science Research Associates, Inc., Chicago, 1956, p. 41.

94 Dempsey, F., and L. Z. Begnoche: "An Early Look at the Employment Market," *Vocational Guidance Quarterly,* Spring 1960, p. 145.

95 *Desk Top Career Kit,* Careers, Inc., Largo, Fla. (see latest edition).

96 Diamond, E.: "Bring the Occupational File Out into the Open," *Vocational Guidance Quarterly,* Summer 1959, p. 219.

97 Dickinson, C.: "How College Seniors' Preferences Compare with Employment and Enrollment Data," *Personnel and Guidance Journal,* April 1954, p. 485.

98 *Dictionary of Occupational Titles,* Government Printing Office, Washington (see new editions and supplements as issued).

99 Diener, T. F., and H. R. Kaczkowski: "Readability of Occupational Information," *Vocational Guidance Quarterly,* Winter 1960, p. 87.

100 DiMinico, G.: "You and Work," *American Vocational Journal,* December 1969, p. 22.

101 *Directory: Employers of New Community College Graduates,* Department of Manpower and Immigration, Ottawa 2, Ontario, Canada (see latest edition).

102 *Directory: Employers of New University Graduates,* Department of Manpower and Immigration, Ottawa 2, Ontario, Canada (see latest edition).

103 *Directory: National Association of Trade and Technical Schools,* Washington (see latest edition).

104 *Directory of Accredited Private Home Study Schools,* Accrediting Commission of the National Home Study Council, Washington (see latest edition).

105 *Directory of National Unions and Employee Associations,* U.S. Bureau of Labor Statistics, Washington (see latest edition).

106 *Directory of Postsecondary Schools with Occupational Programs, Public and Private,* Government Printing Office, Washington (see latest edition).

107 *Directory of Secondary Schools with Occupational Curriculums, Public and Nonpublic,* Government Printing Office, Washington (see latest edition).

108 *Directory: Private Employment Agencies,* National Employment Association, 2000 K St., N.W., Washington (see latest edition).

109 Dittersdorf, H.: "Subject Matter-Centered Career Conferences." *Vocational Guidance Quarterly,* Summer 1962, p. 248.

110 Dodson, A. G.: "An Occupational Exploration Program for Inner-City Elementary Pupils," *Vocational Guidance Quarterly,* September 1971, p. 59.

111   Dresden, K. W.: "High School Seniors Survey Job Opportunities," *Occupations,* October 1950, p. 32.

112   DuBato, G.: "A Vocational Guidance Unit for the Non-College Bound," *Vocational Guidance Quarterly,* Autumn 1961, p. 56.

113   Dunn, C. J., and B. F. Payne: *World of Work: Occupational-Vocational Guidance in the Elementary Grades: A Handbook for Teachers and Counselors,* Leslie Press, Dallas, Tex., 1971.

114   *Education Directory: Higher Education,* Government Printing Office, Washington (see latest edition). Available also on computer tape. Includes name of placement director.

115   *Employment Opportunities Handbook—Canada.* French and English editions in one volume. University and College Placement Association, Markham, Ontario, Canada. Distributed free to universities, institutes of technology, and community colleges in Canada. One copy is sent to each high school vocational guidance department.

116   *Encyclopedia of Associations,* vol. 1, *National Organizations of the U.S.,* Gale Research Company, Detroit, Mich. (see latest edition and supplements in vol. 3, *New Associations).*

117   Engen, M.: "Wyoming High School Seniors Discover Their Community," *Occupations,* March 1948, p. 361.

118   *An Experiment: Job Clinics for the Graduating Senior,* Business Research Station, State College, Miss., 1949.

119   Faul, G. J.: "Vocational Planning and Adjustment Courses at Contra Costa College," in H. T. Morse and P. L. Dressel, *General Education for Personal Maturity,* Wm. C. Brown Company Publishers, Dubuque, Iowa, 1960, p. 161.

120   Fedele, G. M.: "Occupational Information in the Pre-Kindergarten," *Elementary School Guidance and Counseling,* December 1970, p. 153.

121   Feingold, S. N.: *A Career Conference for Your Community,* B'nai B'rith Career and Counseling Services, Washington, 1964.

122   Fick, R. L.: "The Stockton Occupational Survey," *California Journal of Secondary Education,* December 1948, p. 493.

123   Fink, A.: Letter to R. Hoppock, Dec. 2, 1952.

124   Flynn, H. J., N. Saunders, and R. Hoppock: "Course for Dropouts," *Clearing House,* April 1954, p. 486.

125   Forer, B. R.: "Personality Factors in Occupational Choice," *Educational and Psychological Measurement,* Autumn 1953, p. 361.

126   Forrester, G.: *Occupational Literature,* The H. W. Wilson Company, New York (see latest revision).

127   Forte, J.: Memorandum to R. Hoppock, Aug. 6, 1957.

128   Fowler, J. R.: "A Post-Secondary Vocational-Technical Placement Seminar," *Vocational Guidance Quarterly,* September 1972, p. 63.

129   Fox, M. G.: "A Twelfth-grade Course in Occupations," *Bulletin of the National Association of Secondary School Principals,* January 1950, p. 280.

130   Frank, R. L., and B. B. Patten: "A Three-Way Occupational File," *Vocational Guidance Quarterly,* Spring 1960, p. 171.

131   Froehlich, C. P.: "Must Counseling Be Individual?" *Educational and Psychological Measurement,* Winter 1958, p. 681.

132   Gachet, R. R.: "Filing Occupational Information for Women," *Occupations,* March 1944, p. 354.

133   Ganley, A. L.: "Boston Follows through with Its Follow-up," *School Counselor,* no date, p. 1.

134 Gardner, J. W.: *From High School to Job,* reprinted from annual report of the president, Carnegie Corporation of New York, New York, 1960.

135 Gaudet, F. J., and W. Kulick: "Who Comes to a Vocational Guidance Center?" *Personnel and Guidance Journal,* December 1954, p. 211.

136 Gelatt, H. B., B. Varenhorst, and R. Carey: *Deciding,* College Entrance Examination Board, Box 592, Princeton, N.J., 1972.

137 Gelatt, H. B., B. Varenhorst, and R. Carey: *Deciding: A Leader's Guide,* College Entrance Examination Board, Box 592, Princeton, N.J., 1972.

138 Gelatt, H. B., B. Varenhorst, R. Carey, and G. P. Miller: *Decisions and Outcomes,* College Entrance Examination Board, Box 592, Princeton, N.J., 1973.

139 Gelatt, H. B., B. Varenhorst, R. Carey, and G. P. Miller: *Decisions and Outcomes: A Leader's Guide,* College Entrance Examination Board, Box 592, Princeton, N.J., 1973.

140 Ginzberg, E.: "Toward a Theory of Occupational Choice: A Restatement," *Vocational Guidance Quarterly,* March 1972, p. 169.

141 Ginzberg, E., S. W. Ginsburg, S. Axelrad, and J. L. Herma: *Occupational Choice: An Approach to a General Theory,* Columbia University Press, New York, 1951.

142 Goldberg, H. R., and W. T. Brumber: *New Rochester Occupational Reading Series,* Science Research Associates, Inc., Chicago, 1963.

143 Goldman, L.: "Guidance Students Do Research in Occupations," *Personnel and Guidance Journal,* April 1954, p. 475.

144 Greenberg, B.: Memorandum to R. Hoppock, April 20, 1966.

145 *Guidance Exchange,* an annual digest of current literature, 3310 Rochambeau Ave., Bronx, New York,.

146 *Guide to Alternative Service,* National Interreligious Service Board for Conscientious Objectors, Washington, 1972.

147 *Guide to College Majors,* Chronicle Guidance Publications, Inc., Moravia, N.Y. (see latest edition).

148 *A Guide to Graduate Study: Programs Leading to the Ph.D. Degree,* American Council on Education, Washington (see latest edition).

149 *Guide to Indexes as a Resource for Occupations and Careers,* B'nai B'rith Career and Counseling Services, 1640 Rhode Island Av., N.W., Washington (see latest edition).

150 *Guide to Local Occupational Information,* Manpower Administration, U.S. Department of Labor, Washington (see latest edition).

151 *Guide to Minority Business Directories,* National Minority Business Campaign, 1115 Plymouth Ave., Minneapolis, Minn. (see latest edition).

152 *Guidelines for the Preparation and Evaluation of Career Information Media: Films, Filmstrips, and Printed Materials,* National Vocational Guidance Association, Washington, 1971.

153 Hall, R. H.: *Occupations and the Social Structure,* Prentice-Hall, Inc., Englewood Cliffs, N.J., 1969.

154 Hamel, L. B.: "A Survey of the Teaching of Occupations in New York State Secondary Schools," doctoral thesis, St. John's University, Jamaica, N.Y., 1961.

155 *Handbook for Analyzing Jobs,* Government Printing Office, Washington, 1972.

156 *Handbook: A Guide for Group Training in Job Finding,* Bureau of Standards, Methods and Planning, State Employment Service, Trenton, N.J., 1963.

157 Hansen, L. S.: *Career Guidance Practices in School and Community,* National Vocational Guidance Association, Washington, D.C., 1970.

158 Hansen, L. S.: "A Model for Career Development through Curriculum," *Personnel and Guidance Journal,* December 1972, p. 243.

159   Harris, J. (ed.): *Tested Practices: Computer-Assisted Guidance Systems,* National Vocational Guidance Association, Washington, 1972.

160   Hartley, D.: *Guidance Practices in the Schools of New York State: Tentative Report,* State Education Department, Albany, N.Y., 1949.

161   Herr, E. L.: *Review and Synthesis of Foundations for Career Education,* Center for Vocational and Technical Education, Ohio State University, Columbus, 1972.

162   Hewer, V. H.: "Evaluation of Group and Individual Counseling: A Follow-Up," *Journal of College Student Personnel,* July 1967, p. 265.

163   Hewer, V. H.: "Group Counseling," *Vocational Guidance Quarterly,* June 1968, p. 250.

164   Hewer, V. H.: "Vocational Planning Courses at the University of Minnesota," in H. T. Morse and P. L. Dressel, *General Education for Personal Maturity,* Wm. C. Brown Company Publishers, Dubuque, Iowa, 1960.

165   Hill, G. E.: "The Evaluation of Occupational Literature," *Vocational Guidance Quarterly,* Summer 1966, p. 271.

166   Hill, G. E.: *Management and Improvement of Guidance,* Appleton Century Crofts, New York, 1965.

167   Holcomb, J. R.: "College Courses in Careers: An Historical and Evaluative Treatment," unpublished manuscript available from the author at Duquesne University, Pittsburgh, Pa., 1966.

168   Holland, J. L.: *Making Vocational Choices: A Theory of Careers,* Prentice-Hall, Inc., Englewood Cliffs, N.J., 1973.

169   Holland, J. L.: *The Psychology of Vocational Choice,* Blaisdell Publishing Company, Waltham, Mass., 1966.

170   Hollingshead, A. B.: *Elmtown's Youth,* John Wiley & Sons, Inc., New York, 1949.

171   Hopke, W. E.: *The Encyclopedia of Careers and Vocational Guidance,* J. G. Ferguson Publishing Company, Chicago, Ill. (see latest edition).

172   Hopke, W. E. (ed.): *Vocational Development and Career Planning,* State Department of Public Instruction, Raleigh, N.C., 1968.

173   Hoppock, R.: "Courses in Careers," *Journal of Higher Education,* October 1932, p. 365.

174   Hoppock, R.: *Job Satisfaction,* Harper & Row, Publishers, Incorporated, New York, 1935. (Out of print; available from Xerox University Microfilms, Ann Arbor, Mich.)

175   Hoppock, R.: "Teaching Occupations to Counselors," *Vocational Guidance Quarterly,* Spring 1954, p. 74.

176   Hoppock, R.: "Teaching Sources of Occupational Information," *Vocational Guidance Quarterly,* Winter 1953, p. 50.

177   Hoppock, R.: "A Twenty-seven Year Follow-up on Job Satisfaction of Employed Adults," *Personnel and Guidance Journal,* February 1960, p. 489.

178   Hoppock, R.: "Two Methods of Demonstrating Group Guidance to Counselors in Training," *Occupations,* December 1951, p. 195.

179   Hoppock, R.: "Two Methods of Training Counselors for Group Guidance: An Experimental Evaluation," *Occupations,* May 1949, p. 523.

180   Hoppock, R.: "What is the 'Real' Problem?" *American Psychologist,* March 1953, p. 124.

181   Hoppock, R., and S. H. Brown: "Occupational Group Conferences in Grade Two," *Elementary School Guidance and Counseling,* December 1969, p. 150.

182   Hoppock, R., and E. R. Cuony: "Pretesting Equated Groups," *Educational and Psychological Measurement,* Summer 1955, p. 163.

183 Hoppock, R., and M. D. Hardenbergh: "Courses in Careers," *Journal of Higher Education,* March 1944, p. 157.

184 Hoppock, R., and M. E. Hoppock: "Renovating an Occupational Information File," *Vocational Guidance Quarterly,* Winter 1960–1961, p. 84.

185 Hoppock, R., and N. Lowenstein: "The Teaching of Occupations in 1951," *Occupations,* January 1952, p. 274.

186 Hoppock, R., and B. Novick: "The Occupational Information Counsultant: A New Profession?" *Personnel and Guidance Journal,* March 1971, p. 555.

187 Hoppock, R., and N. D. Stevens: "High School Courses in Occupations," *Personnel and Guidance Journal,* May 1954, p. 540.

188 Hoppock, R., and V. Tuxill: "Growth of Courses in Careers," *Journal of Higher Education,* October 1938, p. 357.

189 Hoy, W. C.: "A Survey of the Study of Occupations in Pennsylvania Secondary Schools," doctoral thesis, University of Pittsburgh, Pittsburgh, 1949.

190 Hoyt, D. P.: "An Evaluation of Group and Individual Programs in Vocational Guidance," *Journal of Applied Psychology,* February 1955, p. 26.

191 Hoyt, K. B., and J. G. Ashman: *S.O.S. Guidance Research Information Booklets,* Action Research Service, National Computer Systems, 4401 W. 76 St., Minneapolis, Minn. For sample materials and further information write Mr. Ashman at the address above.

192 Hoyt, K. B., R. N. Evans, E. F. Mackin, and G. L. Mangum: *Career Education: What It Is and How to Do It,* 2d ed., Olympus Publishing Company, Salt Lake City, Utah, 1974.

193 Huey, M. L.: "Filing Occupational Information in the Atlanta Opportunity School," *Occupations,* February 1944, p. 315.

194 Hughbanks, A. W.: "At Purdue, the Recruiters Come to Dinner," *Journal of College Placement,* December 1968–January 1969, p. 119.

195 Hughes, R. G., Jr.: "See for Yourself: A Doing Approach to Vocational Guidance," *Vocational Guidance Quarterly,* Summer 1965, p. 283.

196 Hutson, P. W.: *The Guidance Function in Education,* rev. ed., Appleton Century Crofts, New York, 1968.

197 Hyde, H.: "A Guide for Effective Preparation of New York State Public School Counselors and Utilization of Their Counseling Services," doctoral thesis, New York University School of Education, New York, 1950.

198 "Industry Visits Aid Realistic Counseling and Job Placement," *S.R.A. Guidance Newsletter,* November–December, 1965, p. 3.

199 Isaacson, L. E.: *Career Information in Counseling and Teaching,* Allyn and Bacon, Inc., Boston (see latest edition).

200 Jackson, R. M., and J. W. M. Rothney: "A Comparative Study of the Mailed Questionnaire and the Interview in Follow-up Studies," *Personnel and Guidance Journal,* March 1961, p. 569.

201 Jacobson, T. J.: "Career Centers," *Inform,* American Personnel and Guidance Association, Washington, August 1972, p. 4.

202 Jacobson, T. J.: "Career Guidance Centers," *Personnel and Guidance Journal,* March 1972, p. 599.

203 Janney, A. C.: "Occupational Map," *The Beacon,* Lambertville, N.J., March 15, 1962, p. 8.

204 Jefferies, D.: "The Needs of Inner-City Children for Career Guidance," *Elementary School Guidance and Counseling,* May 1968, p. 268.

205 Jesmur, F. A.: Memoranda to R. Hoppock, Feb. 23 to Apr. 27, 1966.

206 Johnson, B. B.: *Career Information for Counselors and Students,* Occupational Information Center for Education-Industry, 2970 Peachtree Road, N.W., Atlanta, Ga.

207 Johnson, B. B.: "An Occupational Information Center for Education-Industry," *Vocational Guidance Quarterly,* September 1969, p. 41.

208 Johnson, B. B.: "The Occupational Information Center: Where Atlanta Employers and Educators Meet," *Occupational Outlook Quarterly,* Winter 1972, p. 23.

209 Johnson, E., and B. Briggs: "At Our Fingertips," *Vocational Guidance Quarterly,* June 1972, p. 303.

210 Jolles, I.: "An Experiment in Group Guidance," *Journal of Social Psychology,* February 1946, p. 55.

211 *Journal of College Placement,* published quarterly by the College Placement Council, Inc., P.O. Box 2263, Bethlehem, Pa.

212 Kaback, G. R.: "Occupational Information in Elementary Education: What Counselors Do—What Counselors Would Like to Do," *Vocational Guidance Quarterly,* March 1968, p. 203.

213 Kagan, N.: "Three Dimensions of Counselor Encapsulation," *Journal of Counseling Psychology,* Winter 1964, p. 361.

214 Katz, J. K.: "Swarthmore's Extern Program," *Journal of College Placement,* December 1972–January 1973, p. 54.

215 Kearney, N. C.: *A Teacher's Professional Guide,* Prentice-Hall, Inc., Englewood Cliffs, N.J., 1958.

216 Keegan, V.: "Job Strategy: A College Credit Course in Job Hunting Techniques," *School and College Placement,* May 1951, p. 40.

217 Kenyon, L. B.: "A Course in Occupations," *Bulletin of the National Association of Secondary School Principals,* November 1948, p. 131.

218 Kenyon, L. B.: "Dust Off That Tape Recorder," *Occupations,* February 1952, p. 327.

219 Kirk, B. A., and M. E. Michels: *Occupational Information in Counseling,* Consulting Psychologists Press, 270 Town and Country Village, Palo Alto, Calif., 1964.

220 Kline, M. V., and J. M. Schneck: "An Hypnotic Experimental Approach to the Genesis of Occupational Interests and Choice," *British Journal of Medical Hypnotism,* Winter 1950, p. 1.

221 Krause, E. A.: *The Sociology of Occupations,* Little, Brown and Company, Boston, Mass., 1971.

222 Krumboltz, J. D.: "Behavioral Counseling: Rationale and Research," *Personnel and Guidance Journal,* December 1965, p. 383.

223 Krumboltz, J. D.: *Job Experience Kits,* Science Research Associates, Inc., Chicago, 1970.

224 Krumboltz, J. D.: "Parable of the Good Counselor," *Personnel and Guidance Journal,* October 1964, p. 118.

225 Krumboltz, J. D., and R. D. Baker: "Behavioral Counseling for Vocational Decisions," in H. Borow (ed.), *Career Guidance for a New Age,* Houghton Mifflin Company, Boston, Mass., 1973, p. 235.

226 Krumboltz, J. D., and L. E. Sheppard: "Vocational Problem Solving Experiences," in J. D. Krumboltz and C. E. Thoresen, *Behavioral Counseling: Cases and Techniques,* Holt, Rinehart and Winston, Inc., New York, 1969, p. 293.

227 Krumboltz, J. D., and C. E. Thoresen (eds.): *Behavioral Counseling: Cases and Techniques,* Holt, Rinehart and Winston, Inc., New York, 1969.

228 Kuhlin, M. E.: "Bowling Green's Alumni Network," *Journal of College Placement,* December 1970–January 1971, p. 91.

229 Kutner, J. E.: "An Evaluation of Occupational Field Trips Conducted by Paterson Technical and Vocational High School in Terms of Vocational Success," doctoral thesis, New York University School of Education, New York, 1957.

230 Lansner, L. A.: "Helping Seniors to Break the Job Barrier," *Journal of College Placement,* December 1959, p. 27.

231 Lapidos, M.: "Integration of Individual and Group Counseling with a J.V.S.," in *The Latest in Vocational Services: Proceedings of the Midwest Conference of Jewish Vocational Service Agencies, Jan. 12–14, 1951,* sponsored by the Jewish Occupational Council, Cincinnati, Ohio.

232 Laramore, D.: "Career Information Center: An Approach to Occupational Information," *Personnel and Guidance Journal,* September 1969, p. 55.

233 Laramore, D.: "Counselors Make Occupational Information Packages," *Vocational Guidance Quarterly,* March 1971, p. 220.

234 Laramore, D.: "Jobs on Film," *Vocational Guidance Quarterly,* December 1968, p. 87.

235 Laramore, D., and J. Thompson: "Career Experiences Appropriate to Elementary School Grades," *School Counselor,* March 1970, p. 262.

236 Laramore, D., and J. M. Thompson: "Counselors Learn About the World of Work," *Vocational Guidance Quarterly,* December 1970, p. 140.

237 *The Learning Society, Report of the Commission on Post-Secondary Education in Ontario,* Ministry of Government Services, Toronto, Canada, 1972.

238 Leis, W. W.: *Occupational Survey of Pasadena,* City Schools, Pasadena, Calif., 1955.

239 LeMay, M.: "An Inexpensive Address File for Occupational Information," *Vocational Guidance Quarterly,* Autumn 1965, p. 55.

240 LeMay, M. L., and C. F. Warnath: "Student Opinion on the Location of Occupational Information on a University Campus," *Personnel and Guidance Journal,* April 1967, p. 821.

241 Leonard, G. E.: *Developmental Career Guidance in Action. The First Year,* Wayne State University, Detroit, Mich., 1966.

242 Leonard, G. E., and E. Stephens: "Elementary School Employment Service," *Vocational Guidance Quarterly,* September 1967, p. 13.

243 Lifton, W. M.: "The Elementary School's Responsibility for Today's Vocational Misfits," unpublished manuscript, 1959.

244 Likert, R., and W. H. Quasha: *Revised Minnesota Paper Form Board Test,* The Psychological Corporation, New York, 1970.

245 Little, J. K.: *Review and Synthesis of Research on the Placement and Follow-up of Vocational Education Students,* Center for Vocational and Technical Education, Ohio State University, Columbus, 1970.

246 Little, W., and A. L. Chapman: *Developmental Guidance in Secondary Schools,* McGraw-Hill Book Company, New York, 1953.

247 Long, C. D.: *School-leaving Youth and Employment,* Teachers College Press, Columbia University, New York, 1941.

248 *Looking at Private Trade and Correspondence Schools, A Guide for Students,* American Personnel and Guidance Association, Washington (see latest edition).

249 *Lovejoy's College Guide,* Simon & Schuster, Inc., New York (see latest edition).

250 Lowenstein, N.: "The Effect of an Occupations Course in High School on Adjustment to College during the Freshman Year," doctoral thesis, New York University School of Education, New York, 1955; summarized in N. Lowenstein and R. Hoppock, "High School Occupations Course Helps Students Adjust to College," *Personnel and Guidance Journal,* September 1955, p. 21.

251 Lowenstein, N., and R. Hoppock: "The Teaching of Occupations in 1952," *Personnel and Guidance Journal,* April 1953, p. 441.

252 Marland, S. P., Jr.: "Education for More Than One Career," *World,* July 18, 1972, p. 46.

253 Maslow, A. H.: *Motivation and Personality,* Harper & Row, Publishers, Inc., New York, 1954.

254 Maverick, L. A.: *The Vocational Guidance of College Students,* Harvard University Press, Cambridge, Mass., 1926.

255 McCracken, T. C., and H. E. Lamb: *Occupational Information in the Elementary School,* Houghton Mifflin Company, Boston, 1923.

256 McGuire, W. G.: "Getting Out While the Getting's Good," *Journal of College Placement,* December 1972–January 1973, p. 62.

257 McKinlay, B.: *Oregon Career Information System,* University of Oregon, Eugene, 1974.

258 Mellon, S. J., Jr., and J. E. Champagne: *Pre-Employment Group Guidance Program: A Follow-Up Study of the Second Year in Houston,* Center for Human Resources, College of Business Administration, University of Houston, Houston, Tex., 1971.

259 Menninger, K. A.: "Work as a Sublimation," *Bulletin of the Menninger Clinic,* November 1942, p. 170.

260 Meyer, J., and C. Anderson: *Career Guidance through Groups,* National Technical Information Service, Springfield, Va., 1973.

261 Mich, D. D., and E. Eberman: *The Technique of the Picture Story,* McGraw-Hill Book Company, New York, 1945.

262 Miller, A. L., and D. V. Tiedeman: "Decision Making for the '70s: The Cubing of the Tiedeman Paradigm and Its Application in Career Education," *Focus on Guidance,* September 1972, p. 1.

263 Miller, D. C., and W. H. Form: *Industrial Sociology,* 2d ed., Harper & Row, Publishers, Inc., New York, 1964.

264 Miller, H.: "Getting Local Occupational Information through a Volunteer," *Vocational Guidance Quarterly,* Autumn 1952, p. 6.

265 Miller, J. N.: "Seven Steps toward Getting a Job," *Reader's Digest,* March 1963, p. 72.

266 Moore, M.: "A Career Newsletter," *Personnel and Guidance Journal,* March 1973, p. 495.

267 Mooren, R. L., and J. W. M. Rothney: "Personalizing the Follow-up Study," *Personnel and Guidance Journal,* March 1956, p. 409.

268 Morelli, E. A.: "Group Counseling in an Employment Service Setting," *Employment Service Review,* December 1964, p. 17.

269 Morse, H. T., and P. L. Dressel (eds.): *General Education for Personal Maturity,* Wm. C. Brown Company Publishers, Dubuque, Iowa, 1960.

270 *Movies with a Purpose,* Motion Picture and Education Markets Division, Eastman Kodak Company, Rochester, N.Y.

271 Moyer, D.: "Advice from the Apprentices," *Occupations,* March 1940, p. 411.

272 *Multi Media Training Package,* Group Guidance Program, Vocational Guidance Service, 2525 San Jacinto, Houston, Tex., July 1973.

273 Munschauer, J. L.: "Classifying Career Literature," *Journal of College Placement,* December 1971–January 1972, p. 62.

274 Munson, H. L.: *Elementary School Guidance: Concepts, Dimensions, and Practice,* Allyn and Bacon, Inc., Boston, Mass., 1970.

275 Munson, H. L.: *How to Set Up a Guidance Unit,* Science Research Associates, Inc., Chicago, 1957.

276 Münsterberg, H.: *Psychology and Industrial Efficiency,* Houghton Mifflin Company, Boston, 1913.

277 Murphy, G. C.: "Counselor Dominance," doctoral thesis, New York University School of Education, New York, 1957.

278 Musselman, D. L.: "Career Exposition: Big-Time Version of an Old Guidance Technique," *Vocational Guidance Quarterly,* September 1969, p. 49.

279 *National Minority Business Directory,* National Minority Business Campaign, 1115 Plymouth Ave., Minneapolis, Minn. (see latest edition).

280 *National Trade and Professional Associations of the United States and Labor Unions,* Columbia Books, Inc., 734 15 St., N.W., Washington (see latest edition).

281 *NVGA Bibliography of Current Career Information,* American Personnel and Guidance Association, Washington (see latest edition).

282 Neal, E.: "Filing Occupational Information Alphabetically," *Occupations,* May 1944, p. 503.

283 *The New York Times Index,* published periodically by The New York Times, New York.

284 Nolfo, J. A.: "Follow Up Facts and Figures While They're Hot," *Vocational Guidance Quarterly,* Summer 1958, p. 202.

285 Norris, W.: *Occupational Information in the Elementary School,* Science Research Associates, Inc., Chicago (see latest edition).

286 Norris, W., F. R. Zeran, R. N. Hatch, and J. R. Engelkes: *The Information Service in Guidance: Occupational, Educational, Social,* Rand McNally & Company, Chicago (see latest edition).

287 Norton, J. L.: *On the Job,* J. G. Ferguson Publishing Company, Chicago, 1970.

288 Nosow, S., and W. H. Form (eds.): *Man, Work and Society: A Reader in the Sociology of Occupations,* Basic Books, Inc., Publishers, New York, 1962.

289 *Occupational Information Via TV,* Georgia Department of Education, Division of Planning Research and Evaluation, Atlanta, Ga., 1970.

290 *Occupational Library,* Chronicle Guidance Publications, Inc., Moravia, N.Y. (see latest edition).

291 *Occupational Outlook for College Graduates,* Government Printing Office, Washington (see latest edition).

292 *Occupational Outlook Handbook,* Government Printing Office, Washington (see latest edition).

293 *Occupational View-Deck,* Chronicle Guidance Publications, Inc., Moravia, N.Y. (see latest edition).

294 Osipow, S. H.: *Theories of Career Development,* Prentice-Hall, Inc., Englewood Cliffs, N.J. (see latest edition).

295 *Our Youth—Five Years after Graduation: A Follow-up Study of the Class of 1959,* High School, Jamestown, N.Y., no date.

296 Overs, R. P.: "Covert Occupational Information," *Vocational Guidance Quarterly,* September 1967, p. 7.

297 Overs, R. P., and E. C. Deutsch: *Abstracts of Sociological Studies of Occupations,* 2d ed., Curative Workshop of Milwaukee, P.O. Box 7372, Milwaukee, Wis., 1968.

298 Oxhandler, A.: "What Makes an Occupational Information Pamphlet Popular?" *Occupations,* October 1950, p. 26.

299 Panther, E. E.: "Counselors and Legislators: A Case History," *Personnel and Guidance Journal,* April 1972, p. 667.

300 Patterson, C. H.: *Counseling and Guidance in Schools: A First Course,* Harper & Row, Publishers, Inc., New York, 1962.

301 Peagler, O. F.: Memorandum to R. Hoppock, April 30, 1960.

302 Pearson, H. G.: "Career Fields in Industry for the High School Graduate," *Vocational Guidance Quarterly,* December 1969, p. 87.

303 Peters, H. J., and W. Brown, Jr.: "Making a Movie of Local Vocations," *Clearing House,* February 1951, p. 350.

304 Peterson, M., and others: *Bibliography of K-6 Career Education Materials for the Enrichment of Teacher and Counselor Competencies,* Center for Educational Studies, Eastern Illinois University, Charleston, 1972.

305 Pitt, G. A., and R. W. Smith: *The Twenty-minute Lifetime: A Guide to Career Planning,* Prentice-Hall, Inc., Englewood Cliffs, N.J., 1959.

306 *Planning Your Future. Some Career Considerations,* College Placement Council, Inc., P.O. Box 2263, Bethlehem, Pa., no date.

307 Pohlman, E. W.: "Occupations with the Upper Hand," *Vocational Guidance Quarterly,* Winter 1964–1965, p. 103.

308 Porter, L.: *Degrees for Sale,* Arco Publishing Company, Inc., New York, 1972.

309 Powell, C. R., and W. G. McGuire: "Career Planning Courses: A Two-Part Study," *Journal of College Placement,* December 1971–January 1972, p. 30.

310 Prazak, J. A.: "Learning Job-Seeking Interview Skills," in J. D. Krumboltz and C. E. Thoresen, *Behavioral Counseling: Cases and Techniques,* Holt, Rinehart and Winston, Inc., New York, 1969.

311 *Psychological Abstracts,* published periodically by American Psychological Association, Inc., Washington.

312 Purcell, F. E.: "Helping Students Use Occupational Information Files," *Vocational Guidance Quarterly,* Autumn 1961, p. 55.

313 Rauschkolb, J.: "A Key Club Group Conference," *Vocational Guidance Quarterly,* Spring 1960, p. 147.

314 *Readers' Guide to Periodical Literature,* published periodically by The H. W. Wilson Company, New York.

315 Redefer, F. L., and D. Reeves: *Careers in Education,* Harper & Row, Publishers, Inc., New York, 1960.

316 Reed, A. Y.: *Guidance and Personnel Services in Education,* Cornell University Press, Ithaca, N.Y., 1944.

317 Reeves, D.: "A Survey to Ascertain How Widely Job-Getting Techniques Are Presented by Colleges and Universities, the Manner of Presentation, and Reactions to Them," doctoral thesis, New York University School of Education, New York, 1957.

318 Robinson, H. A., R. P. Connors, and G. H. Whitacre: "Job Satisfaction Researches of 1964–65," *Personnel and Guidance Journal,* December 1966, p. 371.

319 Roe, A.: "The Implications of Vocational Interest Theory for Vocational Counseling," unpublished manuscript, 1958.

320 Rogers, C. R.: *Client-centered Therapy,* Houghton Mifflin Company, Boston, 1951.

321 Rogers, C. R.: *Counseling and Psychotherapy,* Houghton Mifflin Company, Boston, 1942.

322 Rogers, C. R.: "Facilitation of Personal Growth," *School Counselor,* January 1955, p. 1.

323 Rosen, S. D., D. J. Weiss, D. D. Hendel, R. V. Dawis, and L. H. Lofquist: *Occupational Reinforcer Patterns,* vol. 2, *Minnesota Studies in Vocational Rehabilitation:* 29, Industrial Relations Center, University of Minnesota, Minneapolis, 1972.

324 Rosengarten, W., Jr.: "The Occupational Orientation of High School Seniors," doctoral thesis, New York University School of Education, New York, 1961, summarized in W. Rosengarten, Jr. and R. Hoppock, "Another Job Course Pays Off," *Personnel and Guidance Journal,* February 1963, p. 531.

325 Ross, M. J.: "Significant Concepts of Occupational Information," *Occupations,* February 1952, p. 323.

326 Ross, R. G.: *Occupational Information,* Guidance Services, State Department of Education, Des Moines, Iowa, 1954.

327 Roth, R. M., D. B. Hershenson, and T. Hilliard: *The Psychology of Vocational Development: Readings in Theory and Research,* Allyn and Bacon, Inc., Boston, 1970.

328 Rothney, J. W. M.: "Interpreting Test Scores to Counselees," *Occupations,* February 1952, p. 320.

329 Rubinfeld, W. A.: "Weekly Group Conferences on Careers," *Personnel and Guidance Journal,* December 1954, p. 223.

330 Ruderman, V.: "A Report on an Occupational Survey of 'Alumni' of a Federal Correctional Institution," master's thesis, New York University School of Education, New York, 1947.

331 Rundquist, R. M.: "Tape-Recorded Interviews Vitalize Occupational Information," *Vocational Guidance Quarterly,* Winter 1955–1956, p. 62.

332 Russell, M. M.: *The College Blue Book: Occupational Education,* CCM Information Corporation, New York, 1972.

333 Ruth, R. A.: "Readability of Occupational Materials," *Vocational Guidance Quarterly,* Autumn 1962, p. 7.

334 *Salary Survey,* prepared and published periodically by the College Placement Council, Inc., P.O. Box 2263, Bethlehem, Pa.

335 Salinger, M. D.: "Adapting a College-Level Occupations Course to Meet Expressed Student Needs," *Personnel and Guidance Journal,* November 1966, p. 272.

336 Samler, J.: "Psycho-Social Aspects of Work: A Critique of Occupational Information," *Personnel and Guidance Journal,* February 1961, p. 458.

337 Saterstrom, M. H., and J. A. Steph: *Educators Guide to Free Guidance Materials,* Educators Progress Service, Randolph, Wis. (see latest edition).

338 Schaffer, R. H.: "Job Satisfaction as Related to Need Satisfaction in Work," *Psychological Monographs,* no. 364, 1953, p. 1.

339 Scherini, R., and B. A. Kirk: "Keeping Current on Occupational Information," *Vocational Guidance Quarterly,* Winter 1963, p. 96.

340 Schreader, B. M.: "The Detroit Job Upgrading Program," *Vocational Guidance Quarterly,* Autumn 1961, p. 53.

341 Schubert, R. M.: "File Your Occupational Information by Student Interests," *Vocational Guidance Quarterly,* Spring 1953, p. 17.

342 Sharp, B. L.: "Readability of Vocational Guidance Materials," *School Counselor,* November 1966, p. 106.

343 Shartle, C. L.: *Occupational Information,* 2d ed., Prentice-Hall, Inc., Englewood Cliffs, N.J., 1952.

344 Sherrill, A. C.: *The 3rd Bridge,* Pittsburgh Plate Glass Company, Pittsburgh, Pa., no date.

345 Shoemaker, W. L.: "Tapping a New Source of Educational Information," *Vocational Guidance Quarterly,* Spring 1960, p. 149.

346 Sinick, D.: *Occupational Information and Guidance,* Houghton Mifflin Company, Boston, Mass., 1970.

347 Sinick, D., W. E. Gorman, and R. Hoppock: "Research on the Teaching of Occupations: 1965–1970," *Vocational Guidance Quarterly,* December 1971, p. 129.

348 Sinick, D., W. E. Gorman, and R. Hoppock: "Research on the Teaching of Occupations: 1963–1964," *Personnel and Guidance Journal,* February 1966, p. 591.

349 Sinick, D., and R. Hoppock: "Research Across the Nation on the Teaching of Occupations," *Vocational Guidance Quarterly,* Autumn 1965, p. 21.

350 Sinick, D., and R. Hoppock: "Research by States on the Teaching of Occupations," *Personnel and Guidance Journal,* November 1960, p. 218.

351 Sinick, D., and R. Hoppock: "Research on the Teaching of Occupations: 1945–1951," *Personnel and Guidance Journal,* November 1953, p. 174.

352 Sinick, D., and R. Hoppock: "Research on the Teaching of Occupations: 1952–1953," *Personnel and Guidance Journal,* October 1954, p. 86.

353 Sinick, D., and R. Hoppock: "Research on the Teaching of Occupations: 1954–1955," *Personnel and Guidance Journal,* November 1956, p. 155.

354 Sinick, D., and R. Hoppock: "Research on the Teaching of Occupations: 1956–1958," *Personnel and Guidance Journal,* October 1959, p. 150.

355 Sinick, D., and R. Hoppock: "Research on the Teaching of Occupations: 1959–1960," *Personnel and Guidance Journal,* October 1961, p. 164.

356 Sinick, D., and R. Hoppock: "Research on the Teaching of Occupations: 1961–1962," *Personnel and Guidance Journal,* January 1964, p. 504.

357 Sinick, D., and R. Hoppock: "States Report Research on the Teaching of Occupations," *Personnel and Guidance Journal,* February 1955, p. 328.

358 Slocum, W. L.: *Occupational Careers: A Sociological Perspective,* Aldine Publishing Company, Chicago, 1966.

359 Slotkin, H.: "New Programs for Dropouts in New York City: A Coordinated Approach," *Vocational Guidance Quarterly,* Summer 1962, p. 235.

360 Slotkin, H.: "A Technique for Self-measurement," *Personnel and Guidance Journal,* March 1954, p. 415.

361 Slotkin, H.: "Three Experimental Programs for Dropouts," *Guidance News,* Board of Education, New York, November 1961, p. 2.

362 Smith, E. D., and R. E. Lindberg: "Innovative Ideas in Vocational Guidance: Project Field Counselors," *American Vocational Journal,* December 1968, p. 21.

363 *Sociological Abstracts,* published periodically by Sociological Abstracts, Inc., 73 Eighth Ave., Brooklyn, N.Y.

364 *Sociological Studies of Occupations: A Bibliography,* Manpower Administration, U.S. Department of Labor, Washington, 1965.

365 Soltys, M. P.: "Video-Taped Role Playing," *Journal of College Placement,* February–March 1971, p. 55.

366 Sondern, F., Jr.: "Judge Cooper's Remarkable Experiment," *Reader's Digest,* June 1956, p. 53.

367 Souther, J. W.: "A Three-Phase Experiment in Minority Placement," *Journal of College Placement,* October–November 1972, p. 59.

368 Southern, J. A., and R. M. Colver: "Looking a Gift Horse in the Mouth," *Vocational Guidance Quarterly,* Winter 1955–1956, p. 46.

369 Splaver, S.: "What High School Freshmen and Seniors Want in Occupational Books," doctoral thesis, New York University School of Education, New York, 1953.

370 Splaver, S.: "What High School Students Want in Occupational Books," *Personnel and Guidance Journal,* September 1954, p. 15.

371 *Standard Industrial Classification Manual,* Government Printing Office, Washington (see latest edition).

372 *The Standard Periodical Directory,* Oxbridge Publishing Company, New York (see latest edition).

373 Stevens, N. D., and R. Hoppock: "College Courses in Careers," *Personnel and Guidance Journal,* April 1956, p. 502.

374 Stevens, N. D., and R. Hoppock: "High School Courses in Occupations," *Personnel and Guidance Journal,* December 1955, p. 213.

375 Stevens, N. D., and R. Hoppock: "Junior College Courses in Careers," *Vocational Guidance Quarterly,* Autumn 1954, p. 21.

376 Stiles, H.: "Career Exploration," *California Guidance Newsletter,* March–May 1961, p. 7.

377 Sudweeks, L. L.: "School Counselors Spend Summer Vacations in the Employment Service," *Vocational Guidance Quarterly,* June 1972, p. 299.

378 *Summary Report of the Seven College Vocational Workshops 1962–1966,* Placement Office, Barnard College, New York, 1966.

379 Super, D. E.: "It's All in the Day's Work," *Personnel and Guidance Journal,* May 1956, p. 541.

380 Super, D. E.: *The Psychology of Careers,* Harper & Row, Publishers, Inc., New York, 1957.

381 Super, D. E.: "A Theory of Vocational Development," *American Psychologist,* May 1953, p. 185.

382 Super, D. E., and J. O. Crites: *Appraising Vocational Fitness by Means of Psychological Tests,* Harper & Row, Publishers, Inc., New York (see latest edition).

383 Super, D. E., and P. L. Overstreet: *The Vocational Maturity of Ninth Grade Boys: Career Pattern Study Monograph 2,* Teachers College Press, Columbia University, New York, 1960.

384 Super, D. E., R. Starishevsky, N. Matlin, and J. P. Jordaan: *Career Development: Self-Concept Theory,* College Entrance Examination Board, Princeton, N.J., 1963.

385 *Supply, Demand and Salaries, New Graduates of Universities and Community Colleges,* Department of Manpower and Immigration, Ottawa, Ontario, Canada (see latest edition).

386 Sutherland, D. M.: "The 'College Opportunities' Course," *Simmons College Bulletin,* February 1949, p. 4.

387 Swain, E.: "A Training Program for Career Exploration Teachers," *American Vocational Journal,* November 1971, p. 81.

388 *Technician Education Yearbook,* Prakken Publications, Ann Arbor, Mich. (see latest edition).

389 Thompson, C. L., and J. L. Parker: "Fifth Graders View the Work World Scene," *Elementary School Guidance and Counseling,* May 1971, p. 281.

390 Tiedeman, D. V.: "Career Pattern Studies: Current Findings with Possibilities," *Harvard Studies in Career Development,* no. 40, Graduate School of Education, Harvard University, Cambridge, Mass., July 20, 1965.

391 Toporowski, T. T.: "A Critical Evaluation of an Experimental Occupational Information Unit Taught to High School Seniors by Social Studies Teachers," doctoral thesis, School of Education, Boston University, Boston, 1961.

392 Travers, R. M. W.: "A Critical Review of Techniques for Evaluating Guidance," *Education and Psychological Measurement,* Summer 1949, p. 211.

393 *Ulrich's International Periodicals Directory,* R. R. Bowker Company, Ann Arbor, Mich. (see latest edition).

394 *Universities and Colleges of Canada,* Association of Universities and Colleges of Canada, Ottawa, Ontario, Canada K1P 5N1 (see latest edition).

395 "Use of Television for ES Recruitment," *Journal of Employment Counseling,* December 1967, p. 112.

396 Valdez, A.: "20 Years of Youth Placement," *Employment Security Review,* March 1963, p. 11.

397 Van Dusen, A. C.: "Group Discussion in an Adult Counseling Program," *Educational and Psychological Measurement,* Autumn 1949, p. 521.

398 Varenhorst, B. B.: "Learning the Consequences of Life's Decisions," in J. D. Krumboltz and C. E. Thoresen, *Behavioral Counseling: Cases and Techniques,* Holt, Rinehart and Winston, Inc., New York, 1969, p. 306.

399 Varenhorst, B. B.: *Life Career Game,* B. B. Varenhorst, 350 Grove Drive, Portola Valley, Calif. (see latest edition).

400 *Vocational Education: Innovations Revolutionize Career Training,* National School Public Relations Association, 1201 16 Street, N.W., Washington, 1971.

401 *Vocational Guidance Quarterly,* National Vocational Guidance Association, Washington.

402 Wagaman, D. F.: Letters to R. Hoppock, November 20, 1968, and January 6, 1969.

403 Warner, W. L., and J. C. Abegglen: *Occupational Mobility in American Business and Industry, 1928–1952,* The University of Minnesota Press, Minneapolis, 1955.

404 Warters, J.: *High School Personnel Work Today,* McGraw-Hill Book Company, New York, 1946.

405 Wasserman, P., and H. W. F. Mason: "A Proposed Method for Finding a Position: Information Sources for Occupational Guidance by Geographic Area," *Personnel and Guidance Journal,* February 1958, p. 408.

406 Watson, D. E., R. M. Rundquist, and W. C. Cottle: "What's Wrong with Occupational Materials?" *Journal of Counseling Psychology,* Winter 1959, p. 288.

407 Weaver, G. L.: *How, When, and Where to Provide Occupational Information,* Science Research Associates, Inc., Chicago, 1955.

408 Weitz, J.: "Job Expectancy and Survival," *Journal of Applied Psychology,* August 1956, p. 245.

409 Wellman, F. E.: "Utilizing a Community Occupational Survey for In-service Education," *Personnel and Guidance Journal,* April 1954, p. 477.

410 White, V.: Letter to R. Hoppock, April 5, 1949.

411 Whiteley, J. M., and A. Resnikoff (eds.): *Perspectives on Vocational Development,* American Personnel and Guidance Association, Washington, 1972.

412 *Why Young People Fail to Get and Hold Jobs,* New York State Employment Service, New York (see latest edition).

413 Williams, F. E.: *Adolescence,* Holt, Rinehart and Winston, Inc., New York, 1930.

414 Williams, H. F.: "The Town Tells Teens about Jobs," *Personnel and Guidance Journal,* January 1954, p. 266.

415 Williamson, E. G.: *Students and Occupations,* Holt, Rinehart and Winston, Inc., New York, 1937.

416 Wilstach, I. M.: "Career Guidance Center Sponsored by Office of Los Angeles County Superintendent of Schools," *Vocational Guidance Quarterly,* Summer 1962, p. 245.

417 Wolfbein, S. L. : "The Outlook for the Skilled Worker in the United States: Implications for Guidance and Counseling," *Personnel and Guidance Journal,* December 1961, p. 334.

418 *Working Loose,* Random House, Inc., New York, 1971.

419 Wright, M.: Letter to R. Hoppock, April 9, 1954, quoting B. H. Reeves, vice-president and general manager of Rockbestos Products Corp.

420 Wyatt, G.: "Who's on Top—You, or Company Literature?" *Journal of College Placement,* May 1957, p. 33.

421 Youngberg, C. F.: "An Experimental Study of 'Job Satisfaction' and Turnover in Relation to Job Expectations and Self Expectations," doctoral thesis, New York University Graduate School of Arts and Science, 1963, summarized in *"Realistic" Job Expectations and Survival,* Life Insurance Agency Management Association, Hartford, Conn., 1964.

422 Youngberg, C. F.: Letter to R. Hoppock, Nov. 30, 1965.

423 Zaccaria, J. S.: *Theories of Occupational Choice and Vocational Development,* Houghton Mifflin Company, Boston, 1970.

424 Ziegler, R. A.: *Creative Job Search Techniques Classes: The 1330 Survey,* State Bureau of Labor, Portland, Oreg., 1968.

425 Ziegler, R. A.: *The Oregon Pilot Project in Teaching Creative Job Search Techniques to the Unemployed and or Underemployed,* and *A Leader's Guide for Group Guidance in Creative Job Search Techniques,* Oregon Bureau of Labor, Portland, Oreg., 1962.

426 Zytowski, D. G.: *Vocational Behavior: Readings in Theory and Research,* Holt, Rinehart and Winston, Inc., New York, 1968.

Name Index

Subject Index